2

My Love Mix-Up!

Art by **Aruko**
Story by **Wataru Hinekure**

Contents

Aoki has fallen for his unrequited love interest Hashimoto, who sits in the seat next to him.♥ But after he borrows an eraser from her and sees the name of another boy in their class—Ida—written on it...his hopes are dashed. Then Ida sees him holding that very eraser. In order to keep Hashimoto's crush a secret, Aoki lies and says the eraser is his. Ida treats the matter seriously and tells Aoki he wants to start as friends. Aoki decides not to clear up the misunderstanding while rooting for Hashimoto's love life. But while he's getting to know Ida, his feelings start slowly changing. Aoki decides to tell Hashimoto that he likes her secret crush too. But it turns out that Hashimoto's crush has been Aoki's best friend Aida all along?!

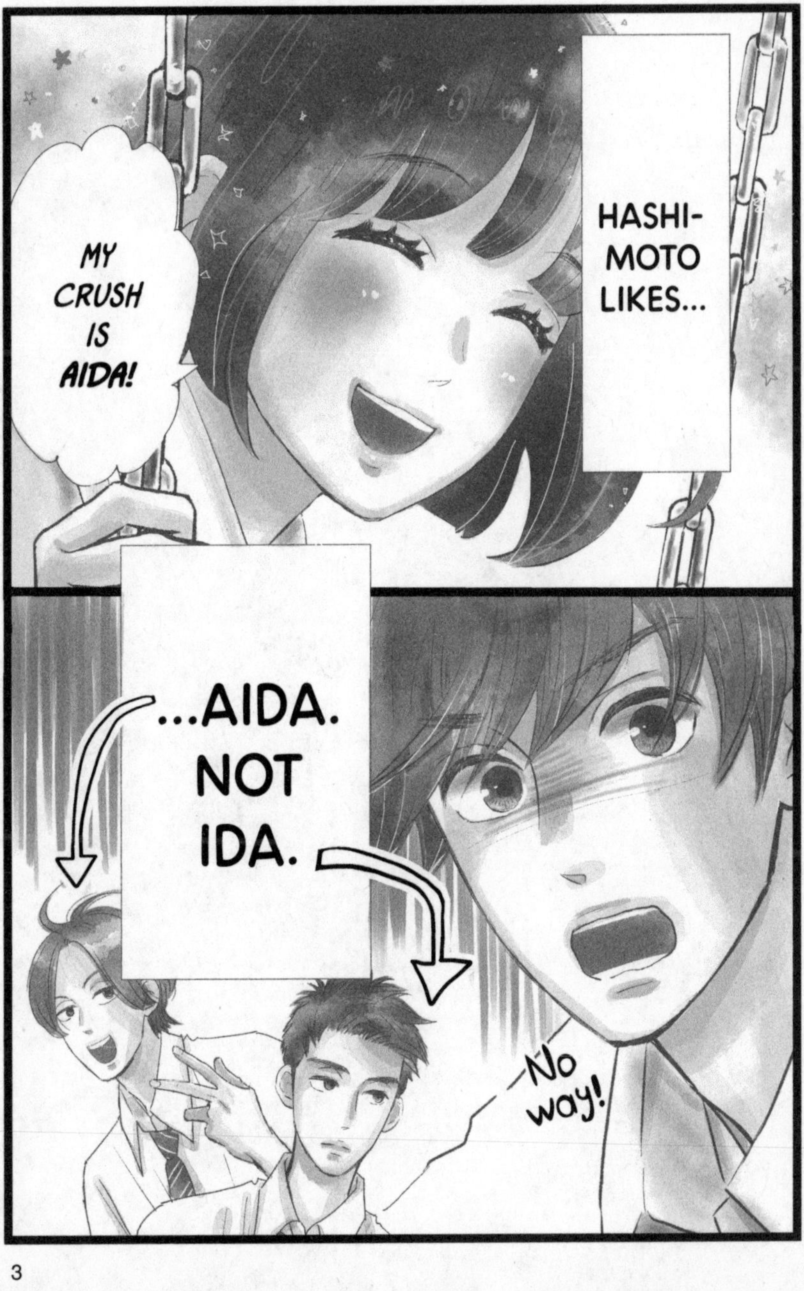
HASHI-MOTO LIKES...
MY CRUSH IS AIDA!
...AIDA. NOT IDA.
No way!

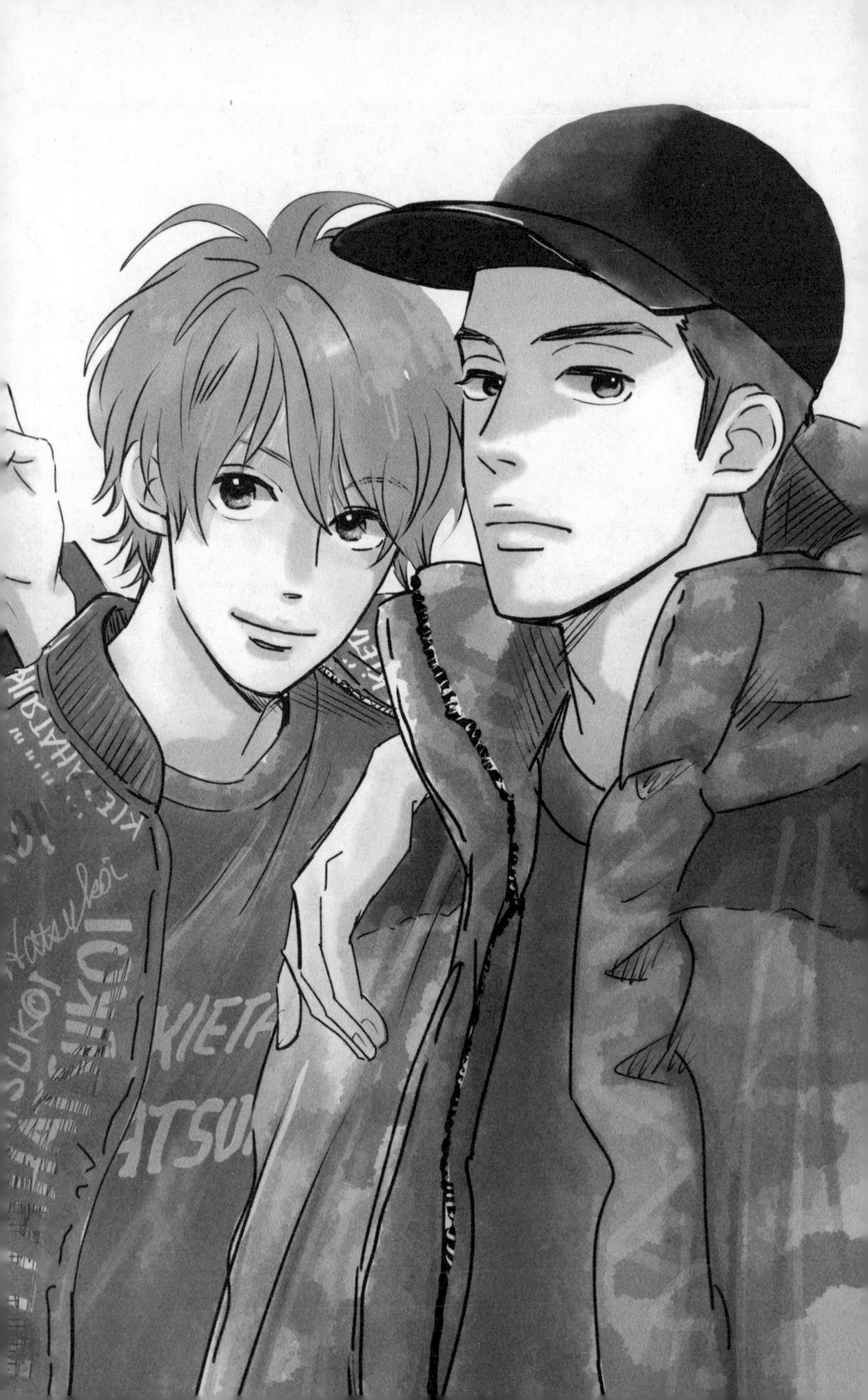

Chapter 6

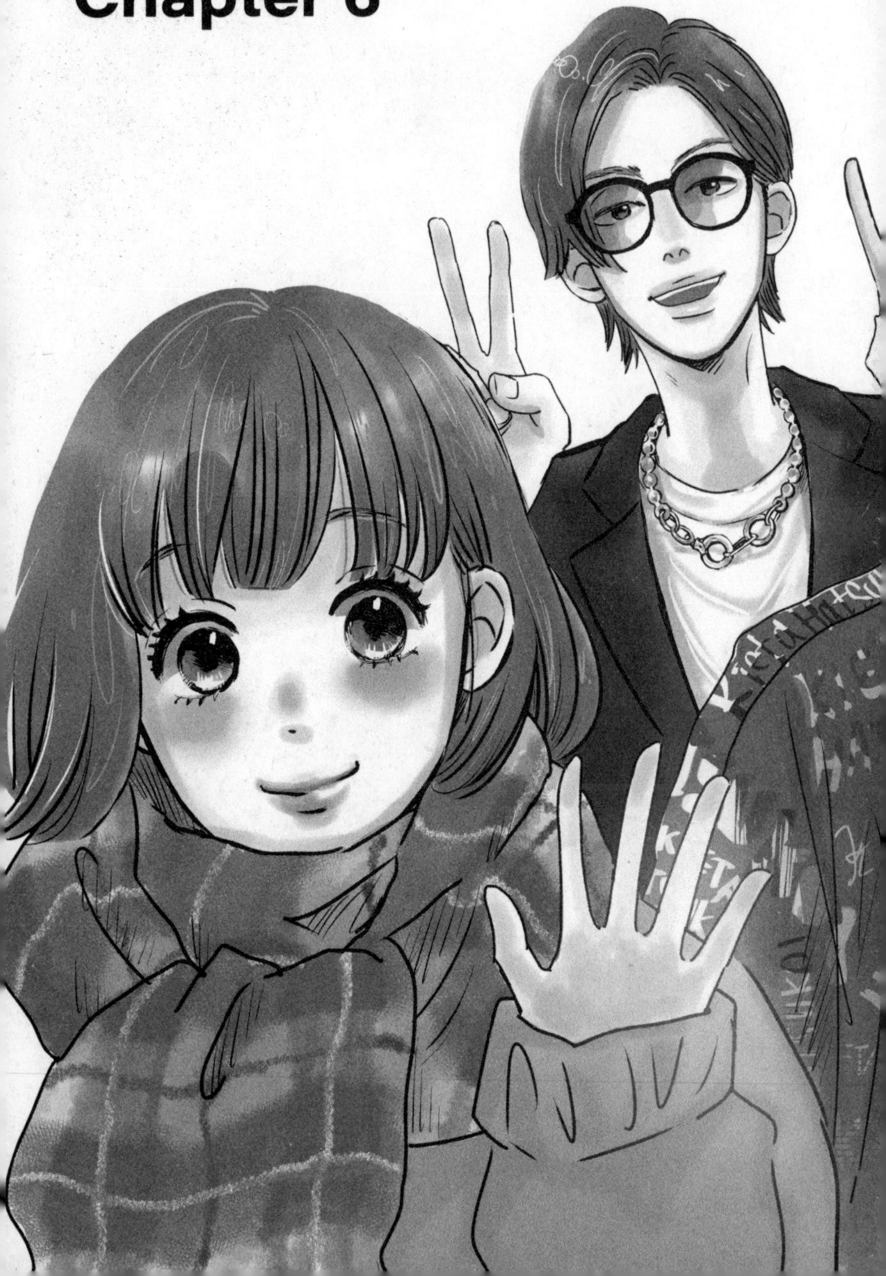

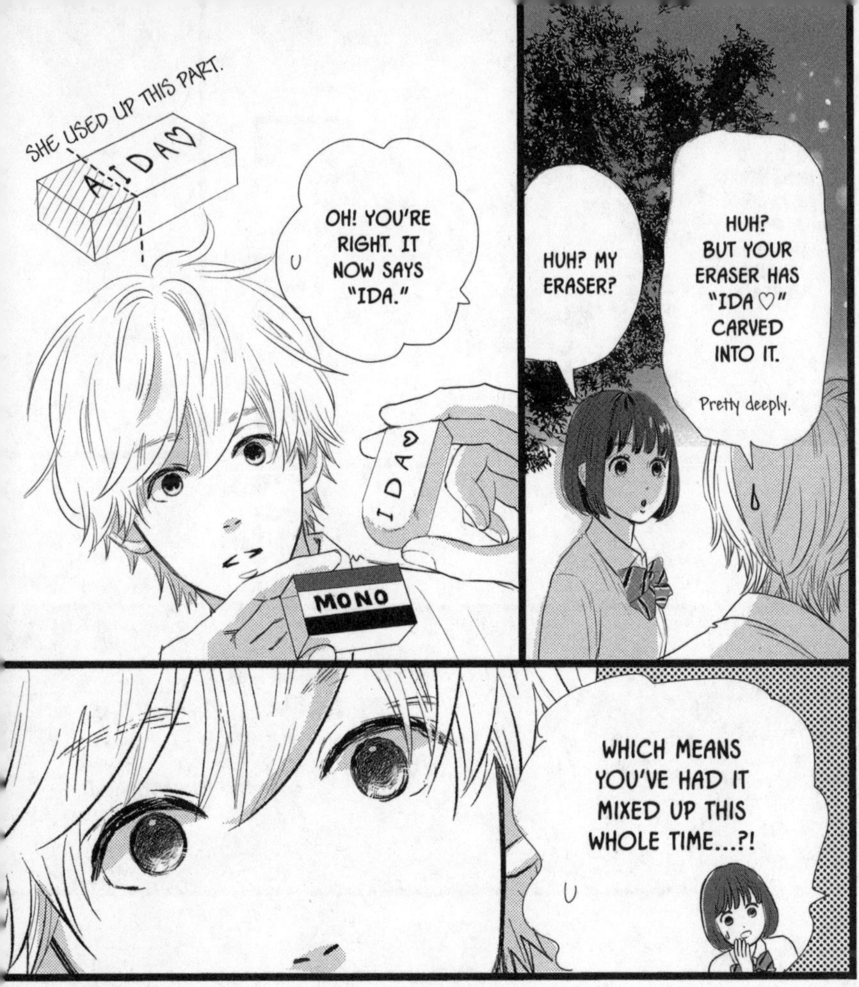
HUH? BUT YOUR ERASER HAS "IDA♡" CARVED INTO IT.
Pretty deeply.
HUH? MY ERASER?
SHE USED UP THIS PART.
AIDA♡
OH! YOU'RE RIGHT. IT NOW SAYS "IDA."
IDA♡
MONO
WHICH MEANS YOU'VE HAD IT MIXED UP THIS WHOLE TIME...?!

My Love Mix-Up!

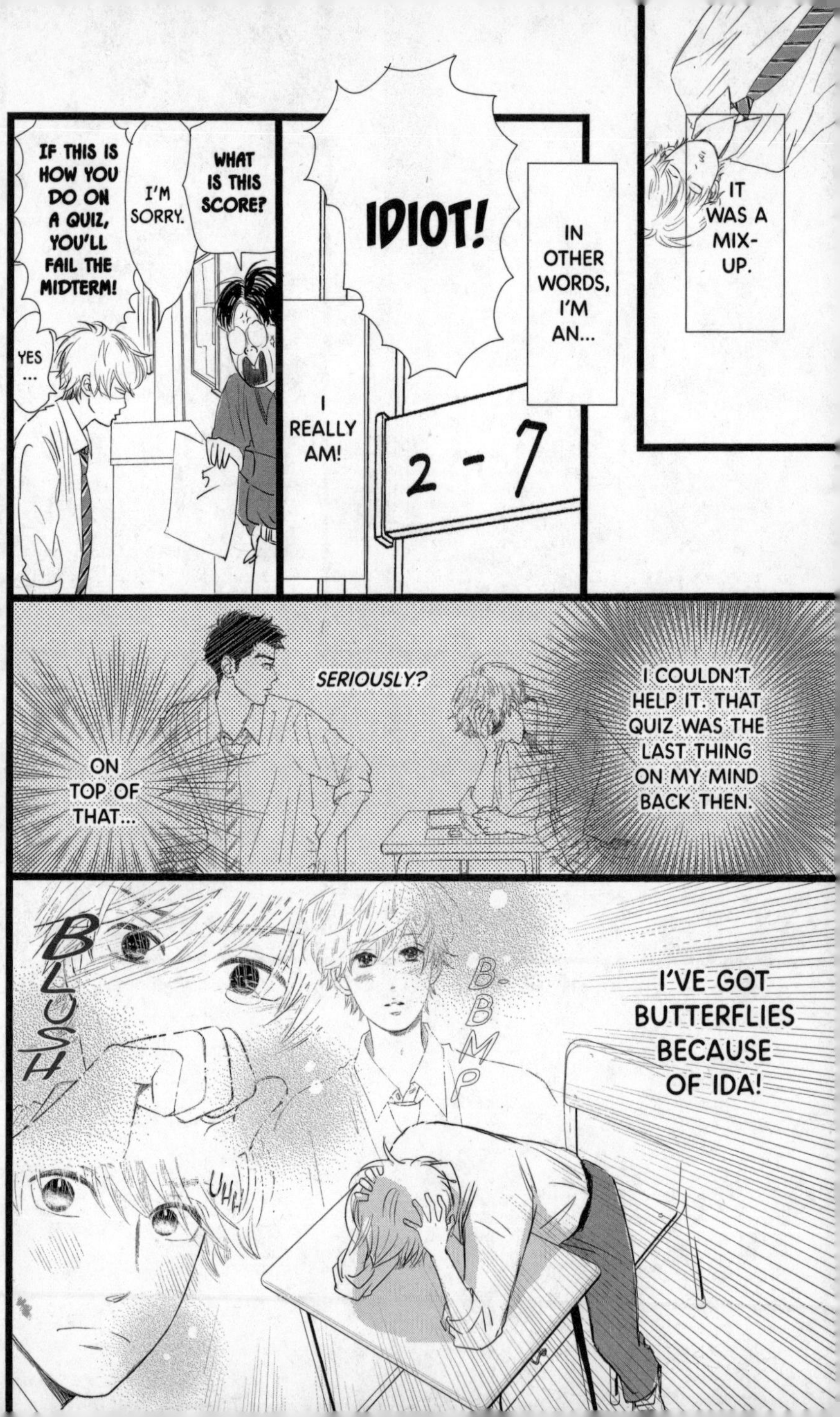
IT WAS A MIX-UP.
IN OTHER WORDS, I'M AN...
IDIOT!
I REALLY AM!
2 - 7
WHAT IS THIS SCORE?
I'M SORRY.
IF THIS IS HOW YOU DO ON A QUIZ, YOU'LL FAIL THE MIDTERM!
YES...
I COULDN'T HELP IT. THAT QUIZ WAS THE LAST THING ON MY MIND BACK THEN.
SERIOUSLY?
ON TOP OF THAT...
I'VE GOT BUTTERFLIES BECAUSE OF IDA!
B-BMP
BLUSH
UHH

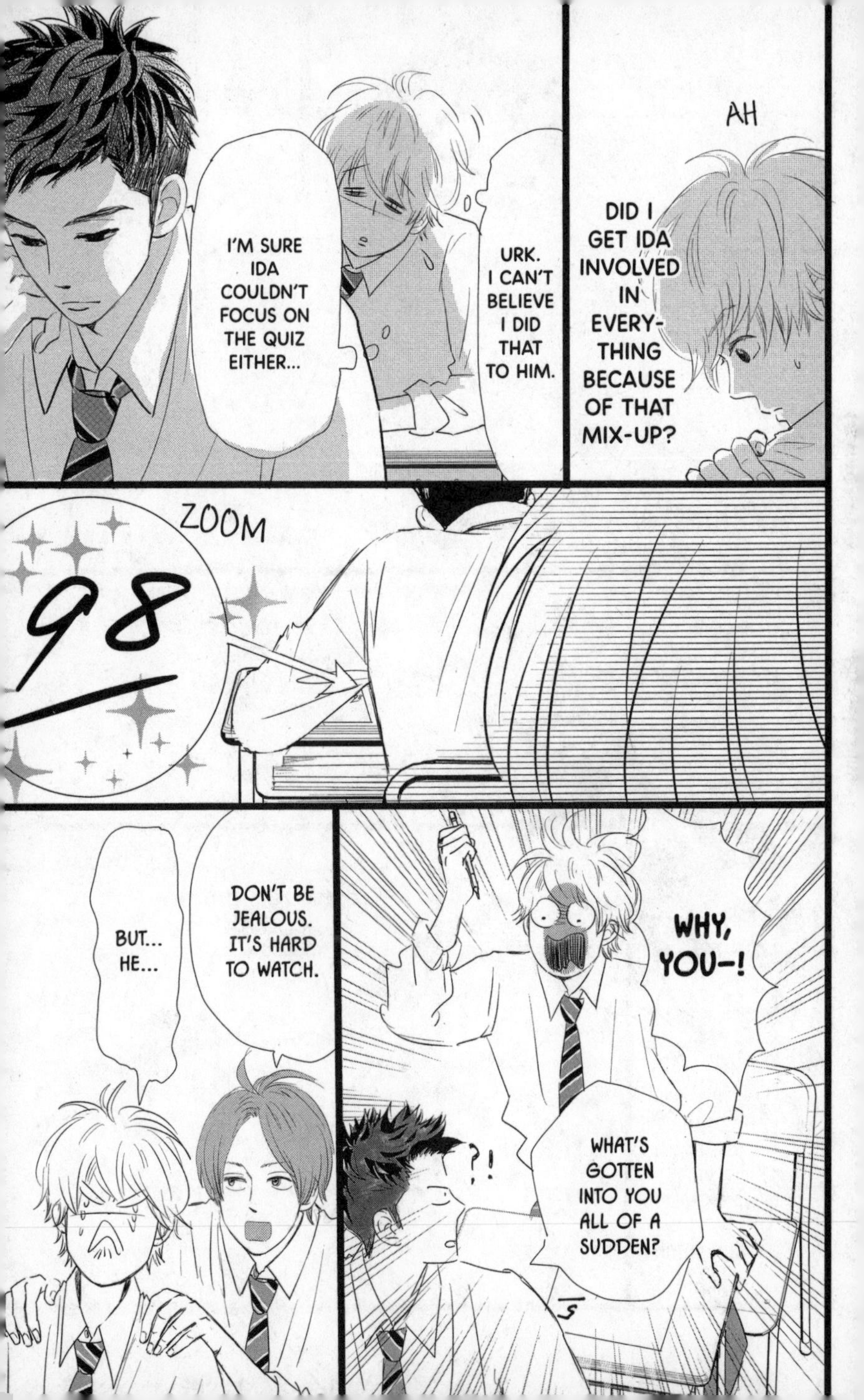
AH
DID I GET IDA INVOLVED IN EVERYTHING BECAUSE OF THAT MIX-UP?
URK. I CAN'T BELIEVE I DID THAT TO HIM.
I'M SURE IDA COULDN'T FOCUS ON THE QUIZ EITHER...
ZOOM
98
WHY, YOU-!
?!
WHAT'S GOTTEN INTO YOU ALL OF A SUDDEN?
DON'T BE JEALOUS. IT'S HARD TO WATCH.
BUT... HE...

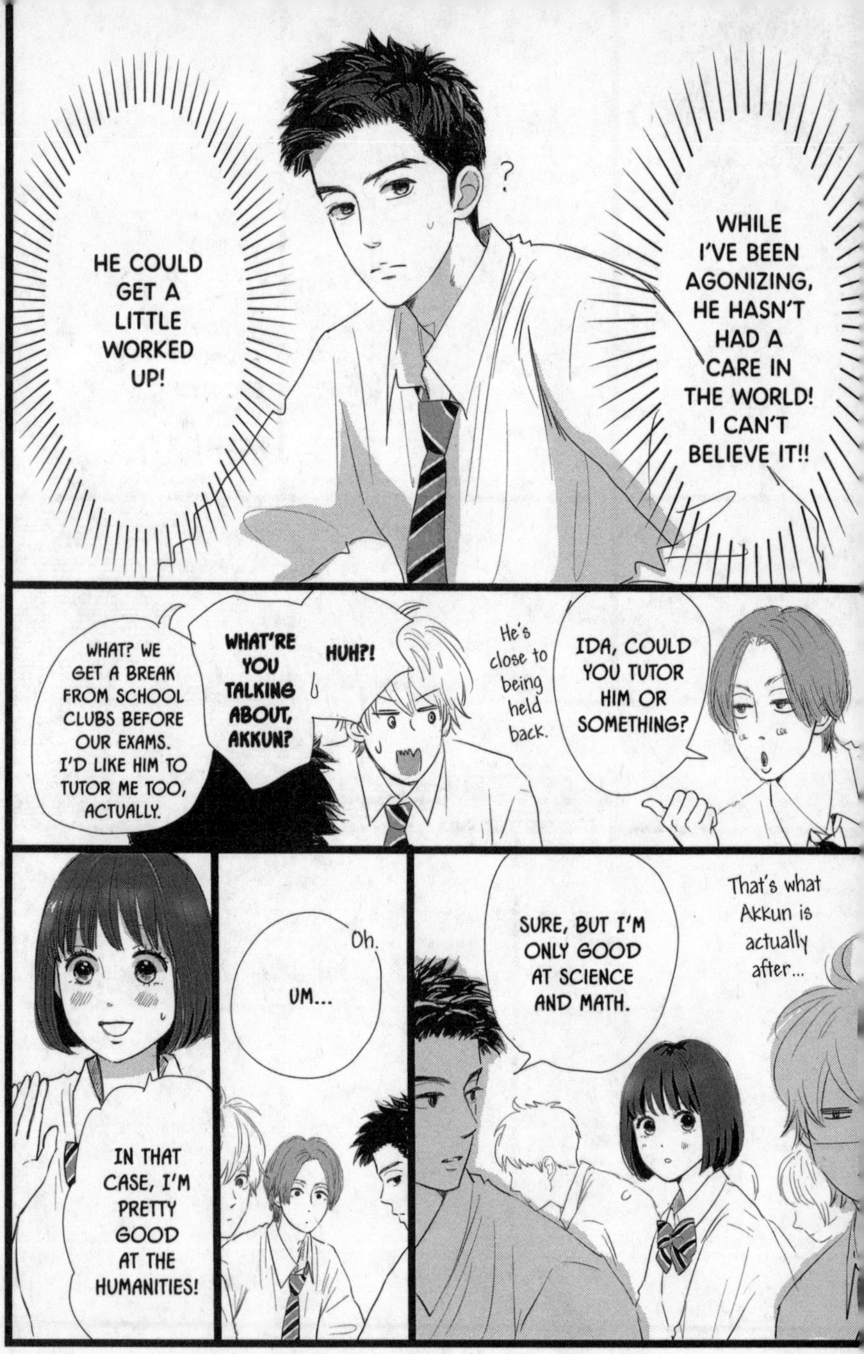
WHILE I'VE BEEN AGONIZING, HE HASN'T HAD A CARE IN THE WORLD! I CAN'T BELIEVE IT!!
?
HE COULD GET A LITTLE WORKED UP!
IDA, COULD YOU TUTOR HIM OR SOMETHING?
He's close to being held back.
HUH?!
WHAT'RE YOU TALKING ABOUT, AKKUN?
WHAT? WE GET A BREAK FROM SCHOOL CLUBS BEFORE OUR EXAMS. I'D LIKE HIM TO TUTOR ME TOO, ACTUALLY.
That's what Akkun is actually after...
SURE, BUT I'M ONLY GOOD AT SCIENCE AND MATH.
Oh.
UM...
IN THAT CASE, I'M PRETTY GOOD AT THE HUMANITIES!

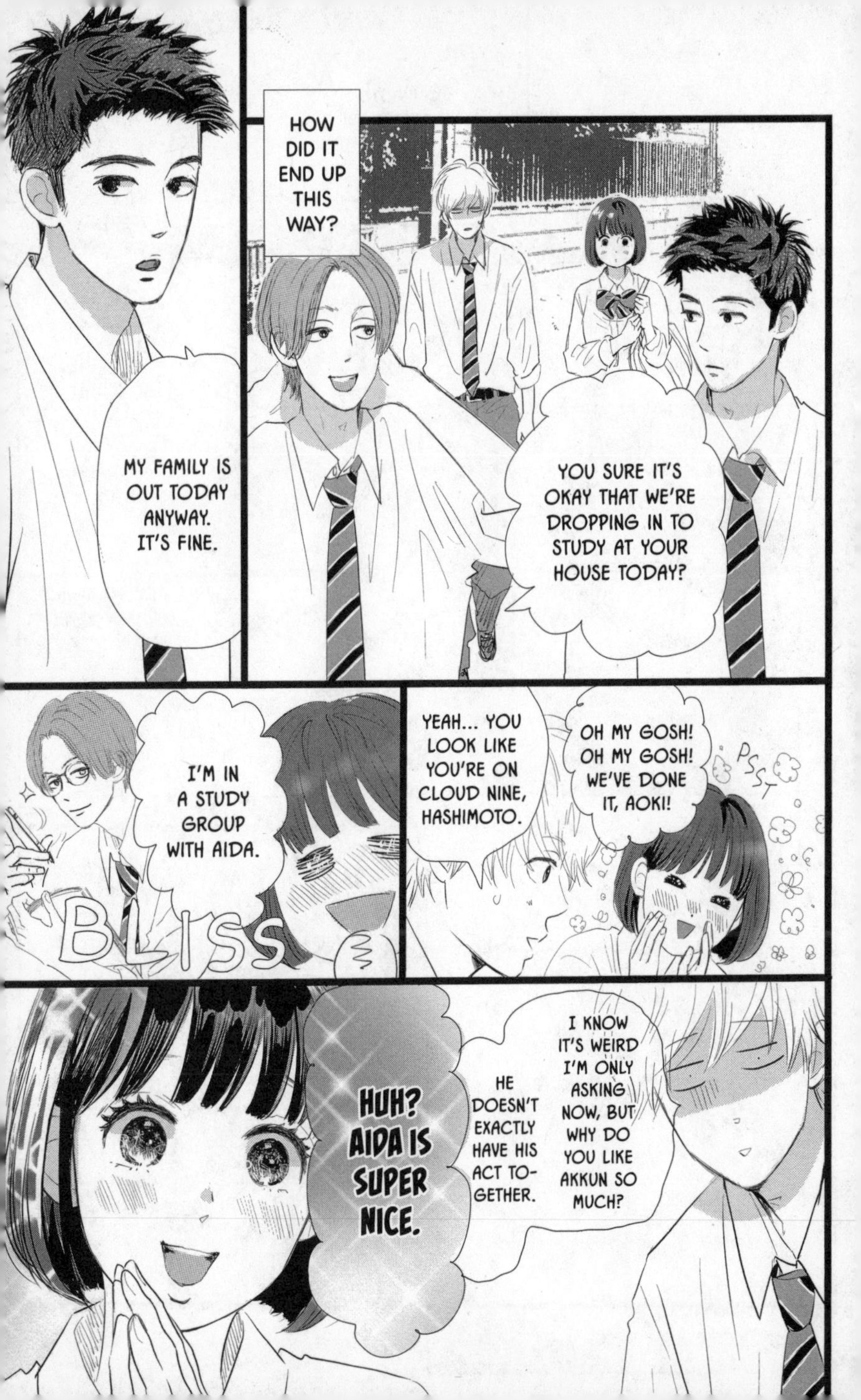
HOW DID IT END UP THIS WAY?
YOU SURE IT'S OKAY THAT WE'RE DROPPING IN TO STUDY AT YOUR HOUSE TODAY?
MY FAMILY IS OUT TODAY ANYWAY. IT'S FINE.
PSST
OH MY GOSH! OH MY GOSH! WE'VE DONE IT, AOKI!
YEAH... YOU LOOK LIKE YOU'RE ON CLOUD NINE, HASHIMOTO.
I'M IN A STUDY GROUP WITH AIDA.
BLISS
I KNOW IT'S WEIRD I'M ONLY ASKING NOW, BUT WHY DO YOU LIKE AKKUN SO MUCH?
HE DOESN'T EXACTLY HAVE HIS ACT TO-GETHER.
HUH? AIDA IS SUPER NICE.

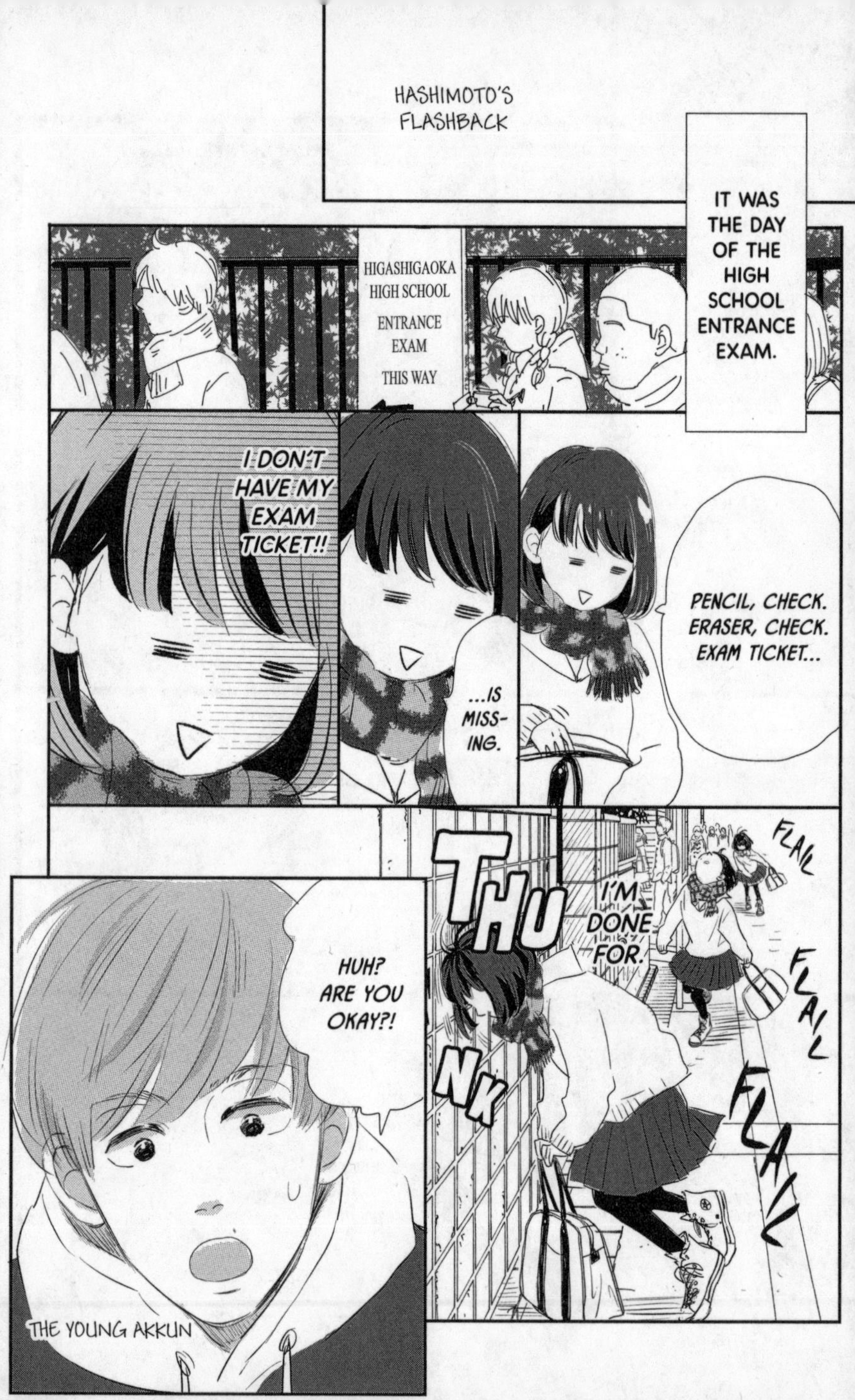
HASHIMOTO'S FLASHBACK
IT WAS THE DAY OF THE HIGH SCHOOL ENTRANCE EXAM.
HIGASHIGAOKA HIGH SCHOOL
ENTRANCE EXAM
THIS WAY
PENCIL, CHECK. ERASER, CHECK. EXAM TICKET...
...IS MISSING.
I DON'T HAVE MY EXAM TICKET!!
FLAIL
FLAIL
FLAIL
I'M DONE FOR.
THUNK
HUH? ARE YOU OKAY?!
THE YOUNG AKKUN

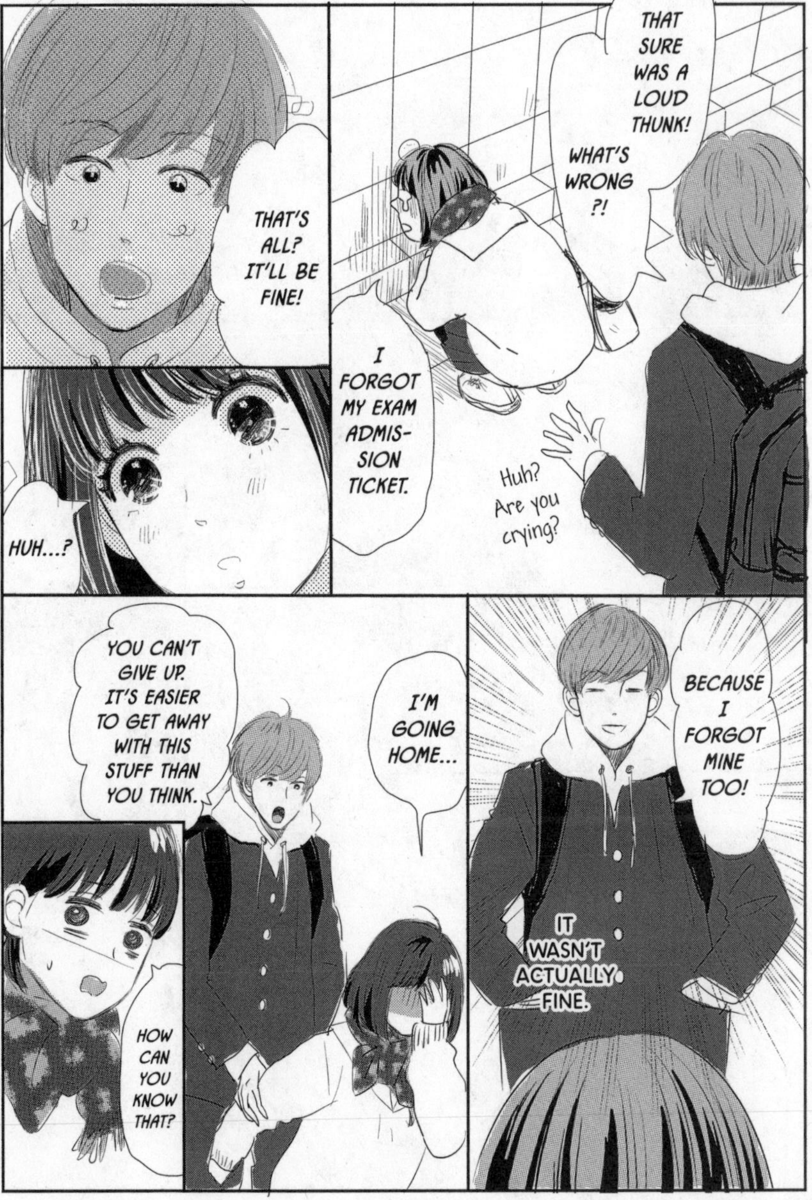
THAT SURE WAS A LOUD THUNK!
WHAT'S WRONG ?!
Huh? Are you crying?
I FORGOT MY EXAM ADMIS-SION TICKET.
THAT'S ALL? IT'LL BE FINE!
HUH...?
BECAUSE I FORGOT MINE TOO!
IT WASN'T ACTUALLY FINE.
I'M GOING HOME...
YOU CAN'T GIVE UP. IT'S EASIER TO GET AWAY WITH THIS STUFF THAN YOU THINK.
HOW CAN YOU KNOW THAT?

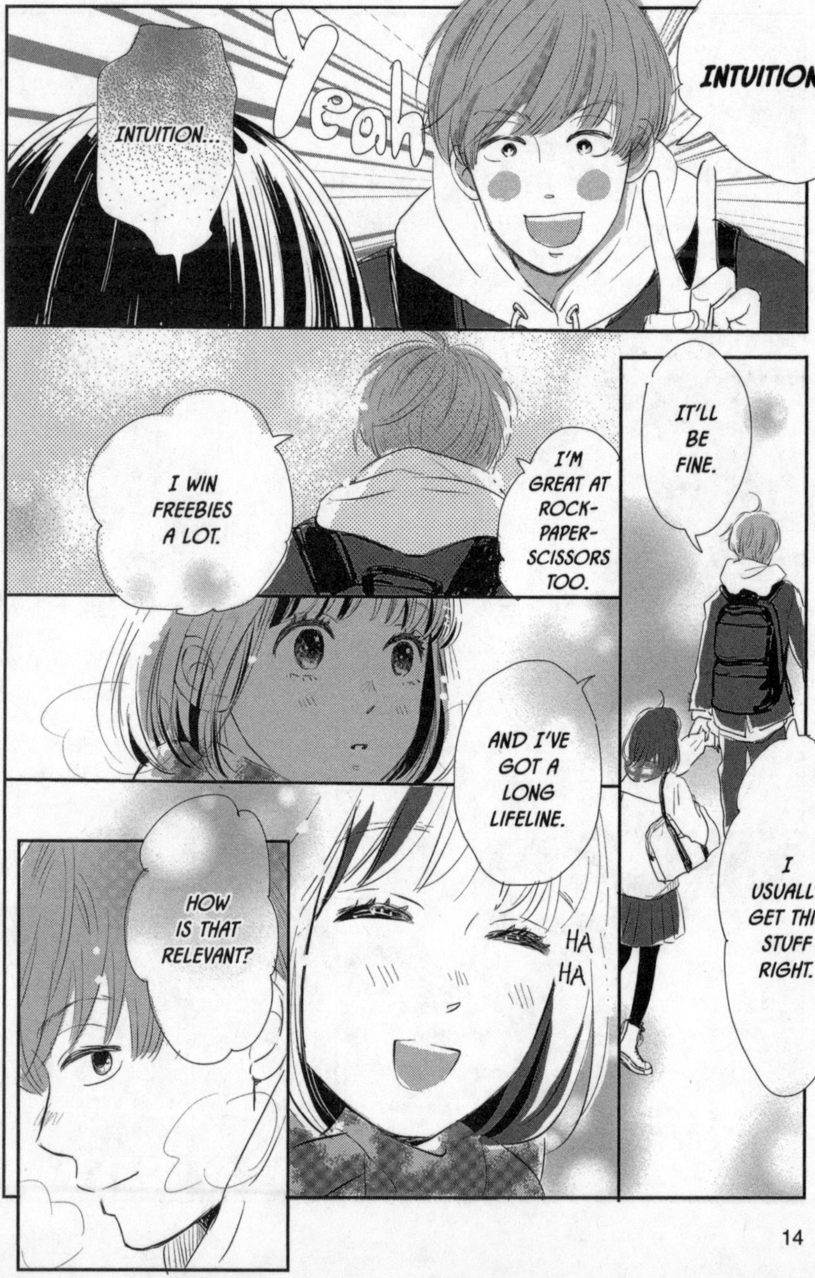
INTUITION!
Yeah
INTUITION...
IT'LL BE FINE.
I USUALLY GET THIS STUFF RIGHT.
I'M GREAT AT ROCK-PAPER-SCISSORS TOO.
I WIN FREEBIES A LOT.
AND I'VE GOT A LONG LIFELINE.
HA HA
HOW IS THAT RELEVANT?

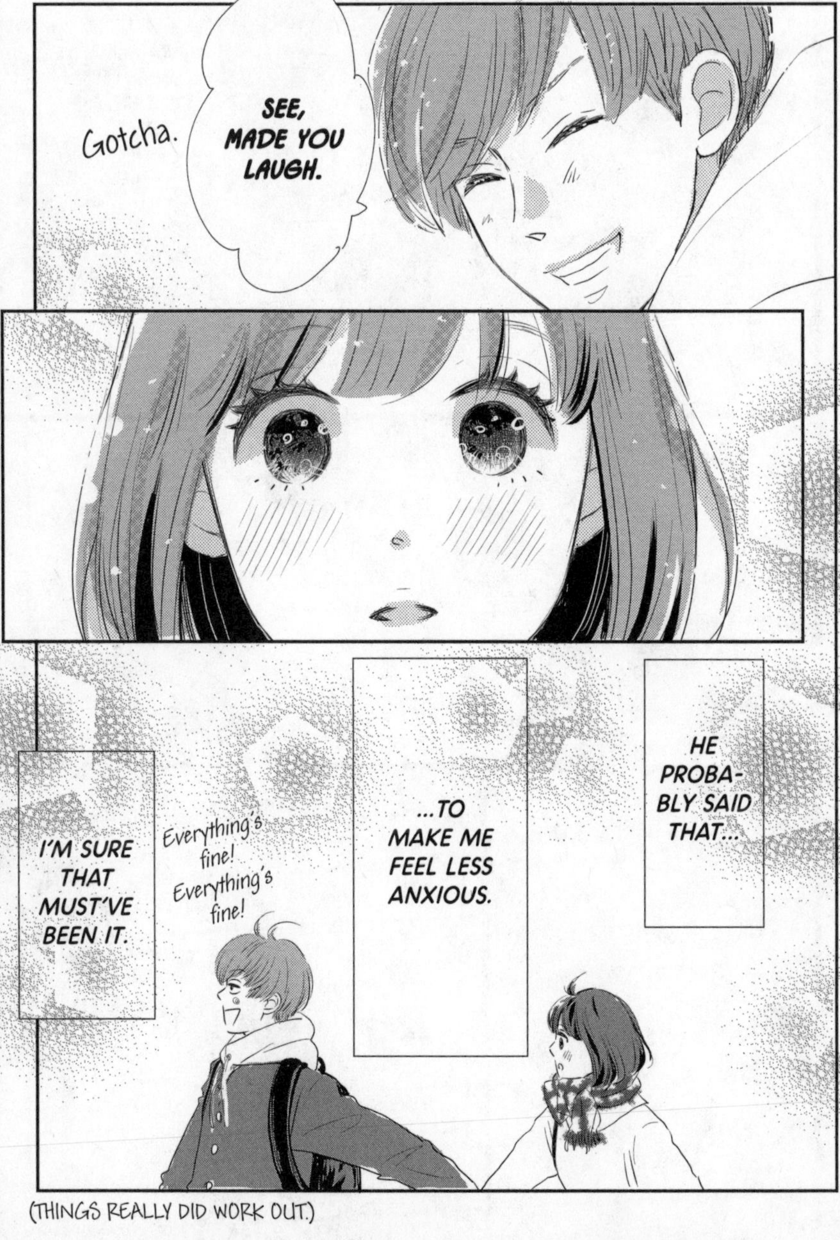
SEE, MADE YOU LAUGH.
Gotcha.
HE PROBABLY SAID THAT...
...TO MAKE ME FEEL LESS ANXIOUS.
Everything's fine! Everything's fine!
I'M SURE THAT MUST'VE BEEN IT.

(THINGS REALLY DID WORK OUT.)

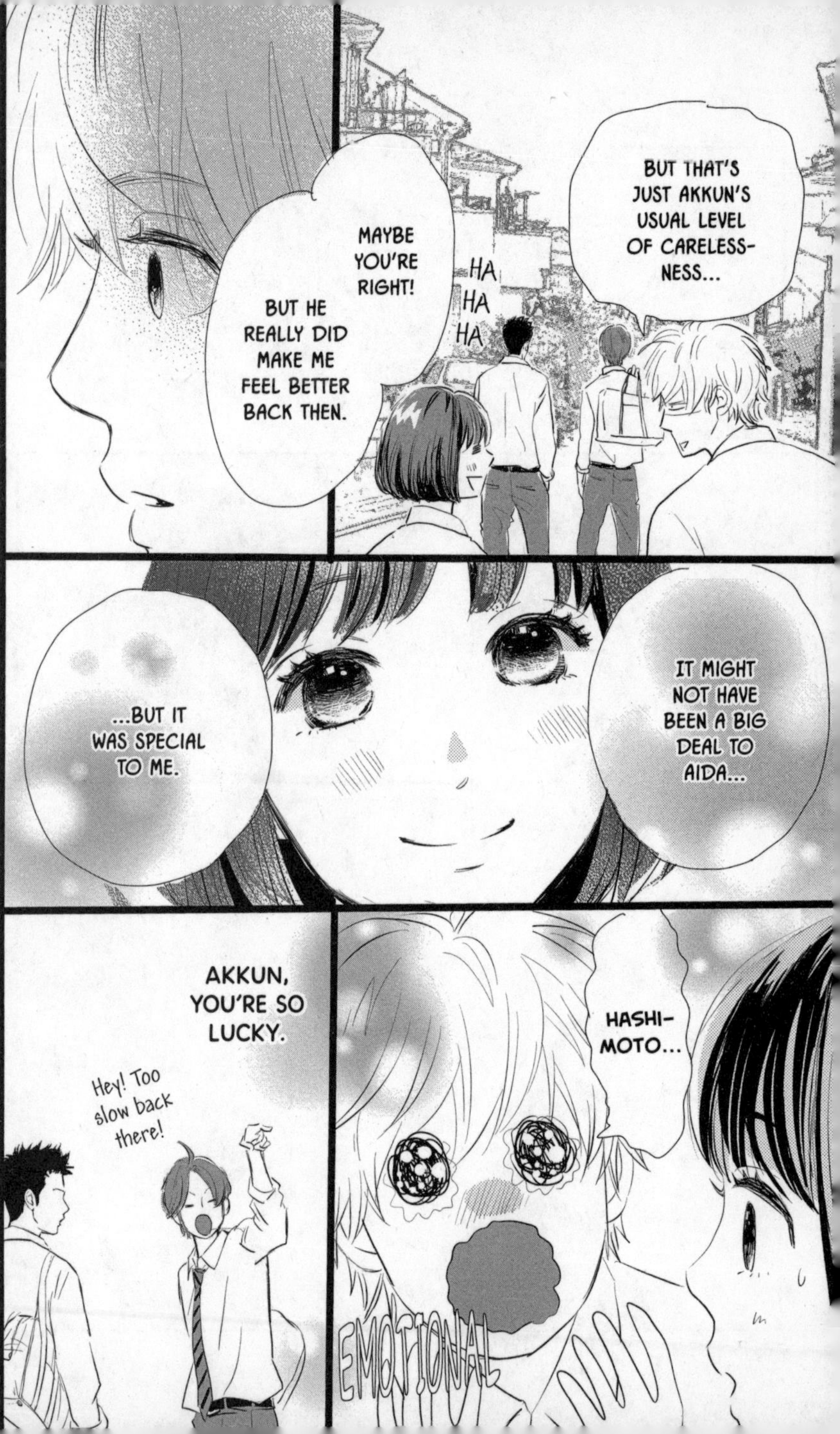

BUT THAT'S JUST AKKUN'S USUAL LEVEL OF CARELESS-NESS...
HA HA HA
MAYBE YOU'RE RIGHT!
BUT HE REALLY DID MAKE ME FEEL BETTER BACK THEN.
IT MIGHT NOT HAVE BEEN A BIG DEAL TO AIDA...
...BUT IT WAS SPECIAL TO ME.
HASHI-MOTO...
EMOTIONAL
AKKUN, YOU'RE SO LUCKY.
Hey! Too slow back there!

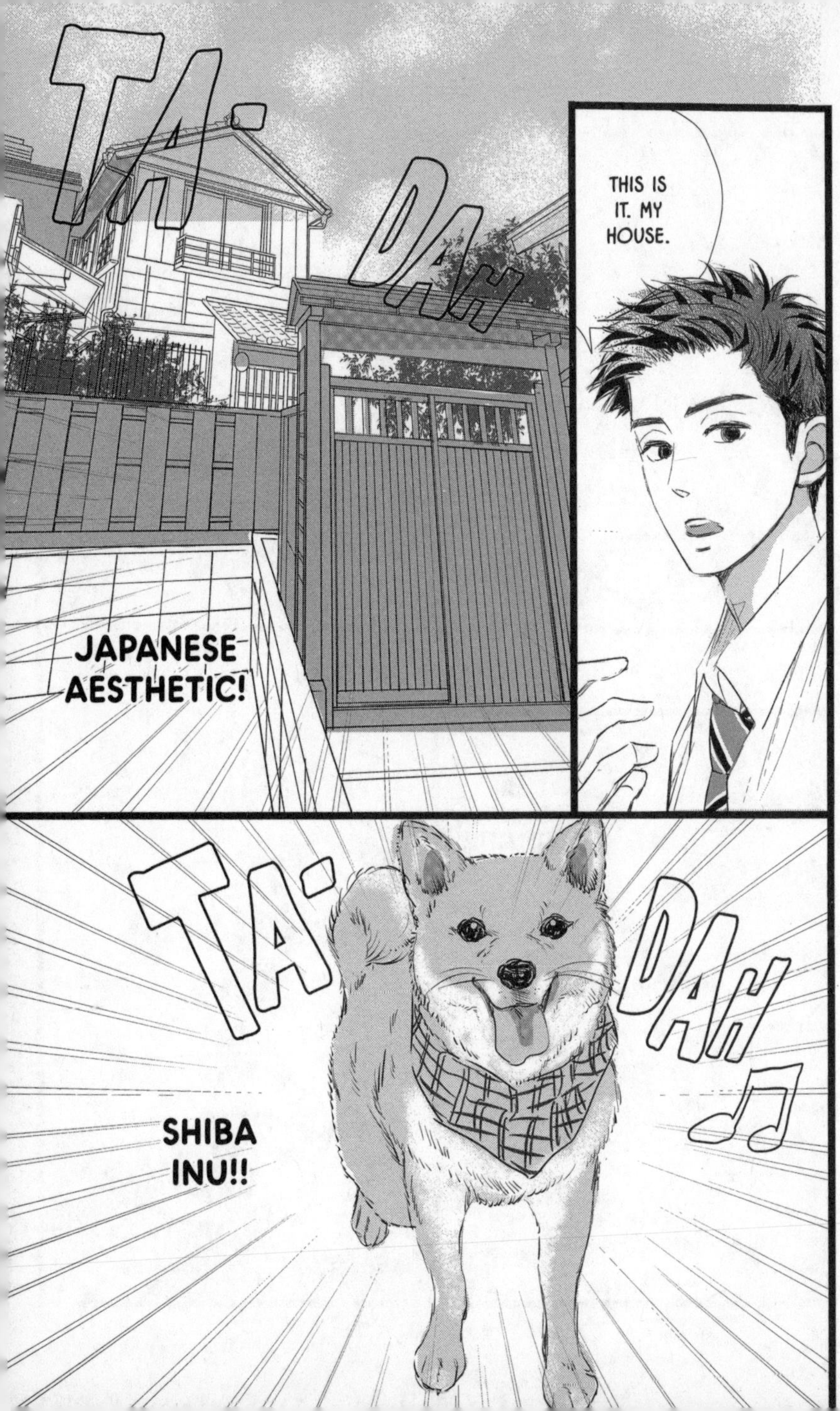
THIS IS IT. MY HOUSE.
TA-DAH
JAPANESE AESTHETIC!
TA-DAH ♫
SHIBA INU!!

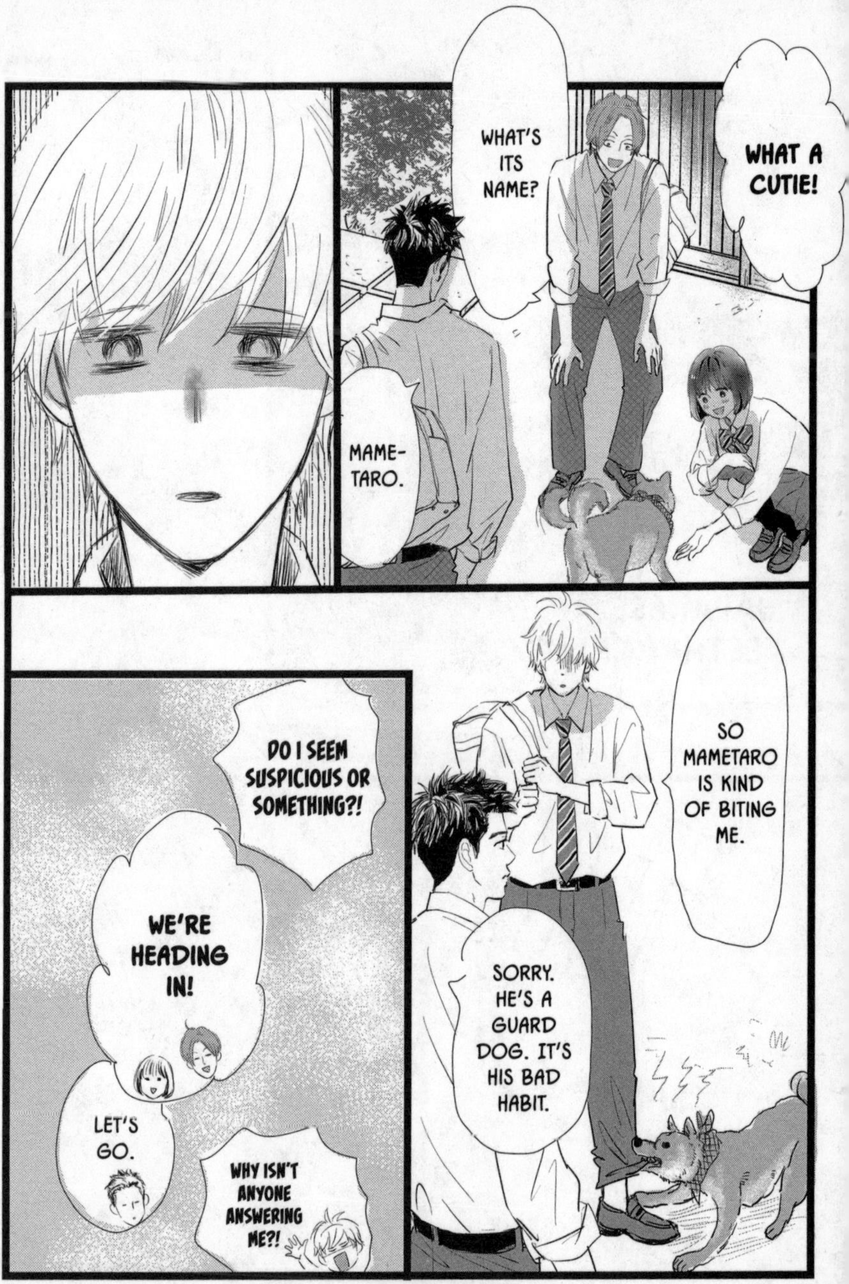
WHAT A CUTIE!
WHAT'S ITS NAME?
MAME-TARO.
SO MAMETARO IS KIND OF BITING ME.
SORRY. HE'S A GUARD DOG. IT'S HIS BAD HABIT.
DO I SEEM SUSPICIOUS OR SOMETHING?!
WE'RE HEADING IN!
LET'S GO.
WHY ISN'T ANYONE ANSWERING ME?!

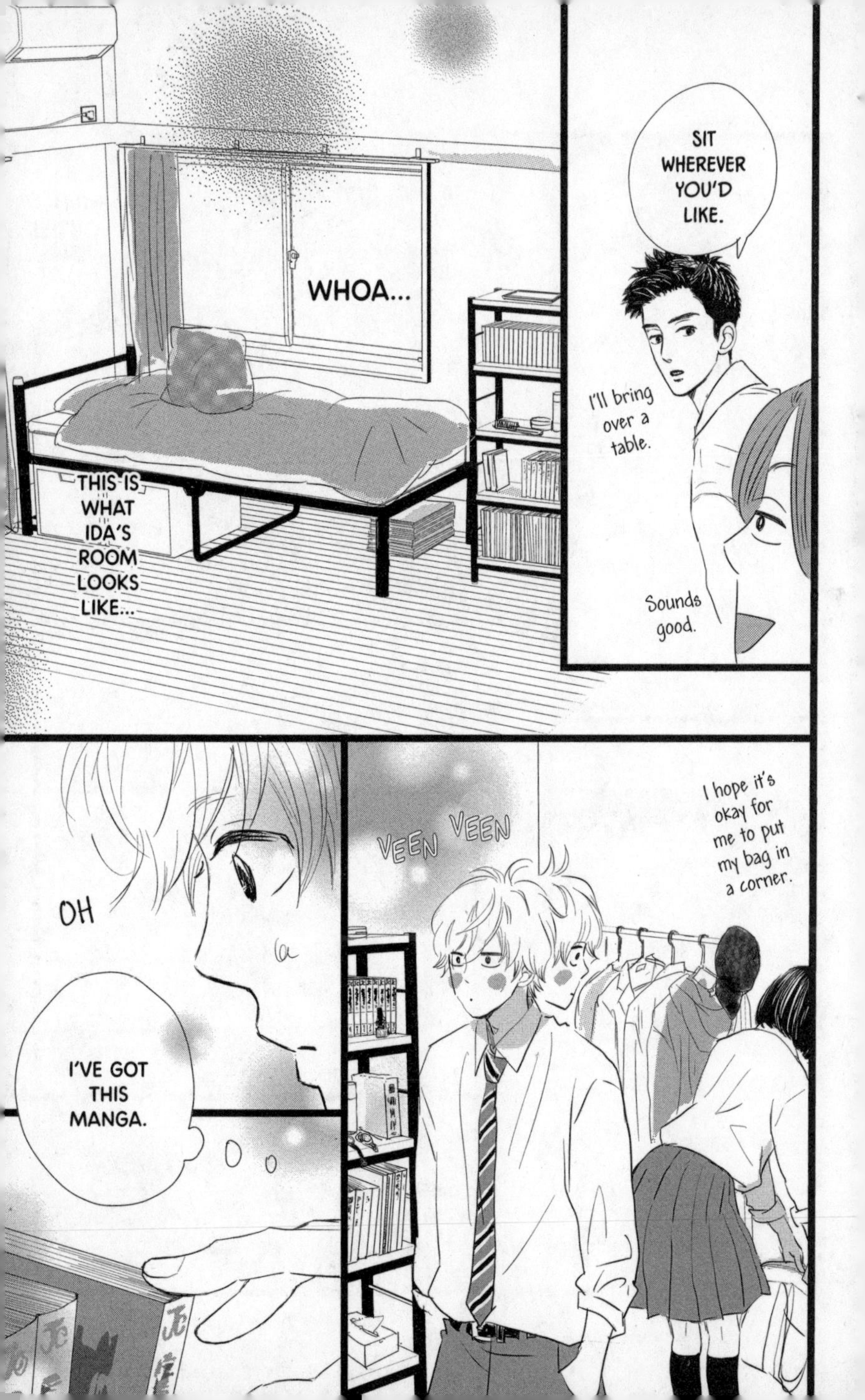
SIT WHEREVER YOU'D LIKE.
I'll bring over a table.
Sounds good.
WHOA...
THIS IS WHAT IDA'S ROOM LOOKS LIKE...
I hope it's okay for me to put my bag in a corner.
VEEN VEEN
OH
I'VE GOT THIS MANGA.

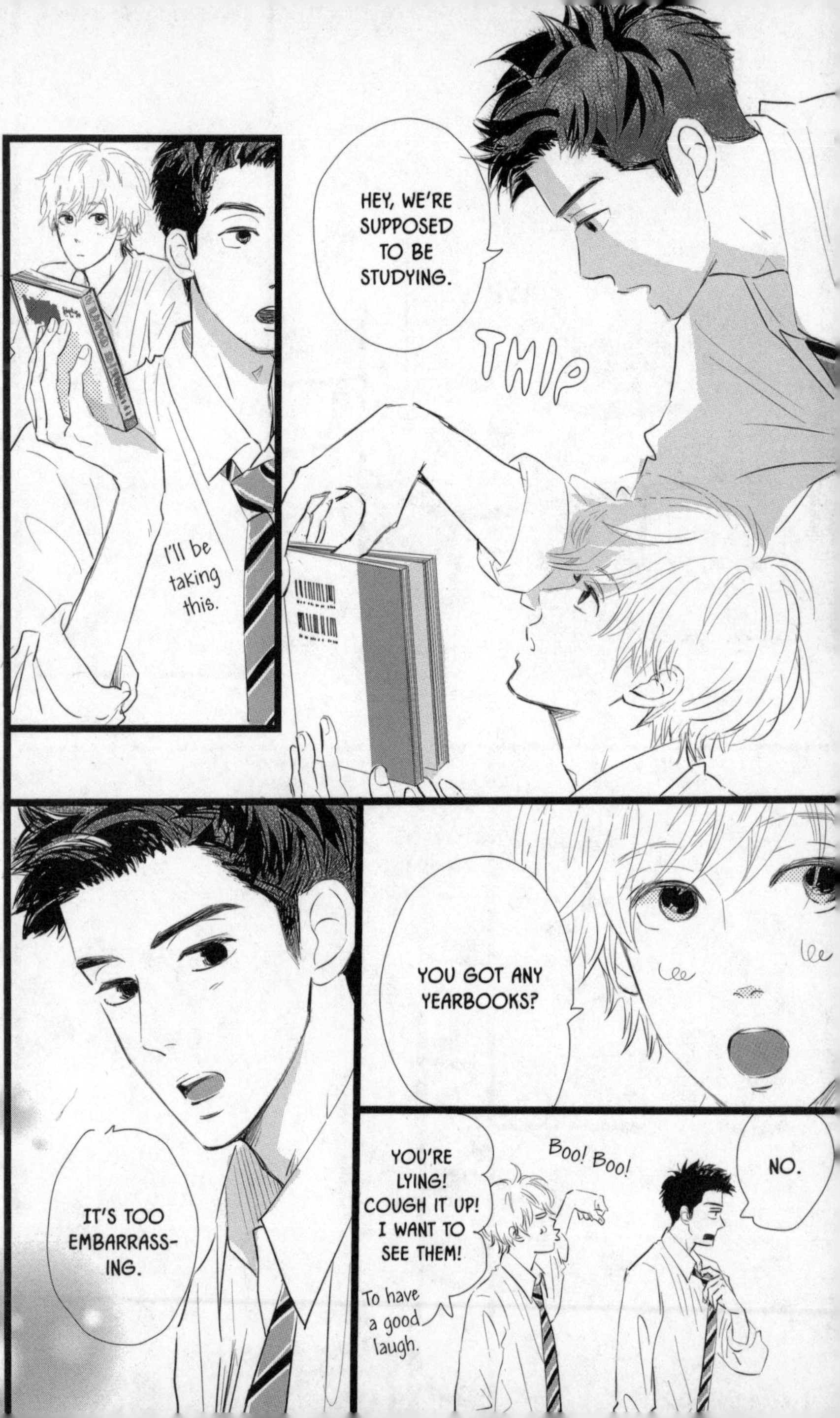
HEY, WE'RE SUPPOSED TO BE STUDYING.
THIP
I'll be taking this.
YOU GOT ANY YEARBOOKS?
NO.
Boo! Boo!
YOU'RE LYING! COUGH IT UP! I WANT TO SEE THEM!
To have a good laugh.
IT'S TOO EMBARRASS-ING.

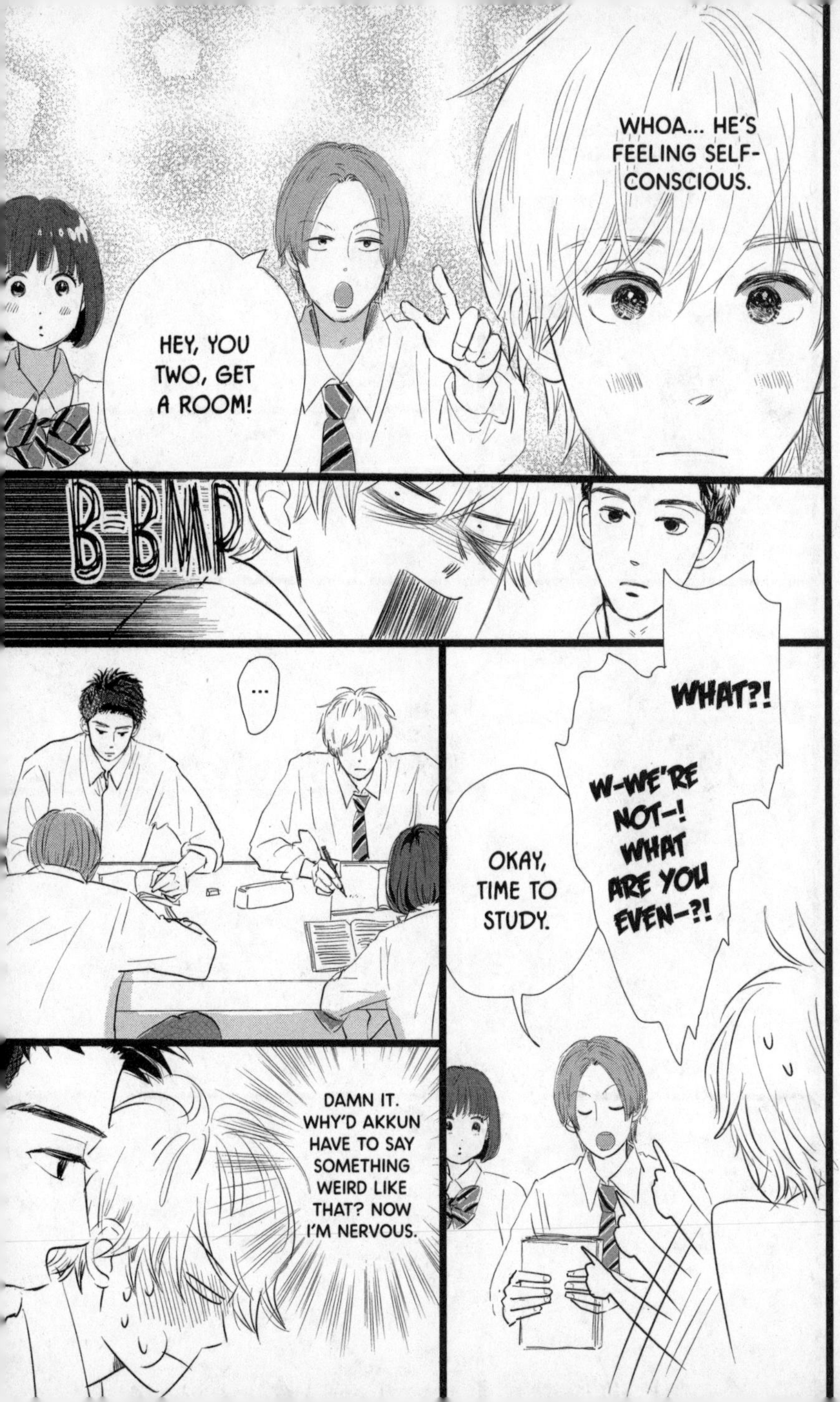
WHOA... HE'S FEELING SELF-CONSCIOUS.
HEY, YOU TWO, GET A ROOM!
B-BMP
WHAT?!
W-WE'RE NOT-! WHAT ARE YOU EVEN-?!
OKAY, TIME TO STUDY.
...
DAMN IT. WHY'D AKKUN HAVE TO SAY SOMETHING WEIRD LIKE THAT? NOW I'M NERVOUS.

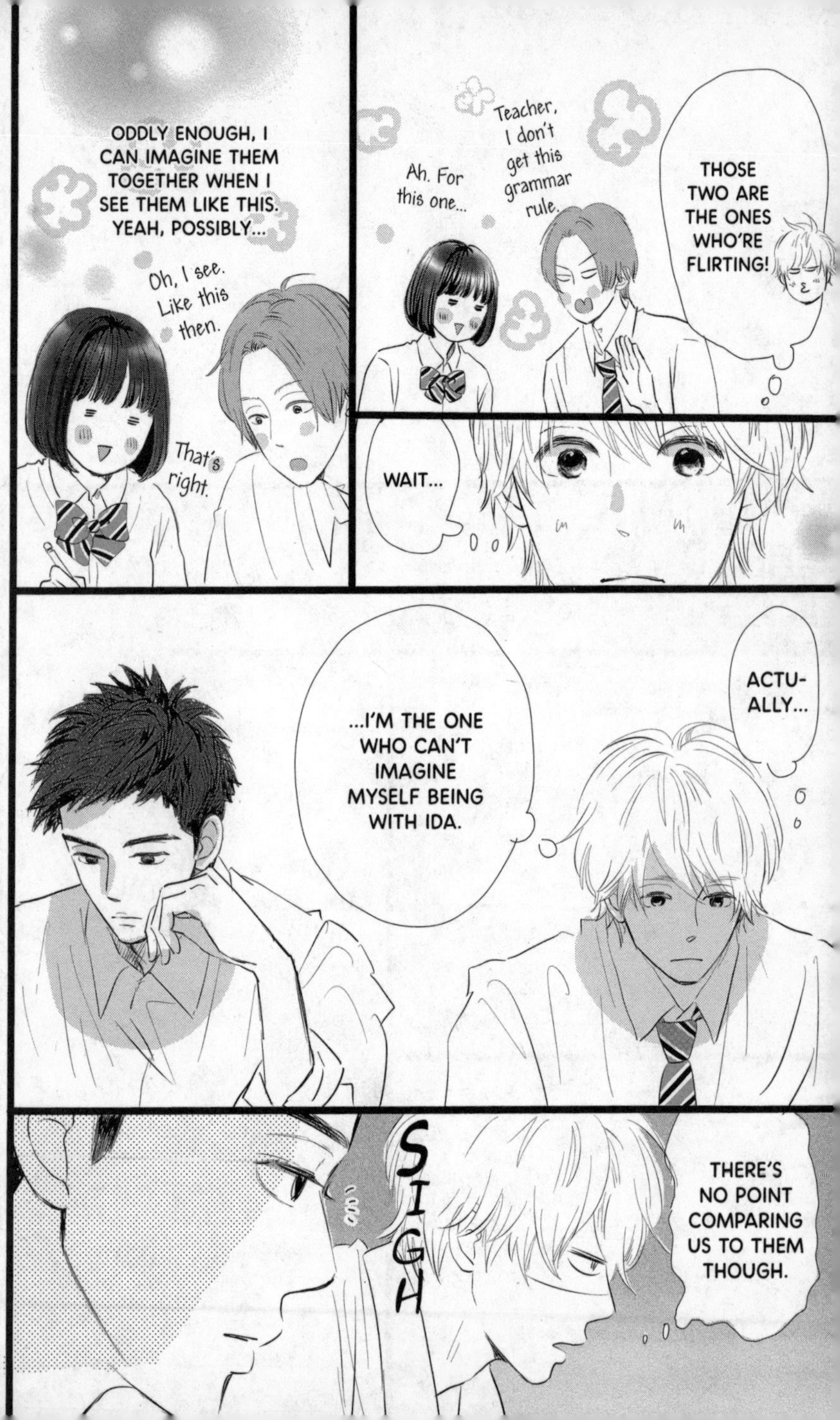
THOSE TWO ARE THE ONES WHO'RE FLIRTING!
Teacher, I don't get this grammar rule.
Ah. For this one...
WAIT...
ODDLY ENOUGH, I CAN IMAGINE THEM TOGETHER WHEN I SEE THEM LIKE THIS. YEAH, POSSIBLY...
Oh, I see. Like this then.
That's right.
ACTU-ALLY...
...I'M THE ONE WHO CAN'T IMAGINE MYSELF BEING WITH IDA.
THERE'S NO POINT COMPARING US TO THEM THOUGH.
SIGH

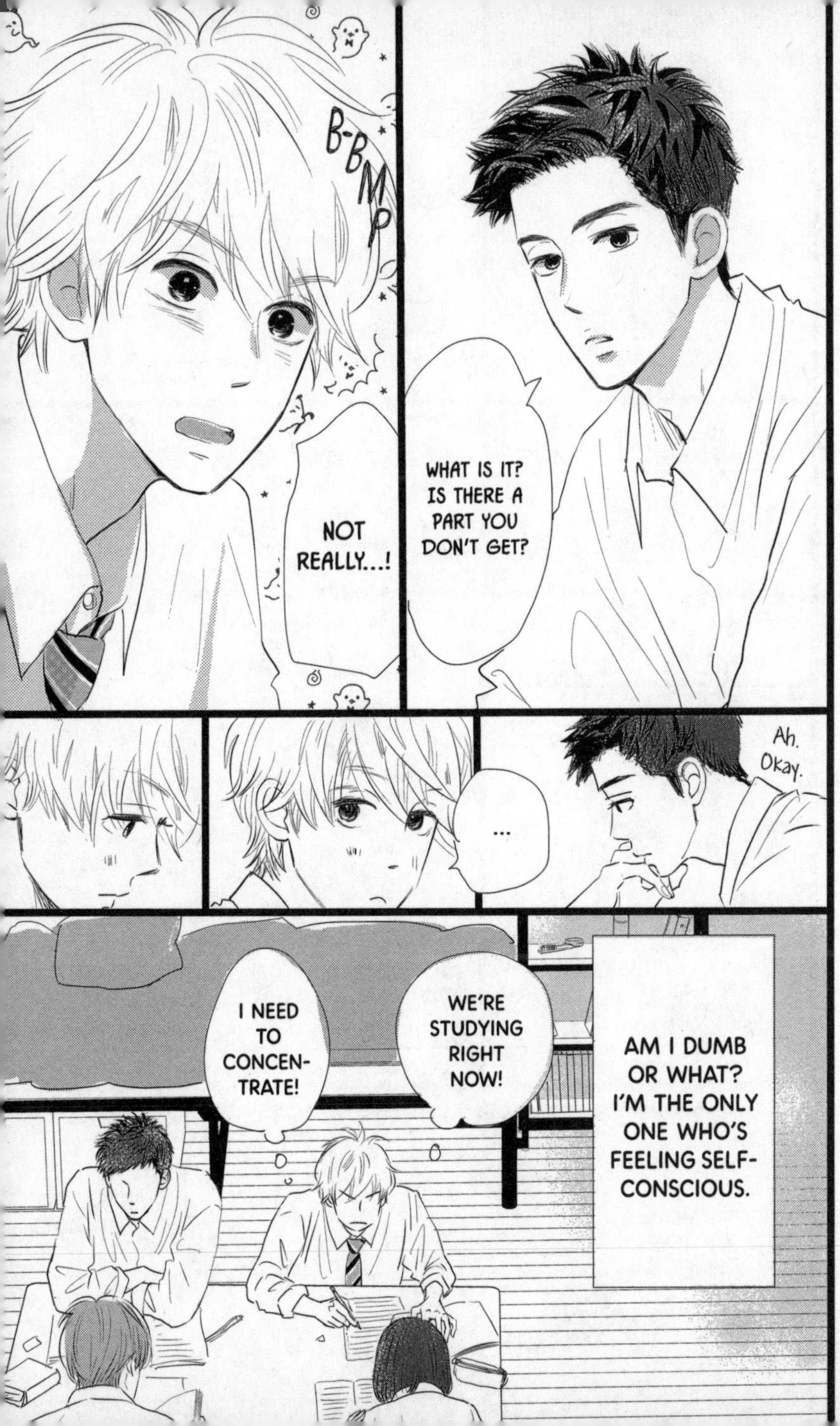
WHAT IS IT? IS THERE A PART YOU DON'T GET?
B-BMP
NOT REALLY...!
Ah. Okay.
...
AM I DUMB OR WHAT? I'M THE ONLY ONE WHO'S FEELING SELF-CONSCIOUS.
WE'RE STUDYING RIGHT NOW!
I NEED TO CONCENTRATE!

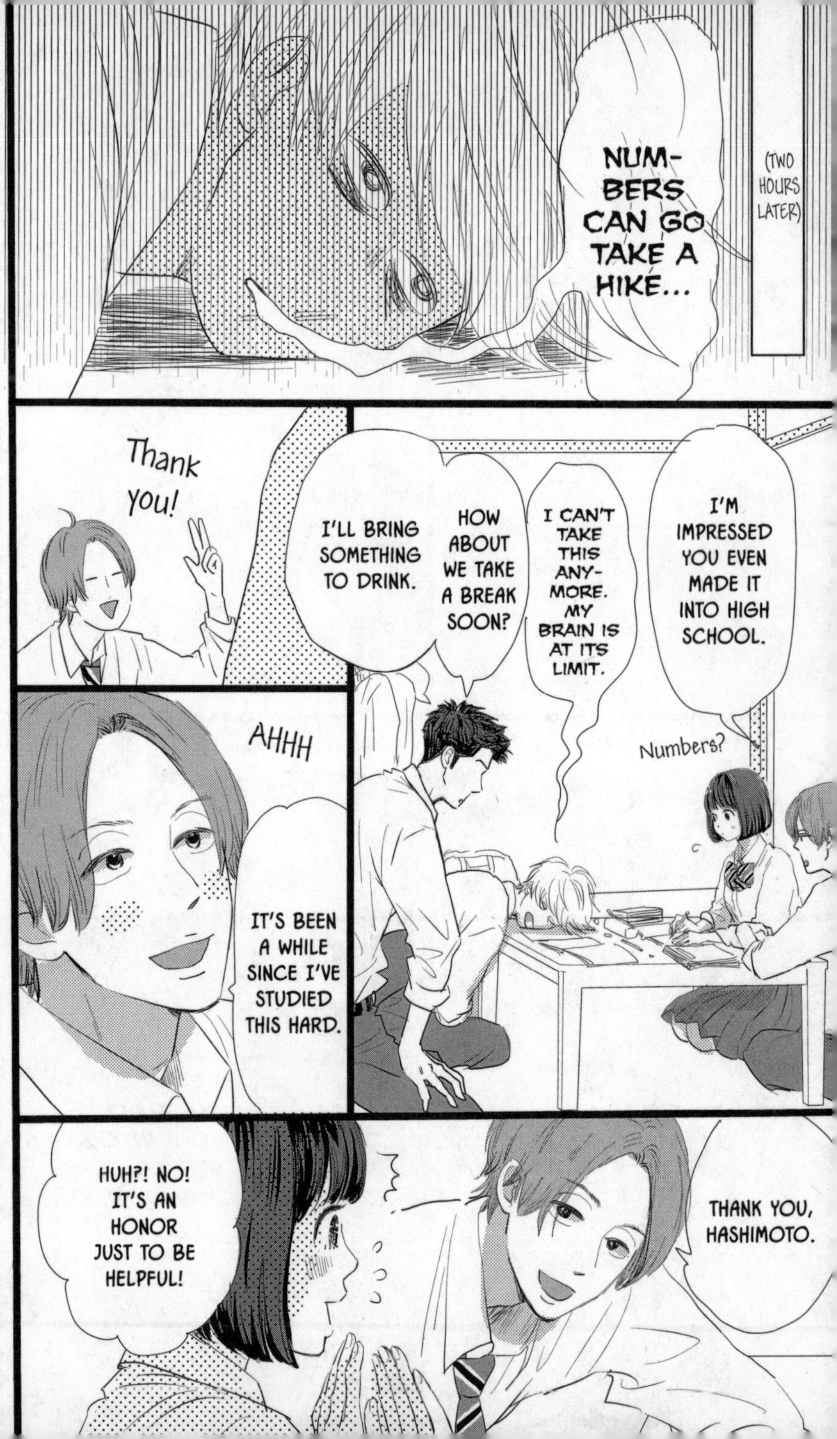
(TWO HOURS LATER)
NUM-BERS CAN GO TAKE A HIKE...
I'M IMPRESSED YOU EVEN MADE IT INTO HIGH SCHOOL.
I CAN'T TAKE THIS ANY-MORE. MY BRAIN IS AT ITS LIMIT.
HOW ABOUT WE TAKE A BREAK SOON?
I'LL BRING SOMETHING TO DRINK.
Numbers?
Thank you!
AHHH
IT'S BEEN A WHILE SINCE I'VE STUDIED THIS HARD.
THANK YOU, HASHIMOTO.
HUH?! NO! IT'S AN HONOR JUST TO BE HELPFUL!

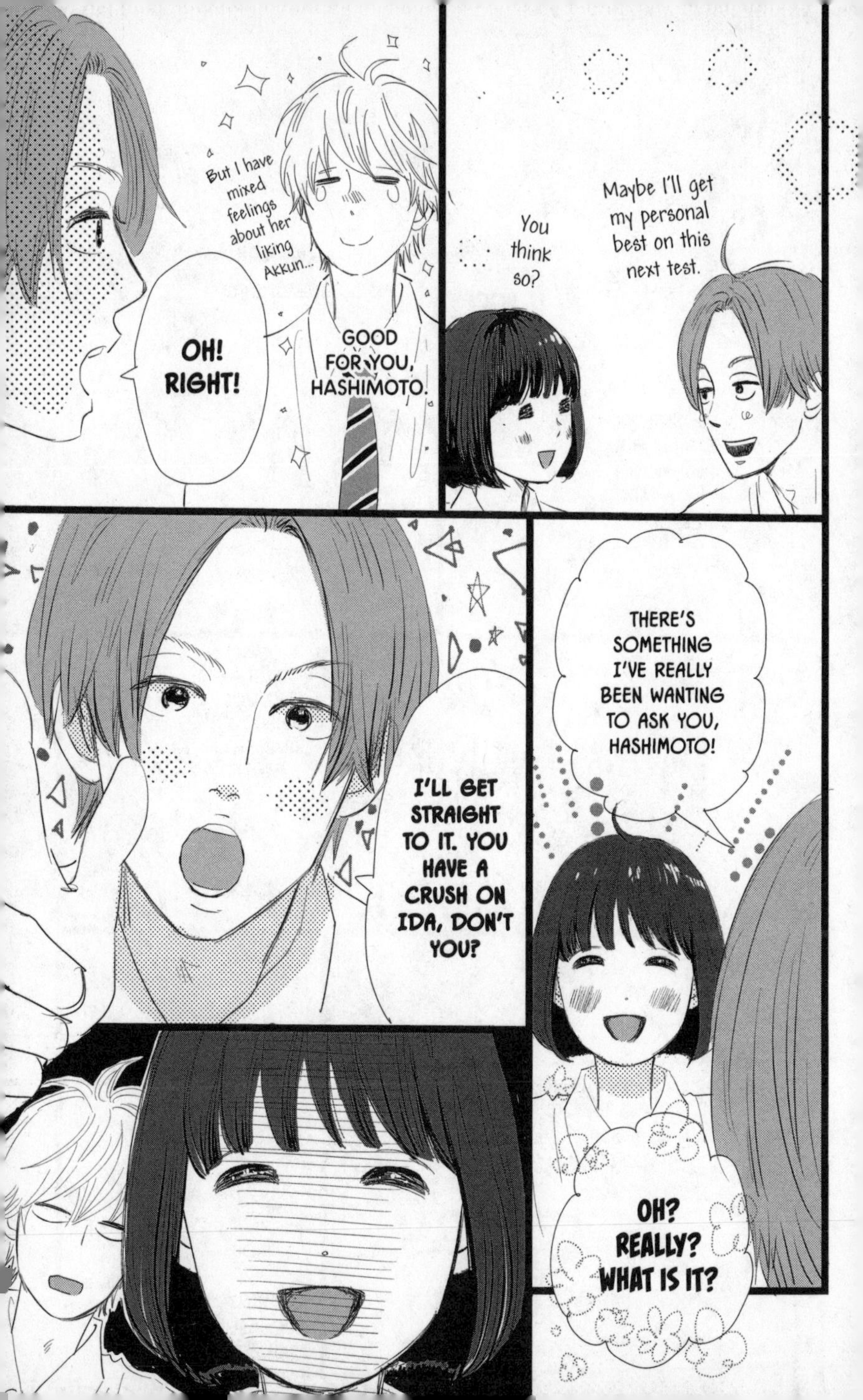
Maybe I'll get my personal best on this next test.
You think so?
But I have mixed feelings about her liking Akkun...
GOOD FOR YOU, HASHIMOTO.
OH! RIGHT!
THERE'S SOMETHING I'VE REALLY BEEN WANTING TO ASK YOU, HASHIMOTO!
OH? REALLY? WHAT IS IT?
I'LL GET STRAIGHT TO IT. YOU HAVE A CRUSH ON IDA, DON'T YOU?

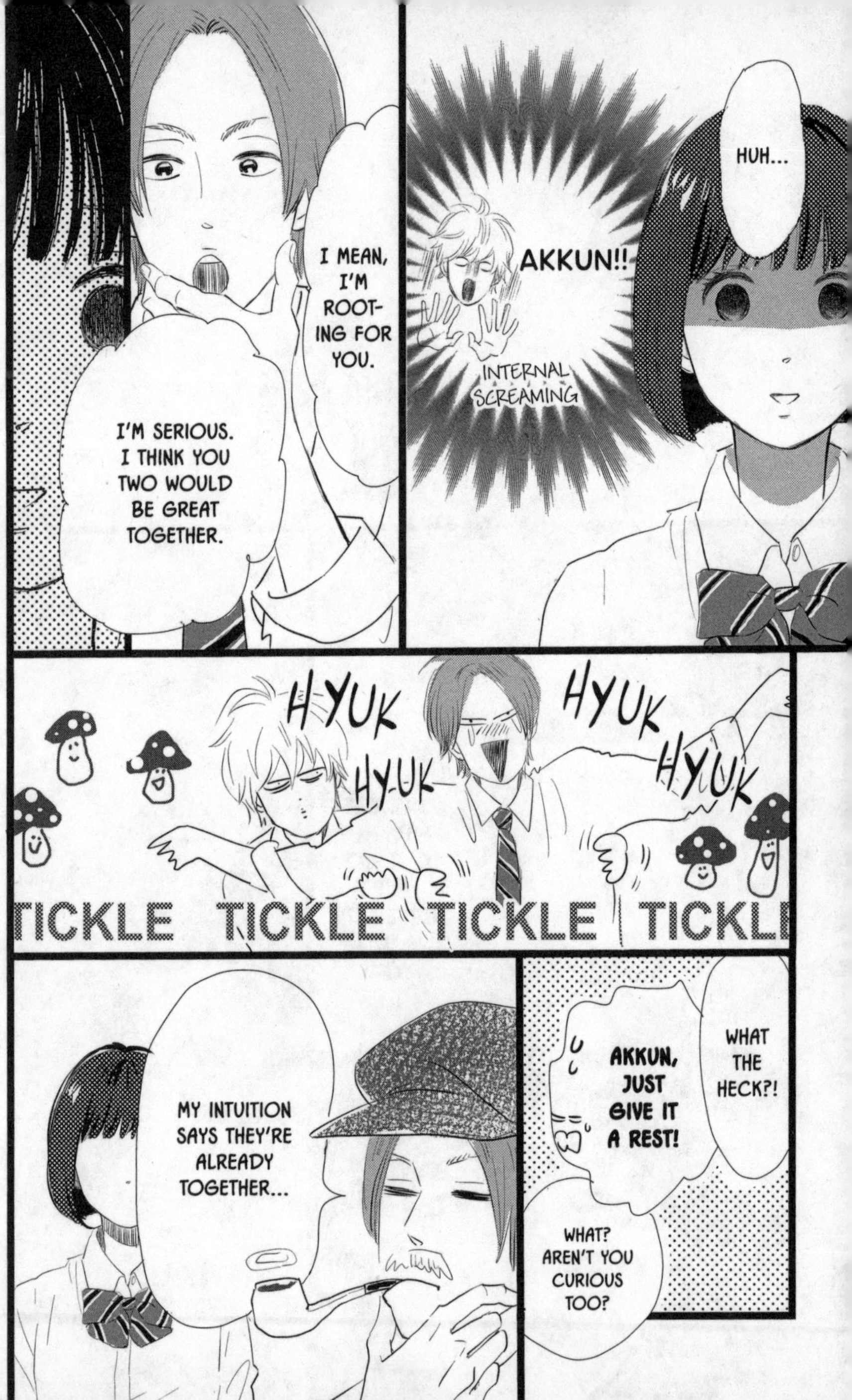
HUH...
AKKUN!!
INTERNAL SCREAMING
I MEAN, I'M ROOT-ING FOR YOU.
I'M SERIOUS. I THINK YOU TWO WOULD BE GREAT TOGETHER.
HYUK
HYUK
HYUK
HYUK
TICKLE
TICKLE
TICKLE
TICKLE
WHAT THE HECK?!
AKKUN, JUST GIVE IT A REST!
WHAT? AREN'T YOU CURIOUS TOO?
MY INTUITION SAYS THEY'RE ALREADY TOGETHER...

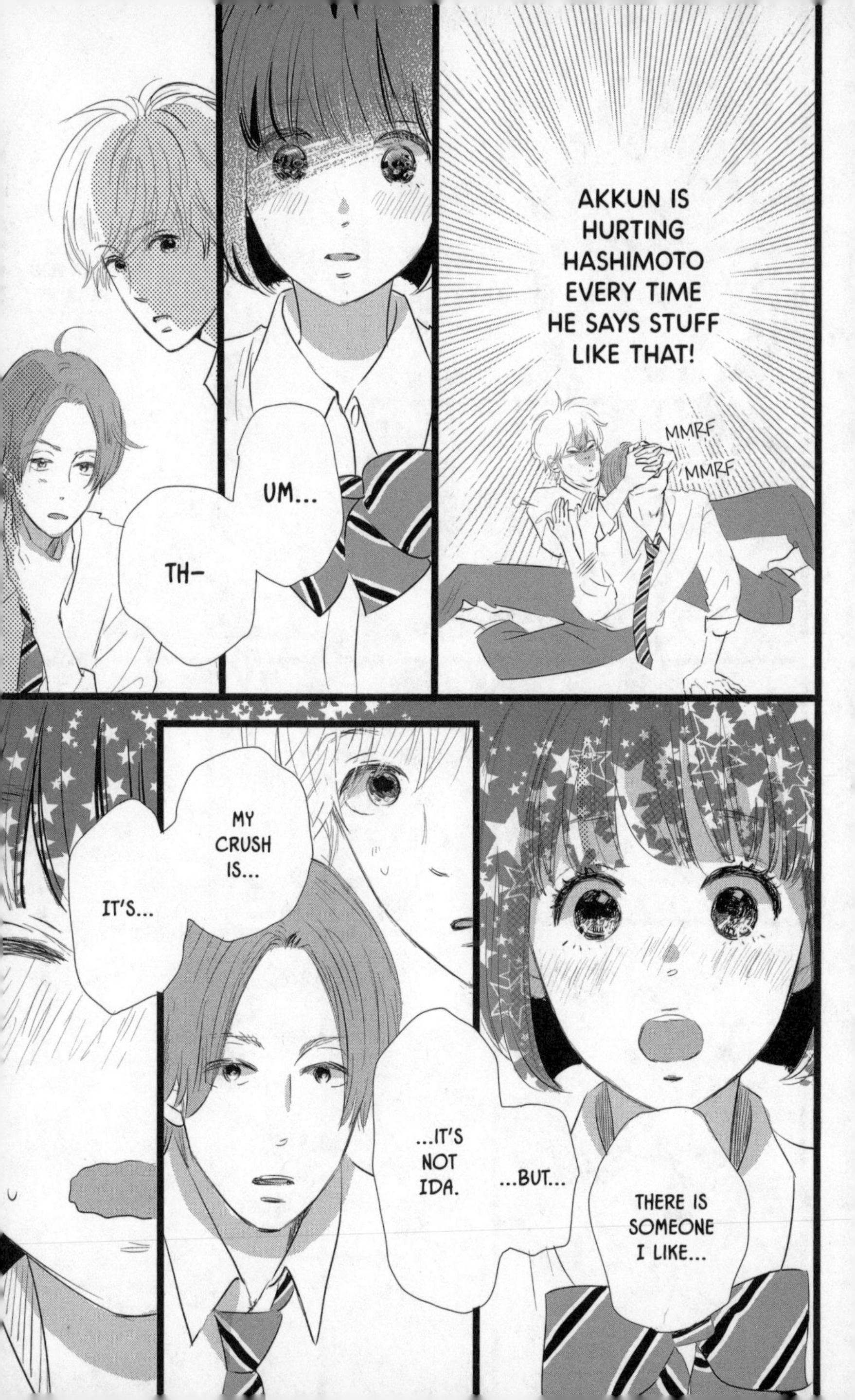
AKKUN IS HURTING HASHIMOTO EVERY TIME HE SAYS STUFF LIKE THAT!
MMRF
MMRF
UM...
TH-
THERE IS SOMEONE I LIKE...
...BUT...
...IT'S NOT IDA.
MY CRUSH IS...
IT'S...

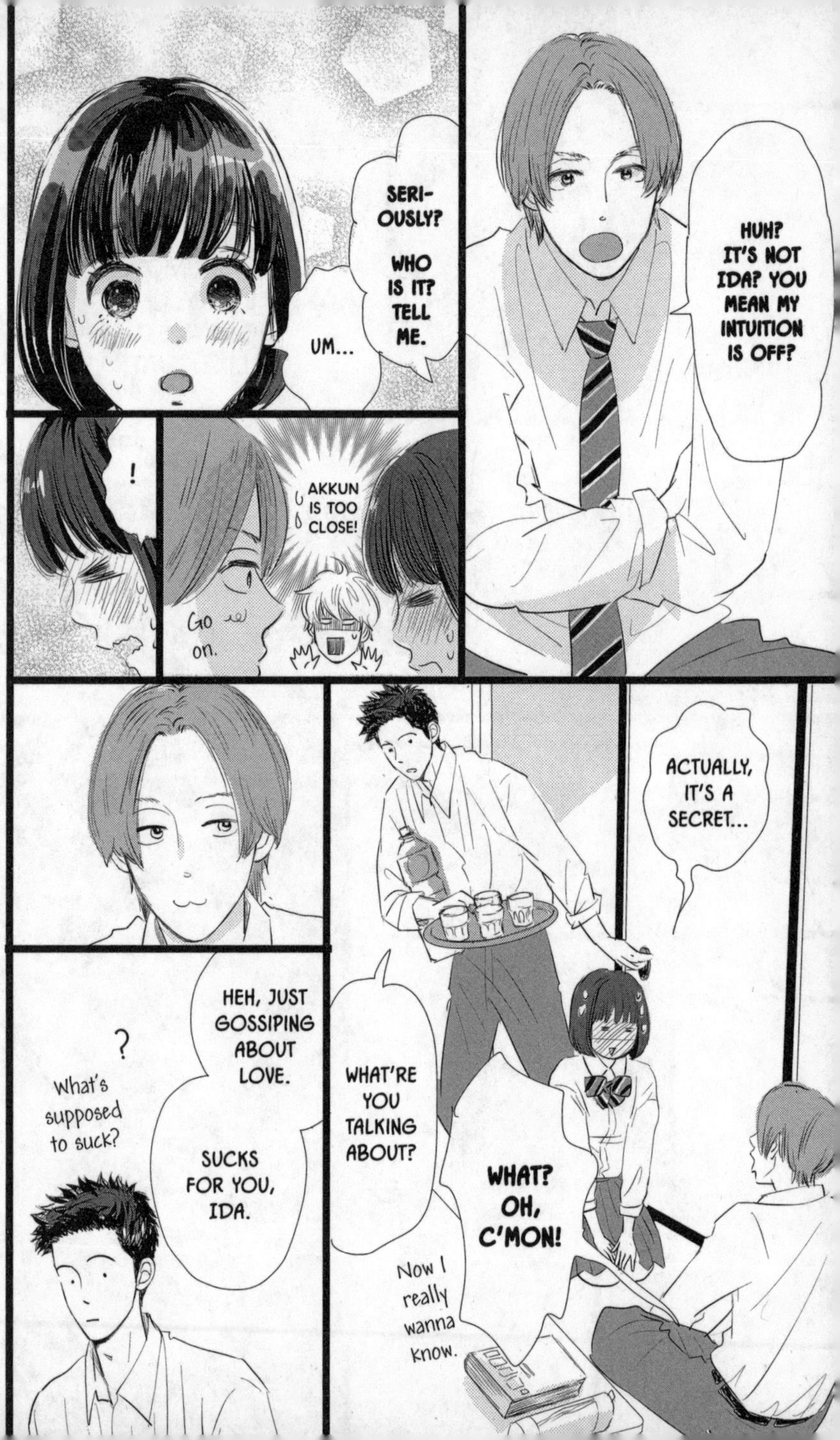
HUH? IT'S NOT IDA? YOU MEAN MY INTUITION IS OFF?
SERI-OUSLY? WHO IS IT? TELL ME.
UM...
AKKUN IS TOO CLOSE!
Go on.
!
ACTUALLY, IT'S A SECRET...
WHAT? OH, C'MON!
Now I really wanna know.
WHAT'RE YOU TALKING ABOUT?
HEH, JUST GOSSIPING ABOUT LOVE.
SUCKS FOR YOU, IDA.
?
What's supposed to suck?

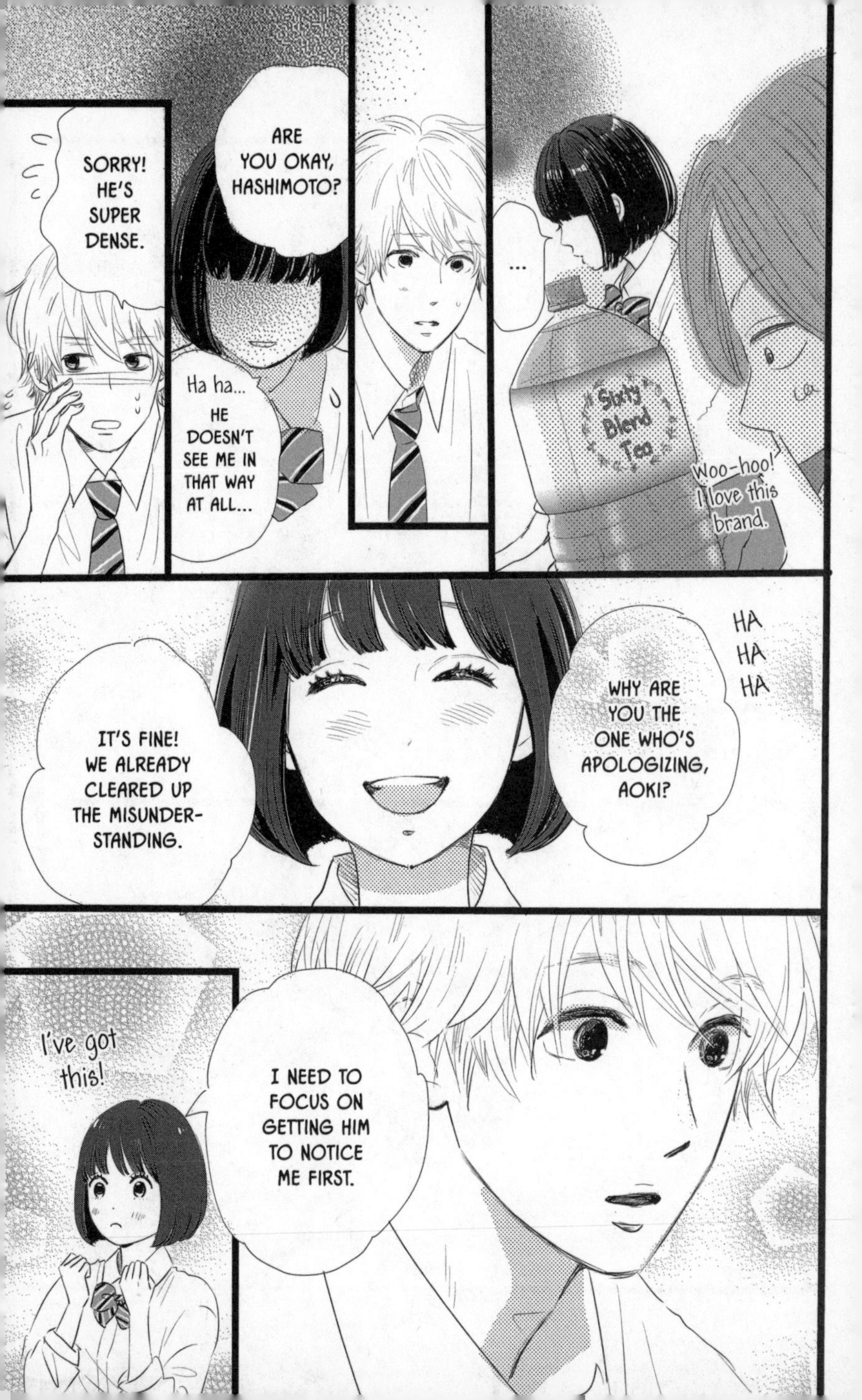
...
Sixty Blend Tea
Woo-hoo! I love this brand.
ARE YOU OKAY, HASHIMOTO?
Ha ha... HE DOESN'T SEE ME IN THAT WAY AT ALL...
SORRY! HE'S SUPER DENSE.
HA HA HA
WHY ARE YOU THE ONE WHO'S APOLOGIZING, AOKI?
IT'S FINE! WE ALREADY CLEARED UP THE MISUNDER-STANDING.
I NEED TO FOCUS ON GETTING HIM TO NOTICE ME FIRST.
I've got this!

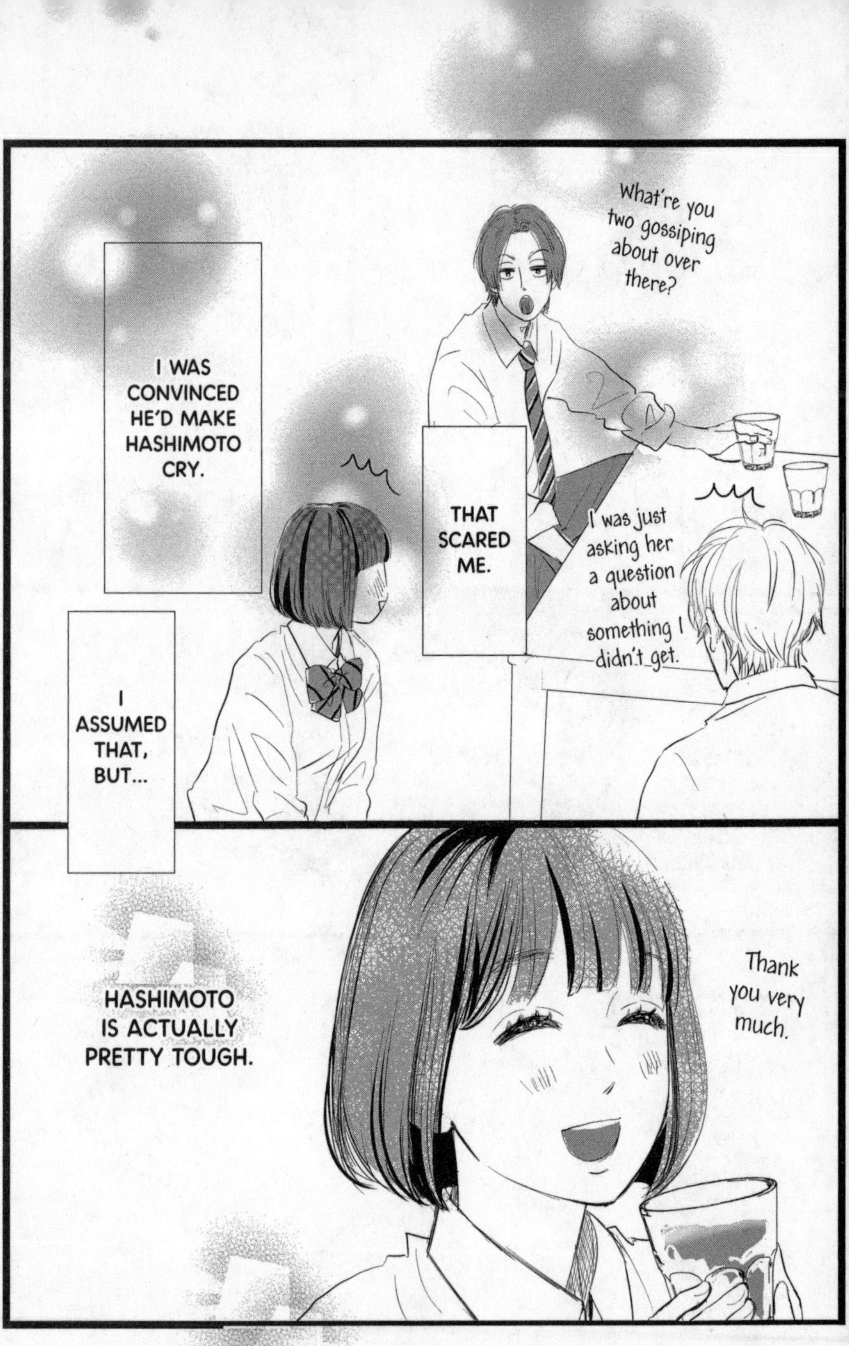
What're you two gossiping about over there?
I was just asking her a question about something I didn't get.
THAT SCARED ME.
I WAS CONVINCED HE'D MAKE HASHIMOTO CRY.
I ASSUMED THAT, BUT...
Thank you very much.
HASHIMOTO IS ACTUALLY PRETTY TOUGH.

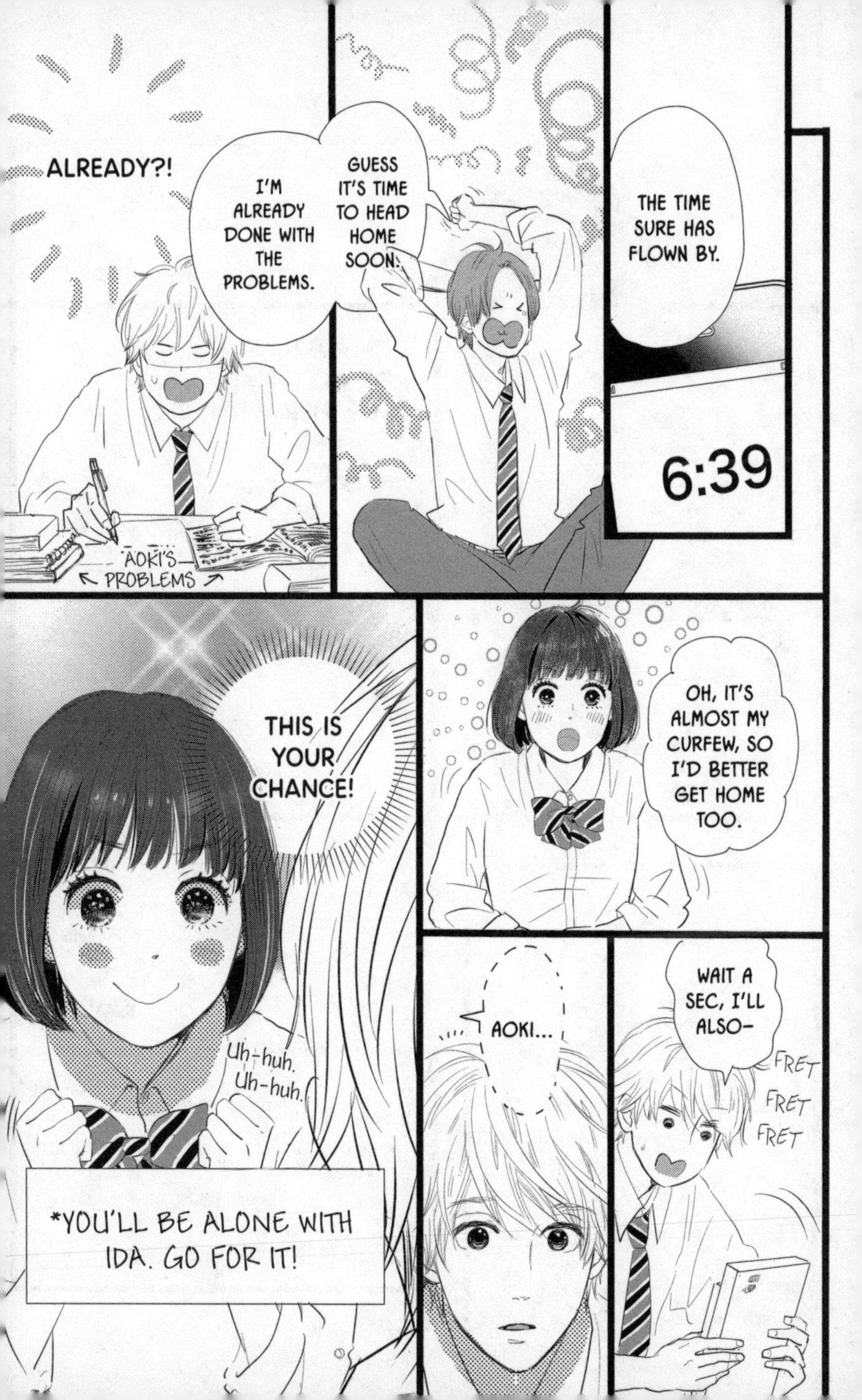
THE TIME SURE HAS FLOWN BY.
6:39
GUESS IT'S TIME TO HEAD HOME SOON.
I'M ALREADY DONE WITH THE PROBLEMS.
ALREADY?!
AOKI'S PROBLEMS
OH, IT'S ALMOST MY CURFEW, SO I'D BETTER GET HOME TOO.
WAIT A SEC, I'LL ALSO-
FRET FRET FRET
... AOKI...
THIS IS YOUR CHANCE!
Uh-huh. Uh-huh.
*YOU'LL BE ALONE WITH IDA. GO FOR IT!

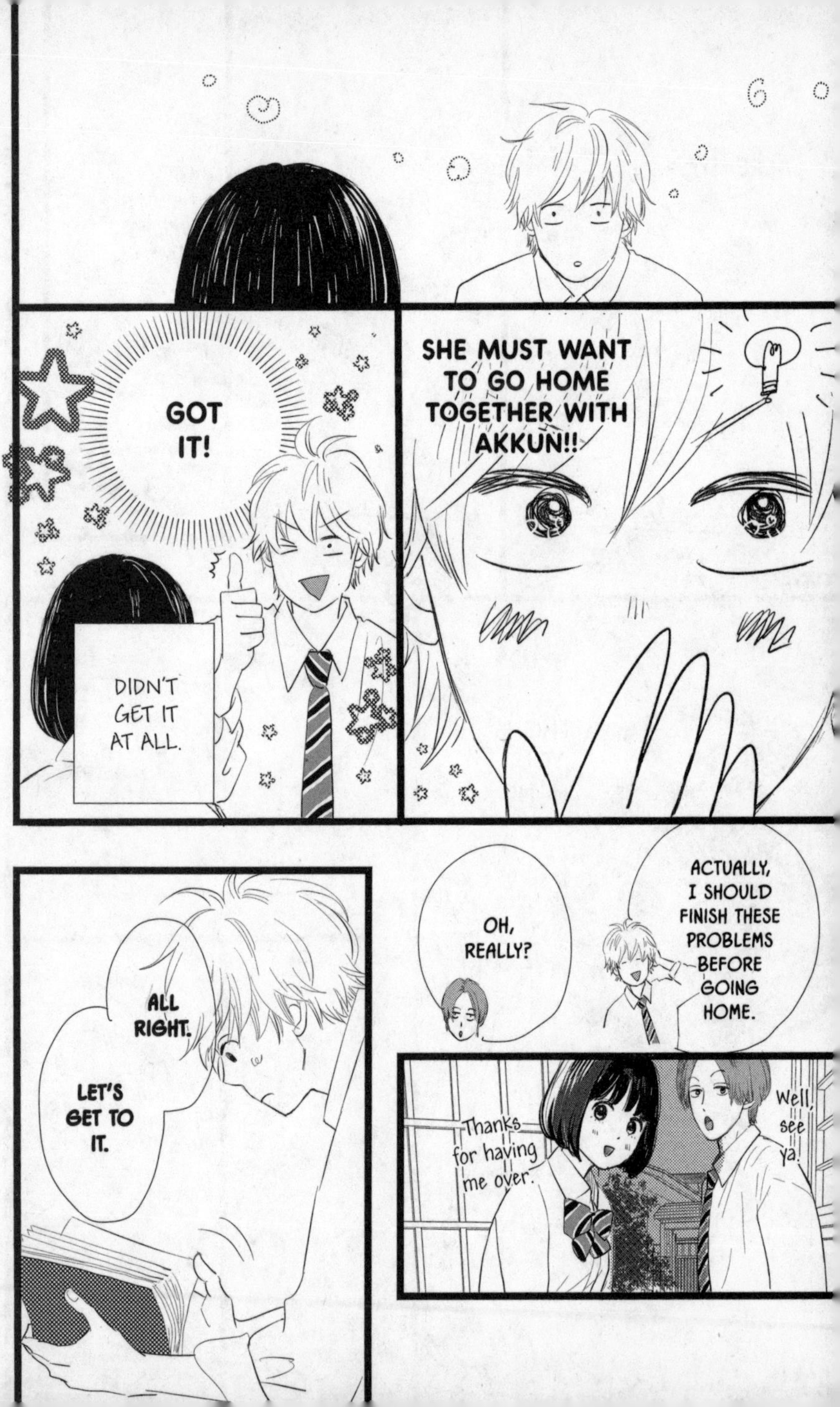
SHE MUST WANT TO GO HOME TOGETHER WITH AKKUN!!
GOT IT!
DIDN'T GET IT AT ALL.
ACTUALLY, I SHOULD FINISH THESE PROBLEMS BEFORE GOING HOME.
OH, REALLY?
Well, see ya!
Thanks for having me over.
ALL RIGHT.
LET'S GET TO IT.

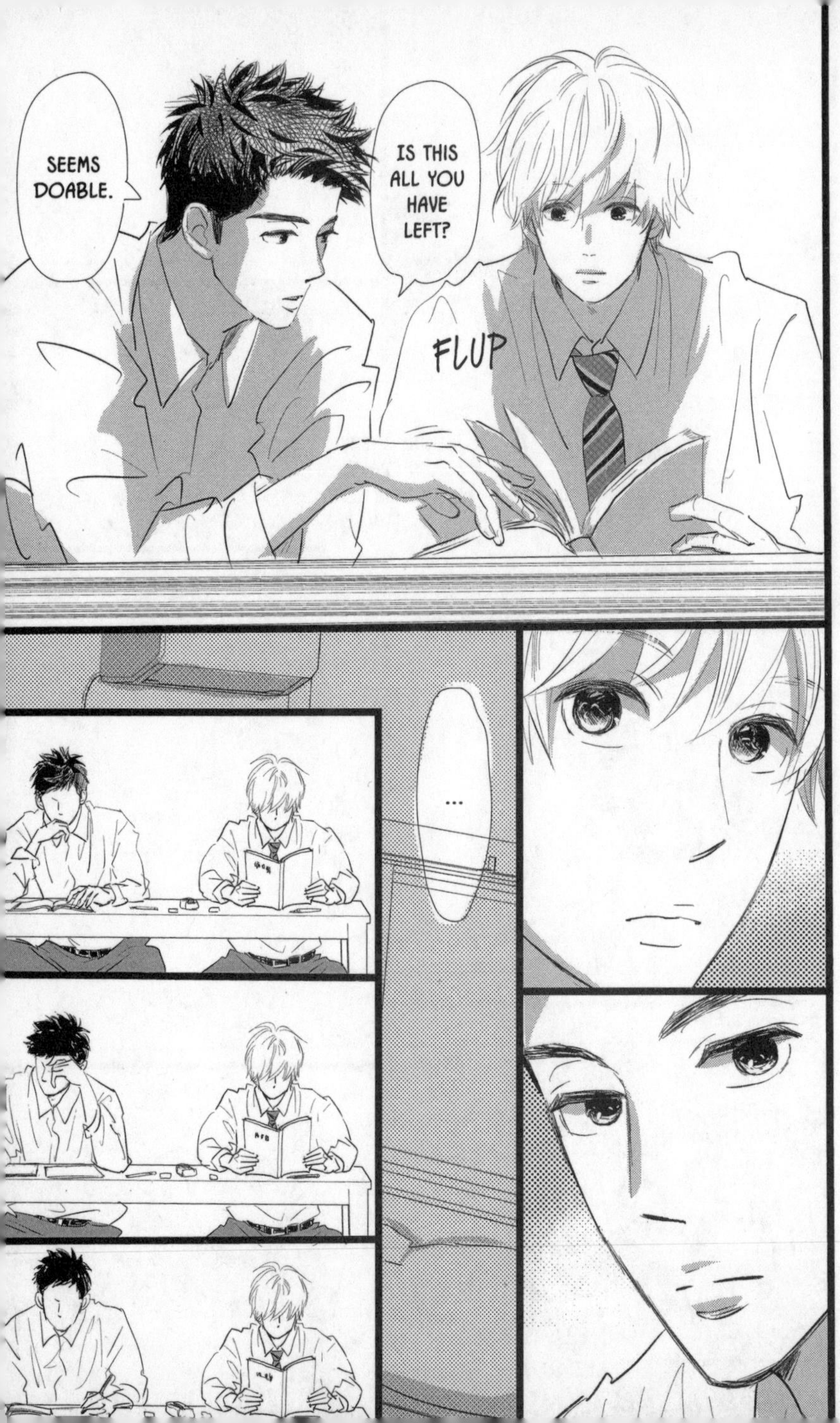
IS THIS ALL YOU HAVE LEFT?
FLUP
SEEMS DOABLE.
...

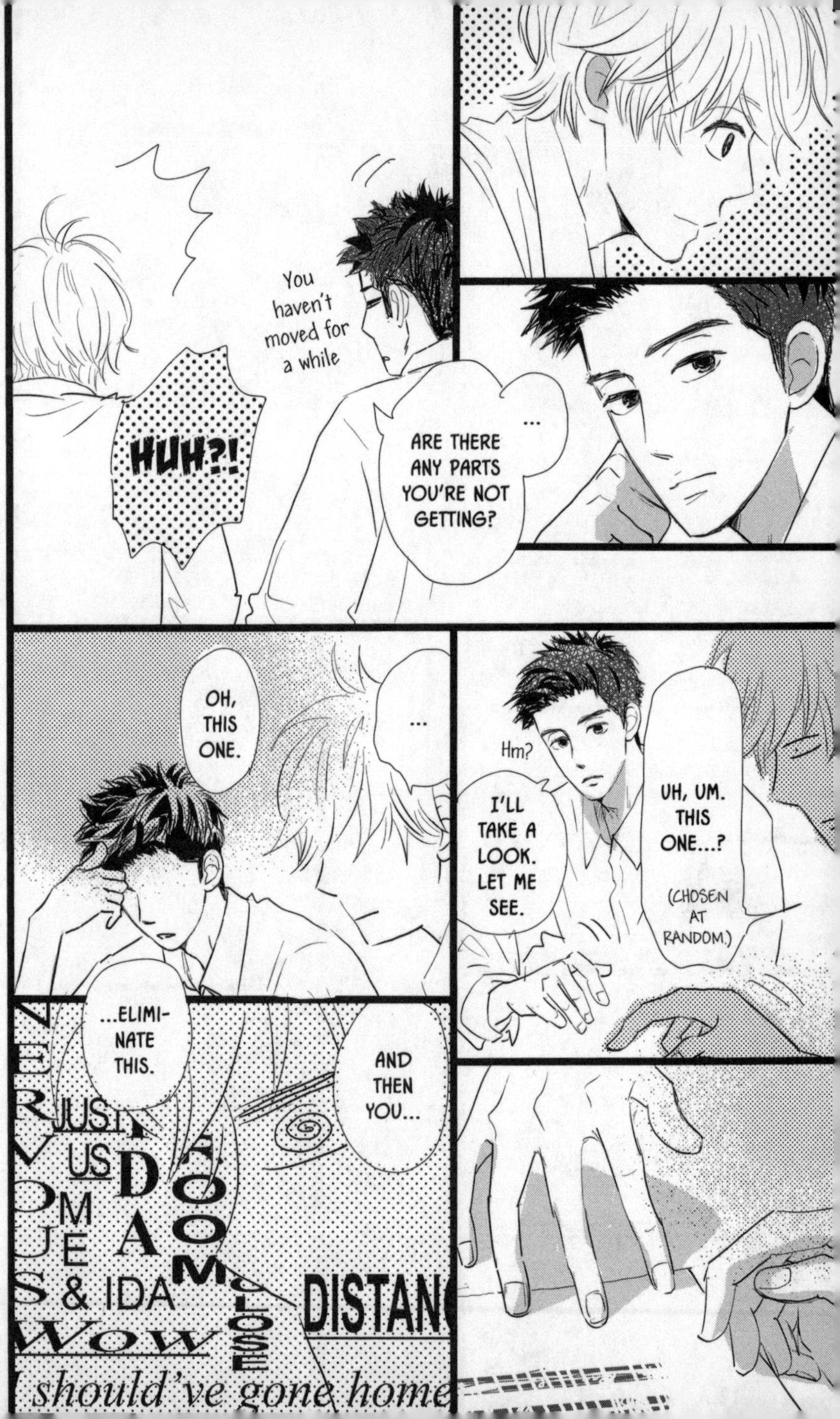
You haven't moved for a while
HUH?!
...
ARE THERE ANY PARTS YOU'RE NOT GETTING?
UH, UM. THIS ONE...?
(CHOSEN AT RANDOM.)
Hm?
I'LL TAKE A LOOK. LET ME SEE.
...
OH, THIS ONE.
AND THEN YOU...
...ELIMINATE THIS.
NERVOUS
JUST US
TOO CLOSE
DISTANC
WOW
I should've gone home

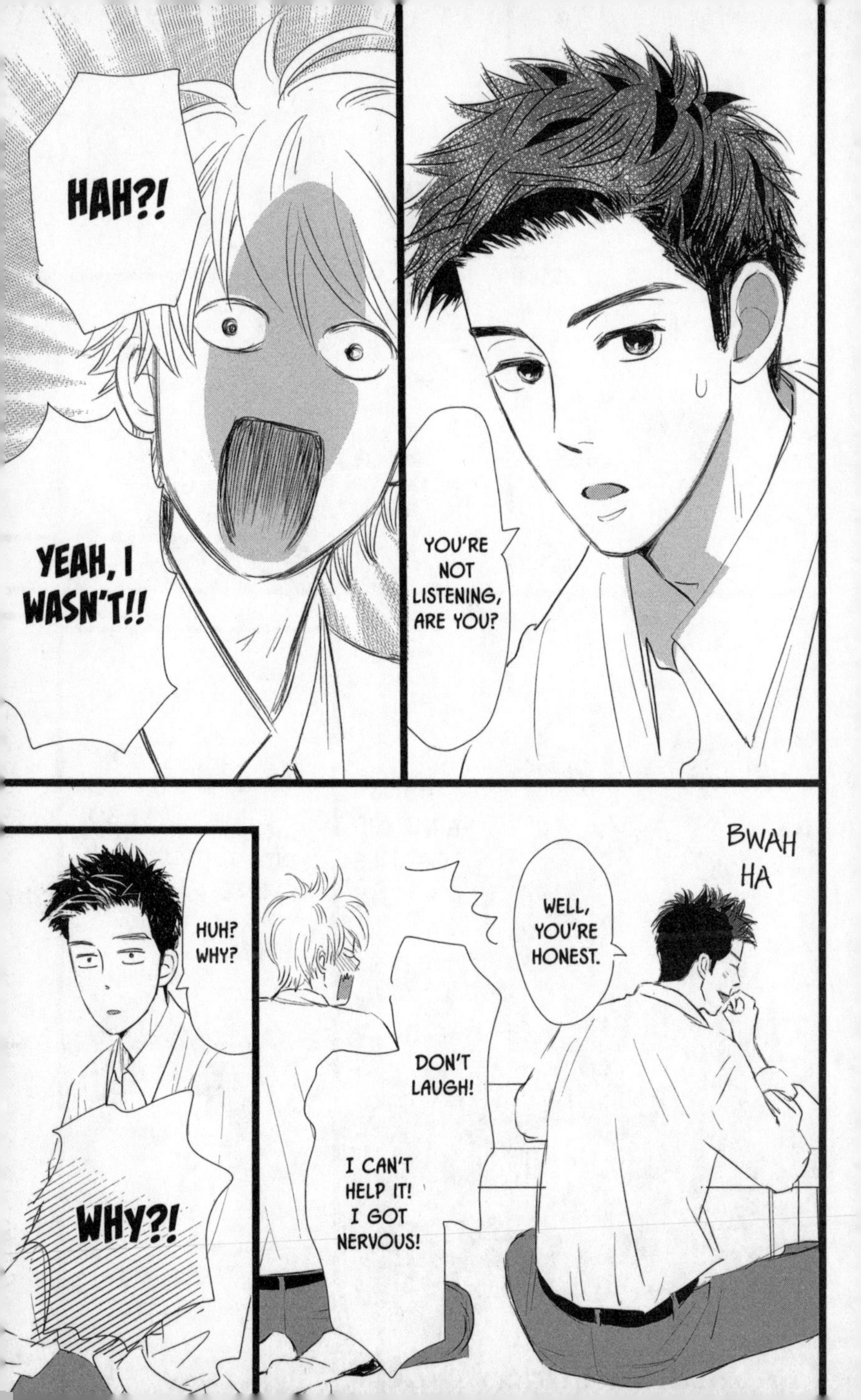
YOU'RE NOT LISTENING, ARE YOU?
HAH?!
YEAH, I WASN'T!!
BWAH HA
WELL, YOU'RE HONEST.
DON'T LAUGH!
I CAN'T HELP IT! I GOT NERVOUS!
HUH? WHY?
WHY?!

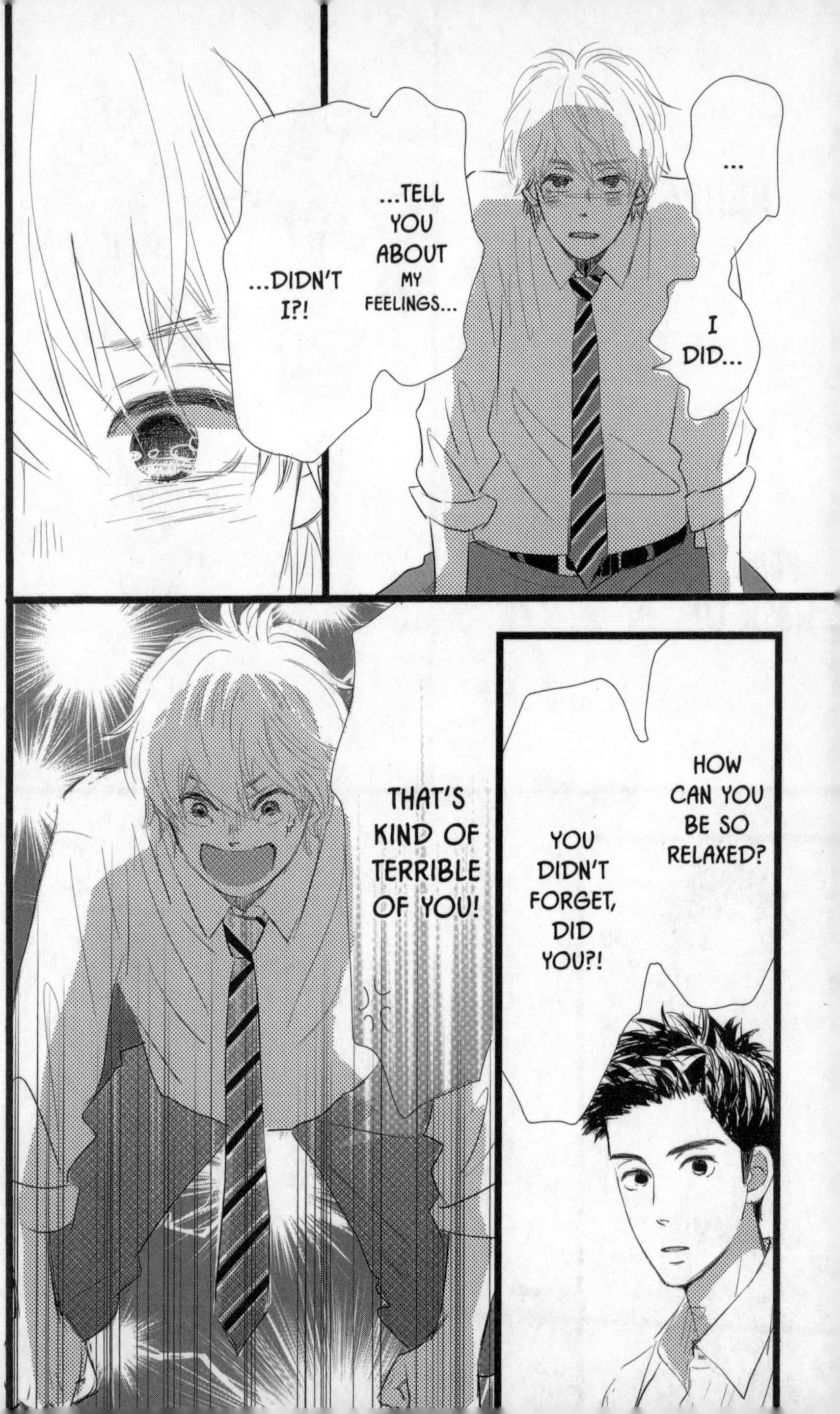
...
I DID...
...TELL YOU ABOUT MY FEELINGS...
...DIDN'T I?!
HOW CAN YOU BE SO RELAXED?
YOU DIDN'T FORGET, DID YOU?!
THAT'S KIND OF TERRIBLE OF YOU!

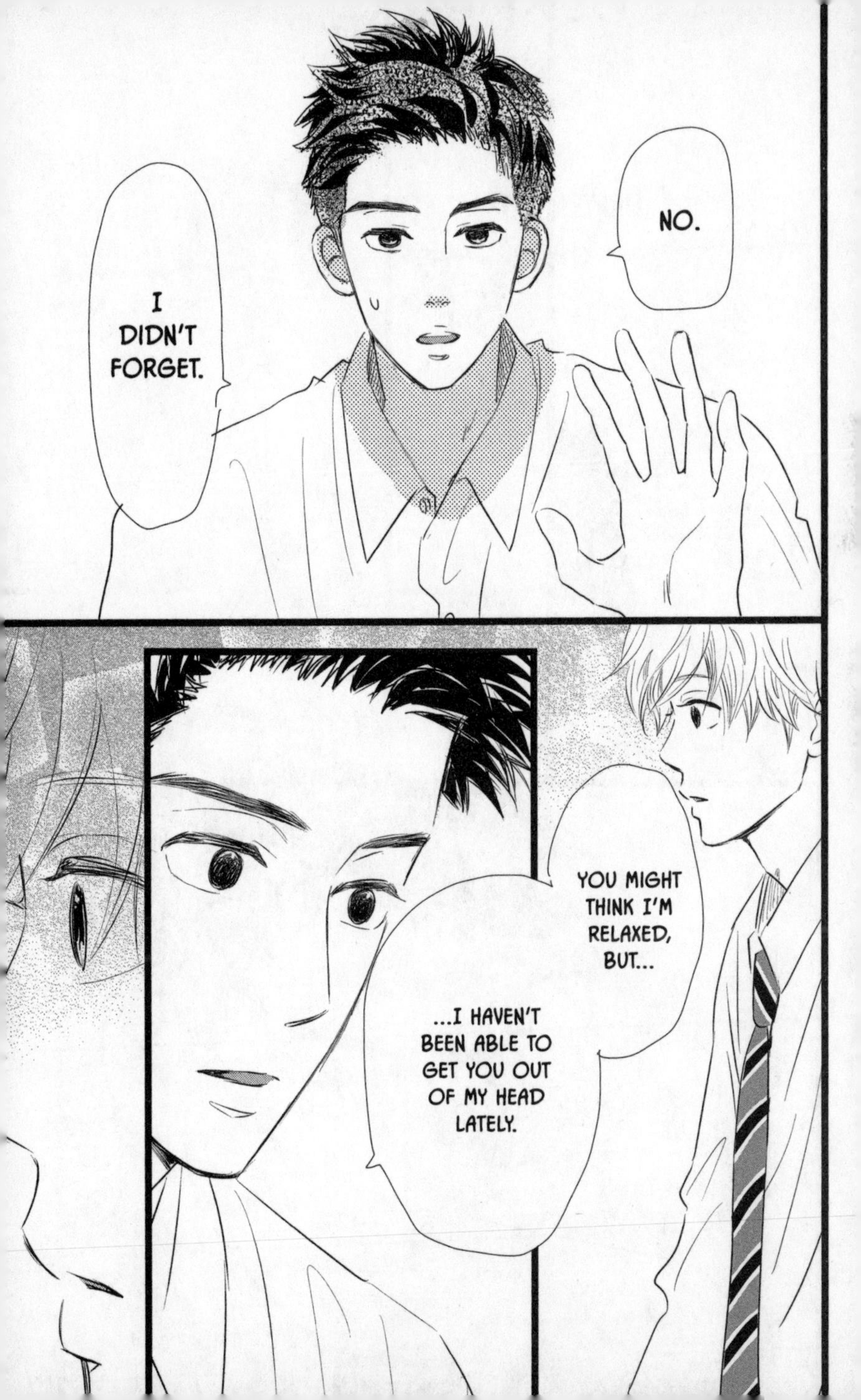
NO.
I DIDN'T FORGET.
YOU MIGHT THINK I'M RELAXED, BUT...
...I HAVEN'T BEEN ABLE TO GET YOU OUT OF MY HEAD LATELY.

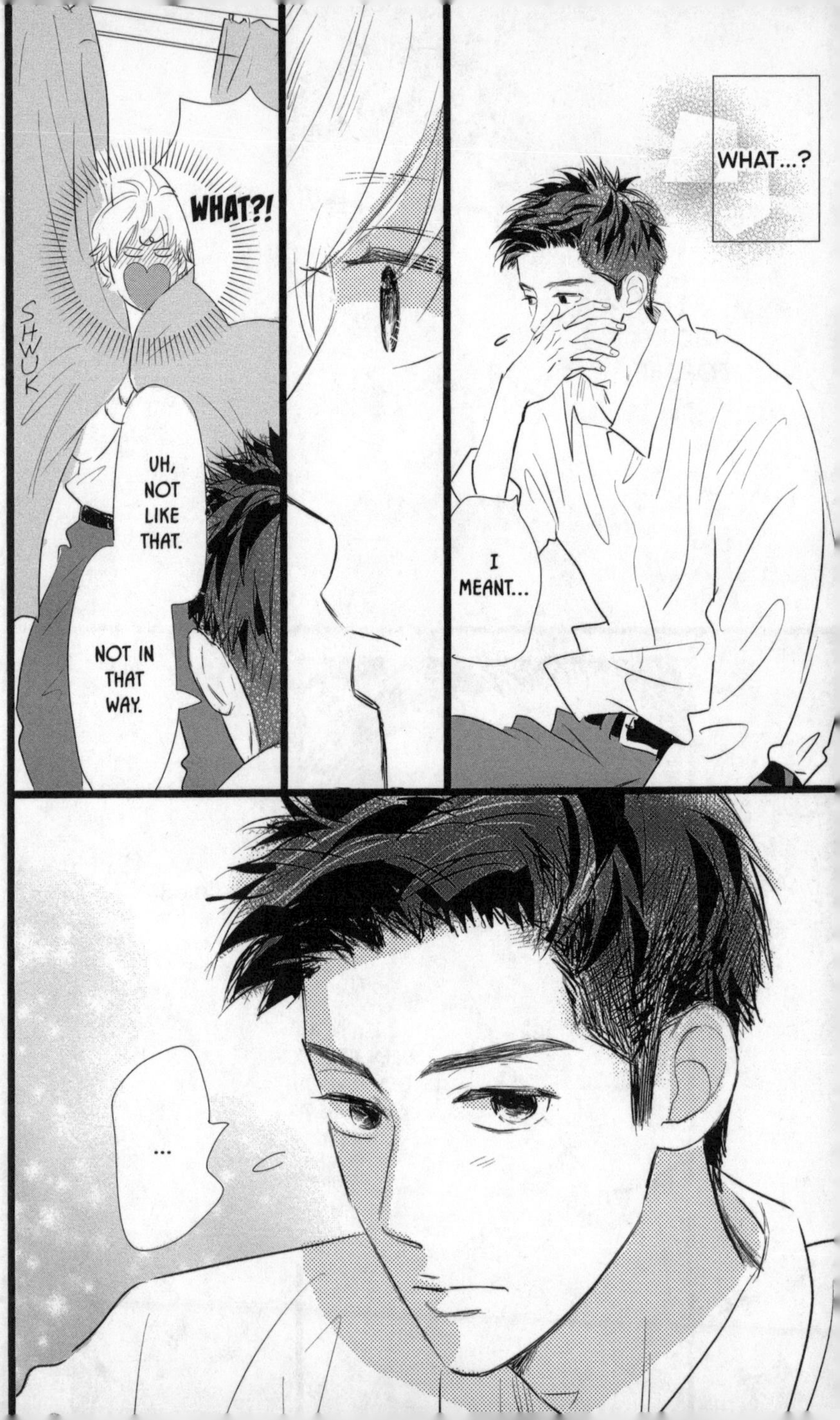
WHAT...?
I MEANT...
WHAT?!
SHWUK
UH, NOT LIKE THAT.
NOT IN THAT WAY.
...

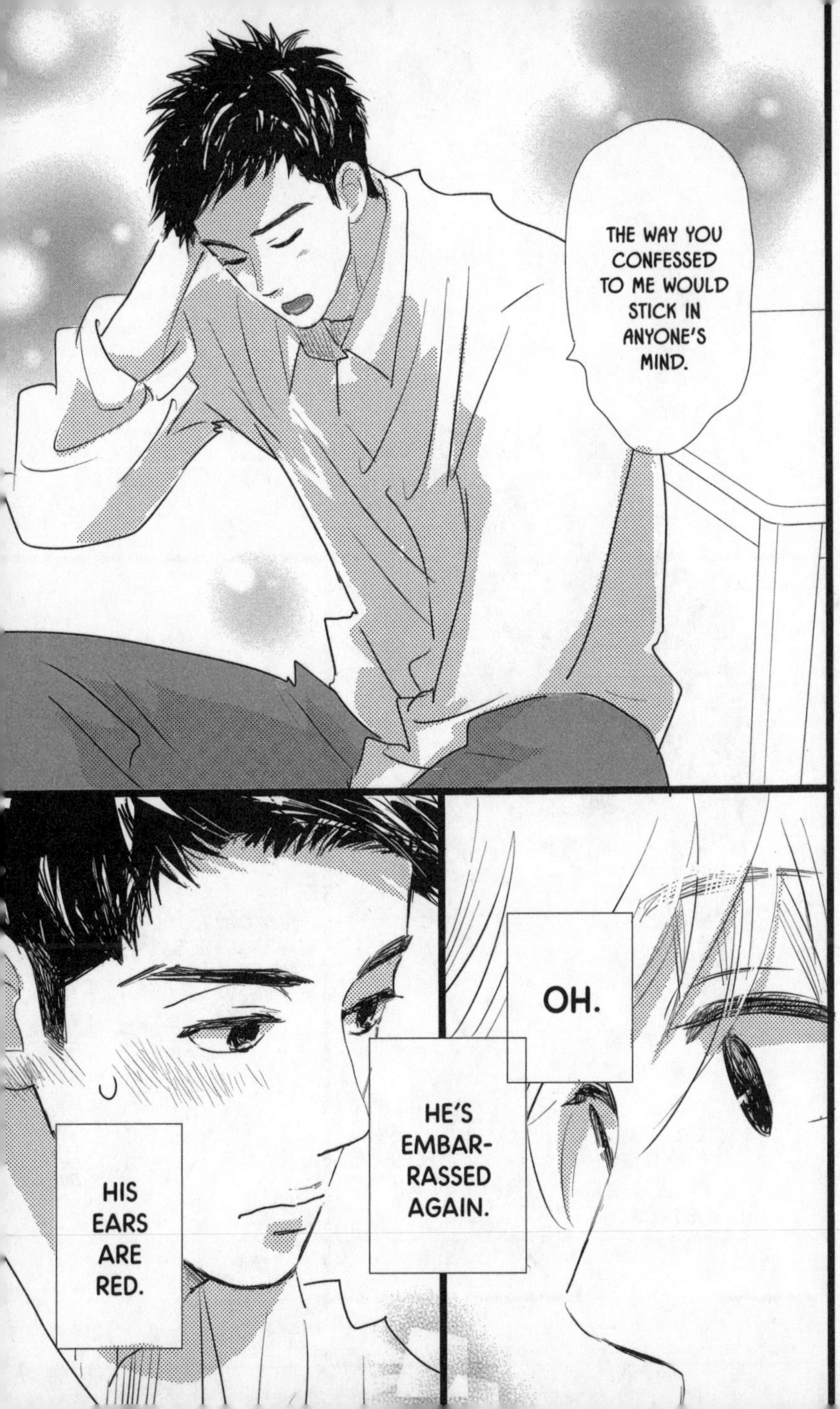
THE WAY YOU CONFESSED TO ME WOULD STICK IN ANYONE'S MIND.
OH.
HE'S EMBAR-RASSED AGAIN.
HIS EARS ARE RED.

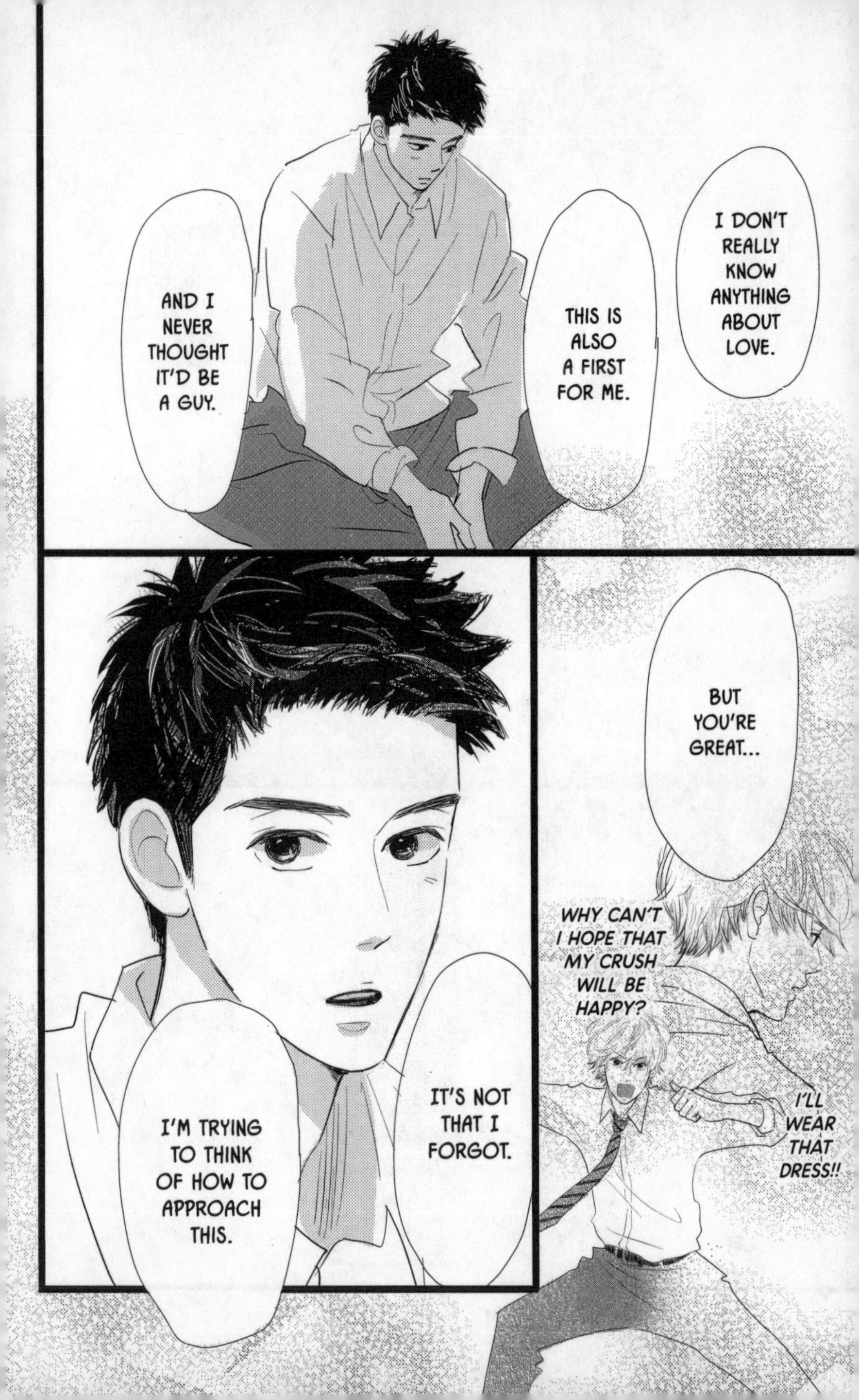
I DON'T REALLY KNOW ANYTHING ABOUT LOVE.
THIS IS ALSO A FIRST FOR ME.
AND I NEVER THOUGHT IT'D BE A GUY.
BUT YOU'RE GREAT...
WHY CAN'T I HOPE THAT MY CRUSH WILL BE HAPPY?
I'LL WEAR THAT DRESS!!
IT'S NOT THAT I FORGOT.
I'M TRYING TO THINK OF HOW TO APPROACH THIS.

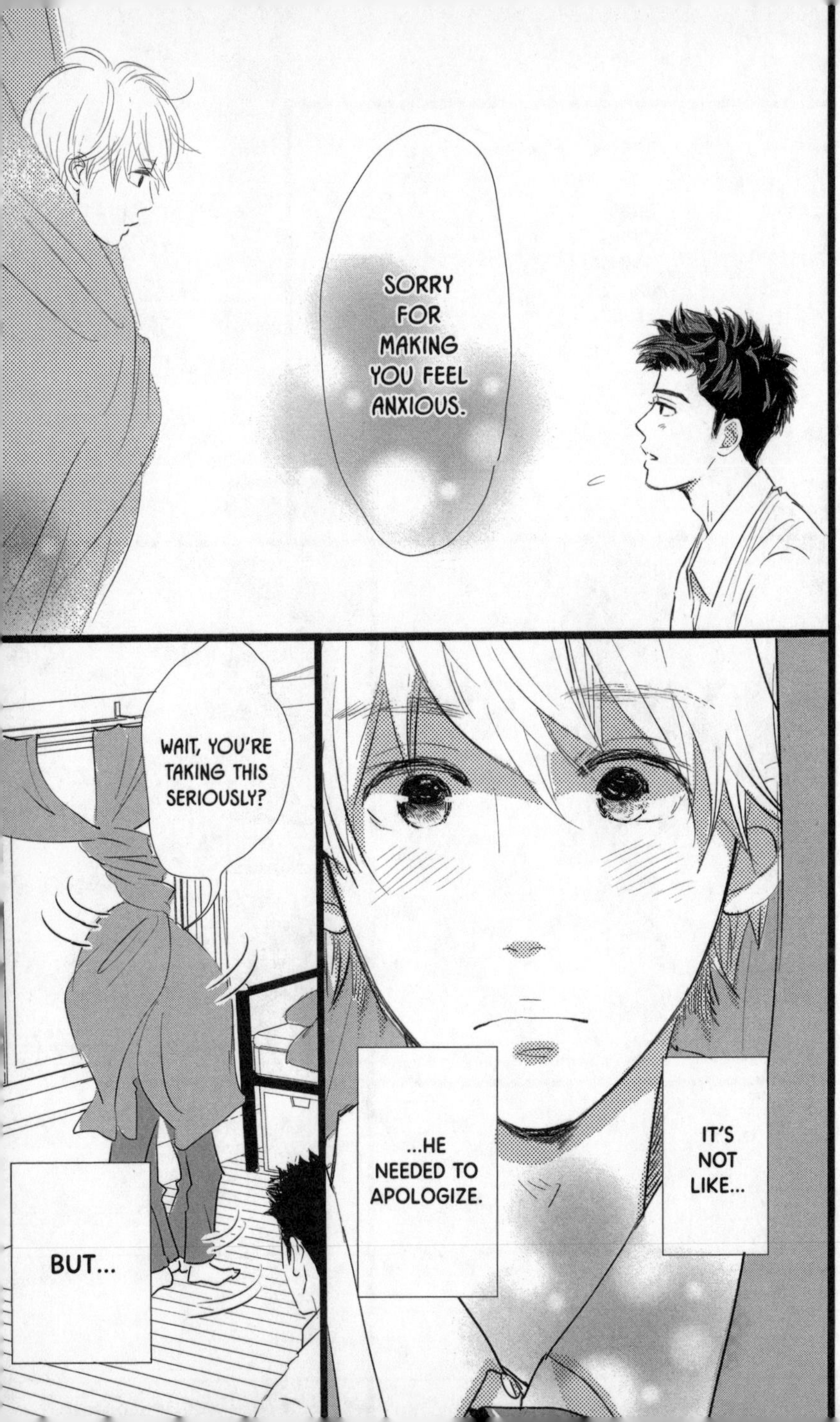
SORRY FOR MAKING YOU FEEL ANXIOUS.
IT'S NOT LIKE...
...HE NEEDED TO APOLOGIZE.
WAIT, YOU'RE TAKING THIS SERIOUSLY?
BUT...

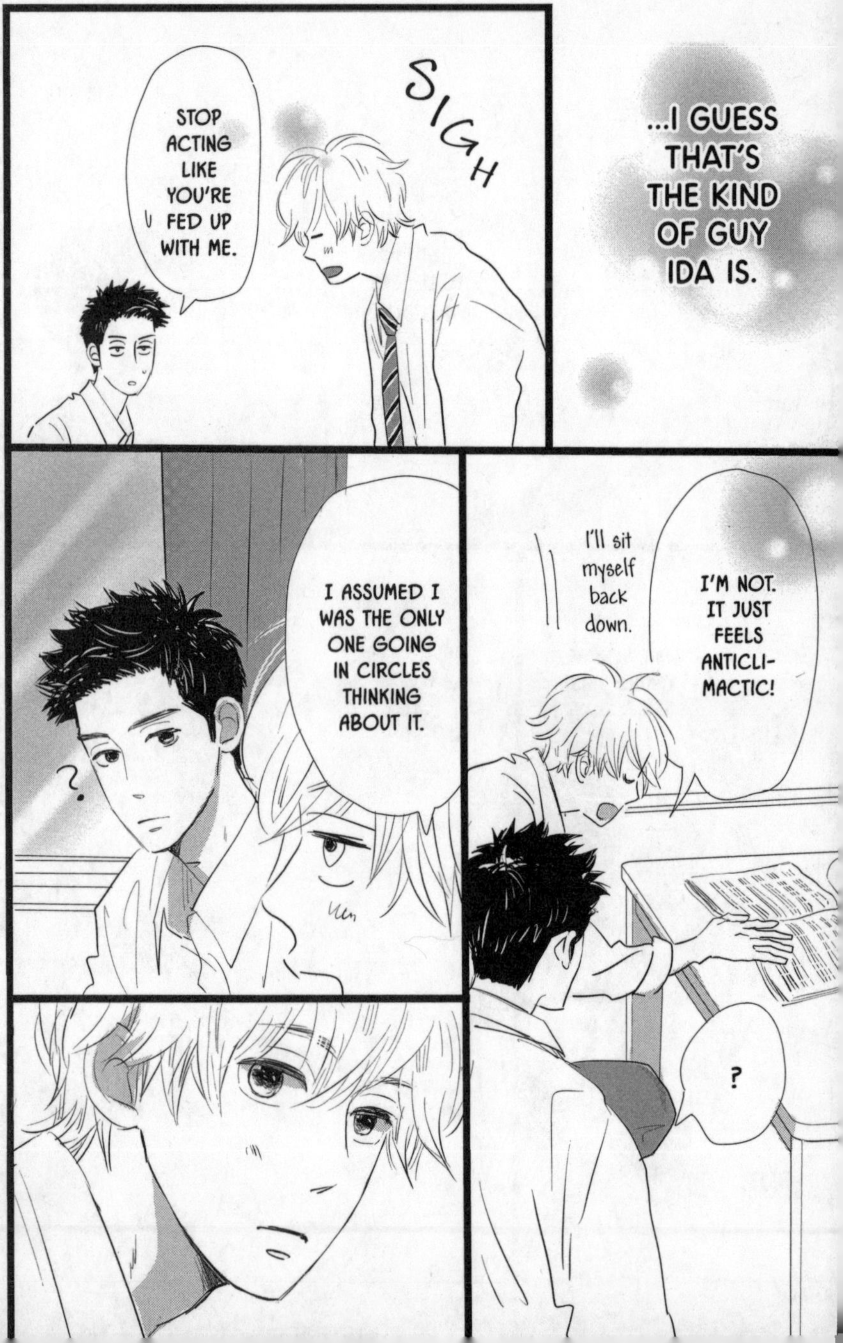
...I GUESS THAT'S THE KIND OF GUY IDA IS.
SIGH
STOP ACTING LIKE YOU'RE FED UP WITH ME.
I'M NOT. IT JUST FEELS ANTICLI-MACTIC!
I'll sit myself back down.
?
I ASSUMED I WAS THE ONLY ONE GOING IN CIRCLES THINKING ABOUT IT.

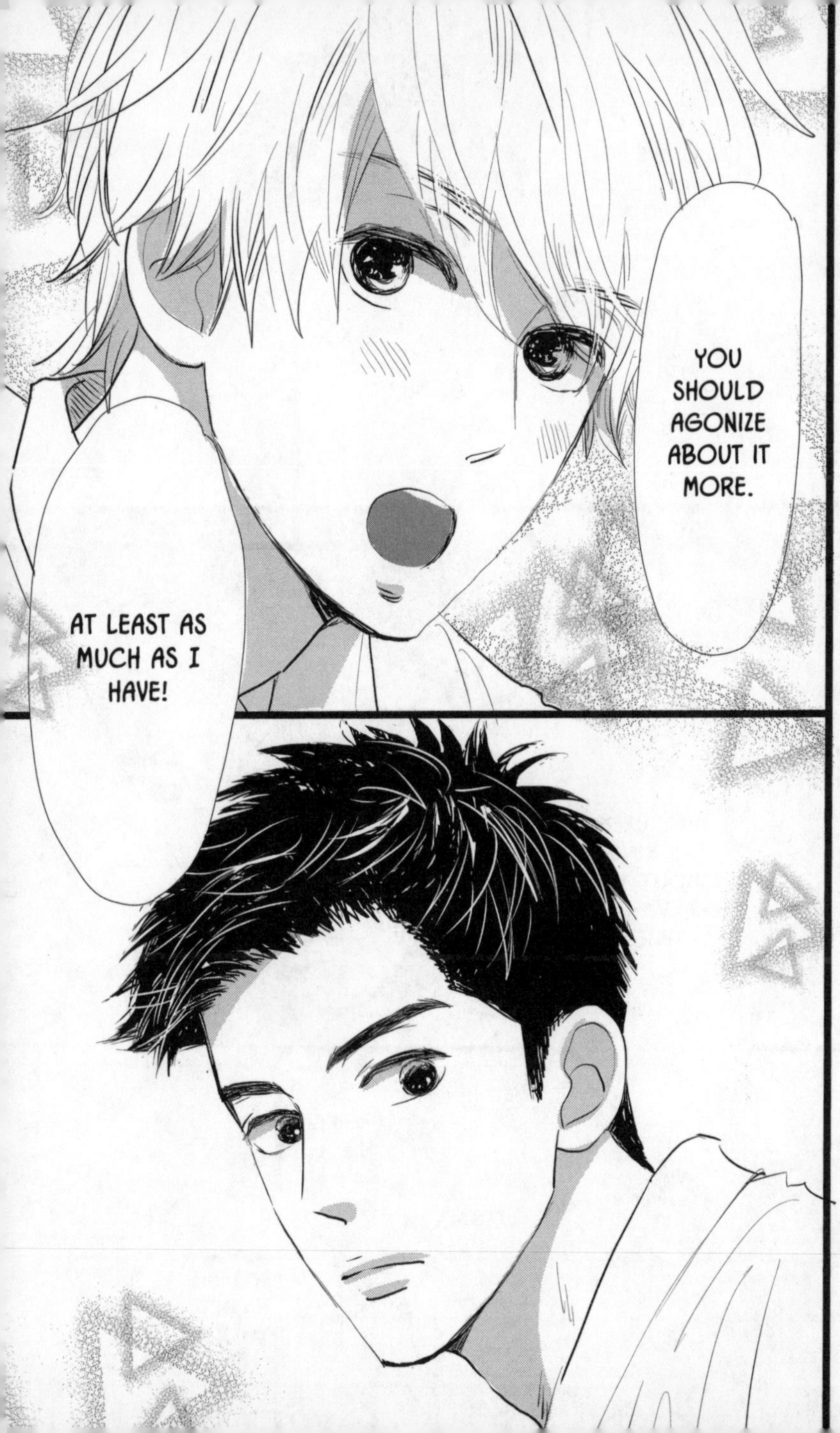
YOU SHOULD AGONIZE ABOUT IT MORE.
AT LEAST AS MUCH AS I HAVE!

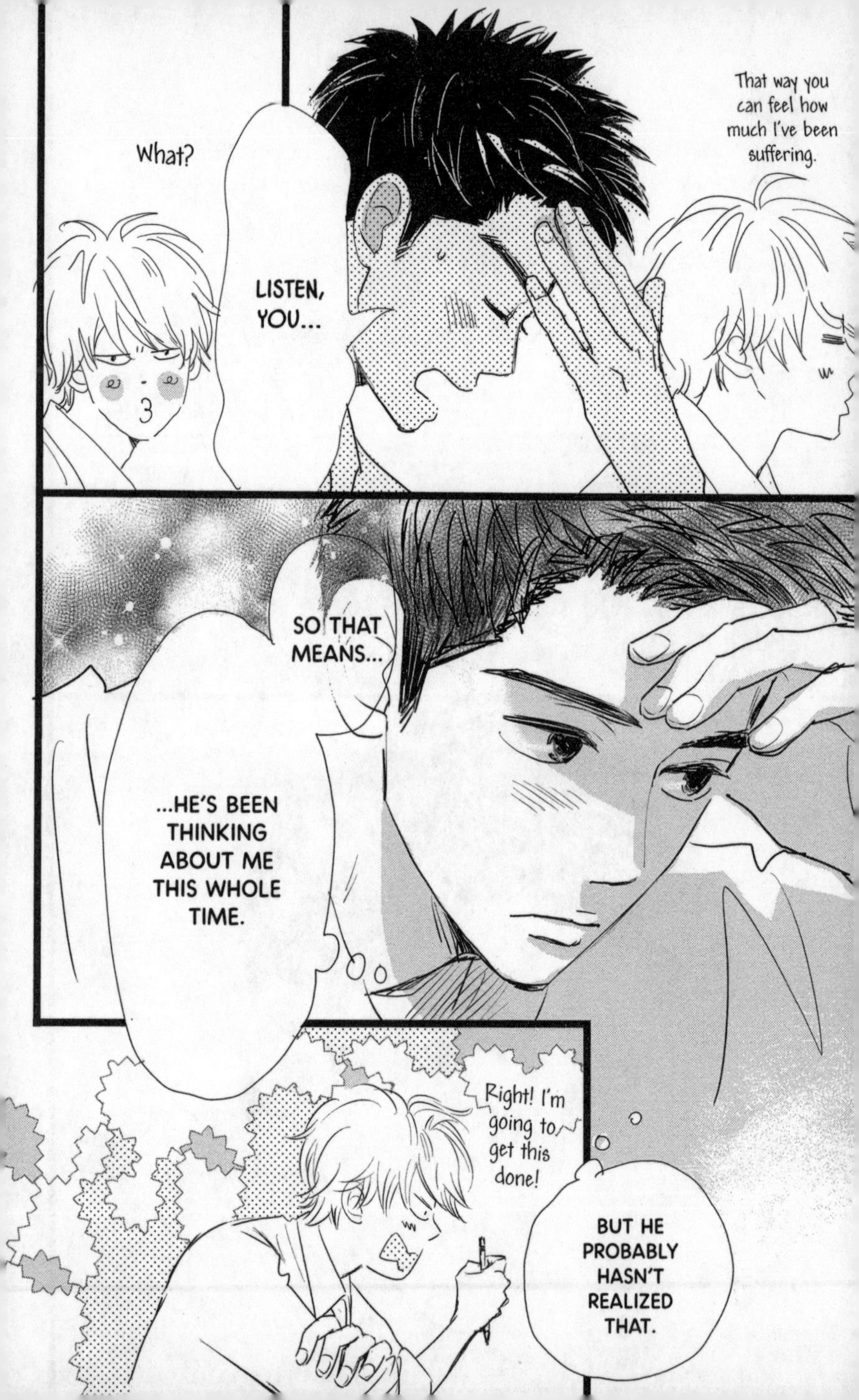
That way you can feel how much I've been suffering.
LISTEN, YOU...
What?
SO THAT MEANS...
...HE'S BEEN THINKING ABOUT ME THIS WHOLE TIME.
BUT HE PROBABLY HASN'T REALIZED THAT.
Right! I'm going to get this done!

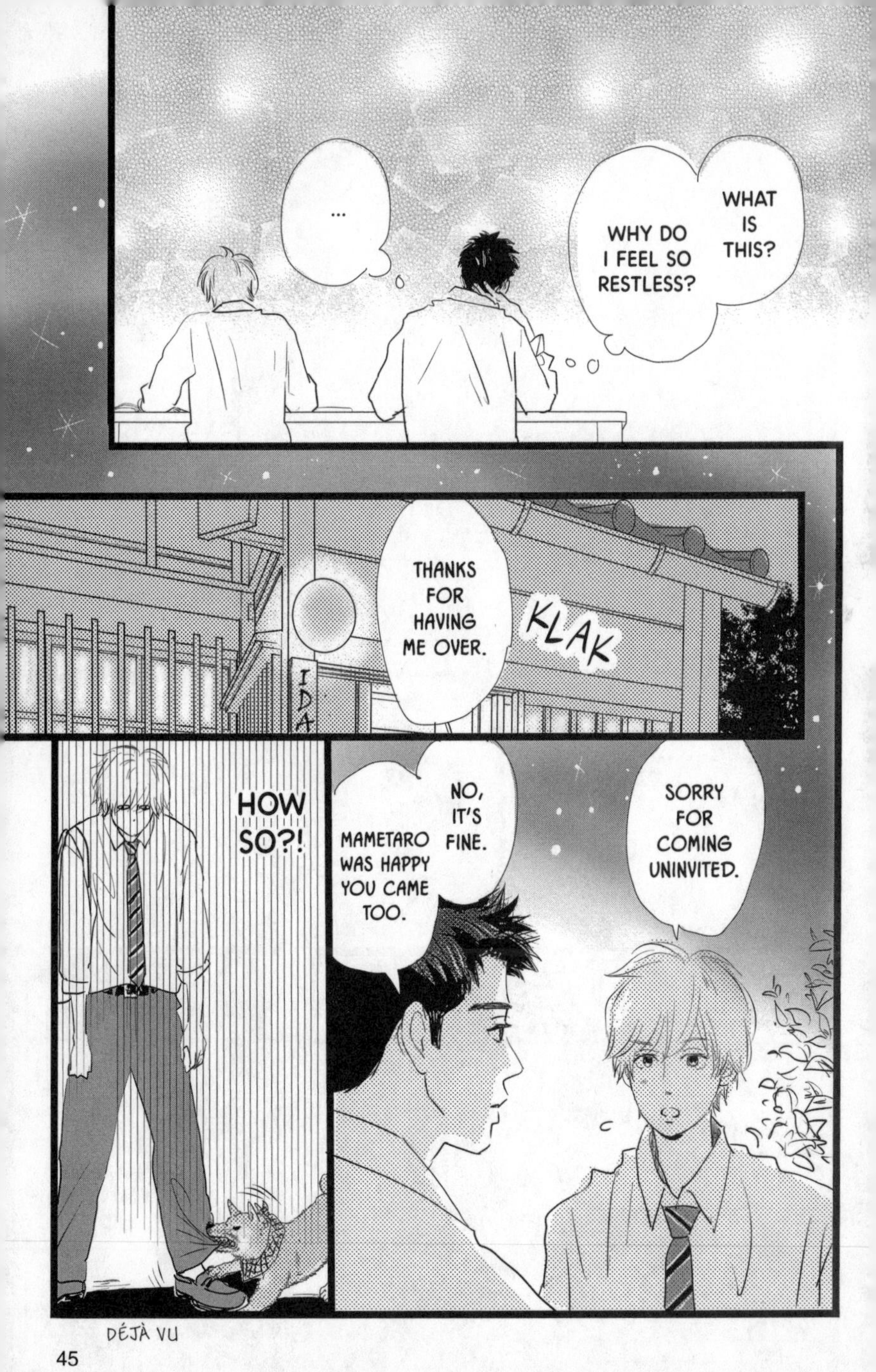
WHAT IS THIS?
WHY DO I FEEL SO RESTLESS?
...
KLAK
THANKS FOR HAVING ME OVER.
SORRY FOR COMING UNINVITED.
NO, IT'S FINE.
MAMETARO WAS HAPPY YOU CAME TOO.
HOW SO?!

DÉJÀ VU

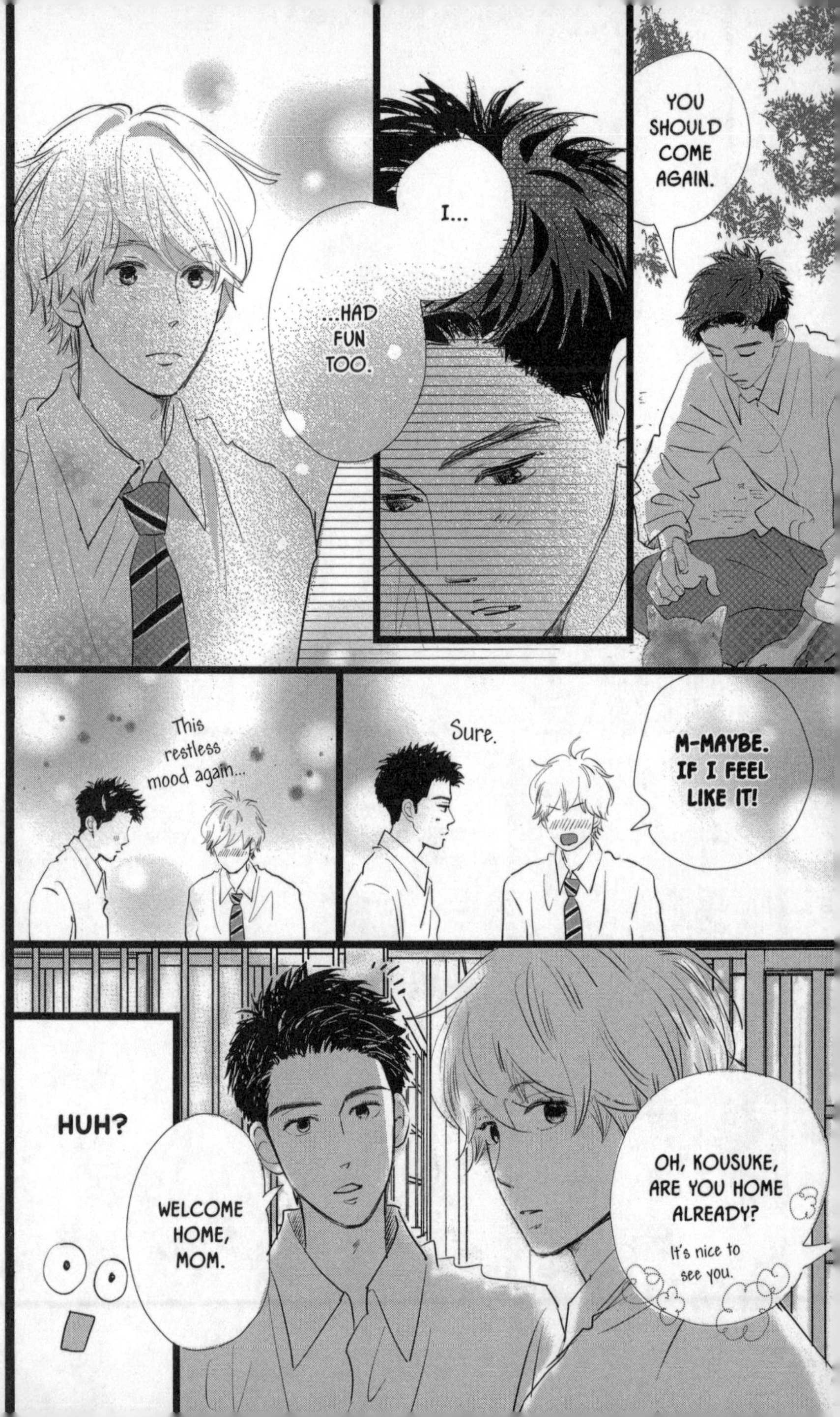
YOU SHOULD COME AGAIN.
I...
...HAD FUN TOO.
M-MAYBE. IF I FEEL LIKE IT!
Sure.
This restless mood again...
OH, KOUSUKE, ARE YOU HOME ALREADY?
It's nice to see you.
WELCOME HOME, MOM.
HUH?

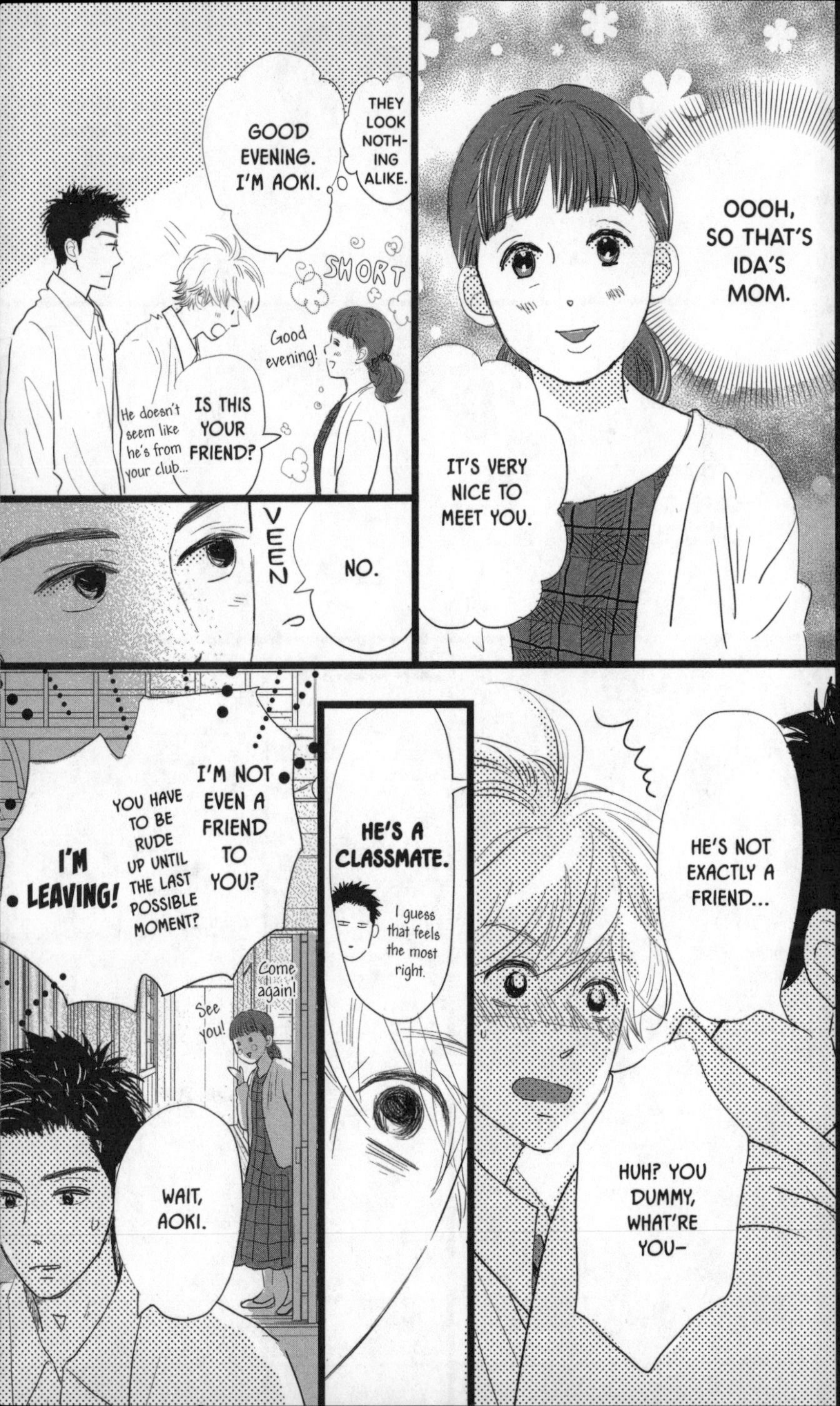

OOOH, SO THAT'S IDA'S MOM.
IT'S VERY NICE TO MEET YOU.
THEY LOOK NOTHING ALIKE.
GOOD EVENING. I'M AOKI.
SHORT
Good evening!
IS THIS YOUR FRIEND?
He doesn't seem like he's from your club...
VEEN
NO.
HE'S NOT EXACTLY A FRIEND...
HUH? YOU DUMMY, WHAT'RE YOU–
HE'S A CLASSMATE.
I guess that feels the most right.
I'M NOT EVEN A FRIEND TO YOU?
YOU HAVE TO BE RUDE UP UNTIL THE LAST POSSIBLE MOMENT?
I'M LEAVING!
Come again!
See you!
WAIT, AOKI.

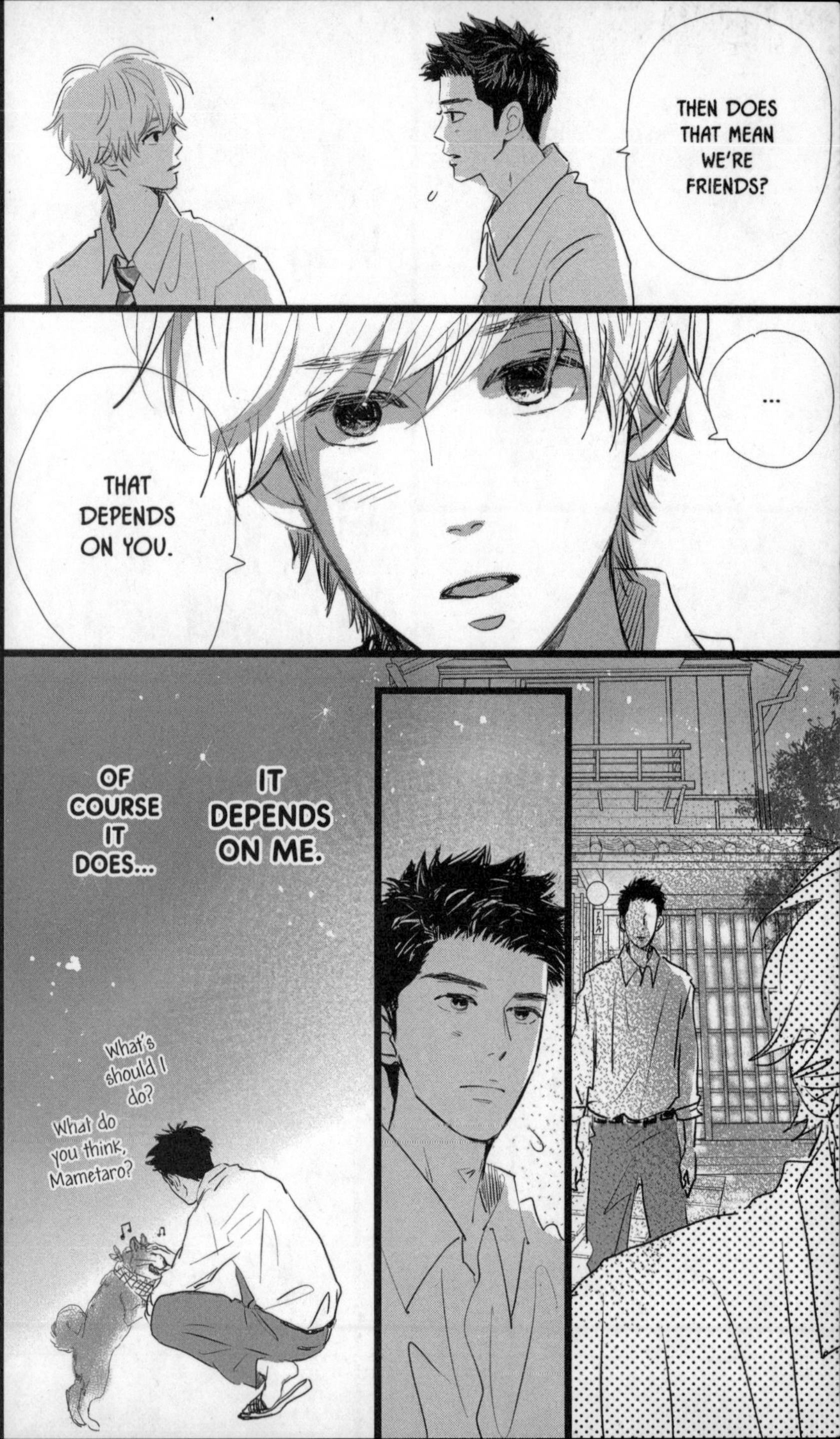
THEN DOES THAT MEAN WE'RE FRIENDS?
...
THAT DEPENDS ON YOU.
IT DEPENDS ON ME.
OF COURSE IT DOES...
What's should I do?
What do you think, Mametaro?

Chapter 7

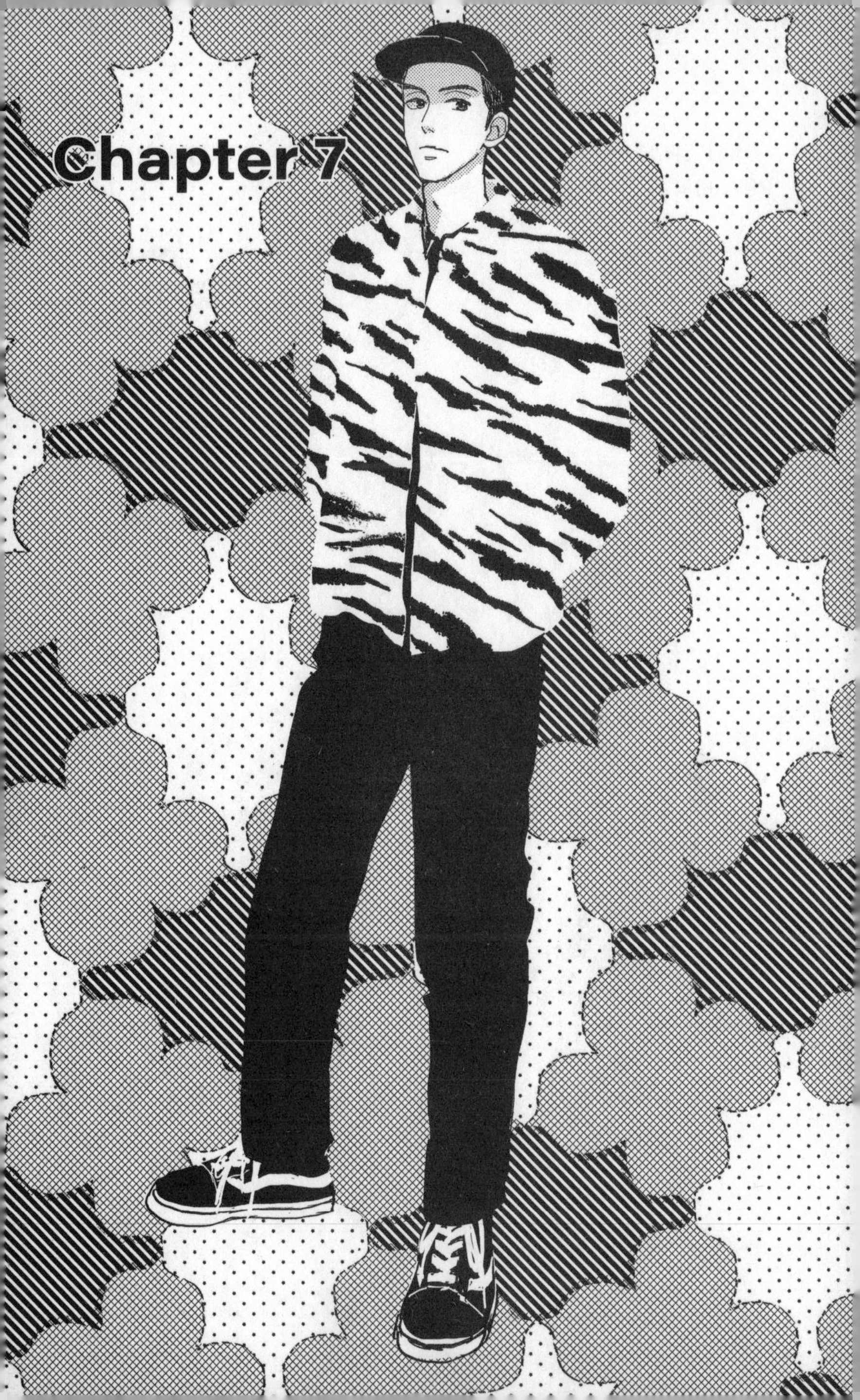

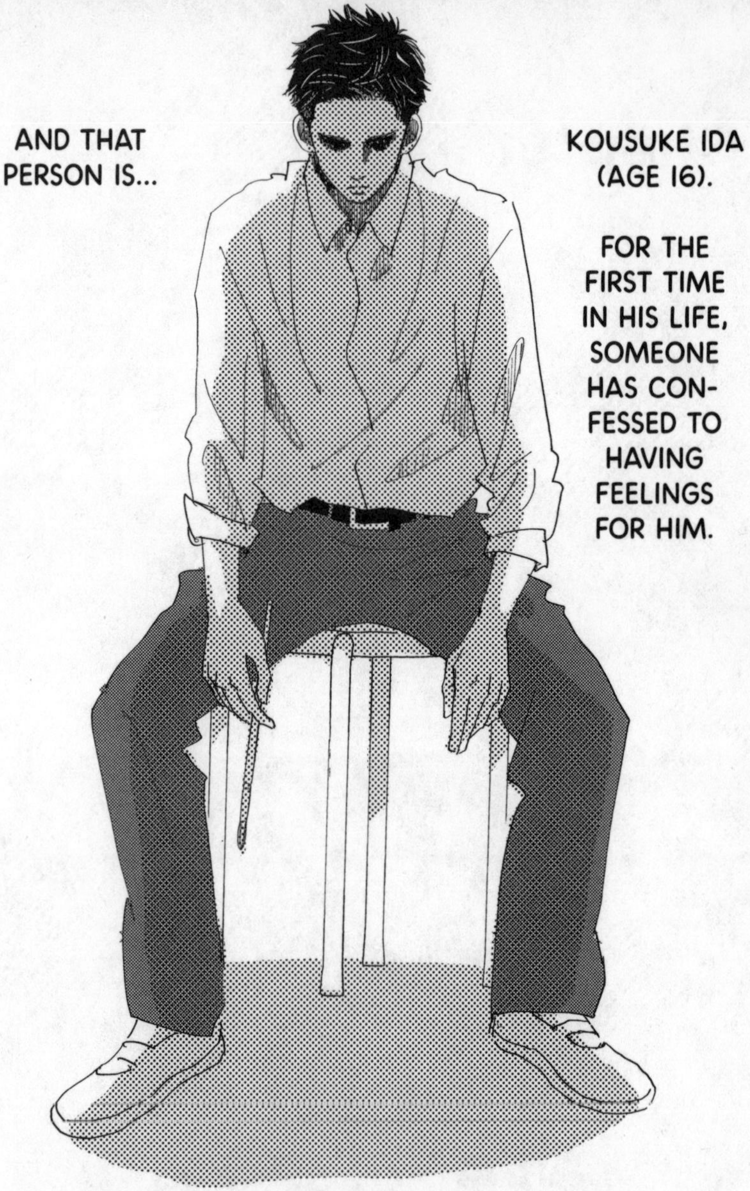
AND THAT PERSON IS...
KOUSUKE IDA (AGE 16).
FOR THE FIRST TIME IN HIS LIFE, SOMEONE HAS CON-FESSED TO HAVING FEELINGS FOR HIM.

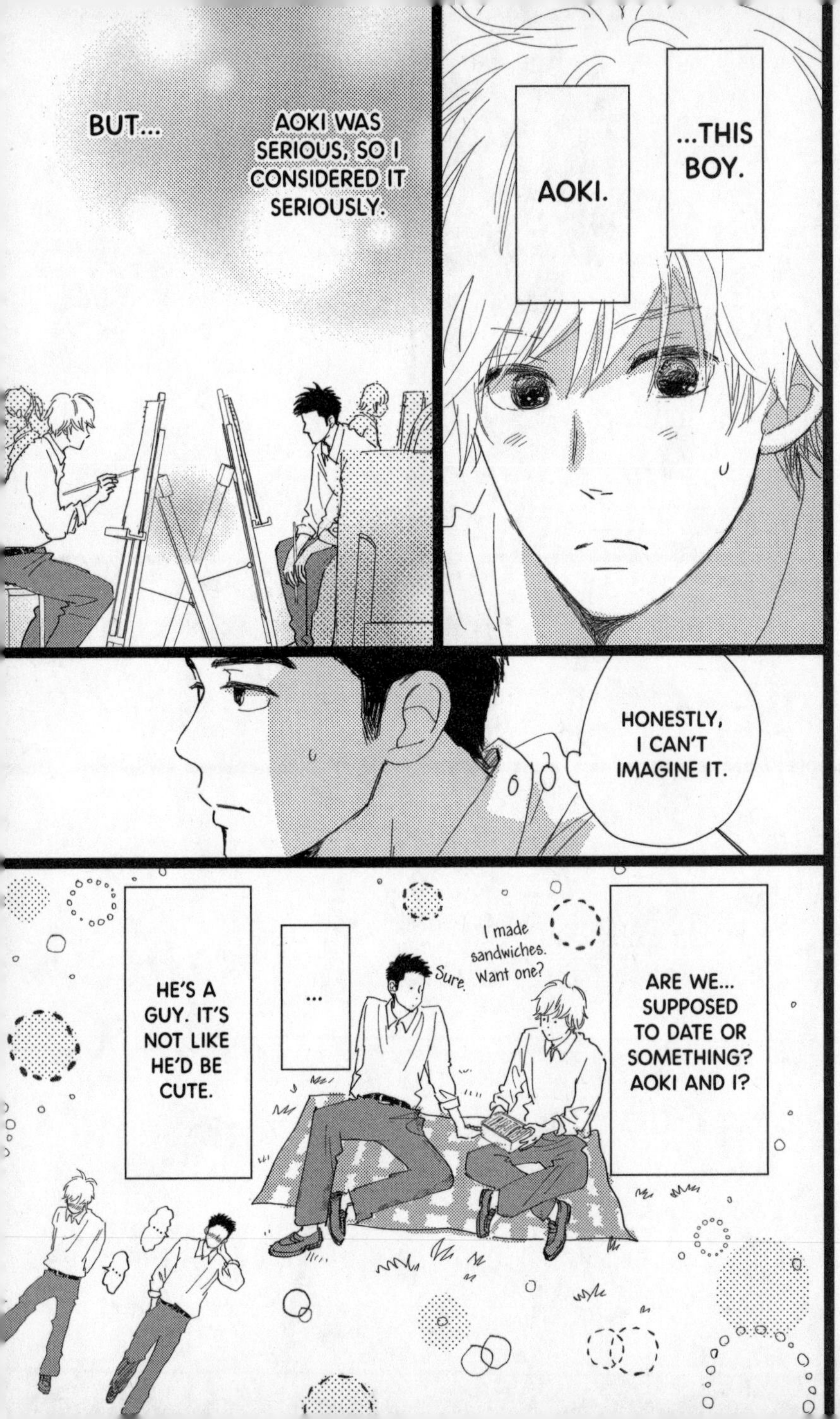
...THIS BOY.
AOKI.
AOKI WAS SERIOUS, SO I CONSIDERED IT SERIOUSLY.
BUT...
HONESTLY, I CAN'T IMAGINE IT.
ARE WE... SUPPOSED TO DATE OR SOMETHING? AOKI AND I?
I made sandwiches. Want one?
Sure.
...
HE'S A GUY. IT'S NOT LIKE HE'D BE CUTE.

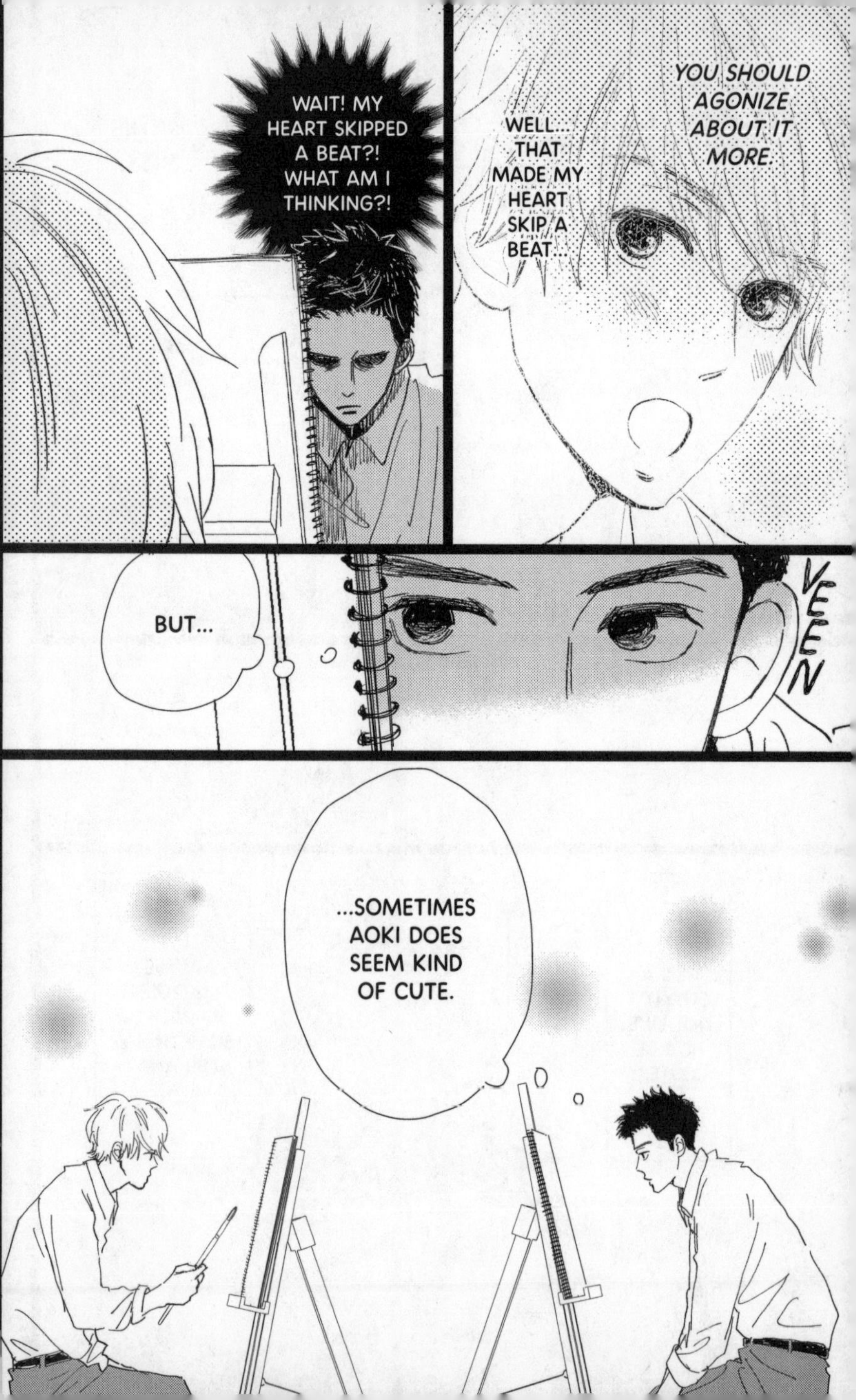
YOU SHOULD AGONIZE ABOUT IT MORE.
WELL... THAT MADE MY HEART SKIP A BEAT...
WAIT! MY HEART SKIPPED A BEAT?! WHAT AM I THINKING?!
VEEN
BUT...
...SOMETIMES AOKI DOES SEEM KIND OF CUTE.

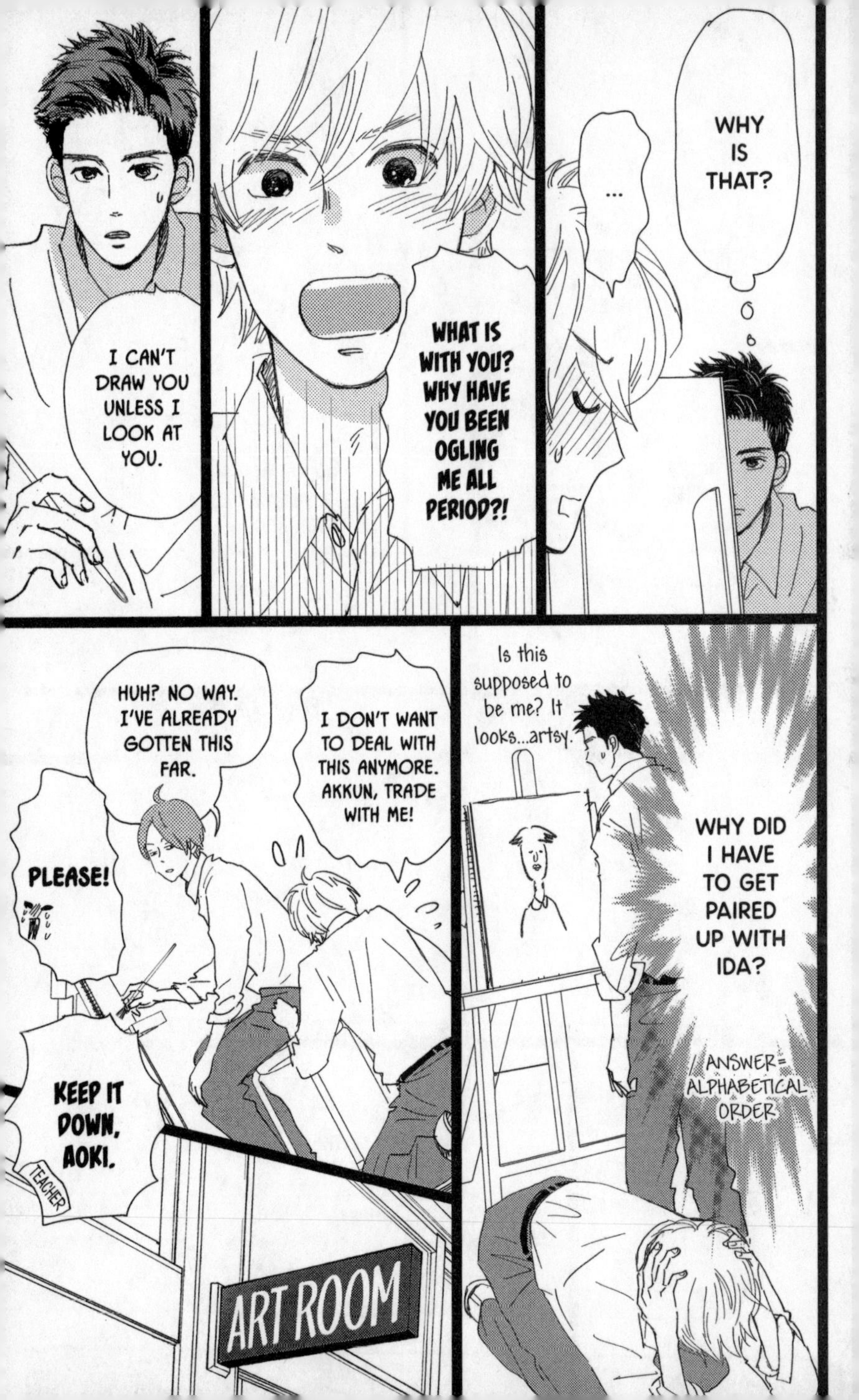
WHY IS THAT?
...
WHAT IS WITH YOU? WHY HAVE YOU BEEN OGLING ME ALL PERIOD?!
I CAN'T DRAW YOU UNLESS I LOOK AT YOU.
Is this supposed to be me? It looks...artsy.
WHY DID I HAVE TO GET PAIRED UP WITH IDA?
ANSWER= ALPHABETICAL ORDER
I DON'T WANT TO DEAL WITH THIS ANYMORE. AKKUN, TRADE WITH ME!
HUH? NO WAY. I'VE ALREADY GOTTEN THIS FAR.
PLEASE!
KEEP IT DOWN, AOKI.
TEACHER
ART ROOM

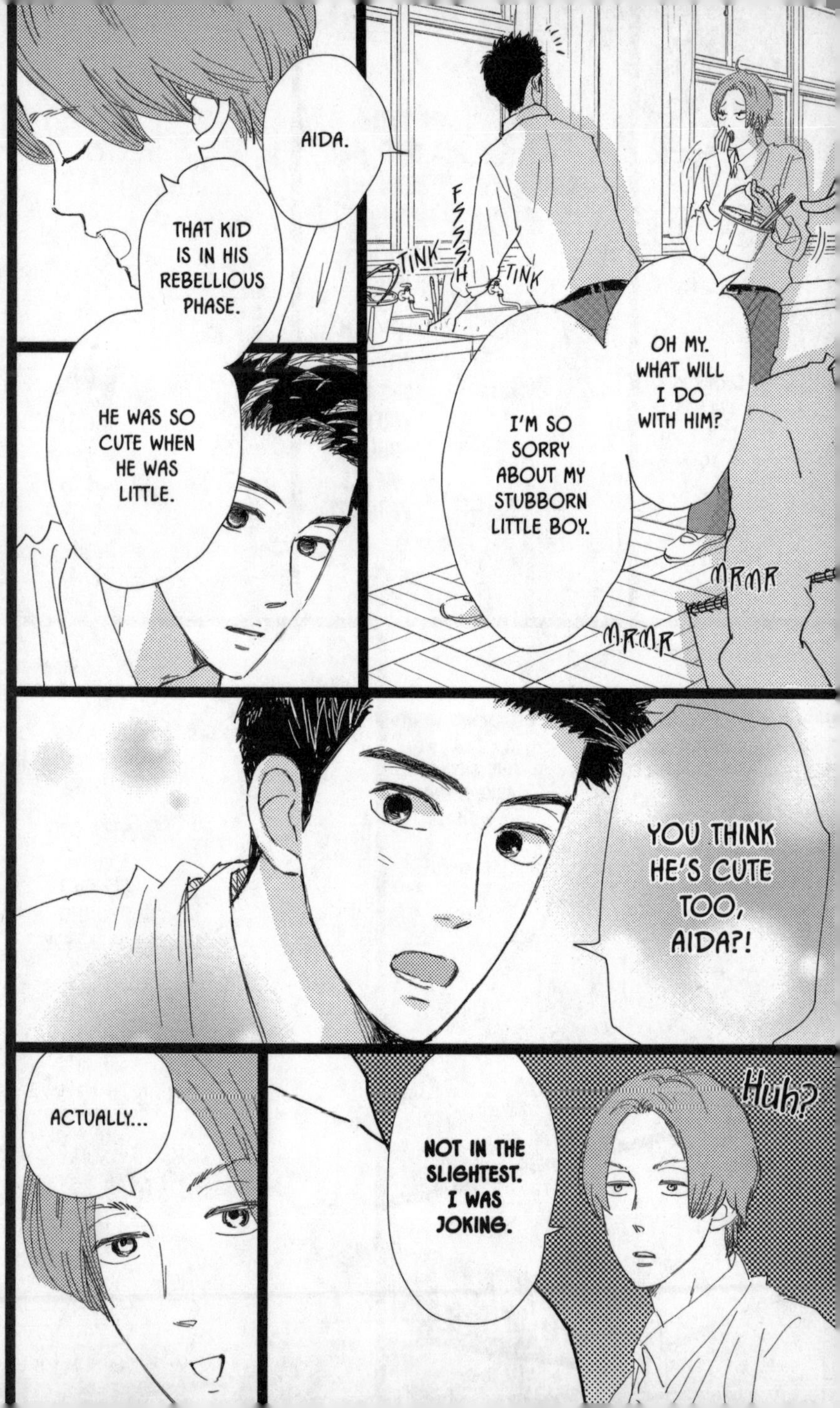
FSSSH
TINK
TINK
OH MY. WHAT WILL I DO WITH HIM?
I'M SO SORRY ABOUT MY STUBBORN LITTLE BOY.
MRMR
MRMR
AIDA.
THAT KID IS IN HIS REBELLIOUS PHASE.
HE WAS SO CUTE WHEN HE WAS LITTLE.
YOU THINK HE'S CUTE TOO, AIDA?!
Huh?
NOT IN THE SLIGHTEST. I WAS JOKING.
ACTUALLY...

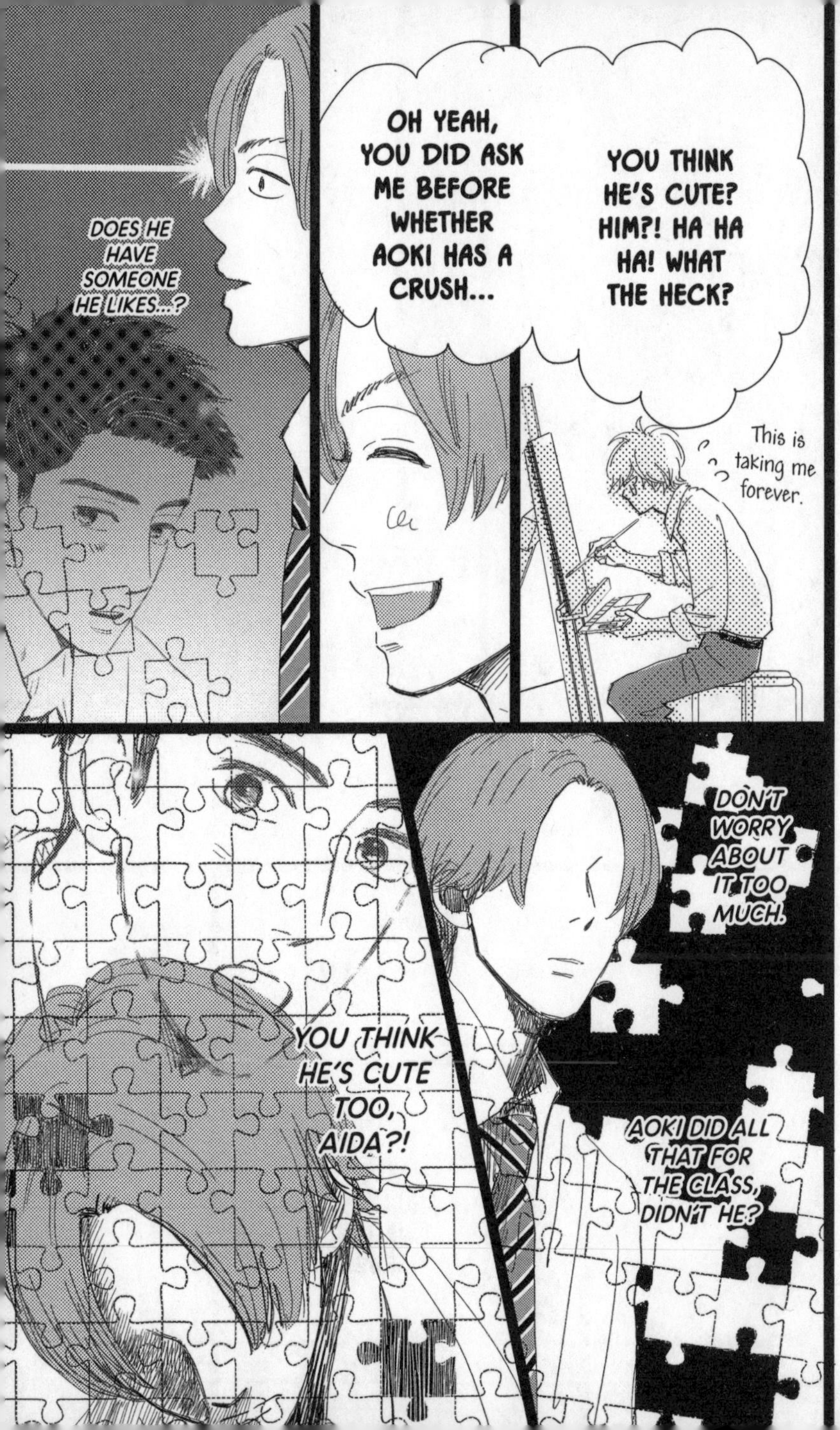
This is taking me forever.
YOU THINK HE'S CUTE? HIM?! HA HA HA! WHAT THE HECK?
OH YEAH, YOU DID ASK ME BEFORE WHETHER AOKI HAS A CRUSH...
DOES HE HAVE SOMEONE HE LIKES...?
DON'T WORRY ABOUT IT TOO MUCH.
AOKI DID ALL THAT FOR THE CLASS, DIDN'T HE?
YOU THINK HE'S CUTE TOO, AIDA?!

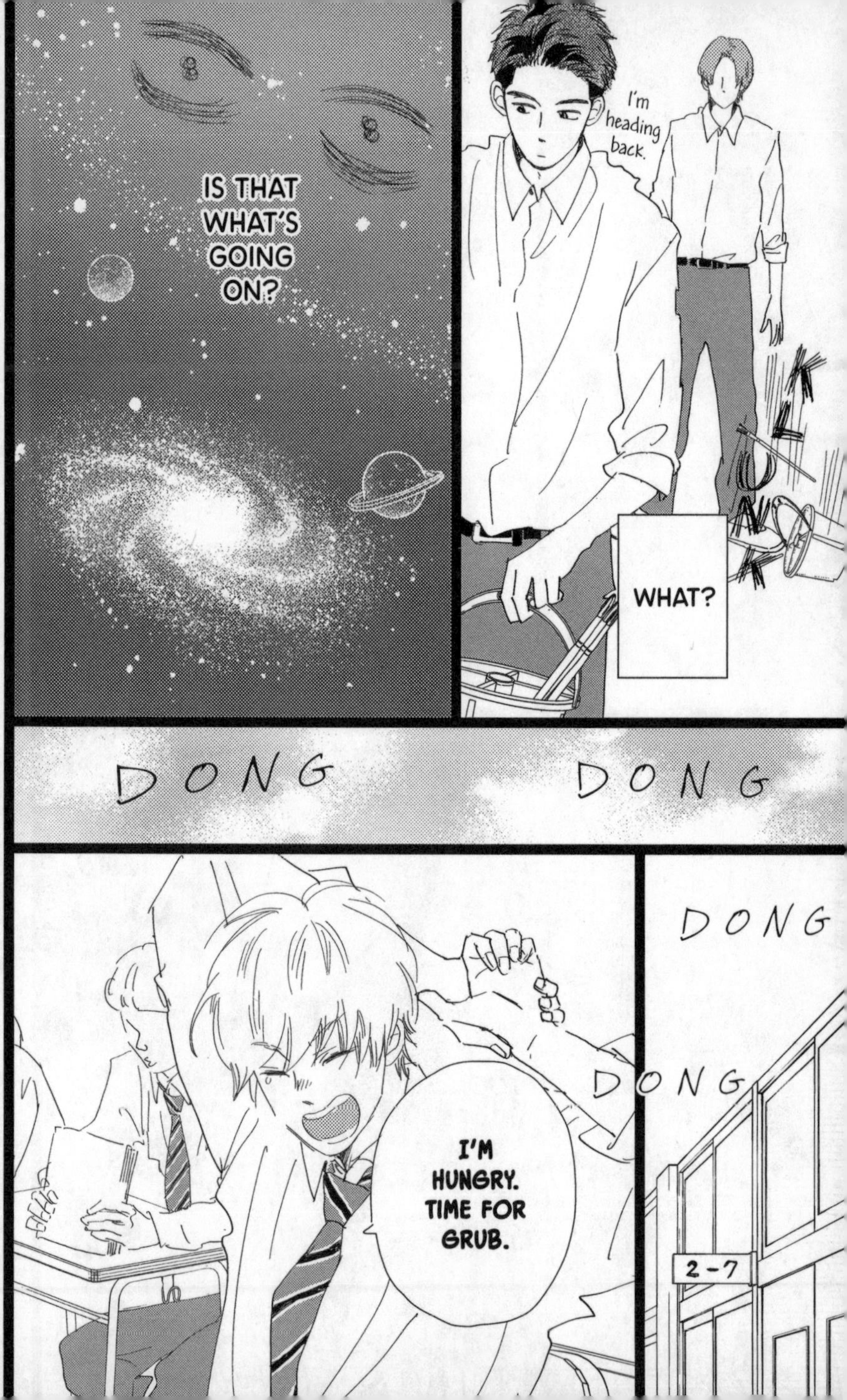
I'm heading back.
WHAT?
IS THAT WHAT'S GOING ON?
DONG DONG
DONG
DONG
2-7
I'M HUNGRY. TIME FOR GRUB.

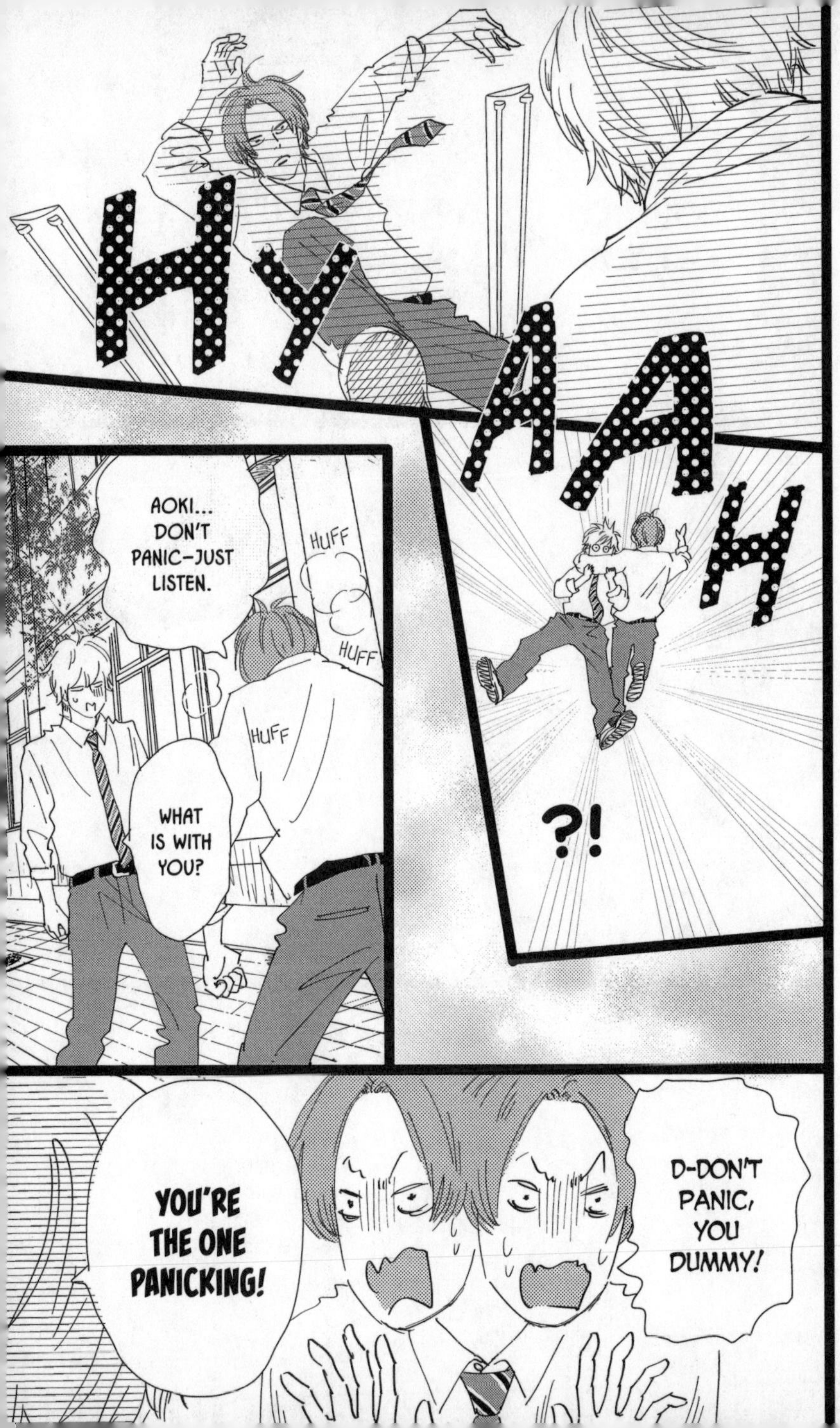
HYAAH
?!
HUFF
HUFF
AOKI... DON'T PANIC—JUST LISTEN.
HUFF
WHAT IS WITH YOU?
D-DON'T PANIC, YOU DUMMY!
YOU'RE THE ONE PANICKING!

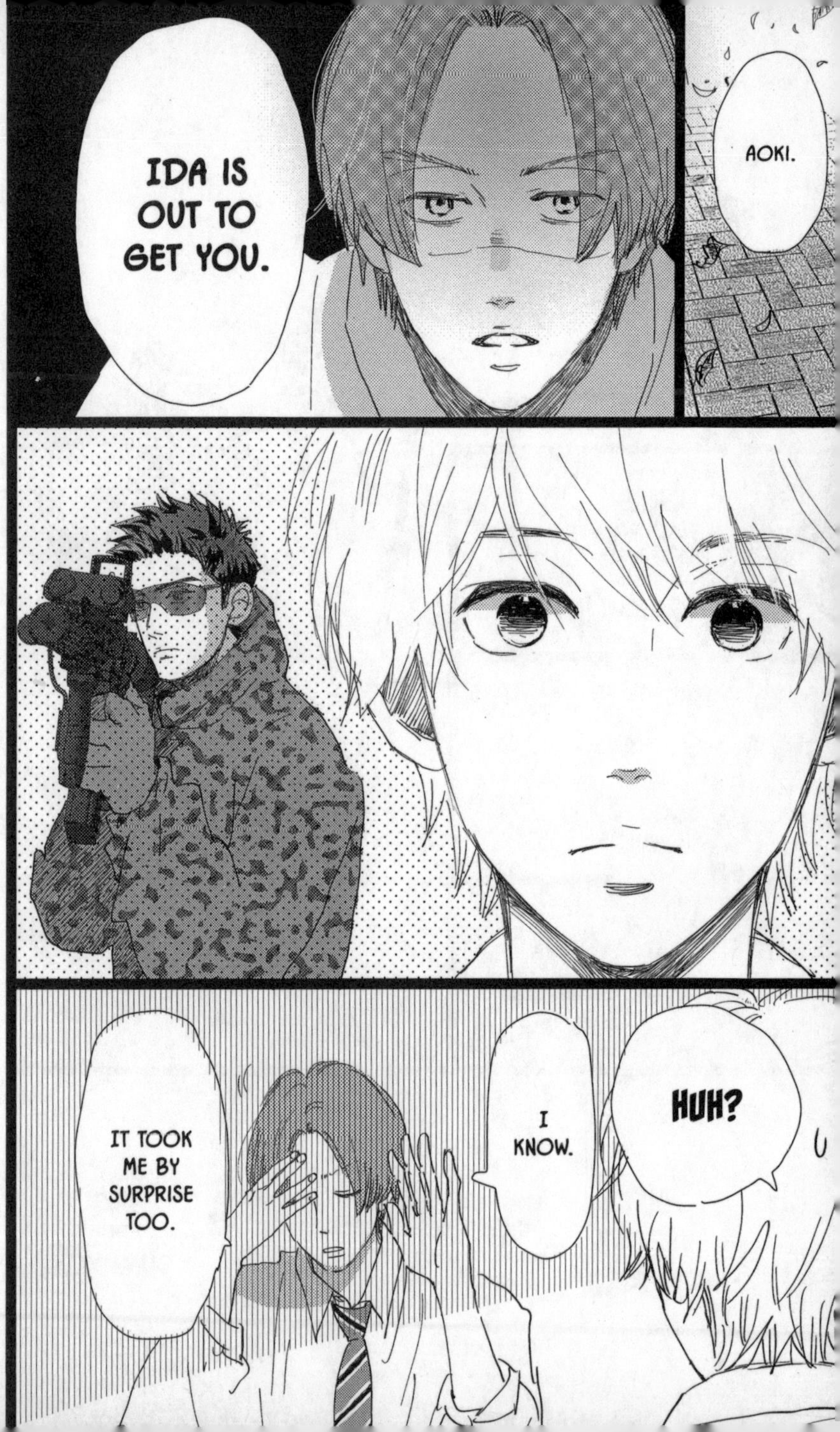
AOKI.
IDA IS OUT TO GET YOU.
HUH?
I KNOW.
IT TOOK ME BY SURPRISE TOO.

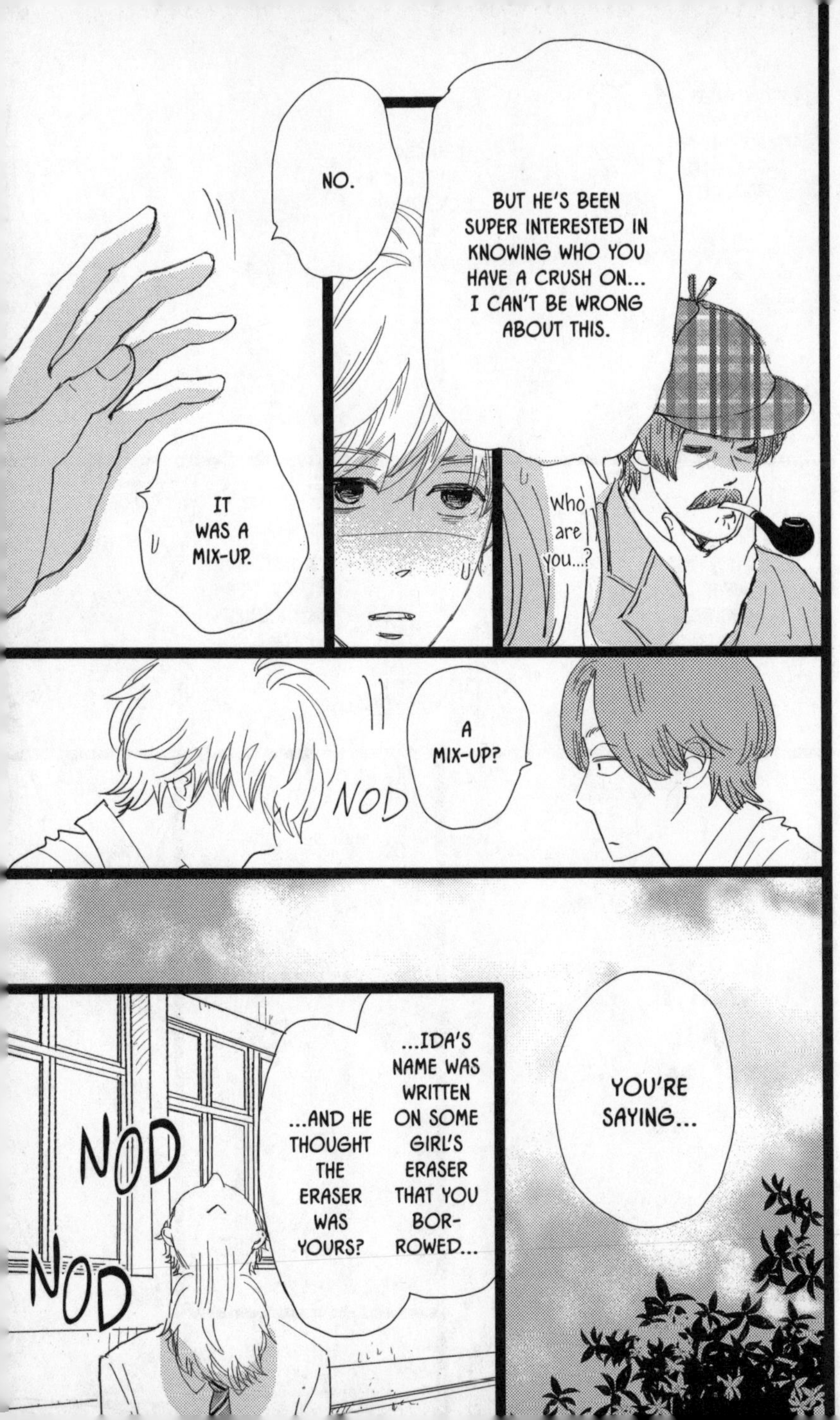
BUT HE'S BEEN SUPER INTERESTED IN KNOWING WHO YOU HAVE A CRUSH ON... I CAN'T BE WRONG ABOUT THIS.
Who are you...?
NO.
IT WAS A MIX-UP.
A MIX-UP?
NOD
YOU'RE SAYING...
...IDA'S NAME WAS WRITTEN ON SOME GIRL'S ERASER THAT YOU BOR-ROWED...
...AND HE THOUGHT THE ERASER WAS YOURS?
NOD
NOD

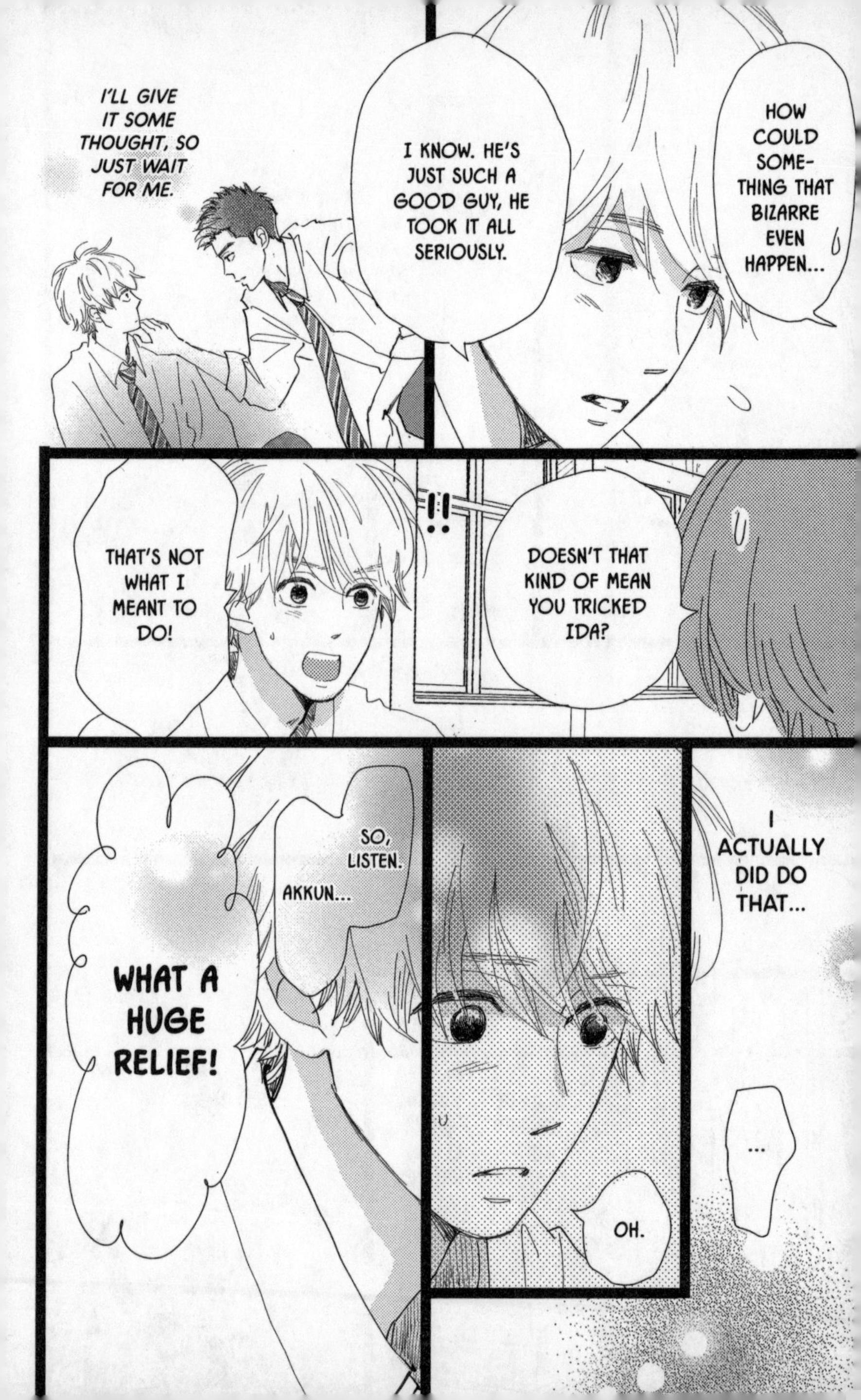
HOW COULD SOME- THING THAT BIZARRE EVEN HAPPEN...
I KNOW. HE'S JUST SUCH A GOOD GUY, HE TOOK IT ALL SERIOUSLY.
I'LL GIVE IT SOME THOUGHT, SO JUST WAIT FOR ME.
DOESN'T THAT KIND OF MEAN YOU TRICKED IDA?
!!
THAT'S NOT WHAT I MEANT TO DO!
I ACTUALLY DID DO THAT...
...
OH.
SO, LISTEN.
AKKUN...
WHAT A HUGE RELIEF!

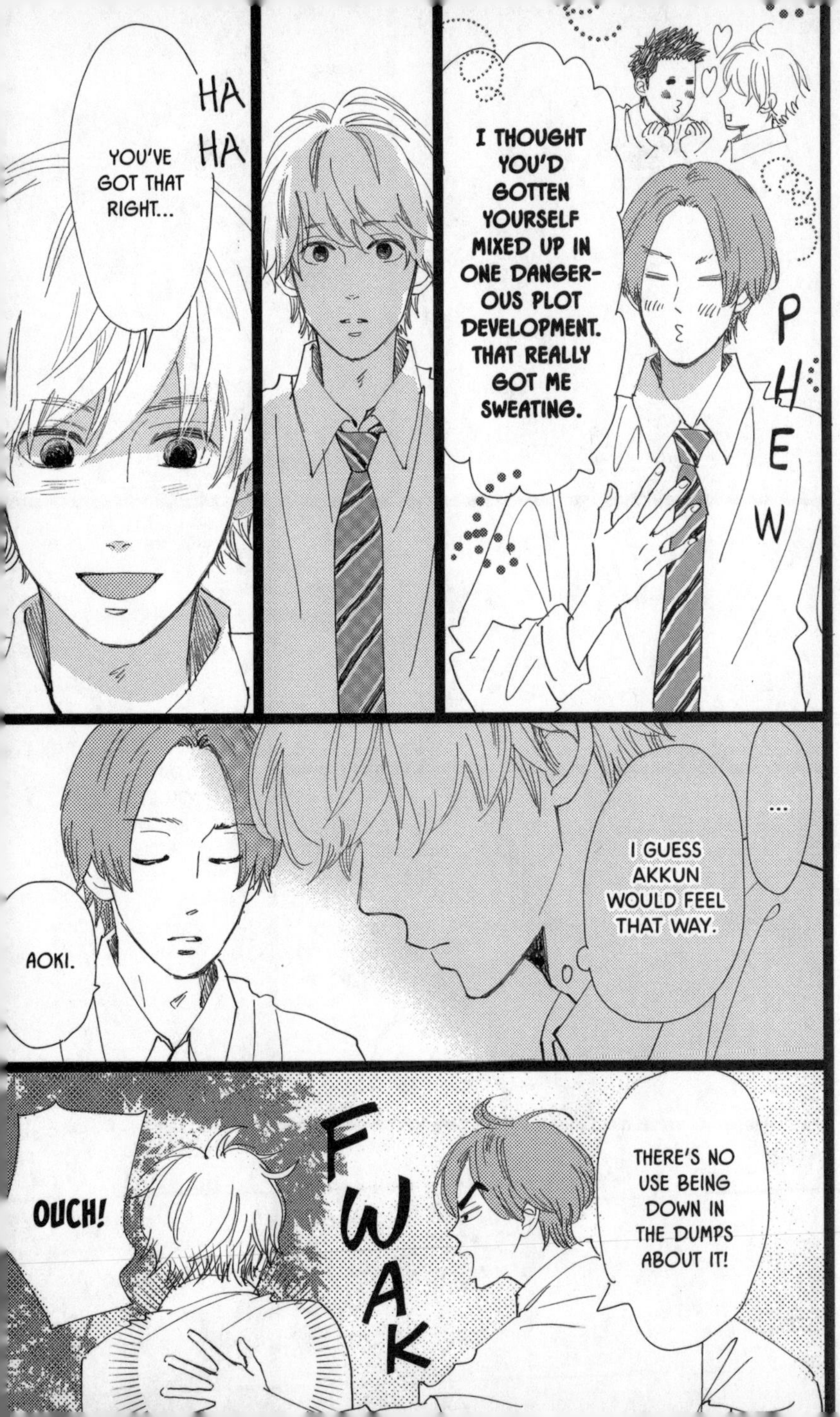
I THOUGHT YOU'D GOTTEN YOURSELF MIXED UP IN ONE DANGEROUS PLOT DEVELOPMENT. THAT REALLY GOT ME SWEATING.
PHEW
HA HA
YOU'VE GOT THAT RIGHT...
...
I GUESS AKKUN WOULD FEEL THAT WAY.
AOKI.
THERE'S NO USE BEING DOWN IN THE DUMPS ABOUT IT!
FWAK
OUCH!

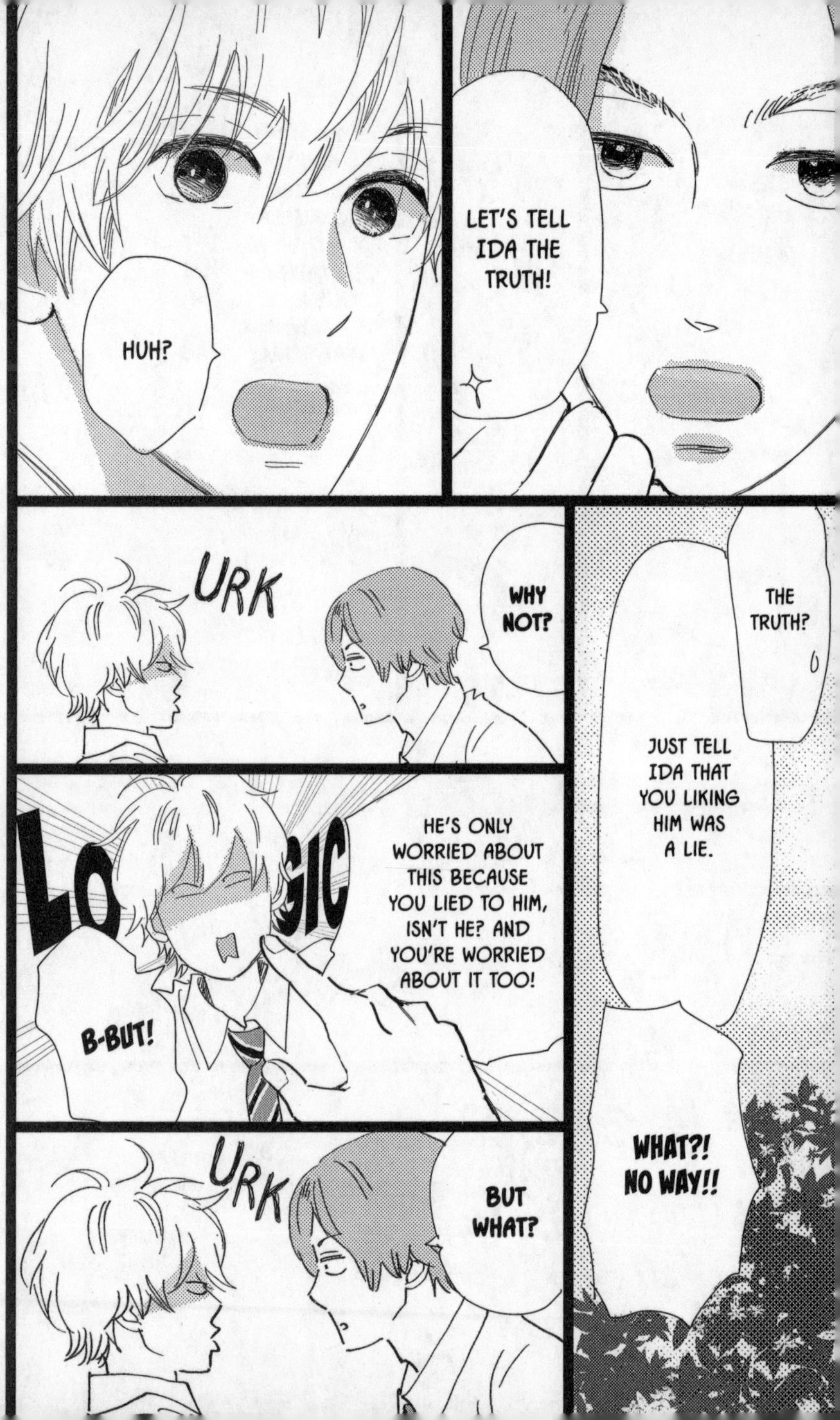
LET'S TELL IDA THE TRUTH!
HUH?
THE TRUTH?
JUST TELL IDA THAT YOU LIKING HIM WAS A LIE.
WHAT?! NO WAY!!
WHY NOT?
URK
HE'S ONLY WORRIED ABOUT THIS BECAUSE YOU LIED TO HIM, ISN'T HE? AND YOU'RE WORRIED ABOUT IT TOO!
LOGIC
B-BUT!
BUT WHAT?
URK

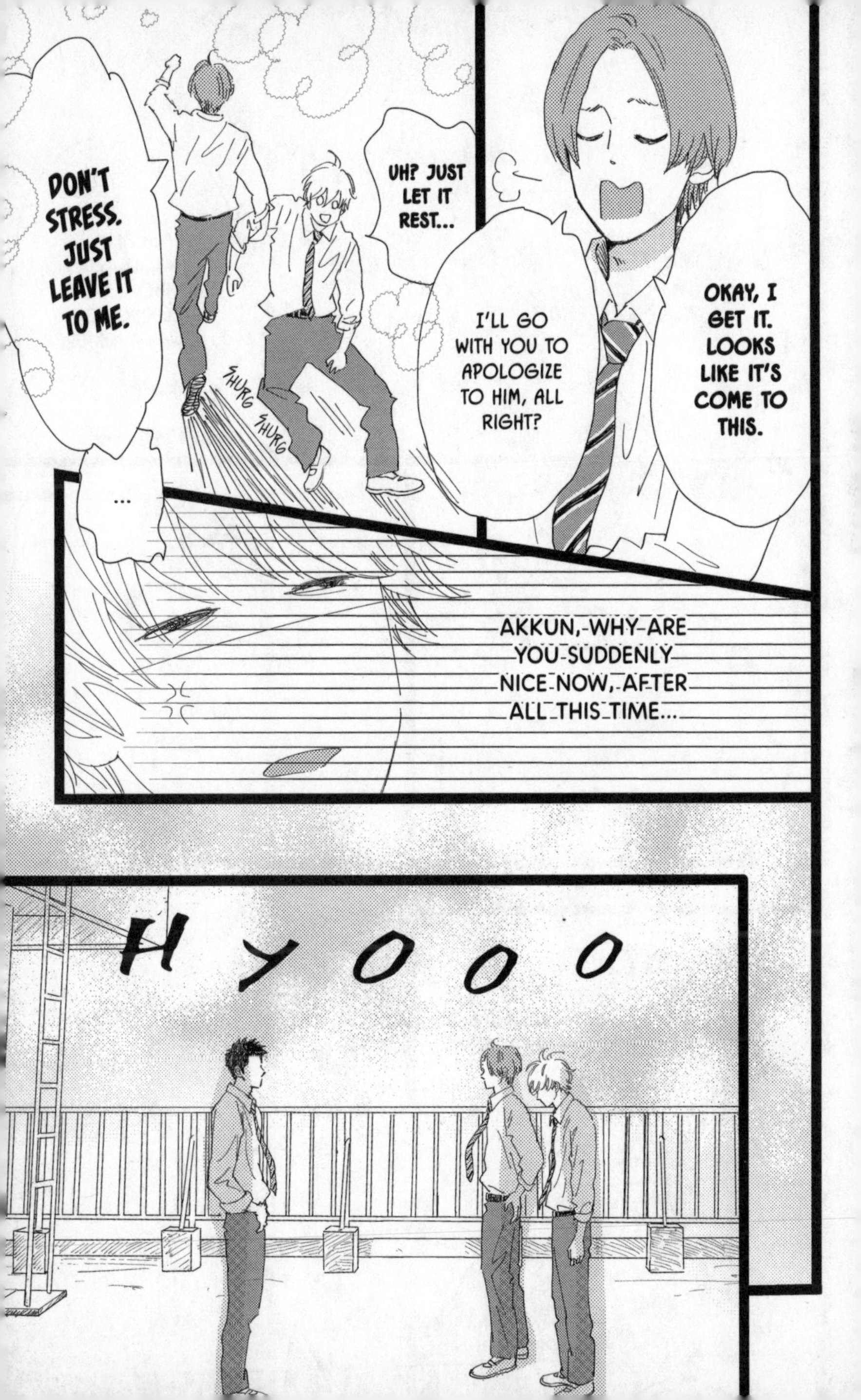
OKAY, I GET IT. LOOKS LIKE IT'S COME TO THIS.
I'LL GO WITH YOU TO APOLOGIZE TO HIM, ALL RIGHT?
UH? JUST LET IT REST...
DON'T STRESS. JUST LEAVE IT TO ME.
SHURG
SHURG
...
AKKUN, WHY ARE YOU SUDDENLY NICE NOW, AFTER ALL THIS TIME...
HYOOO

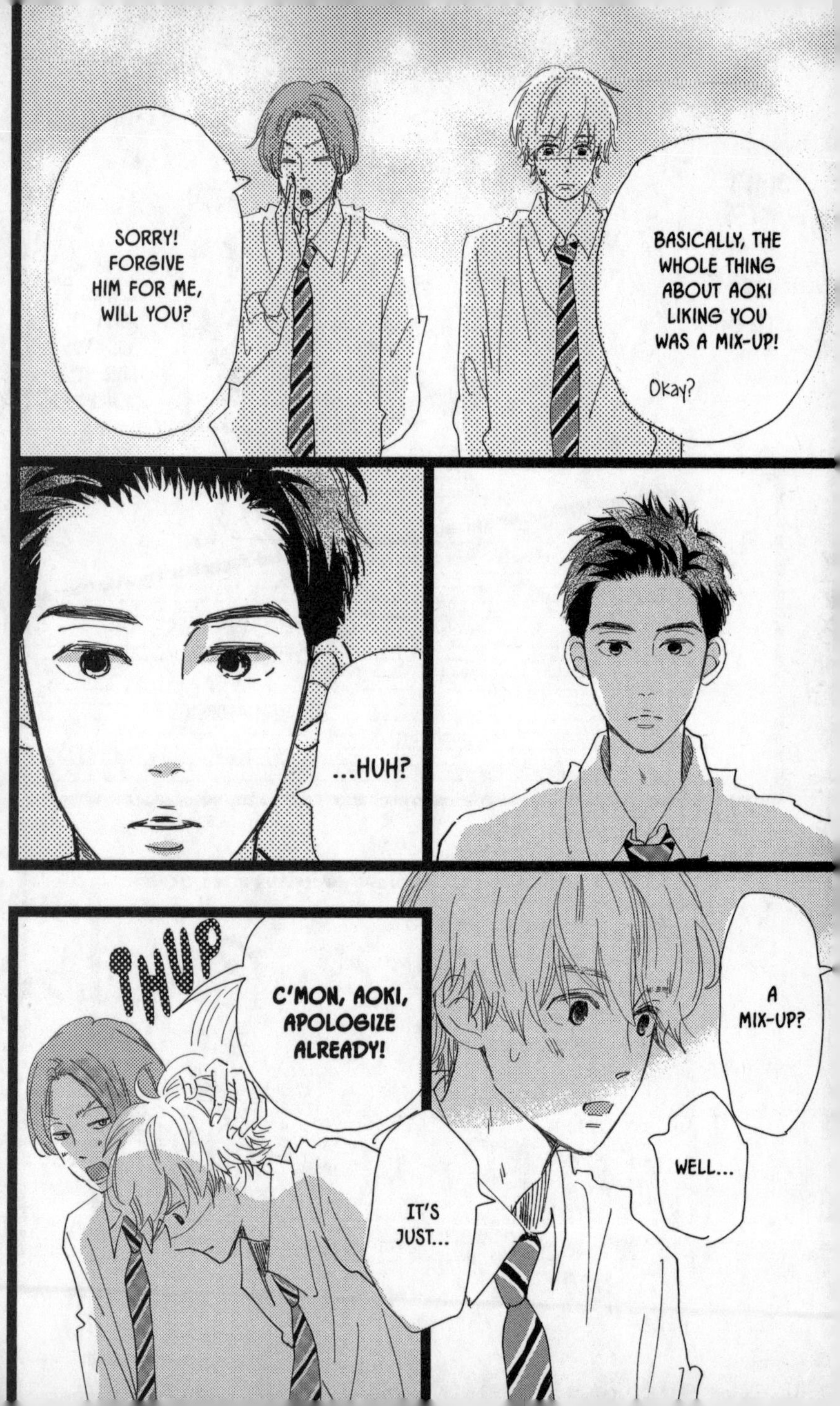
BASICALLY, THE WHOLE THING ABOUT AOKI LIKING YOU WAS A MIX-UP!
Okay?
SORRY! FORGIVE HIM FOR ME, WILL YOU?
...HUH?
A MIX-UP?
WELL...
IT'S JUST...
THUP
C'MON, AOKI, APOLOGIZE ALREADY!

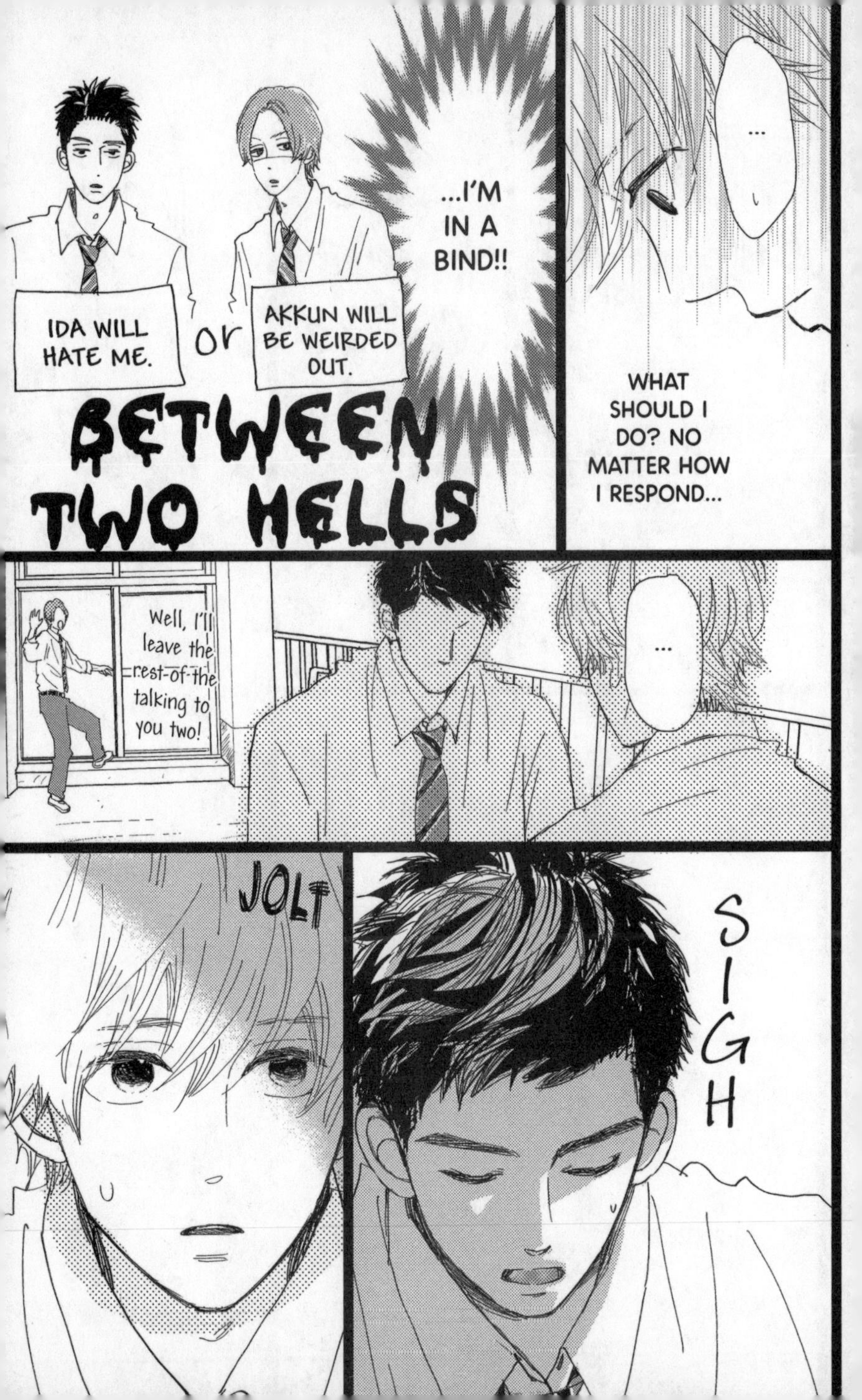
...
WHAT SHOULD I DO? NO MATTER HOW I RESPOND...
...I'M IN A BIND!!
IDA WILL HATE ME.
or
AKKUN WILL BE WEIRDED OUT.
BETWEEN TWO HELLS
...
Well, I'll leave the rest of the talking to you two!
SIGH
JOLT

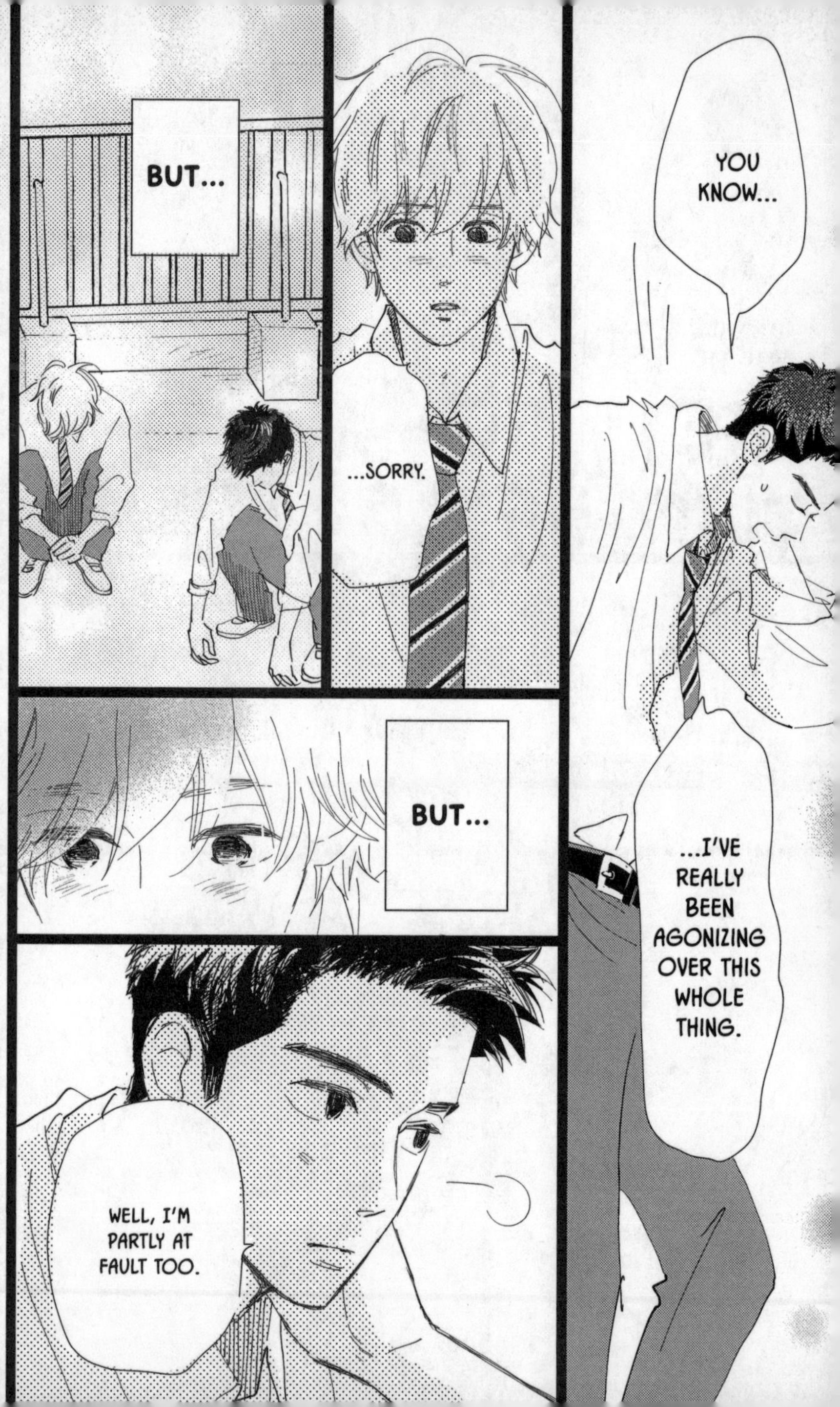
YOU KNOW...
...I'VE REALLY BEEN AGONIZING OVER THIS WHOLE THING.
...SORRY.
BUT...
BUT...
WELL, I'M PARTLY AT FAULT TOO.

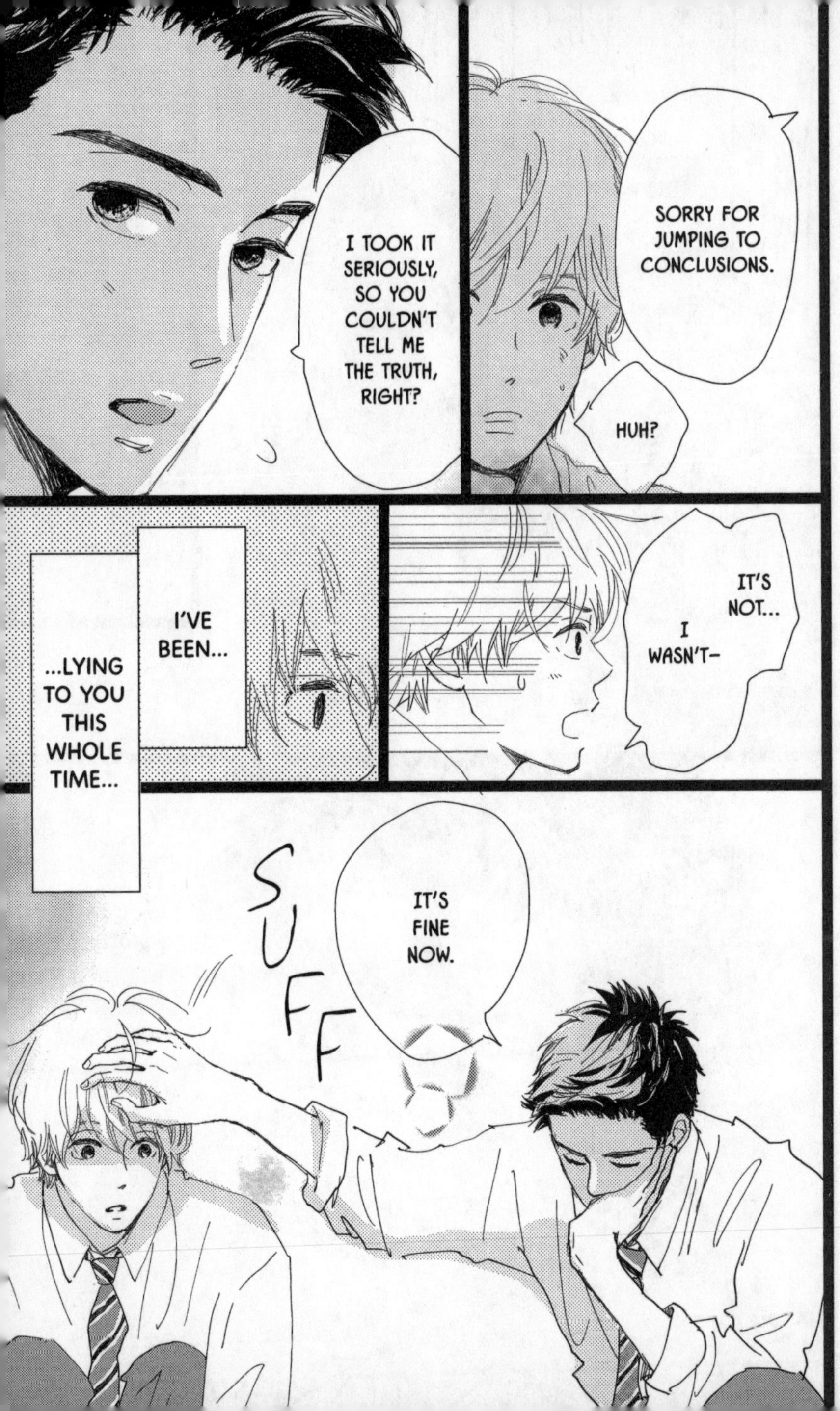
SORRY FOR JUMPING TO CONCLUSIONS.
HUH?
I TOOK IT SERIOUSLY, SO YOU COULDN'T TELL ME THE TRUTH, RIGHT?
IT'S NOT...
I WASN'T-
I'VE BEEN...
...LYING TO YOU THIS WHOLE TIME...
IT'S FINE NOW.
SUFF

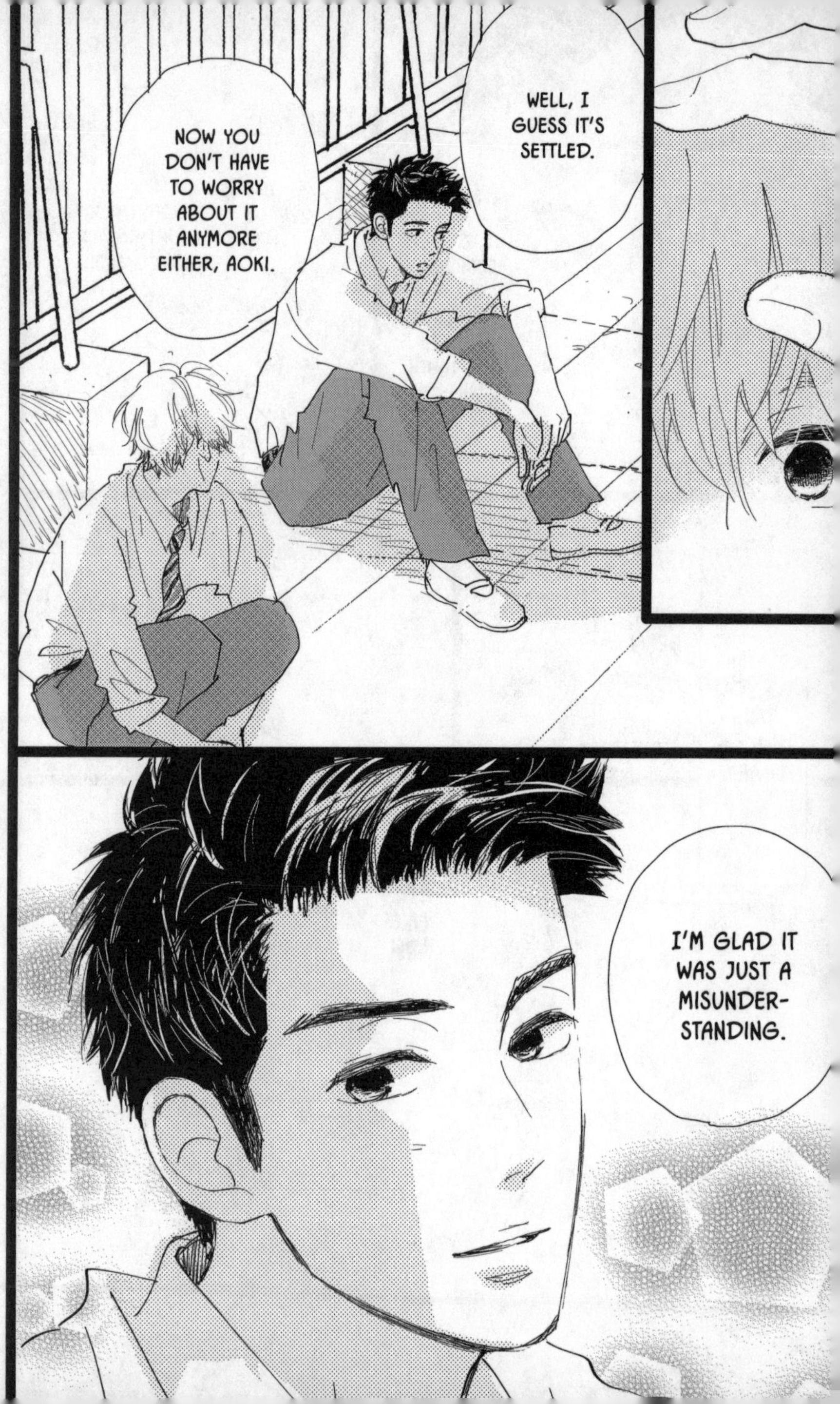
WELL, I GUESS IT'S SETTLED.
NOW YOU DON'T HAVE TO WORRY ABOUT IT ANYMORE EITHER, AOKI.
I'M GLAD IT WAS JUST A MISUNDER-STANDING.

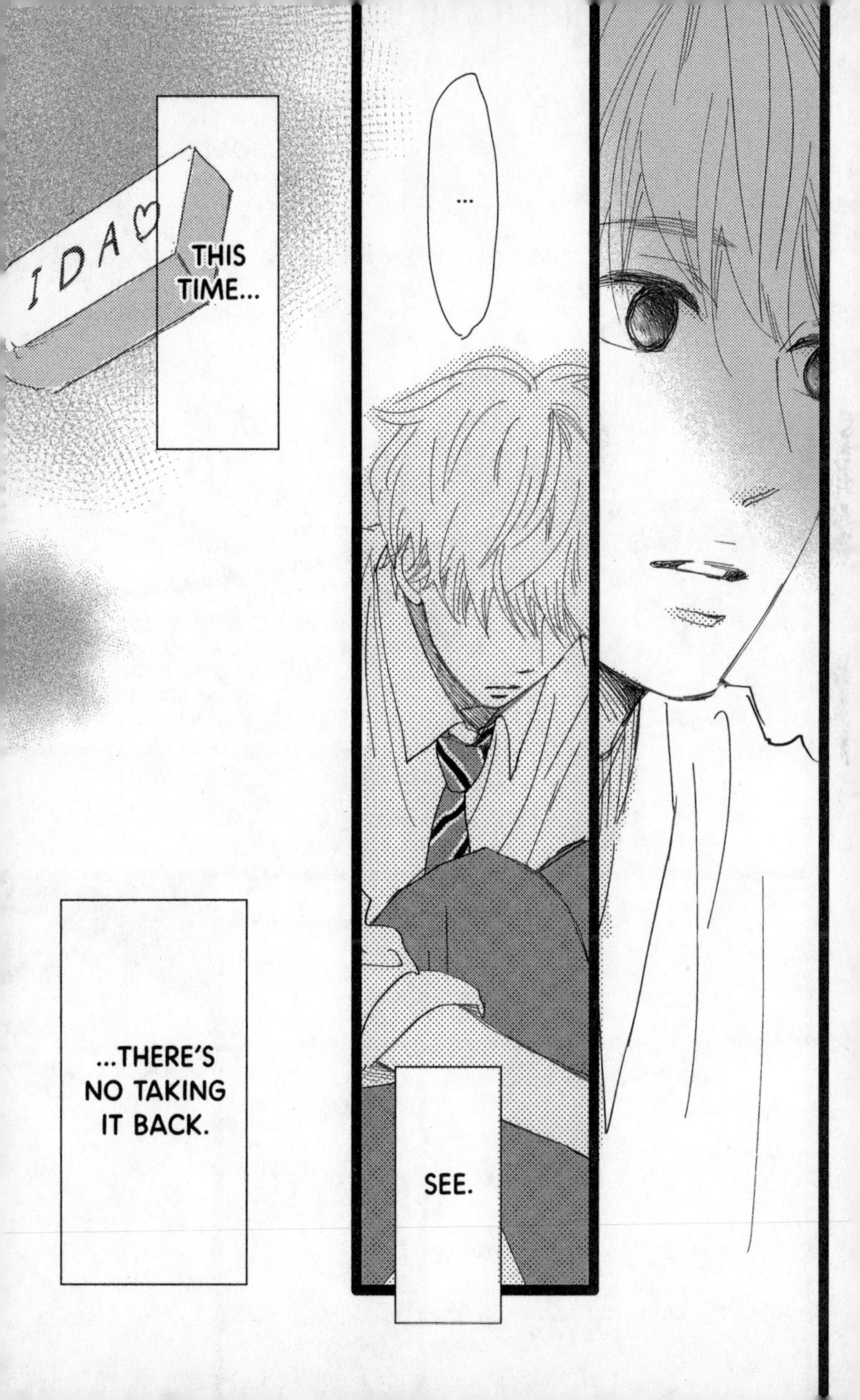
...
SEE.
THIS TIME...
IDA♡
...THERE'S NO TAKING IT BACK.

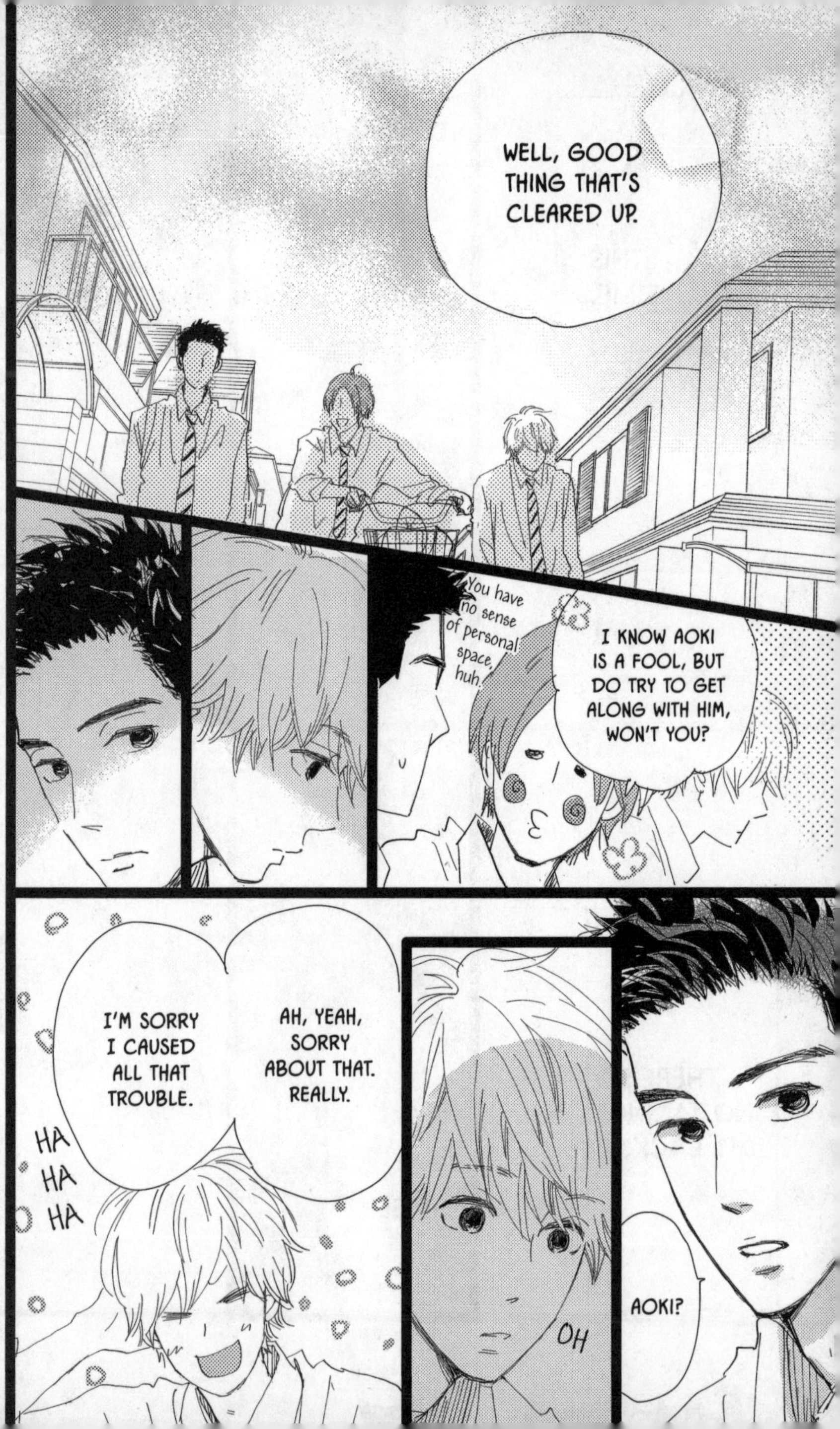
WELL, GOOD THING THAT'S CLEARED UP.
I KNOW AOKI IS A FOOL, BUT DO TRY TO GET ALONG WITH HIM, WON'T YOU?
You have no sense of personal space, huh.
AOKI?
OH
AH, YEAH, SORRY ABOUT THAT. REALLY.
I'M SORRY I CAUSED ALL THAT TROUBLE.
HA HA HA

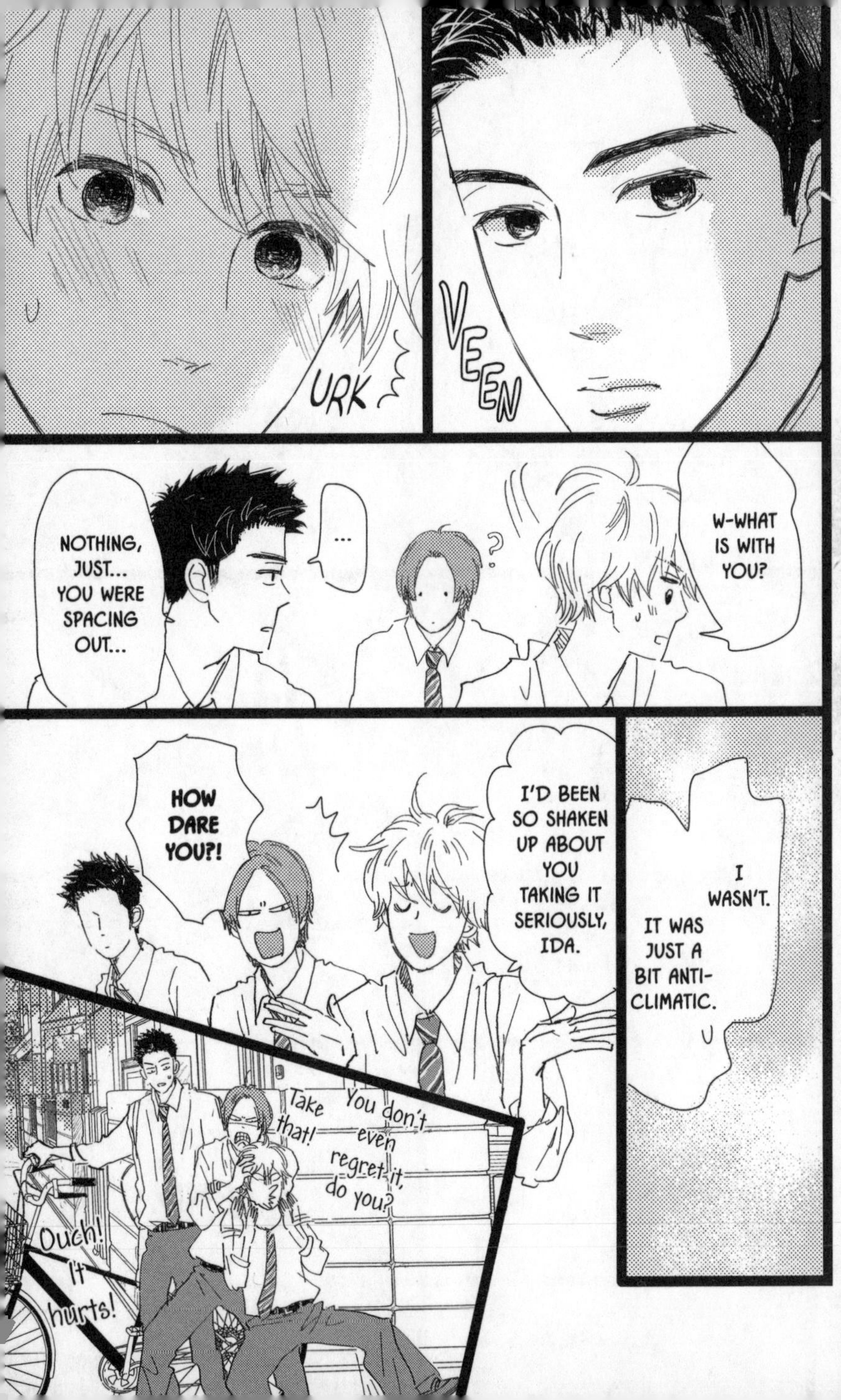
VEEN
URK
W-WHAT IS WITH YOU?
?
...
NOTHING, JUST... YOU WERE SPACING OUT...
I WASN'T.
IT WAS JUST A BIT ANTI-CLIMATIC.
I'D BEEN SO SHAKEN UP ABOUT YOU TAKING IT SERIOUSLY, IDA.
HOW DARE YOU?!
You don't even regret it, do you?
Take that!
Ouch! It hurts!

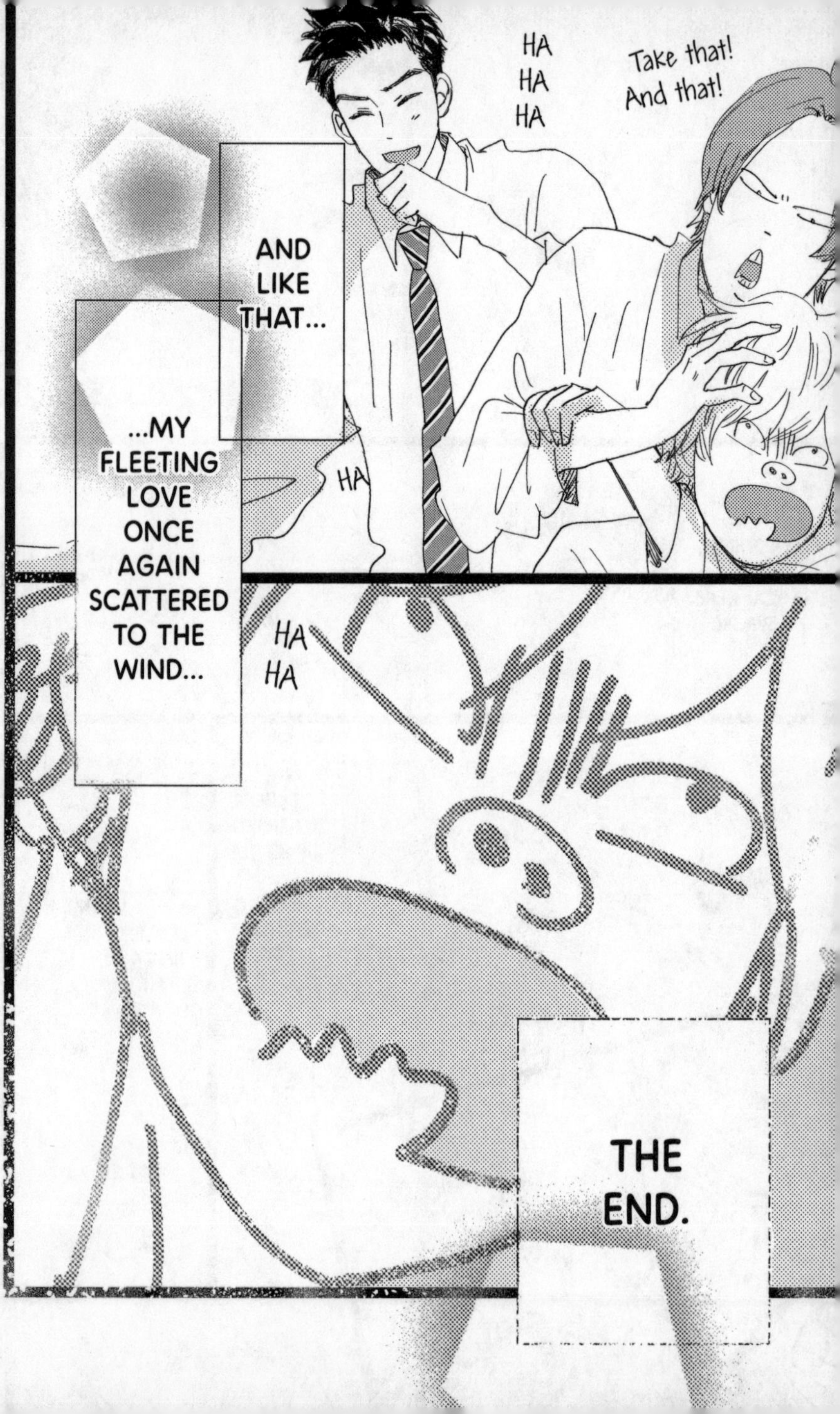
Take that! And that!
HA HA HA
AND LIKE THAT...
HA
...MY FLEETING LOVE ONCE AGAIN SCATTERED TO THE WIND...
HA HA
THE END.

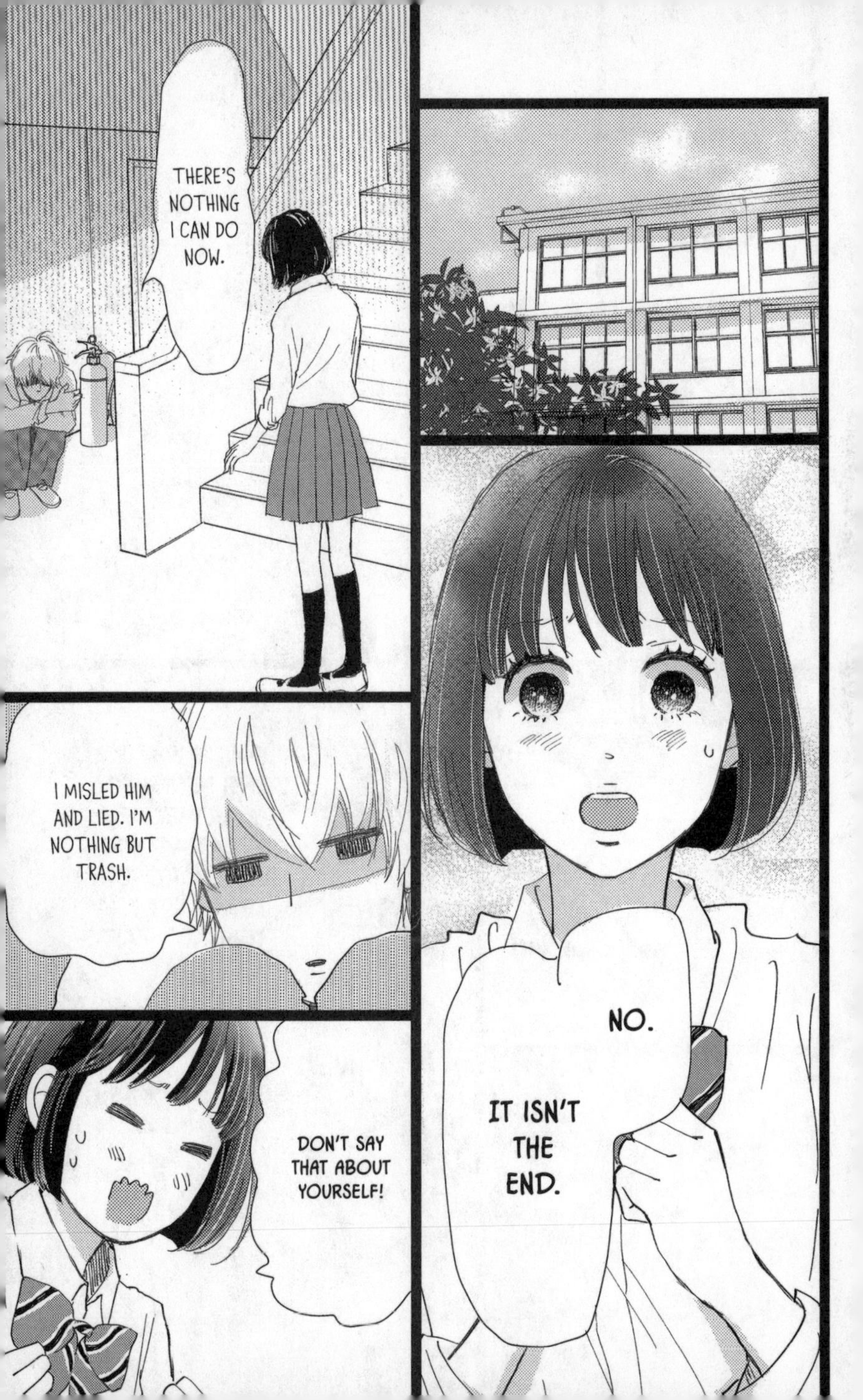
NO.
IT ISN'T THE END.
THERE'S NOTHING I CAN DO NOW.
I MISLED HIM AND LIED. I'M NOTHING BUT TRASH.
DON'T SAY THAT ABOUT YOURSELF!

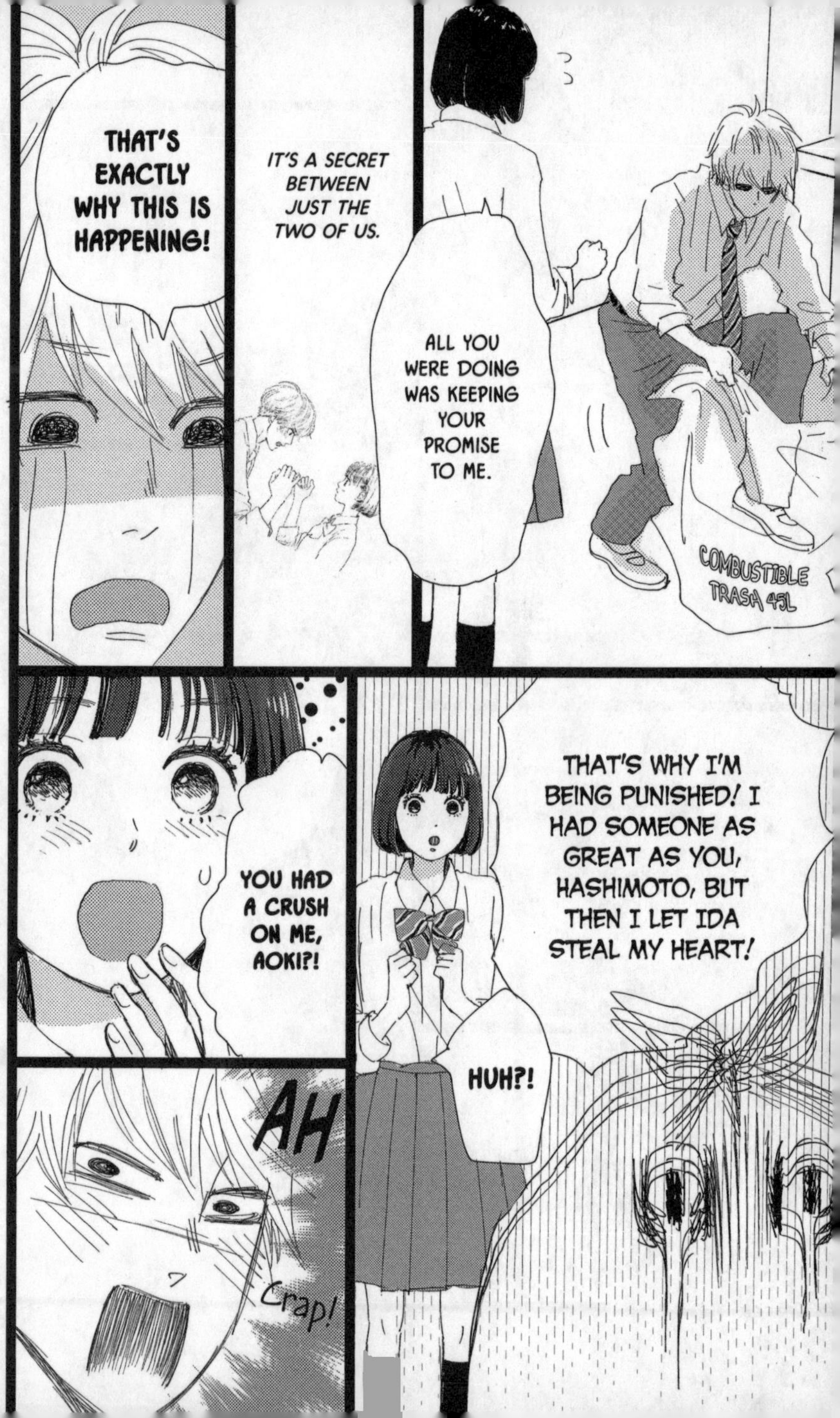
ALL YOU WERE DOING WAS KEEPING YOUR PROMISE TO ME.
COMBUSTIBLE TRASA 45L
IT'S A SECRET BETWEEN JUST THE TWO OF US.
THAT'S EXACTLY WHY THIS IS HAPPENING!
THAT'S WHY I'M BEING PUNISHED! I HAD SOMEONE AS GREAT AS YOU, HASHIMOTO, BUT THEN I LET IDA STEAL MY HEART!
HUH?!
YOU HAD A CRUSH ON ME, AOKI?!
AH
Crap!

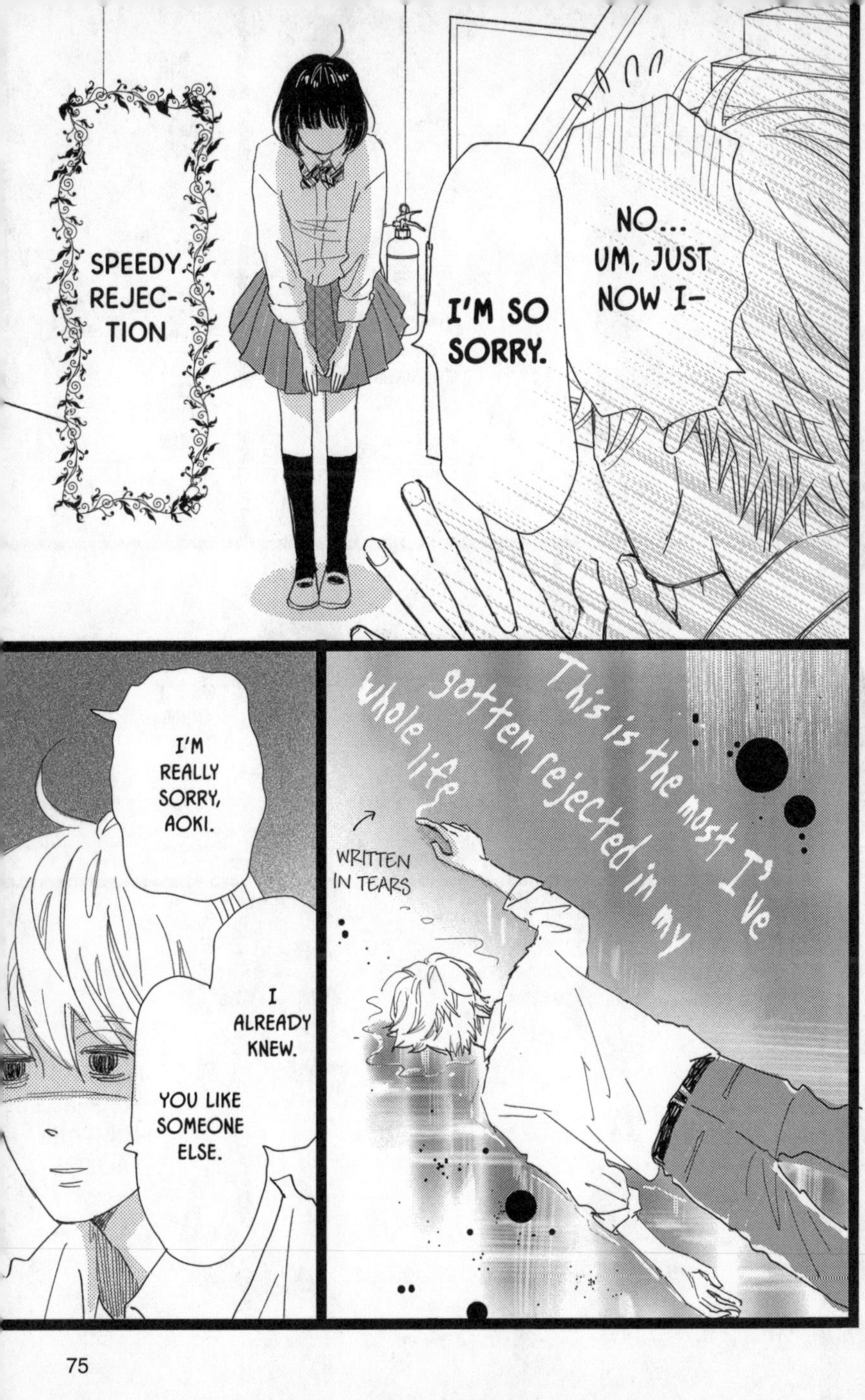
NO... UM, JUST NOW I-
I'M SO SORRY.
SPEEDY REJECTION
This is the most I've gotten rejected in my whole life
WRITTEN IN TEARS
I'M REALLY SORRY, AOKI.
I ALREADY KNEW.
YOU LIKE SOMEONE ELSE.

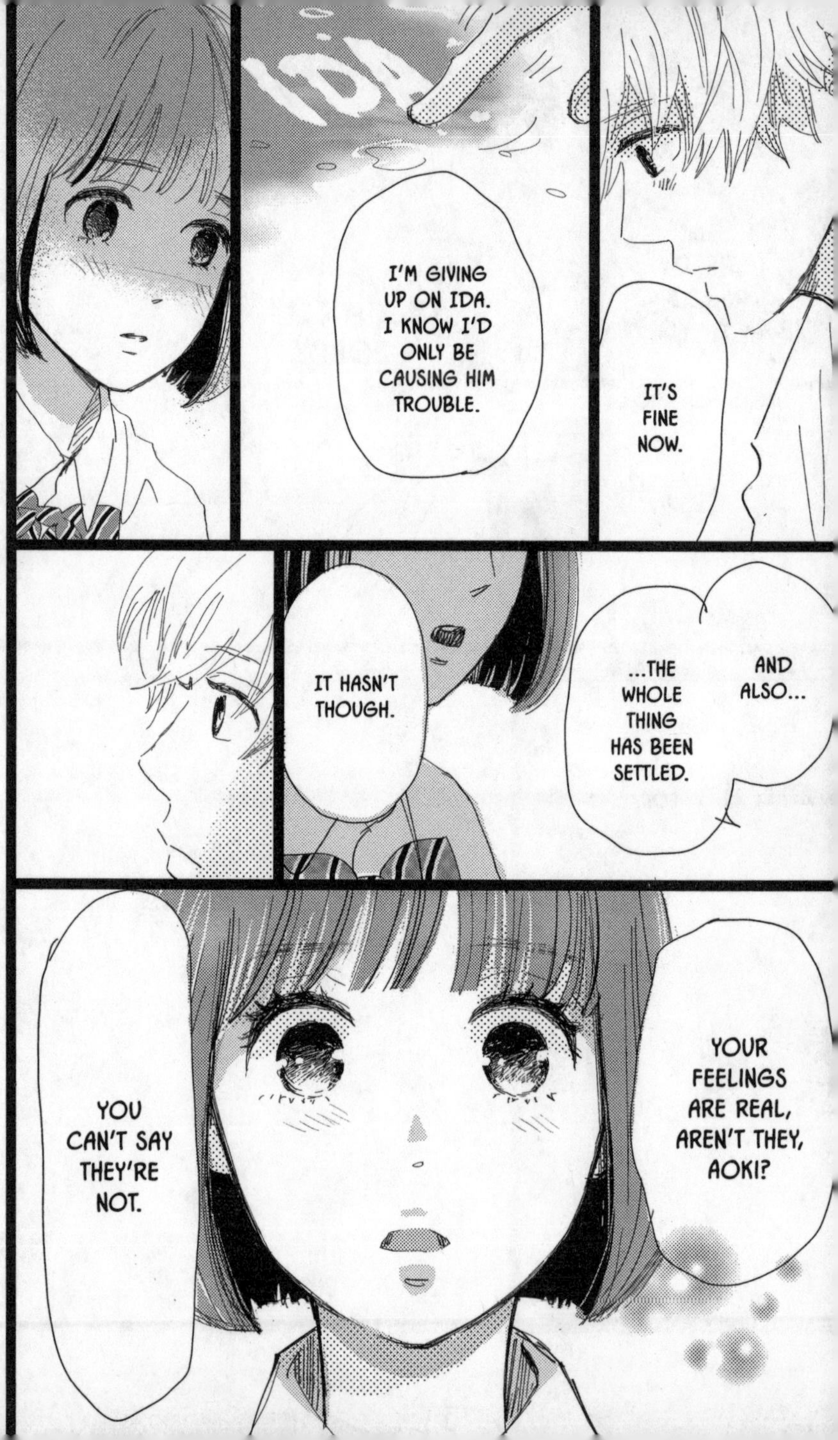
IT'S FINE NOW.
I'M GIVING UP ON IDA. I KNOW I'D ONLY BE CAUSING HIM TROUBLE.
AND ALSO...
...THE WHOLE THING HAS BEEN SETTLED.
IT HASN'T THOUGH.
YOUR FEELINGS ARE REAL, AREN'T THEY, AOKI?
YOU CAN'T SAY THEY'RE NOT.

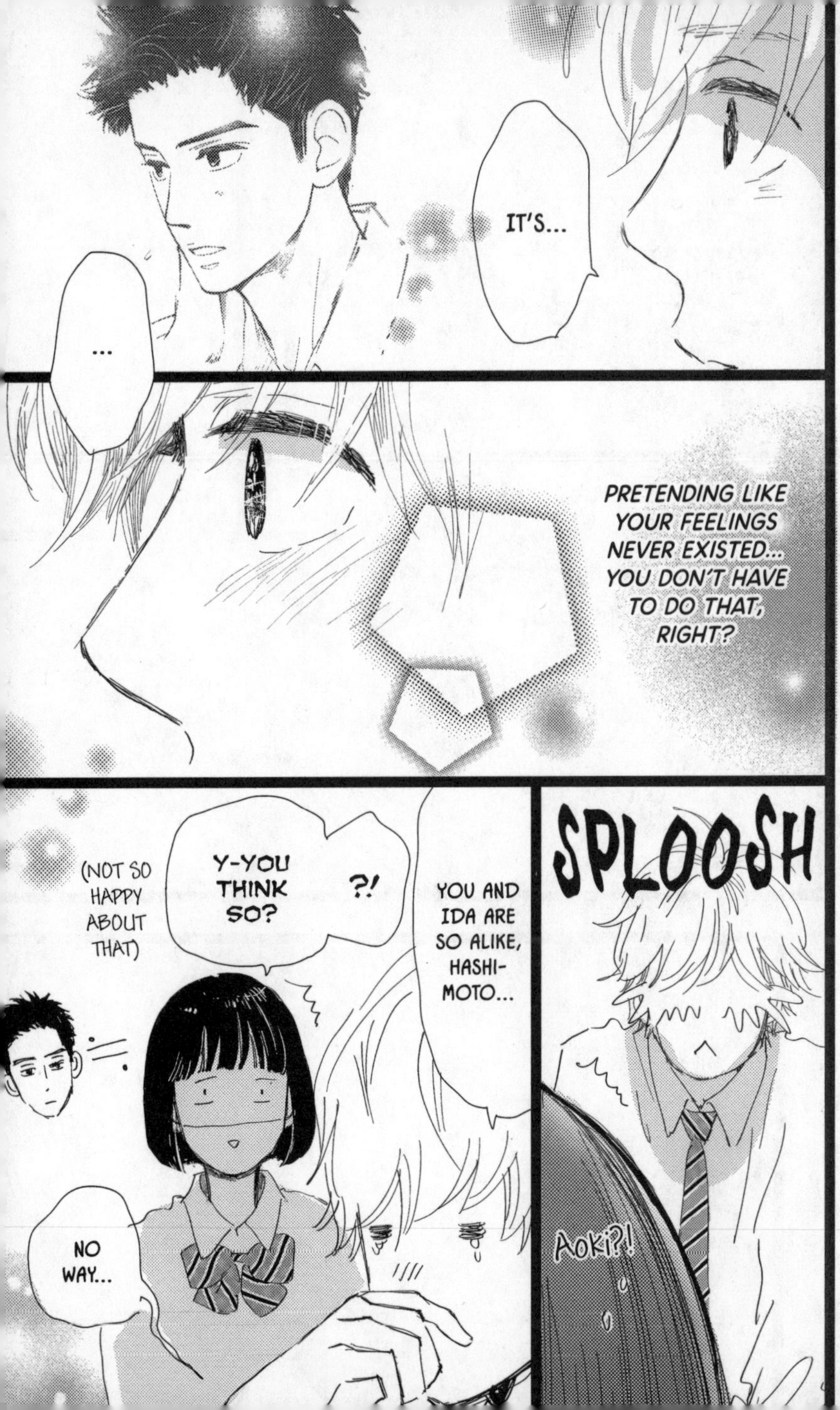

IT'S...
...
PRETENDING LIKE YOUR FEELINGS NEVER EXISTED... YOU DON'T HAVE TO DO THAT, RIGHT?
SPLOOSH
Aoki?!
YOU AND IDA ARE SO ALIKE, HASHIMOTO...
?!
Y-YOU THINK SO?
(NOT SO HAPPY ABOUT THAT)
NO WAY...

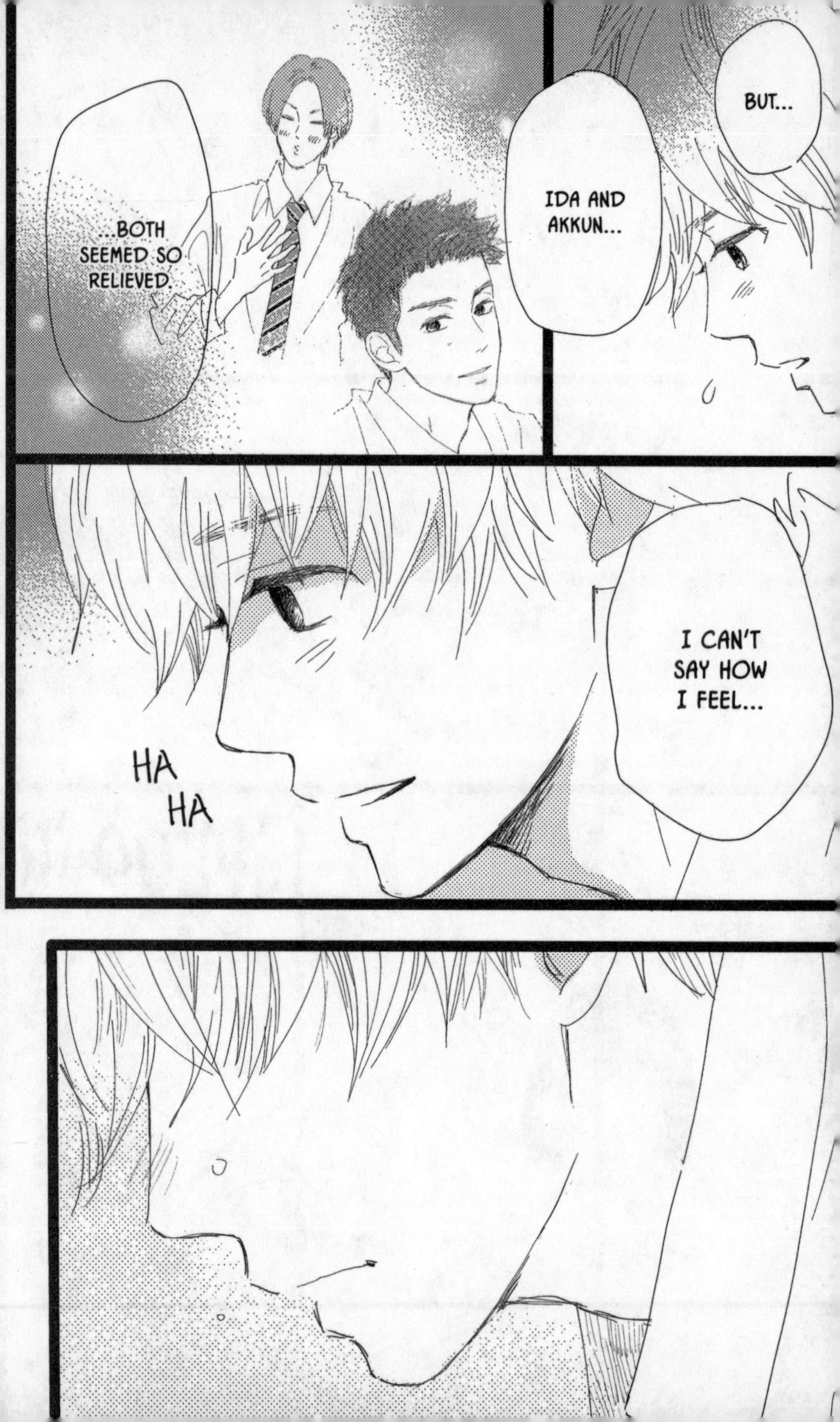
BUT...
IDA AND AKKUN...
...BOTH SEEMED SO RELIEVED.
I CAN'T SAY HOW I FEEL...
HA HA

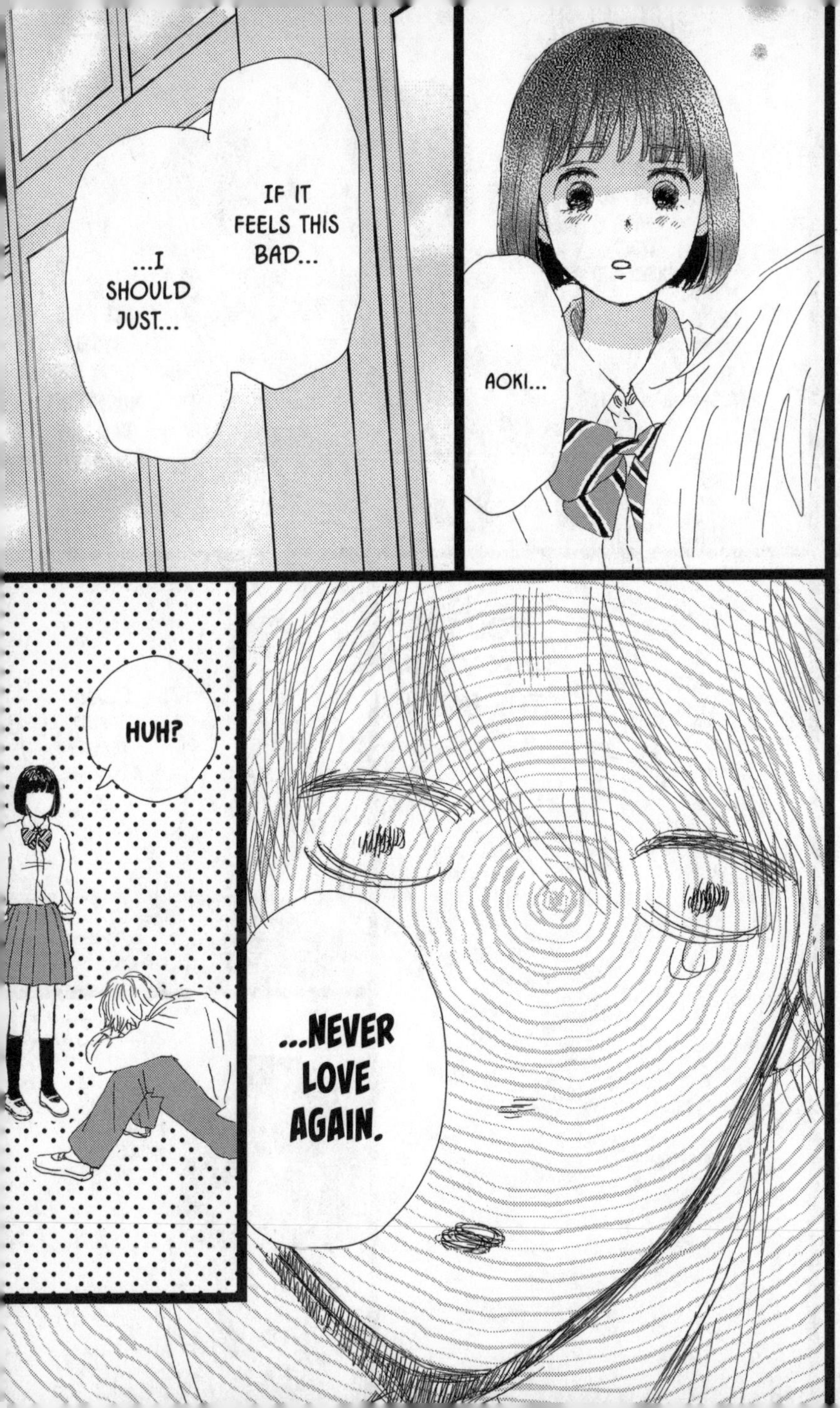
AOKI...
IF IT FEELS THIS BAD...
...I SHOULD JUST...
...NEVER LOVE AGAIN.
HUH?

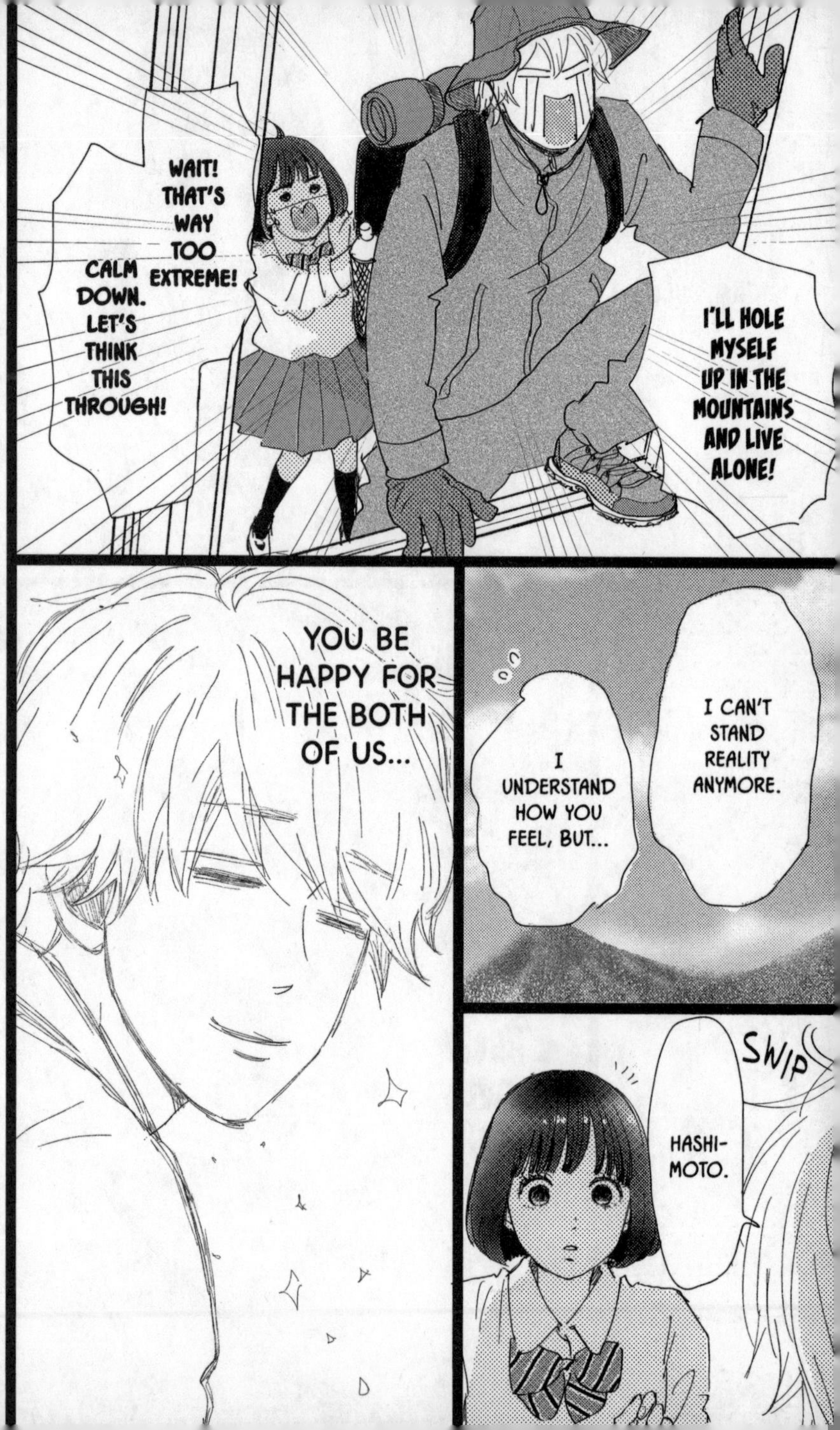
I'LL HOLE MYSELF UP IN THE MOUNTAINS AND LIVE ALONE!
WAIT! THAT'S WAY TOO EXTREME!
CALM DOWN. LET'S THINK THIS THROUGH!
I CAN'T STAND REALITY ANYMORE.
I UNDERSTAND HOW YOU FEEL, BUT...
SWIP
HASHI-MOTO.
YOU BE HAPPY FOR THE BOTH OF US...

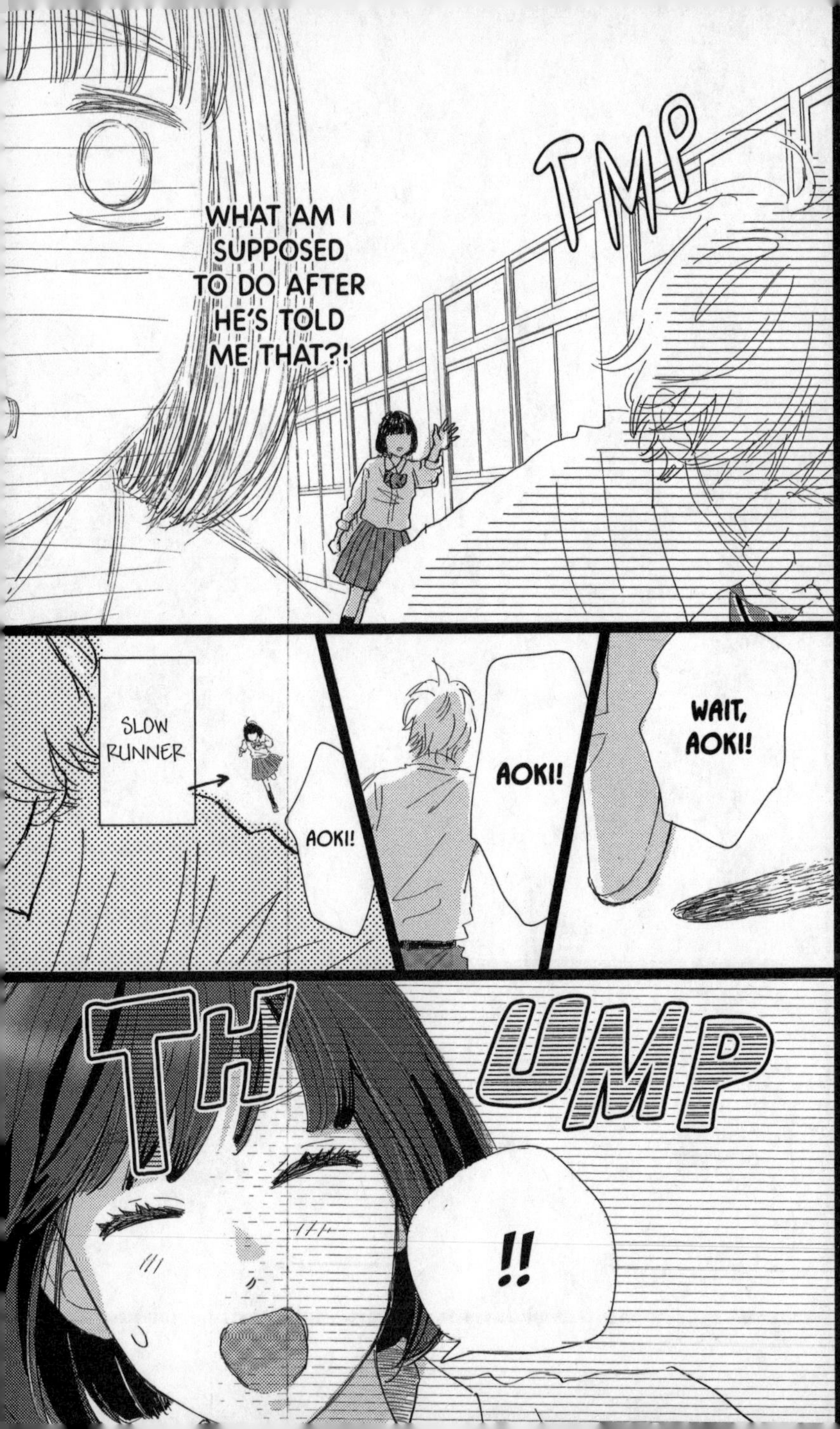
TMP
WHAT AM I SUPPOSED TO DO AFTER HE'S TOLD ME THAT?!
WAIT, AOKI!
AOKI!
AOKI!
SLOW RUNNER
THUMP
!!

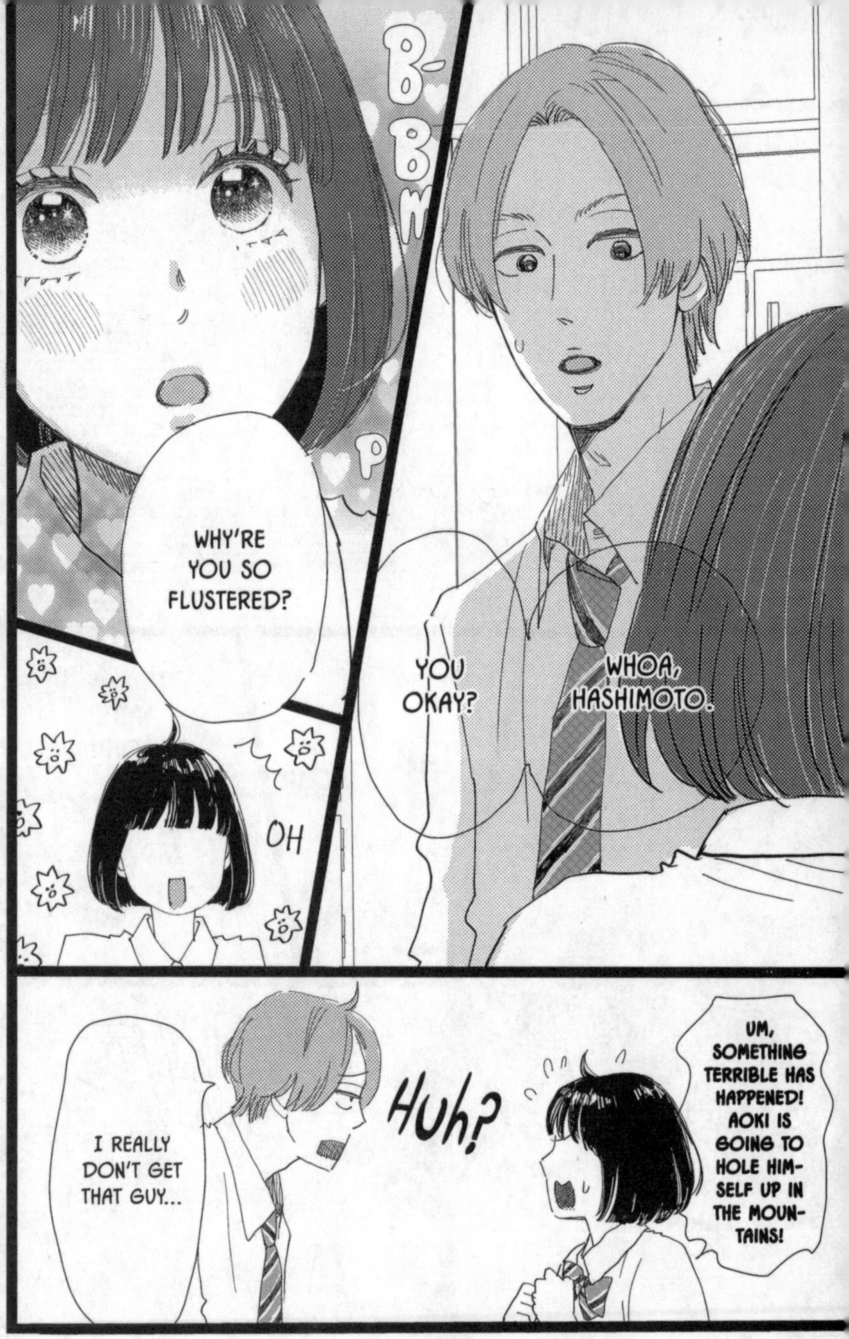

WHOA, HASHIMOTO.
YOU OKAY?
B-BUMP
WHY'RE YOU SO FLUSTERED?
OH
UM, SOMETHING TERRIBLE HAS HAPPENED! AOKI IS GOING TO HOLE HIMSELF UP IN THE MOUNTAINS!
HUH?
I REALLY DON'T GET THAT GUY...

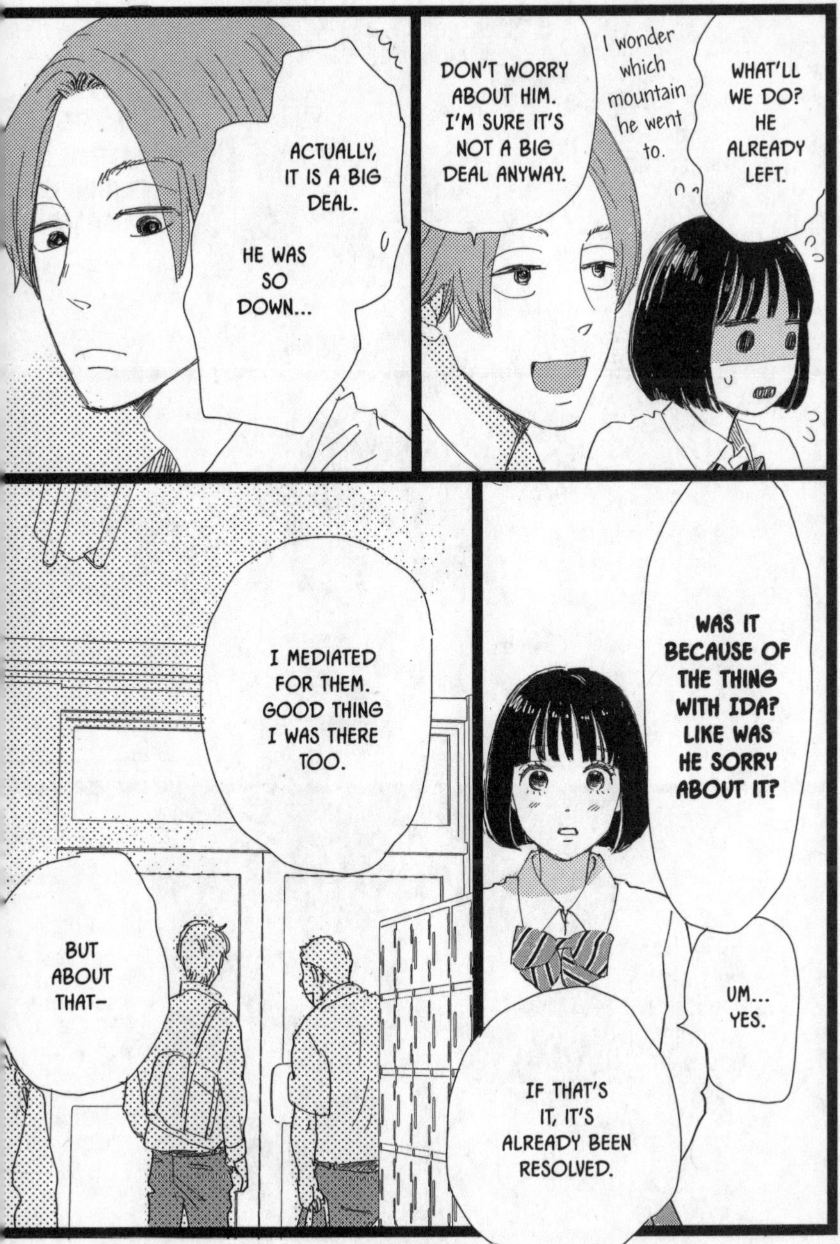
WHAT'LL WE DO? HE ALREADY LEFT.
I wonder which mountain he went to.
DON'T WORRY ABOUT HIM. I'M SURE IT'S NOT A BIG DEAL ANYWAY.
ACTUALLY, IT IS A BIG DEAL.
HE WAS SO DOWN...
WAS IT BECAUSE OF THE THING WITH IDA? LIKE WAS HE SORRY ABOUT IT?
UM... YES.
IF THAT'S IT, IT'S ALREADY BEEN RESOLVED.
I MEDIATED FOR THEM. GOOD THING I WAS THERE TOO.
BUT ABOUT THAT–

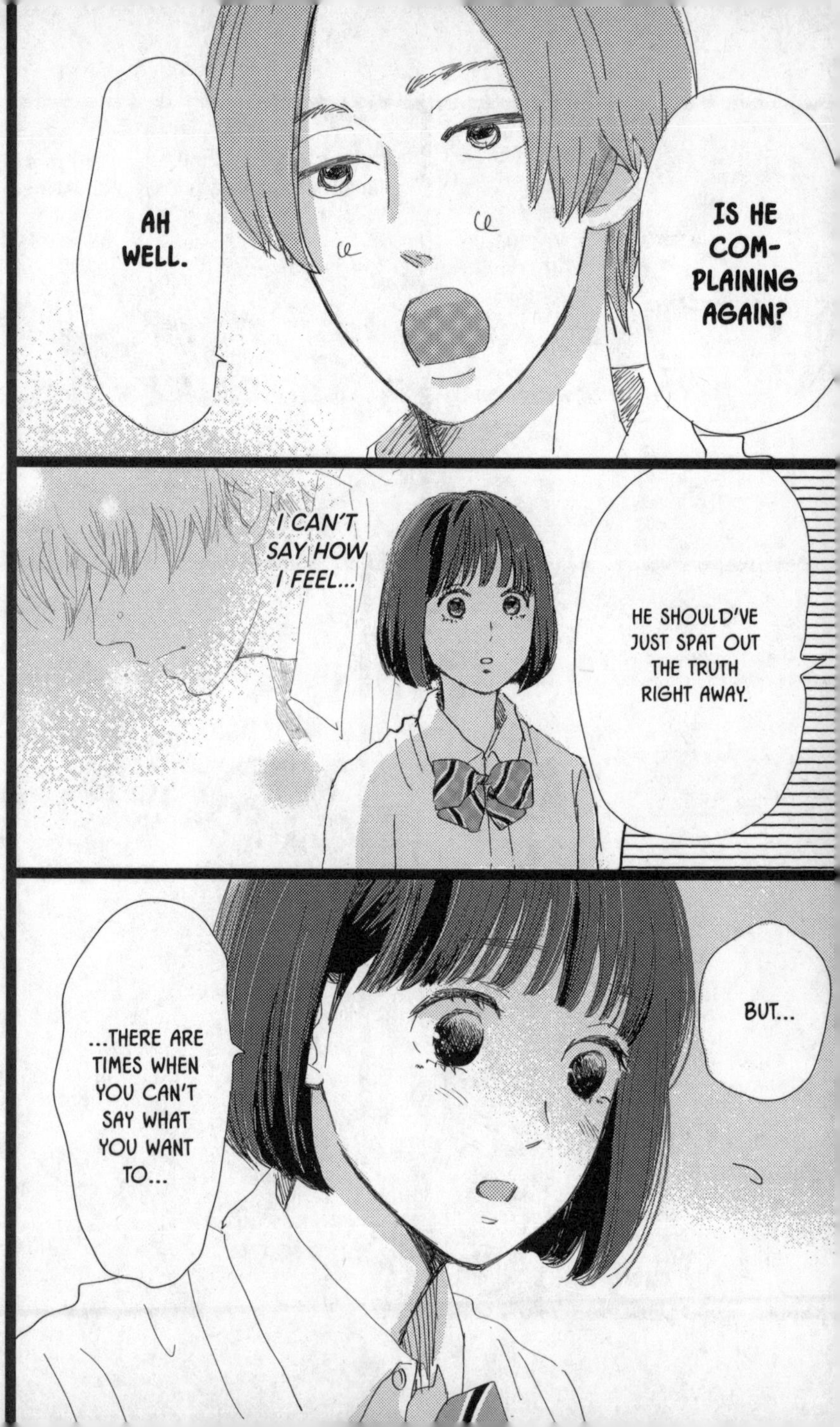
IS HE COMPLAINING AGAIN?
AH WELL.
HE SHOULD'VE JUST SPAT OUT THE TRUTH RIGHT AWAY.
I CAN'T SAY HOW I FEEL...
BUT...
...THERE ARE TIMES WHEN YOU CAN'T SAY WHAT YOU WANT TO...

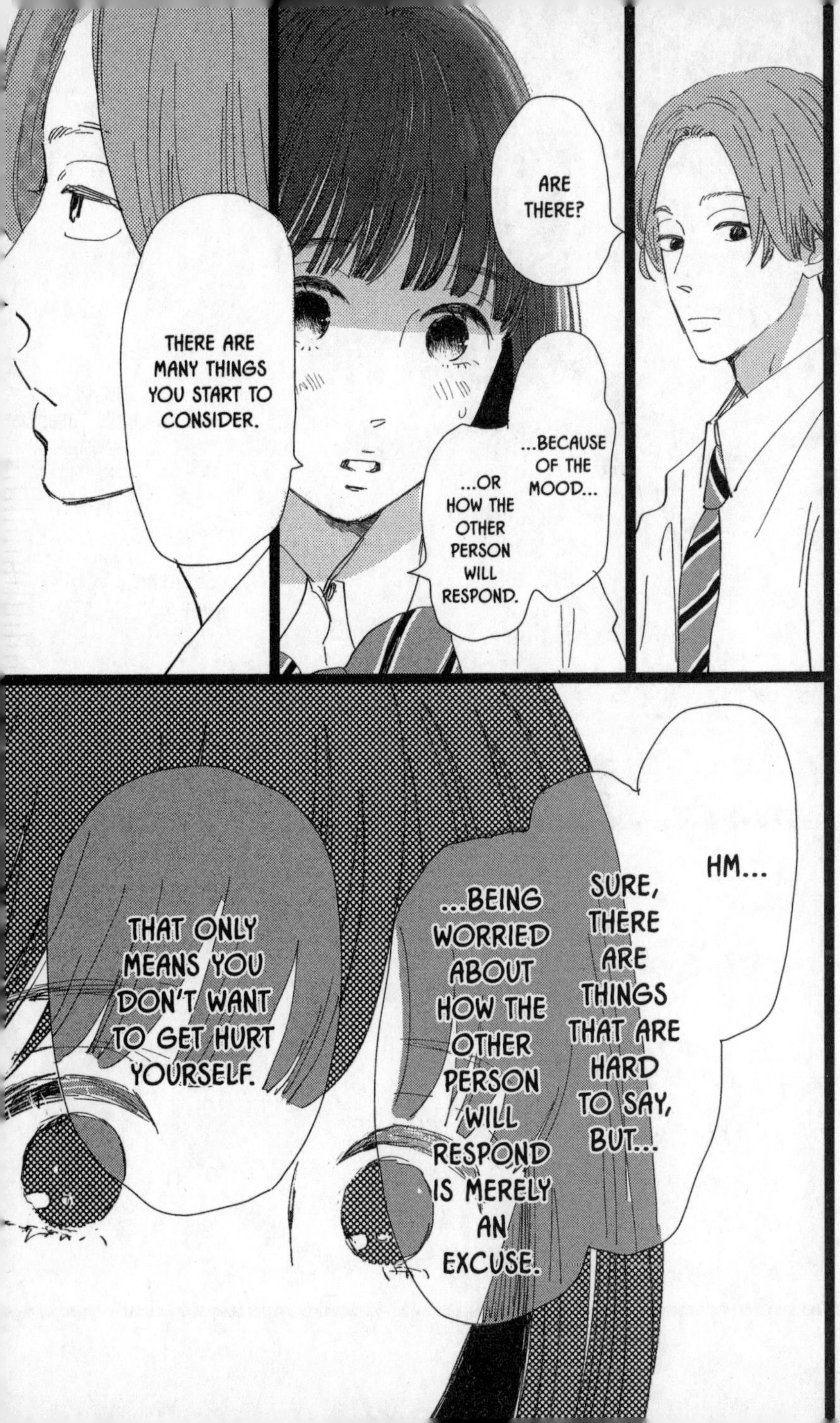
ARE THERE?
...BECAUSE OF THE MOOD...
...OR HOW THE OTHER PERSON WILL RESPOND.
THERE ARE MANY THINGS YOU START TO CONSIDER.
HM...
SURE, THERE ARE THINGS THAT ARE HARD TO SAY, BUT...
...BEING WORRIED ABOUT HOW THE OTHER PERSON WILL RESPOND IS MERELY AN EXCUSE.
THAT ONLY MEANS YOU DON'T WANT TO GET HURT YOURSELF.

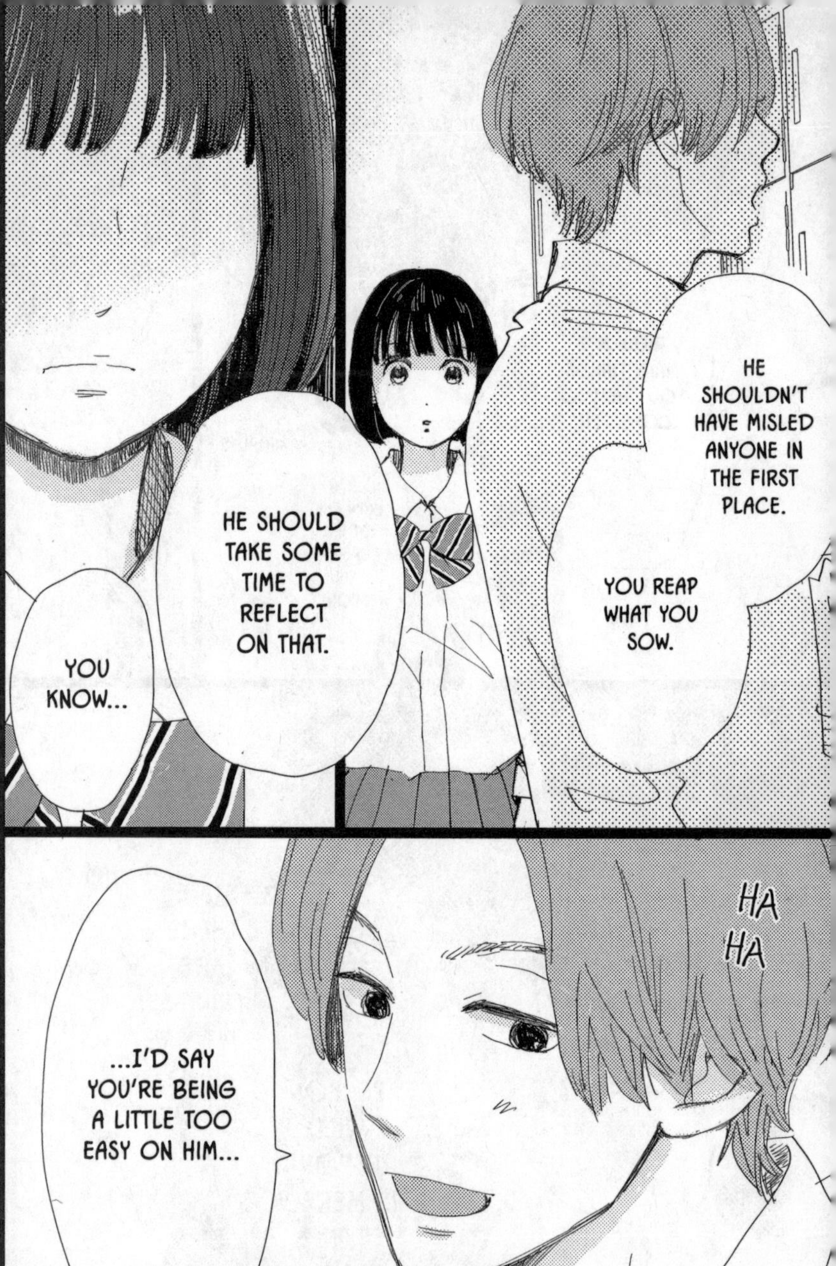
HE SHOULDN'T HAVE MISLED ANYONE IN THE FIRST PLACE.
YOU REAP WHAT YOU SOW.
HE SHOULD TAKE SOME TIME TO REFLECT ON THAT.
YOU KNOW...
HA HA
...I'D SAY YOU'RE BEING A LITTLE TOO EASY ON HIM...

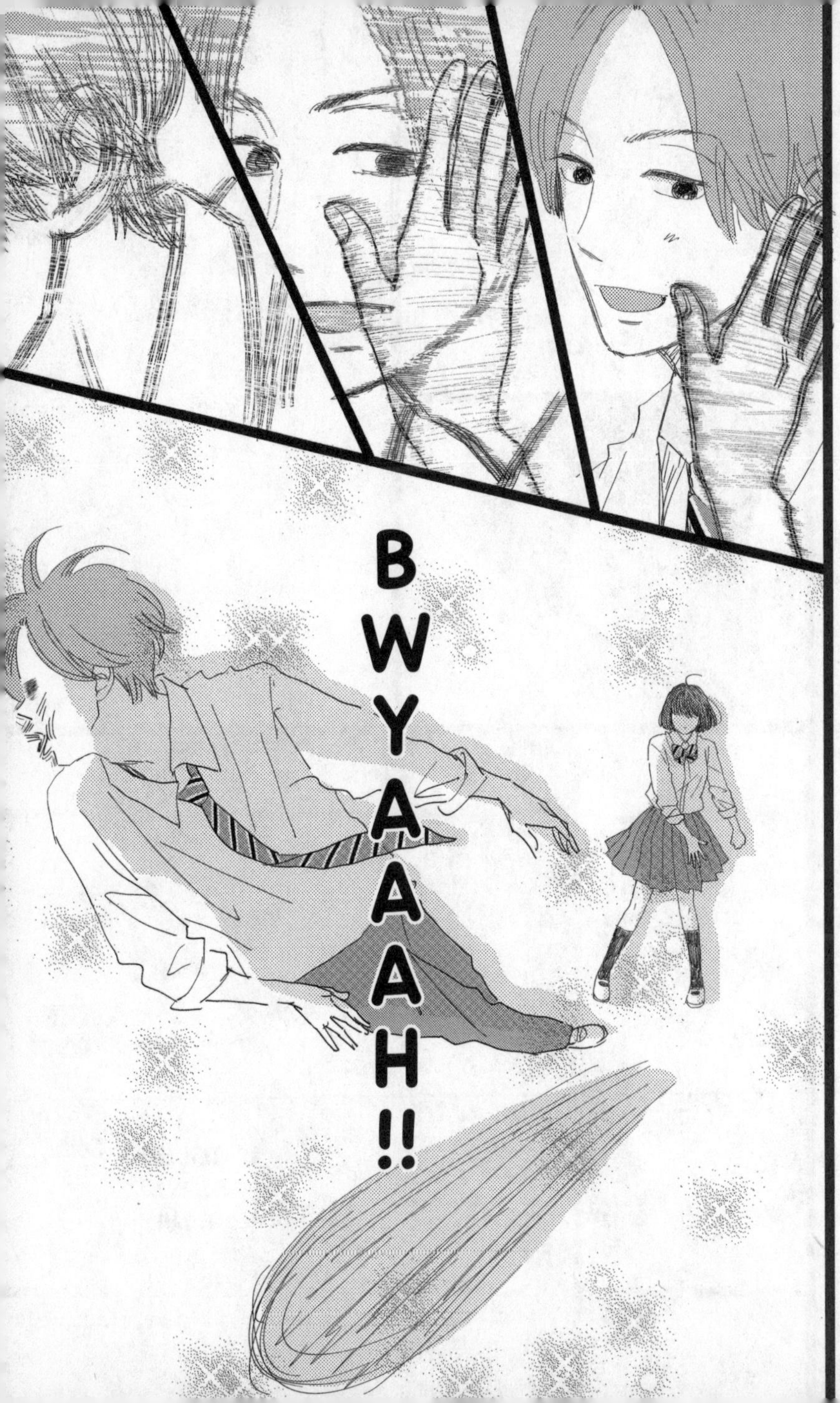
BWYAAAH!!

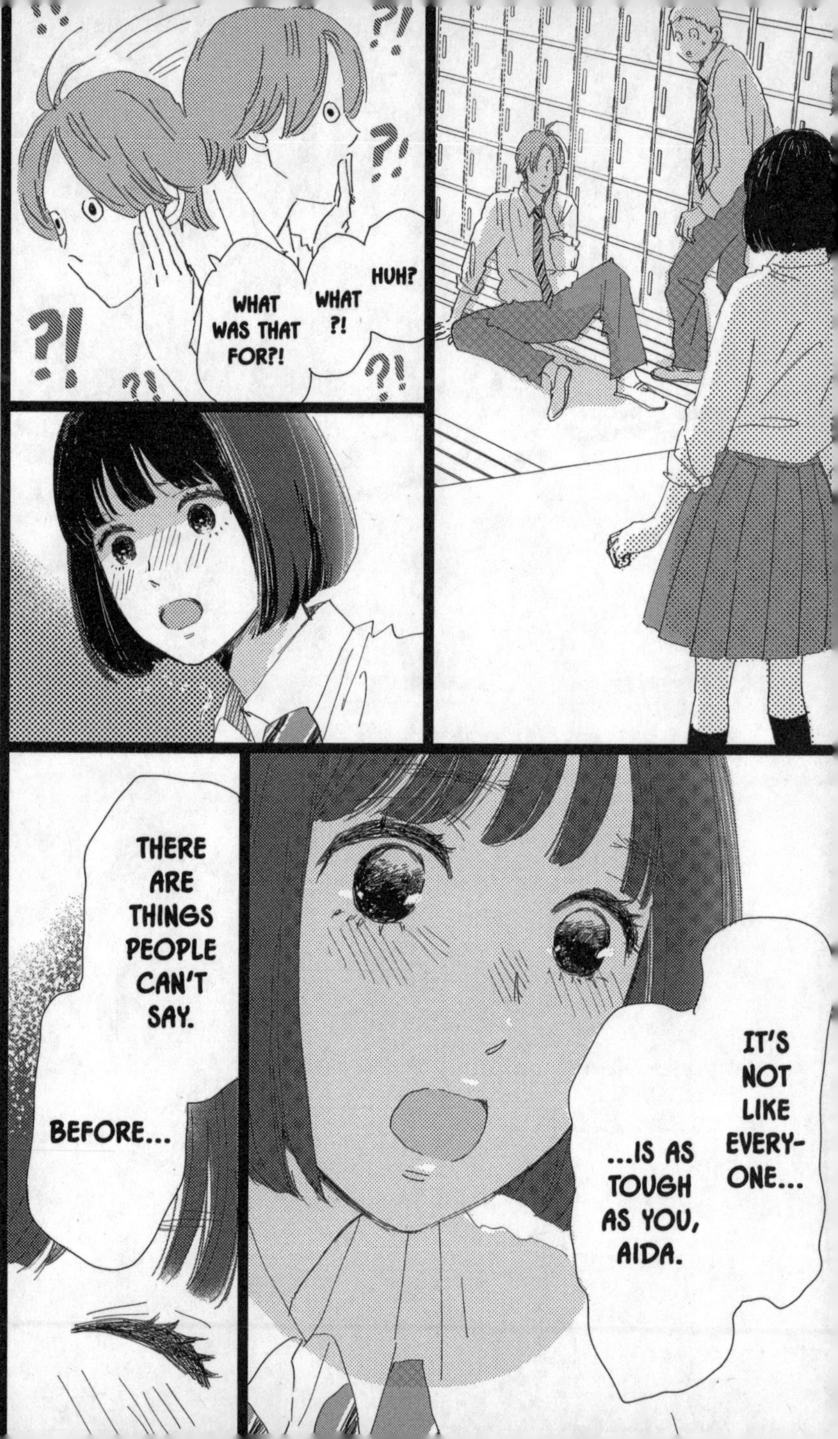
?!
?!
HUH?
WHAT ?!
WHAT WAS THAT FOR?!
?!
?!
?!
IT'S NOT LIKE EVERYONE...
...IS AS TOUGH AS YOU, AIDA.
THERE ARE THINGS PEOPLE CAN'T SAY.
BEFORE...

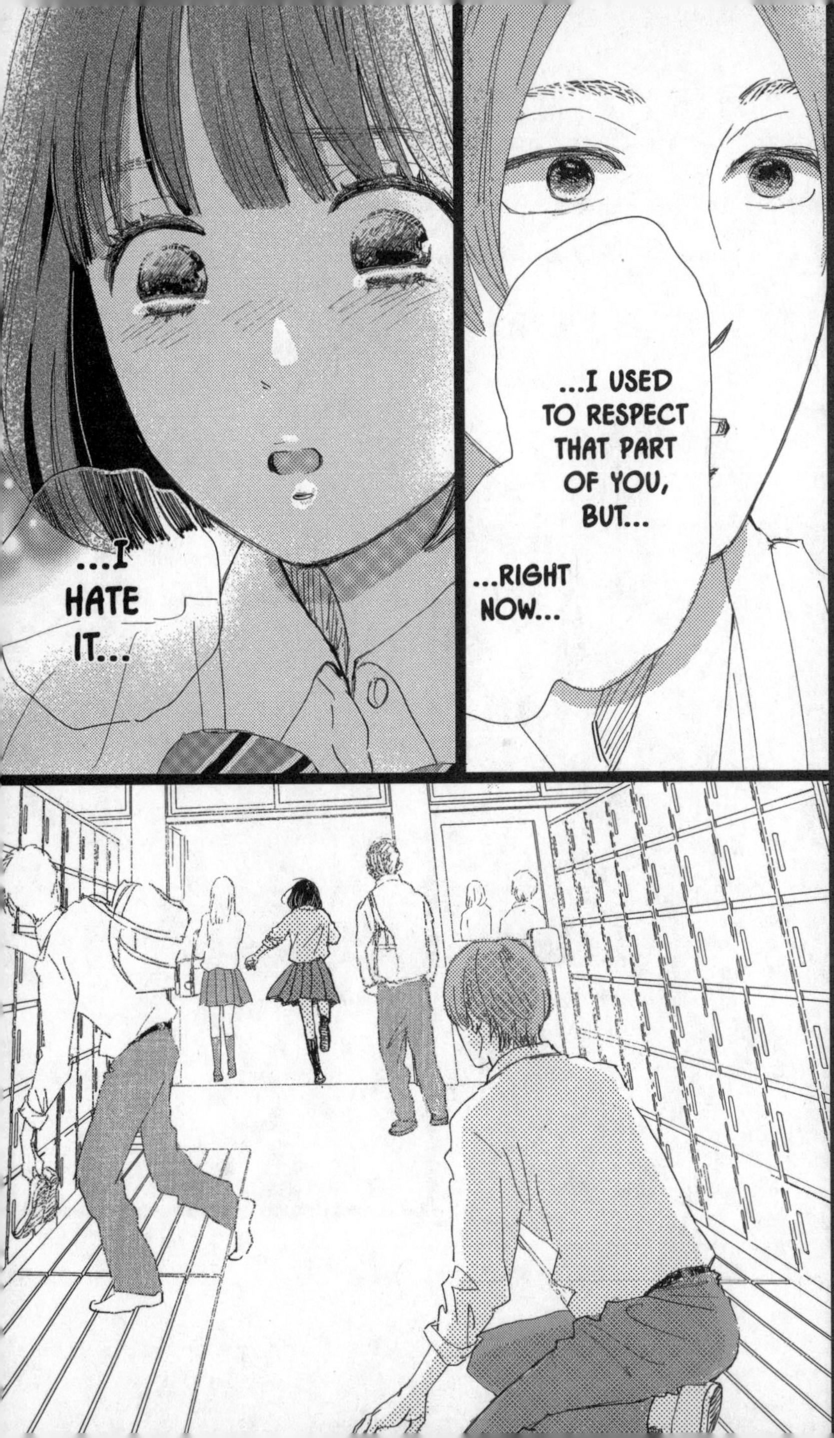
...I USED TO RESPECT THAT PART OF YOU, BUT...
...RIGHT NOW...
...I HATE IT...

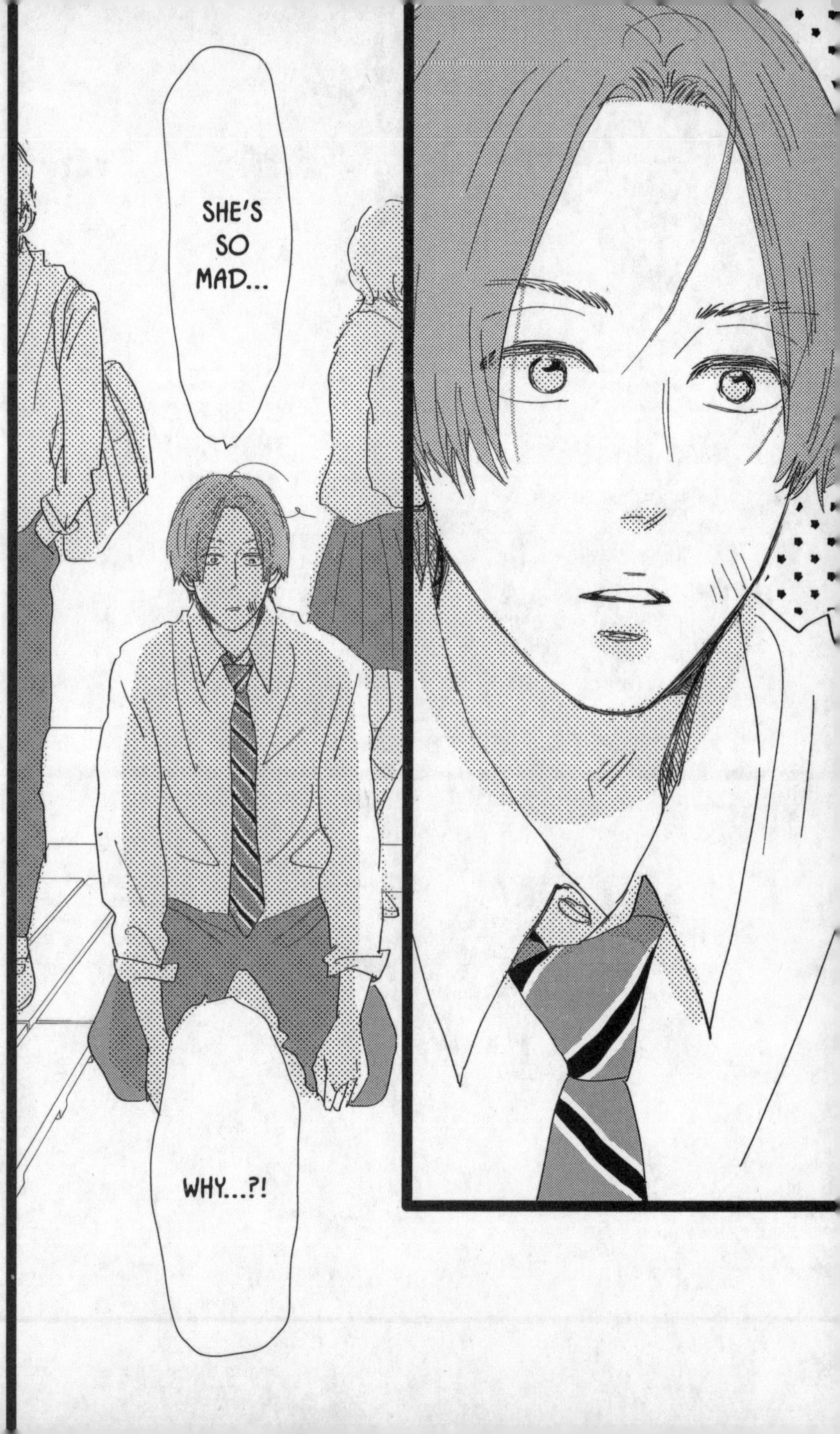
SHE'S SO MAD...
WHY...?!

Chapter 8

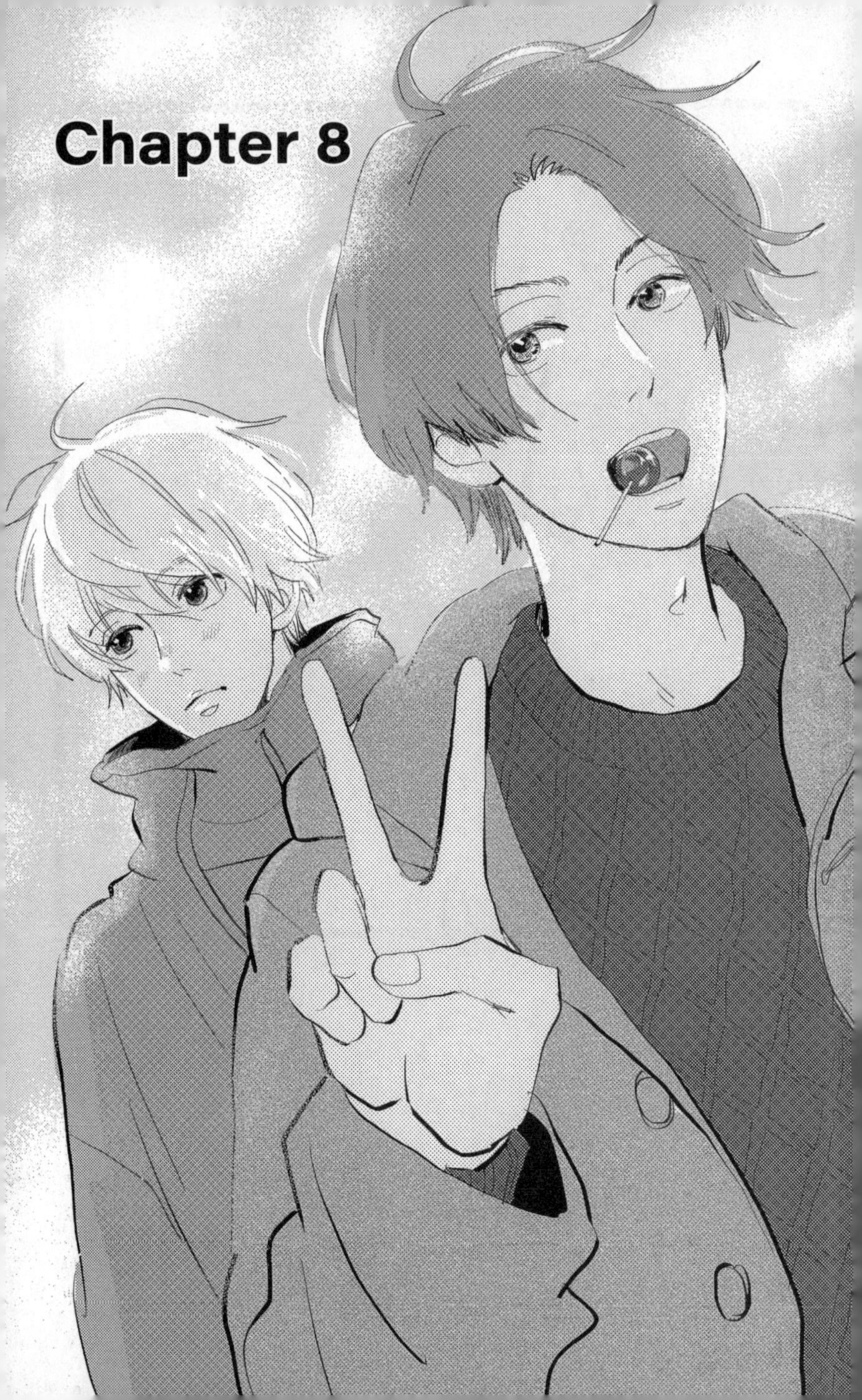

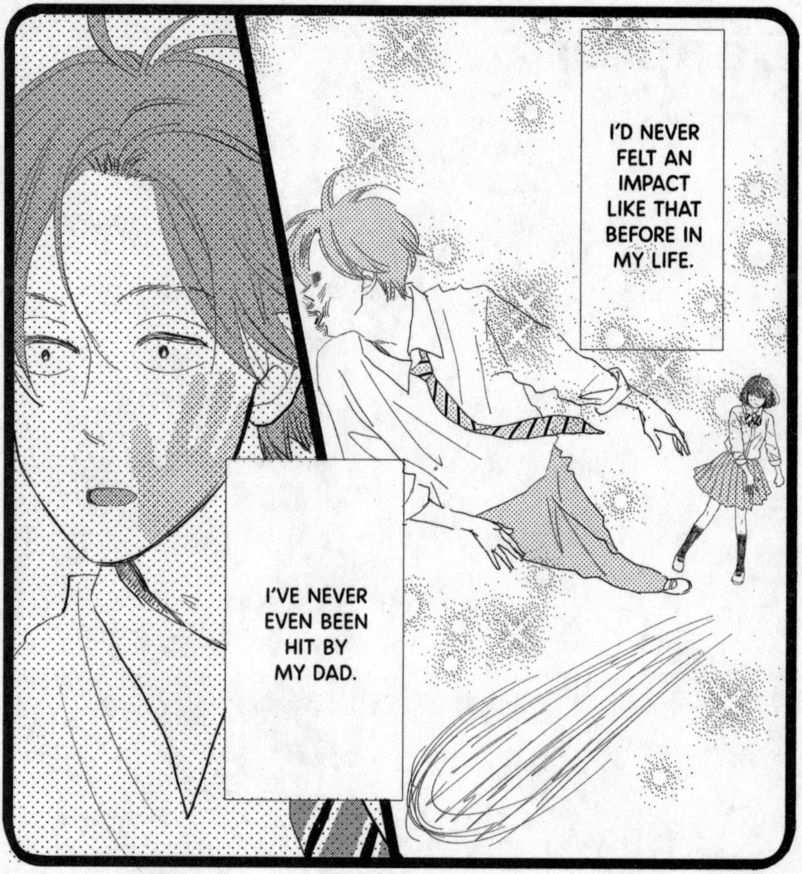
I'D NEVER FELT AN IMPACT LIKE THAT BEFORE IN MY LIFE.
I'VE NEVER EVEN BEEN HIT BY MY DAD.

My Love Mix-Up!

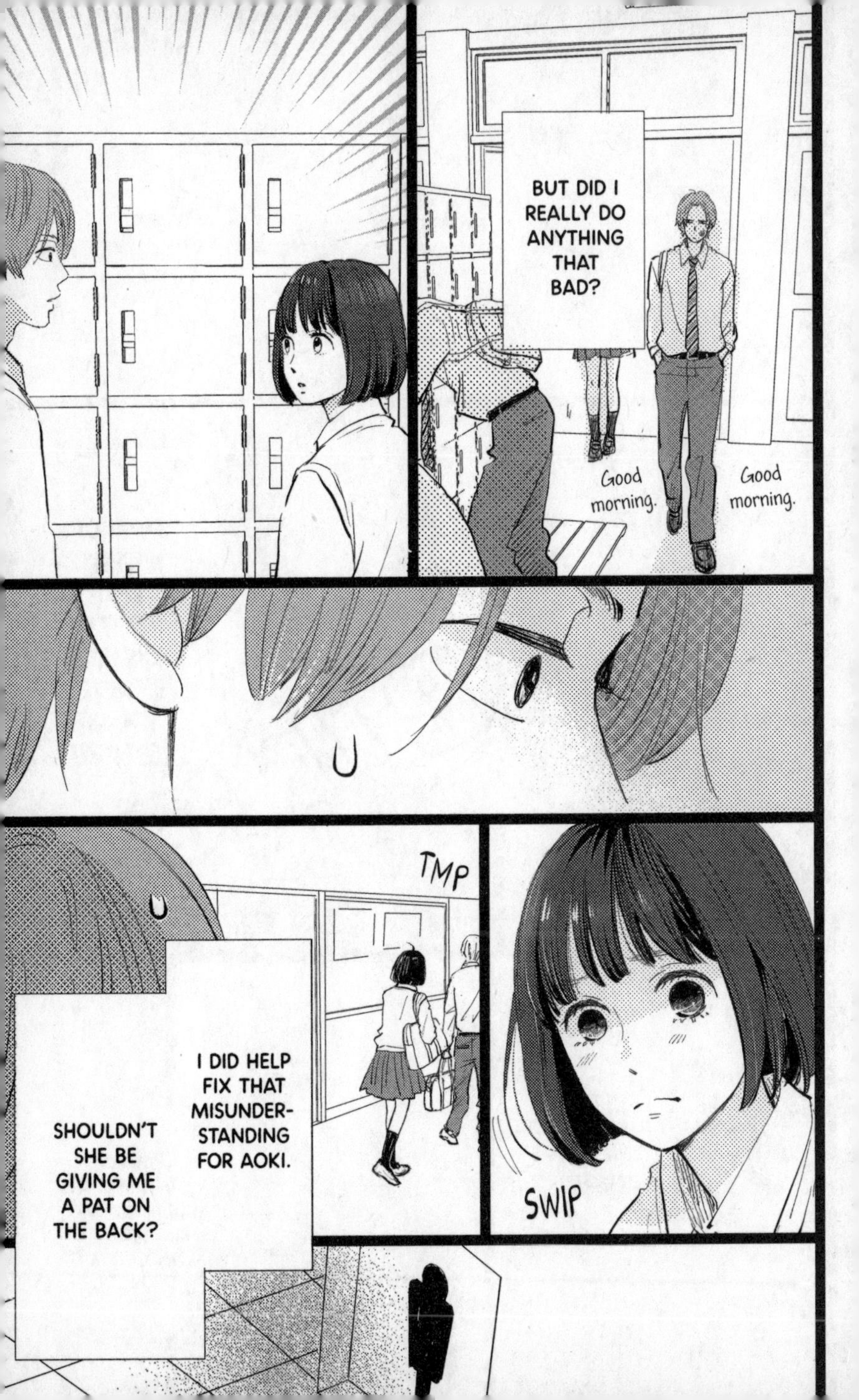
BUT DID I REALLY DO ANYTHING THAT BAD?
Good morning.
Good morning.
SWIP
TMP
I DID HELP FIX THAT MISUNDER-STANDING FOR AOKI.
SHOULDN'T SHE BE GIVING ME A PAT ON THE BACK?

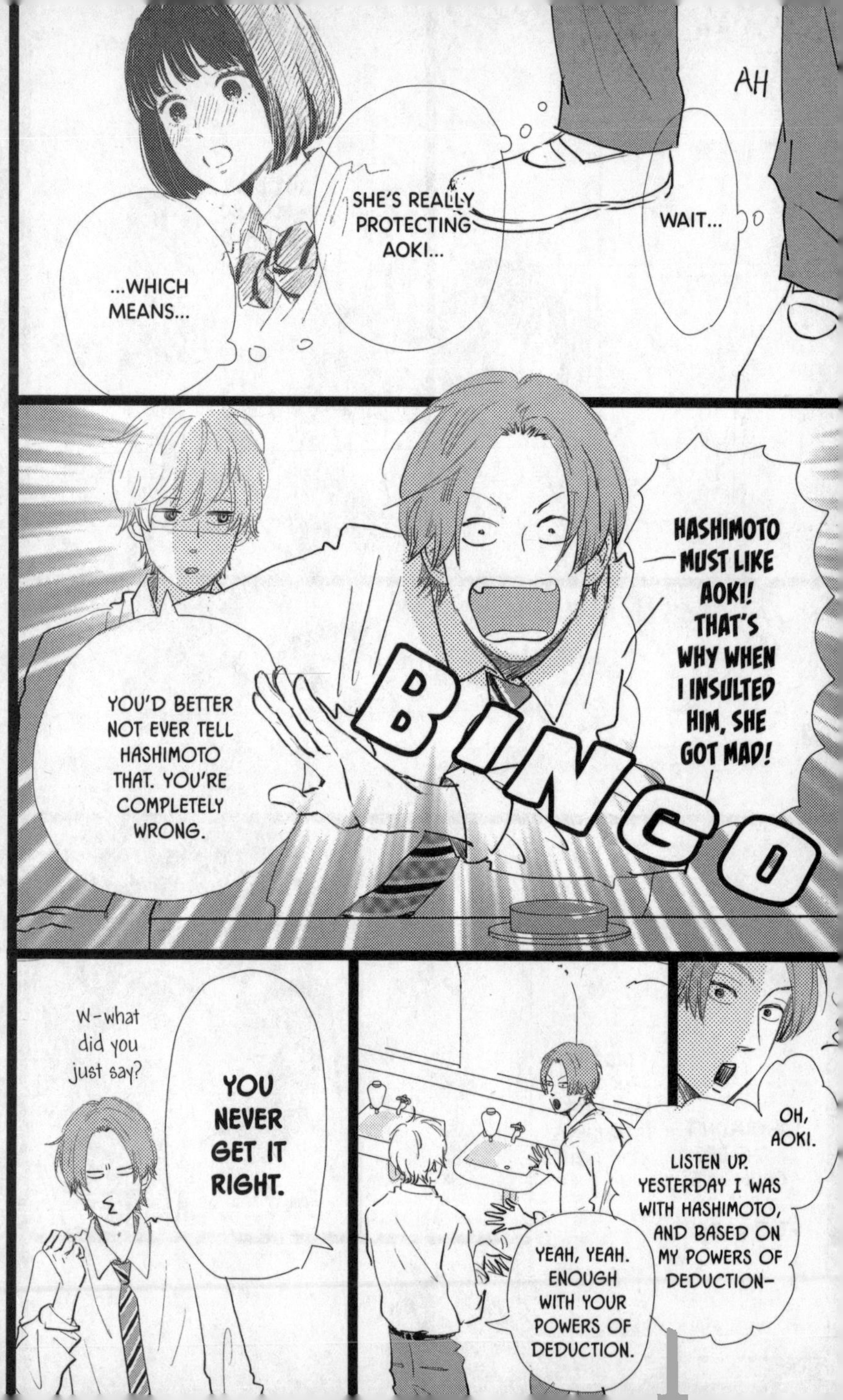
AH
WAIT...
SHE'S REALLY PROTECTING AOKI...
...WHICH MEANS...
HASHIMOTO MUST LIKE AOKI! THAT'S WHY WHEN I INSULTED HIM, SHE GOT MAD!
BINGO
YOU'D BETTER NOT EVER TELL HASHIMOTO THAT. YOU'RE COMPLETELY WRONG.
OH, AOKI.
LISTEN UP. YESTERDAY I WAS WITH HASHIMOTO, AND BASED ON MY POWERS OF DEDUCTION–
YEAH, YEAH. ENOUGH WITH YOUR POWERS OF DEDUCTION.
YOU NEVER GET IT RIGHT.
W-what did you just say?

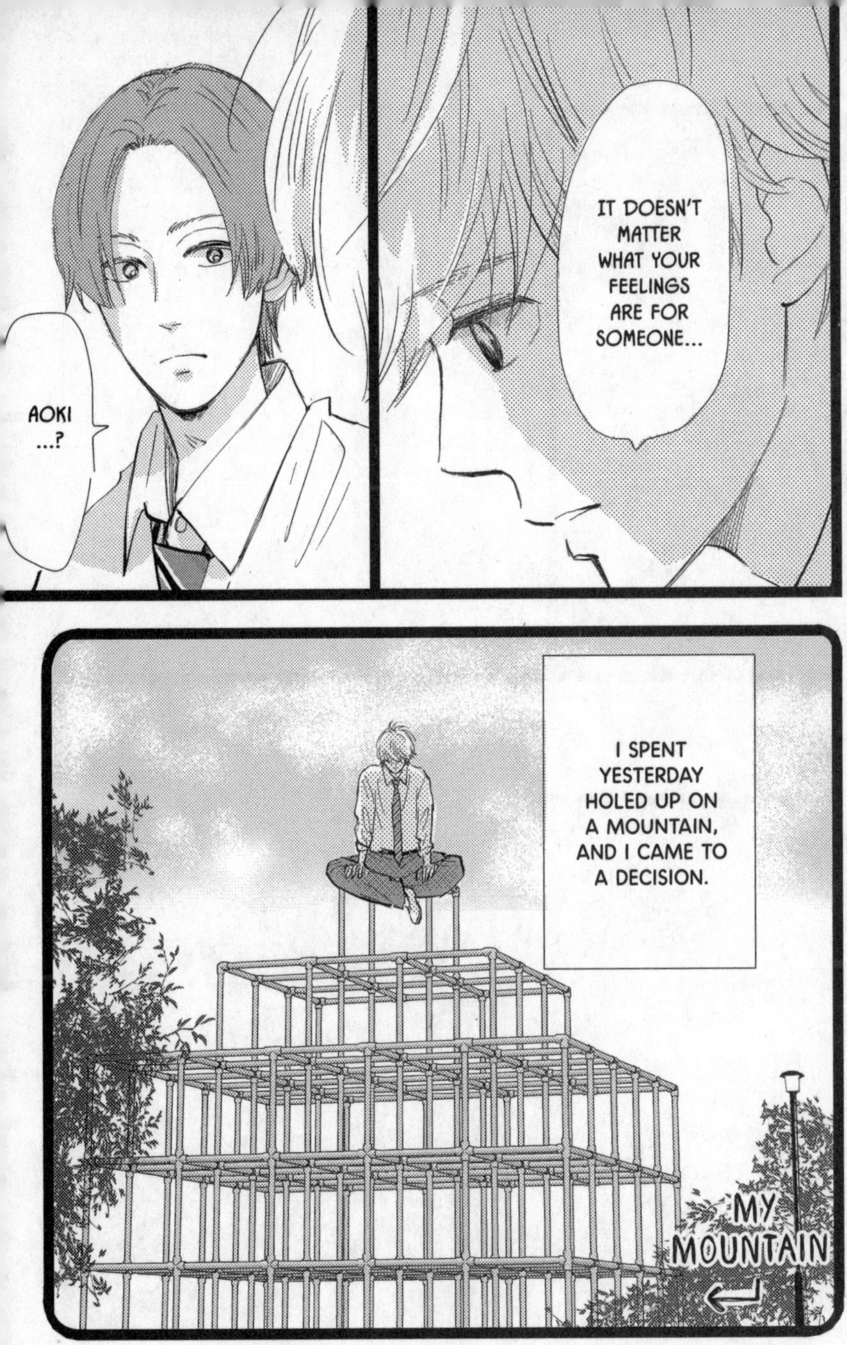
IT DOESN'T MATTER WHAT YOUR FEELINGS ARE FOR SOMEONE...
AOKI ...?
I SPENT YESTERDAY HOLED UP ON A MOUNTAIN, AND I CAME TO A DECISION.
MY MOUNTAIN

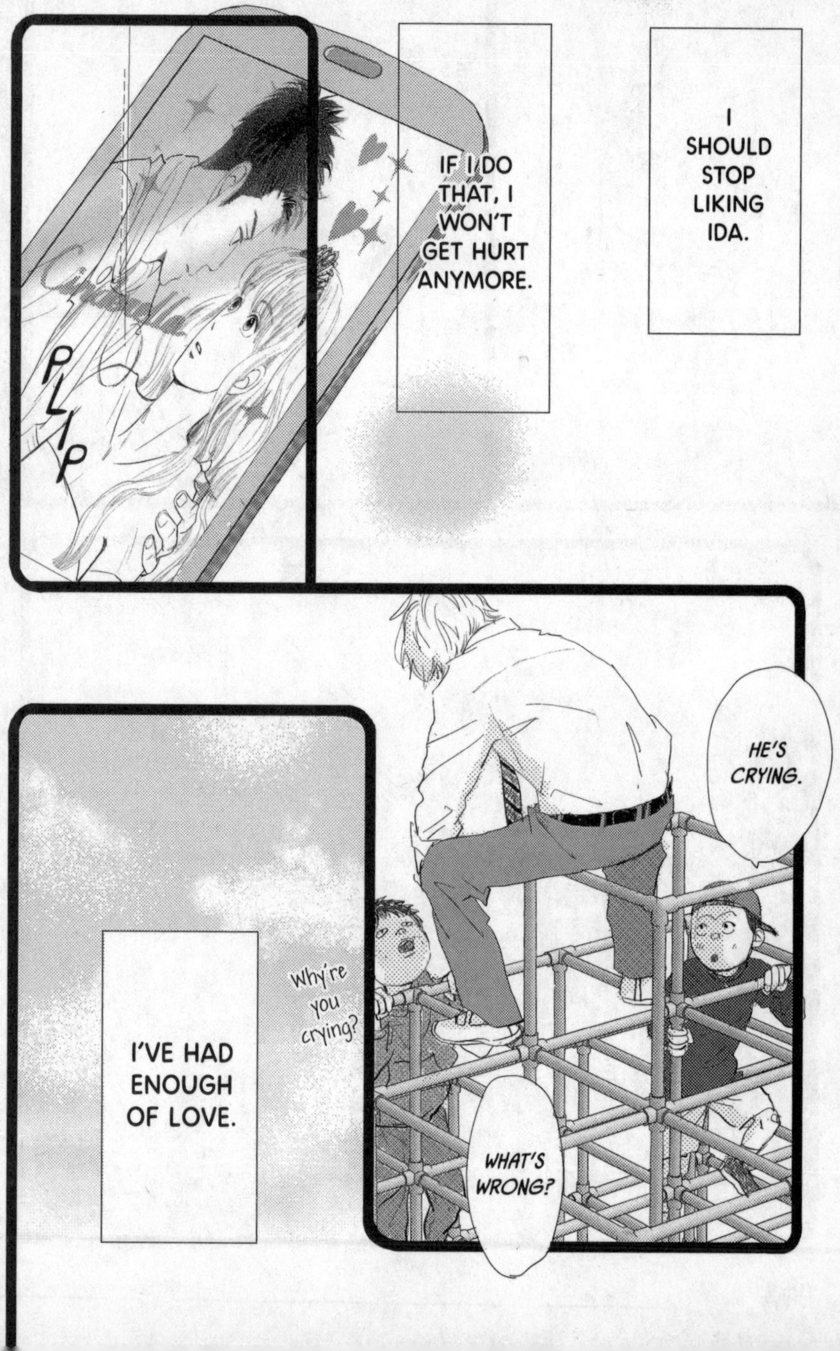
I SHOULD STOP LIKING IDA.
IF I DO THAT, I WON'T GET HURT ANYMORE.
PLIP
HE'S CRYING.
Why're you crying?
WHAT'S WRONG?
I'VE HAD ENOUGH OF LOVE.

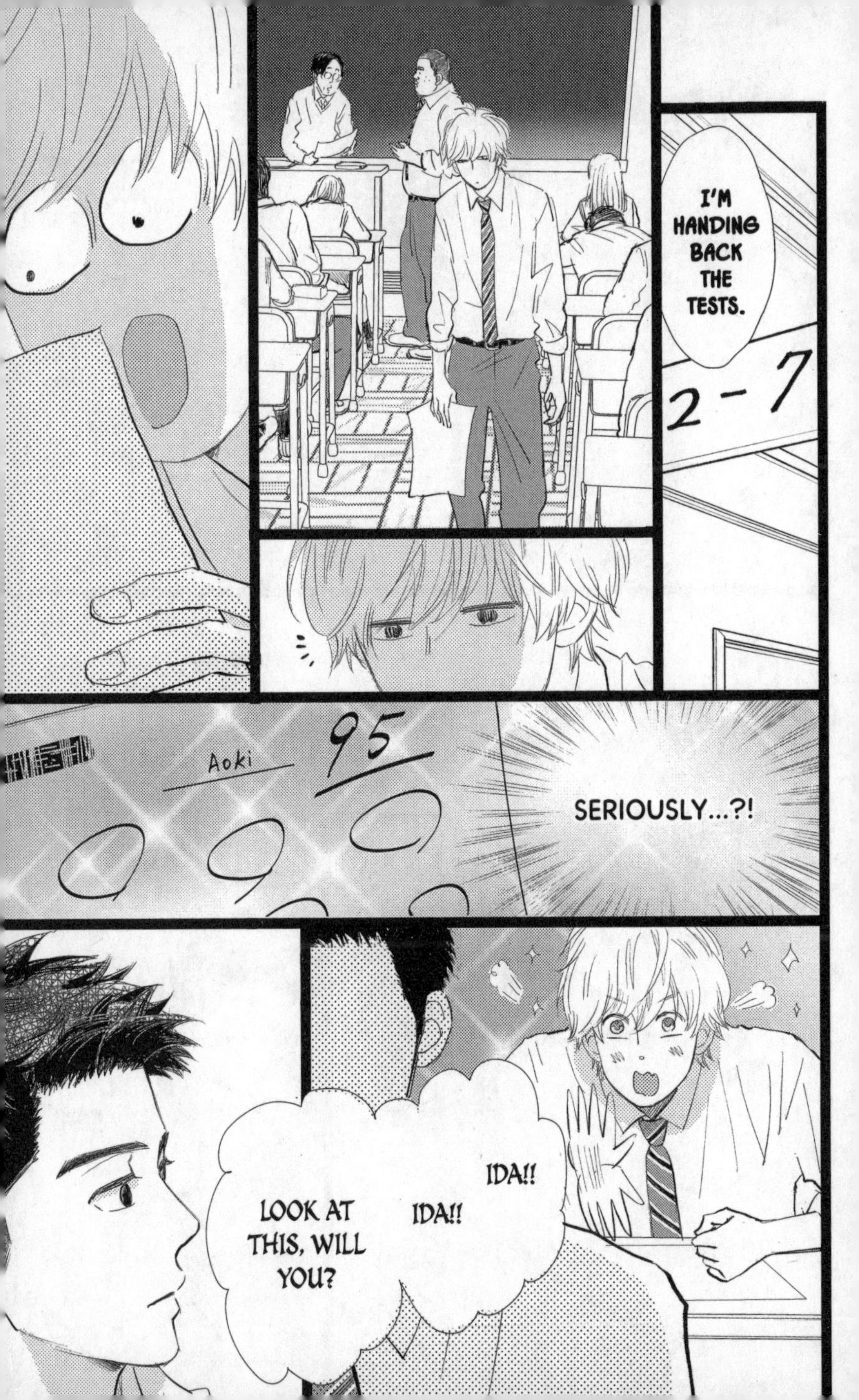
I'M HANDING BACK THE TESTS.
2 - 7
SERIOUSLY...?!
Aoki
95
IDA!!
IDA!!
LOOK AT THIS, WILL YOU?

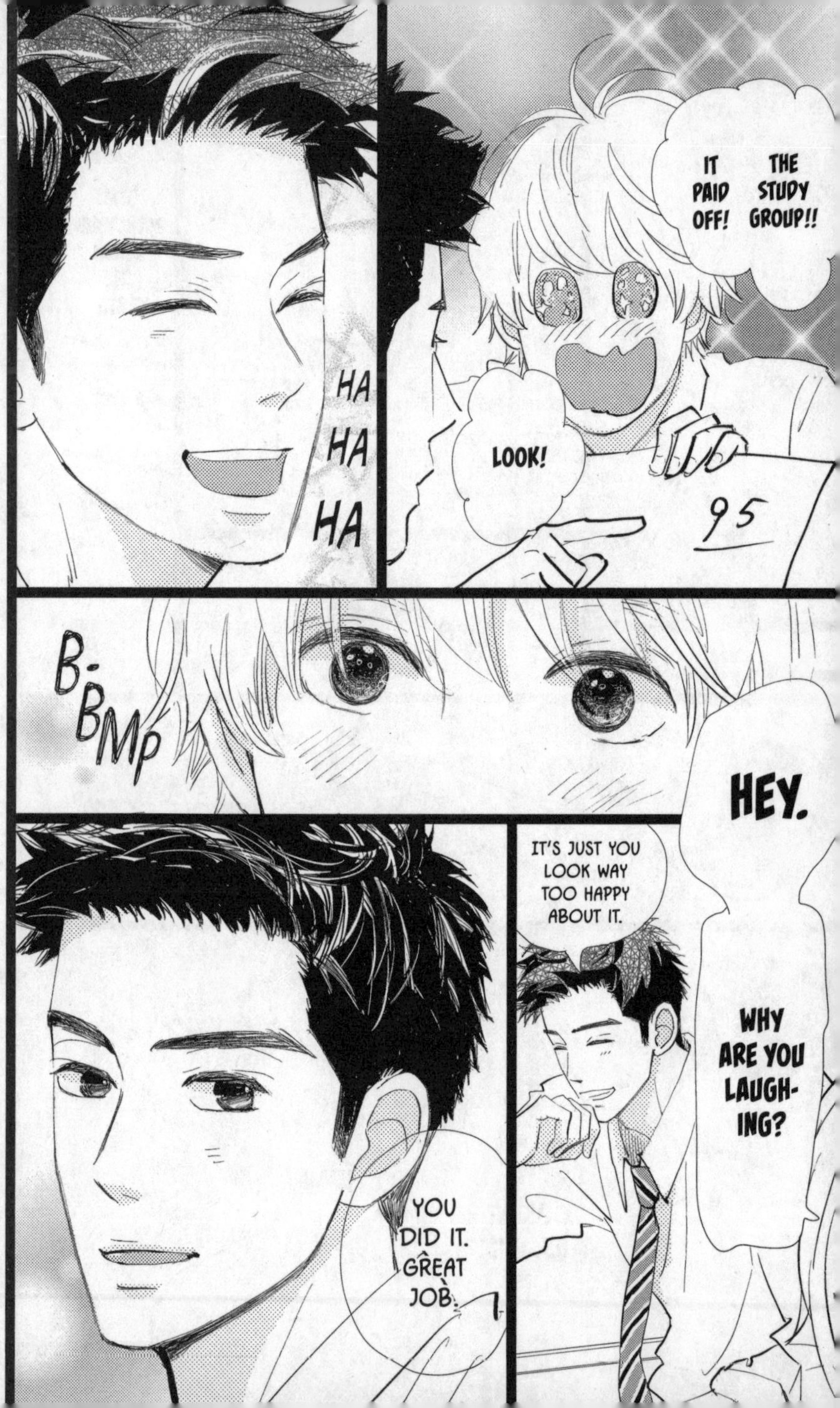
THE STUDY GROUP!!
IT PAID OFF!
LOOK!
HA HA HA
B-BMP
HEY.
WHY ARE YOU LAUGH-ING?
IT'S JUST YOU LOOK WAY TOO HAPPY ABOUT IT.
YOU DID IT. GREAT JOB.

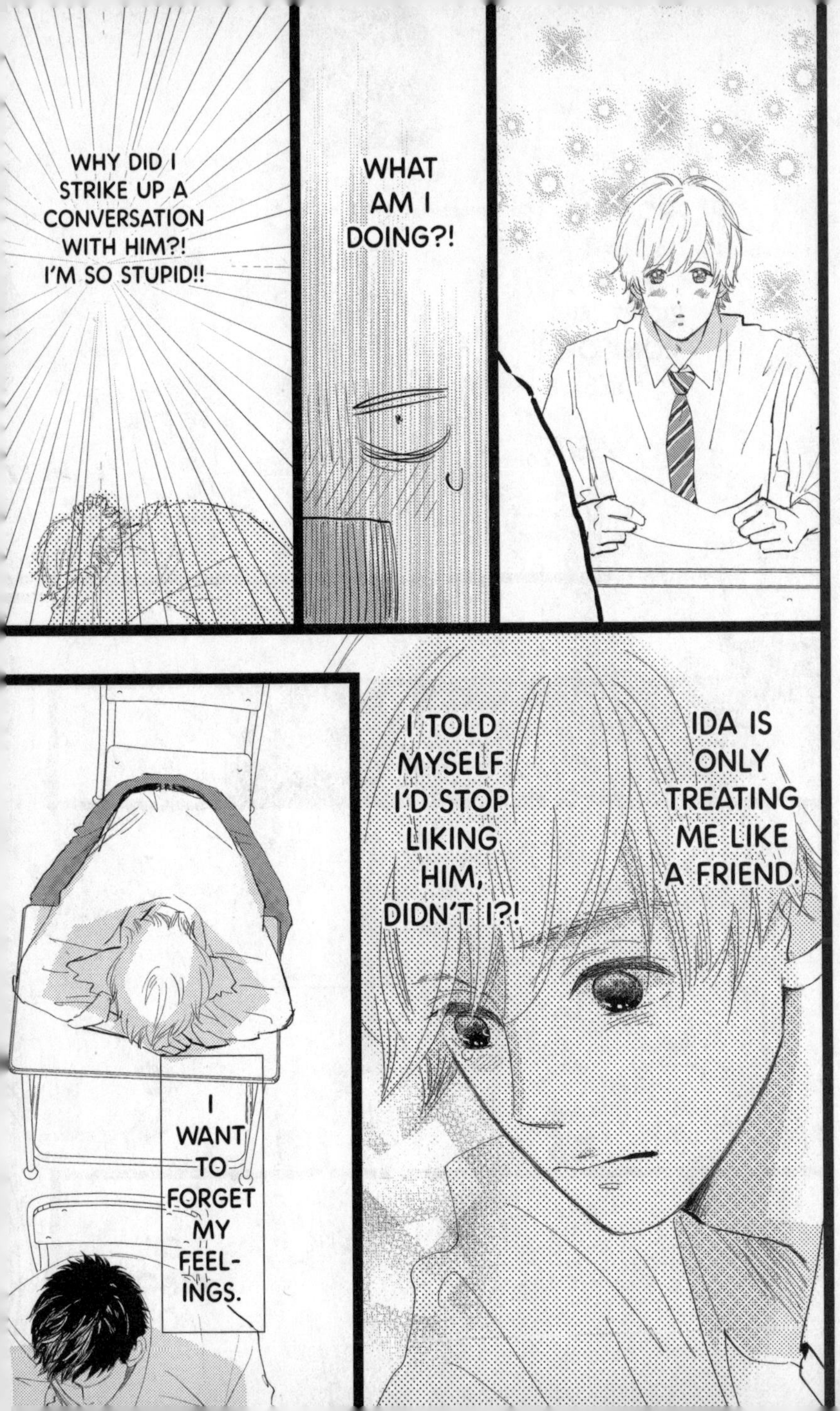
WHAT AM I DOING?!
WHY DID I STRIKE UP A CONVERSATION WITH HIM?! I'M SO STUPID!!
IDA IS ONLY TREATING ME LIKE A FRIEND.
I TOLD MYSELF I'D STOP LIKING HIM, DIDN'T I?!
I WANT TO FORGET MY FEEL-INGS.

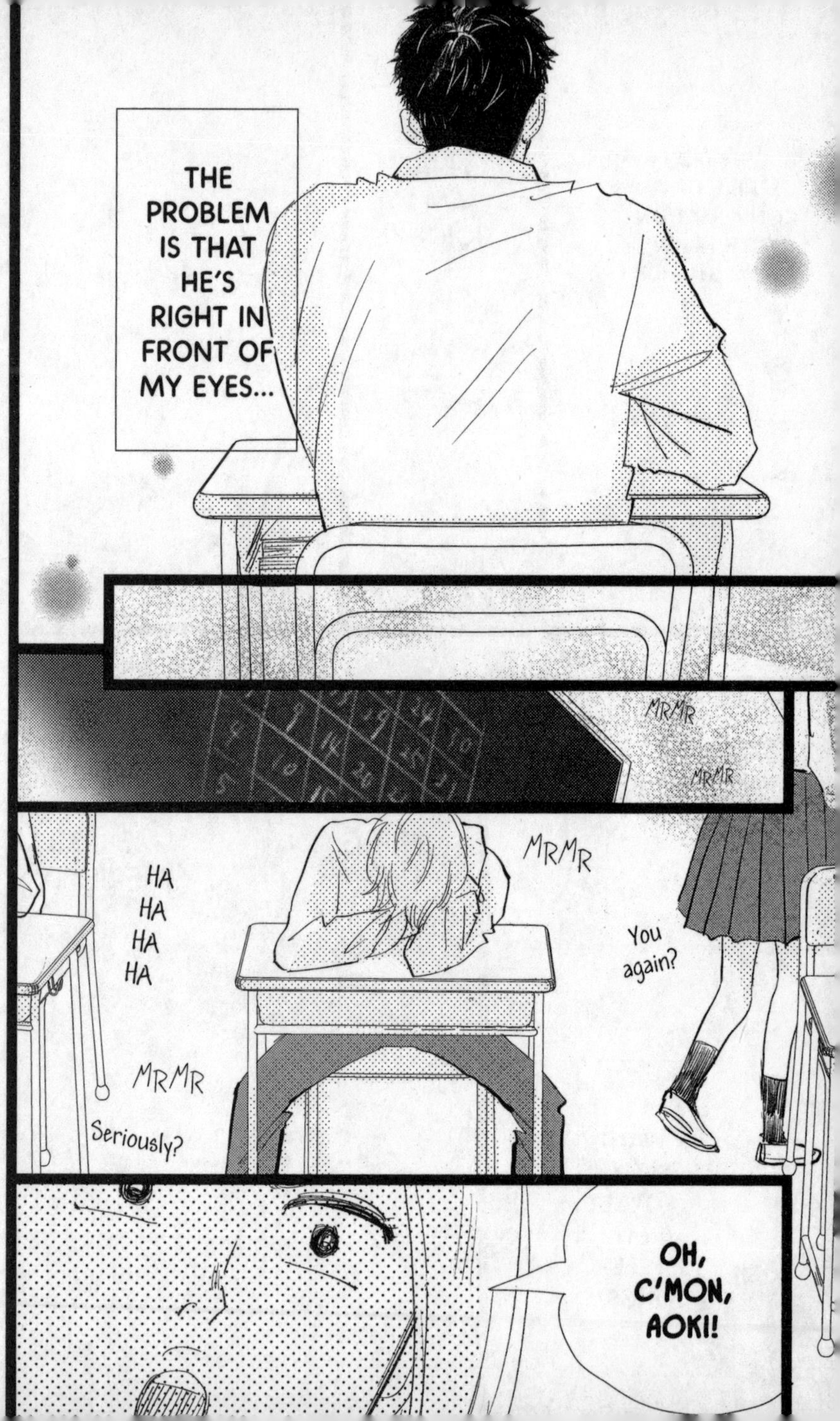
THE PROBLEM IS THAT HE'S RIGHT IN FRONT OF MY EYES...
MRMR
MRMR
You again?
MRMR
HA HA HA HA
MRMR
Seriously?
OH, C'MON, AOKI!

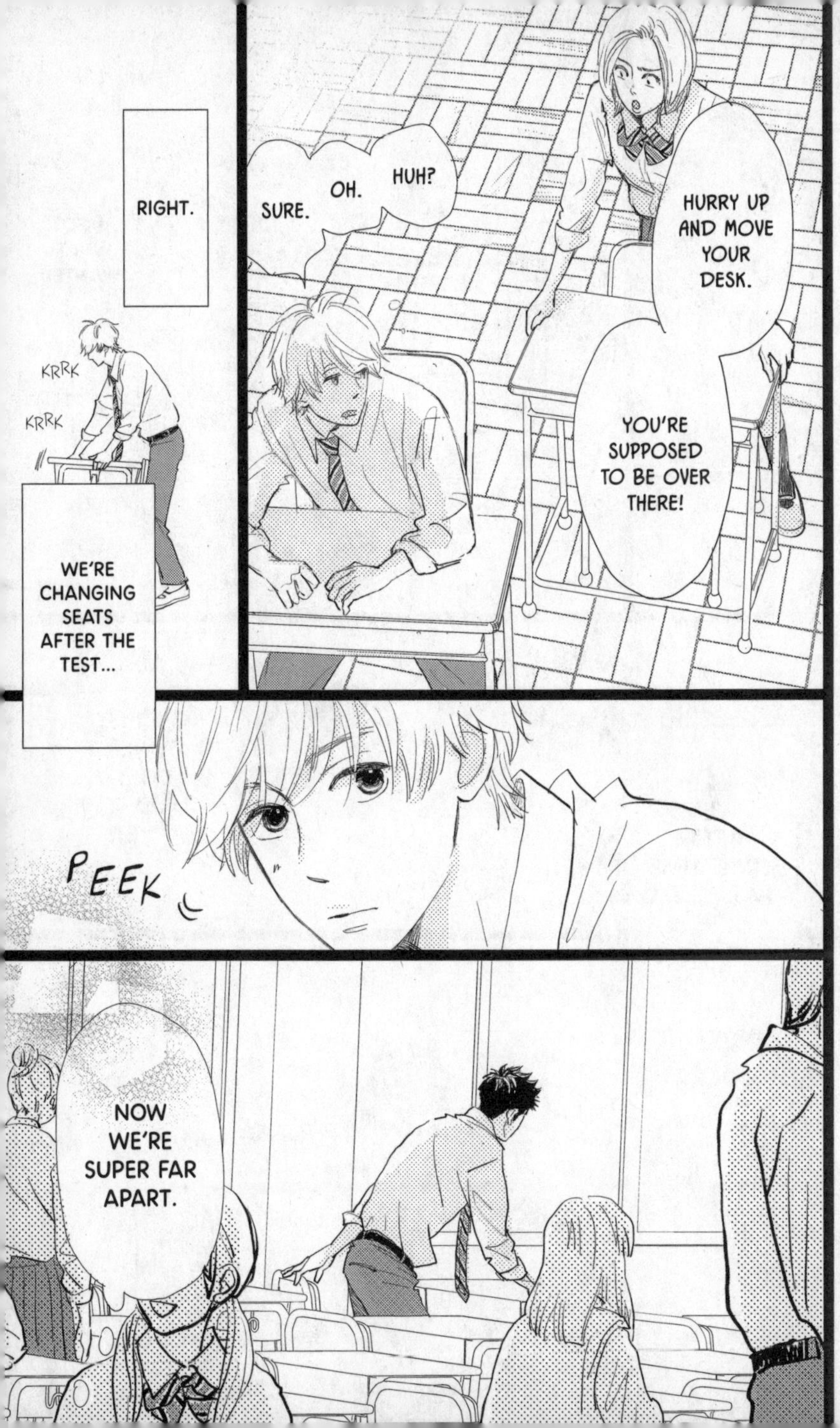
HURRY UP AND MOVE YOUR DESK.
YOU'RE SUPPOSED TO BE OVER THERE!
HUH? OH. SURE.
RIGHT.
KRRK
KRRK
WE'RE CHANGING SEATS AFTER THE TEST...
PEEK
NOW WE'RE SUPER FAR APART.

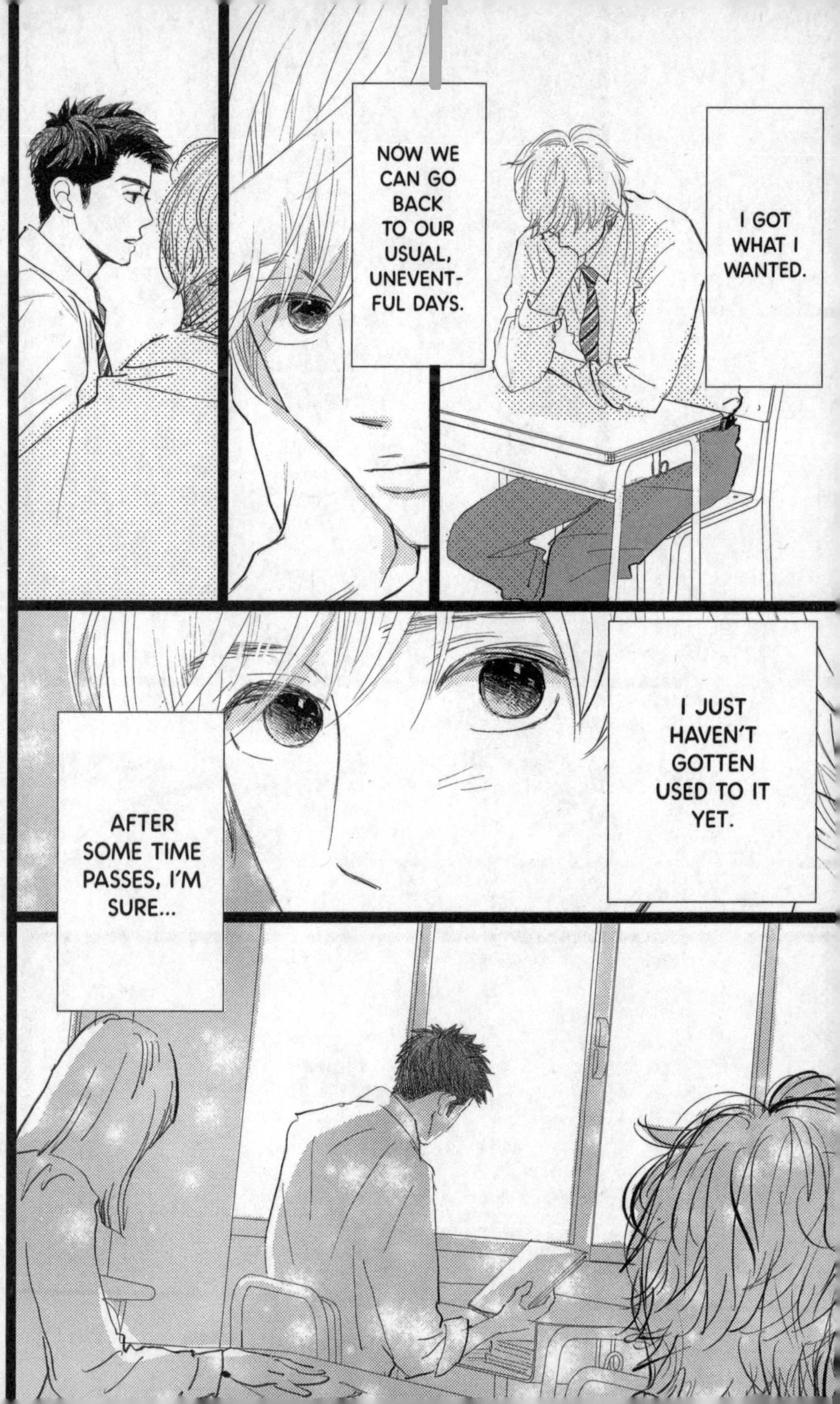
I GOT WHAT I WANTED.
NOW WE CAN GO BACK TO OUR USUAL, UNEVENTFUL DAYS.
I JUST HAVEN'T GOTTEN USED TO IT YET.
AFTER SOME TIME PASSES, I'M SURE...

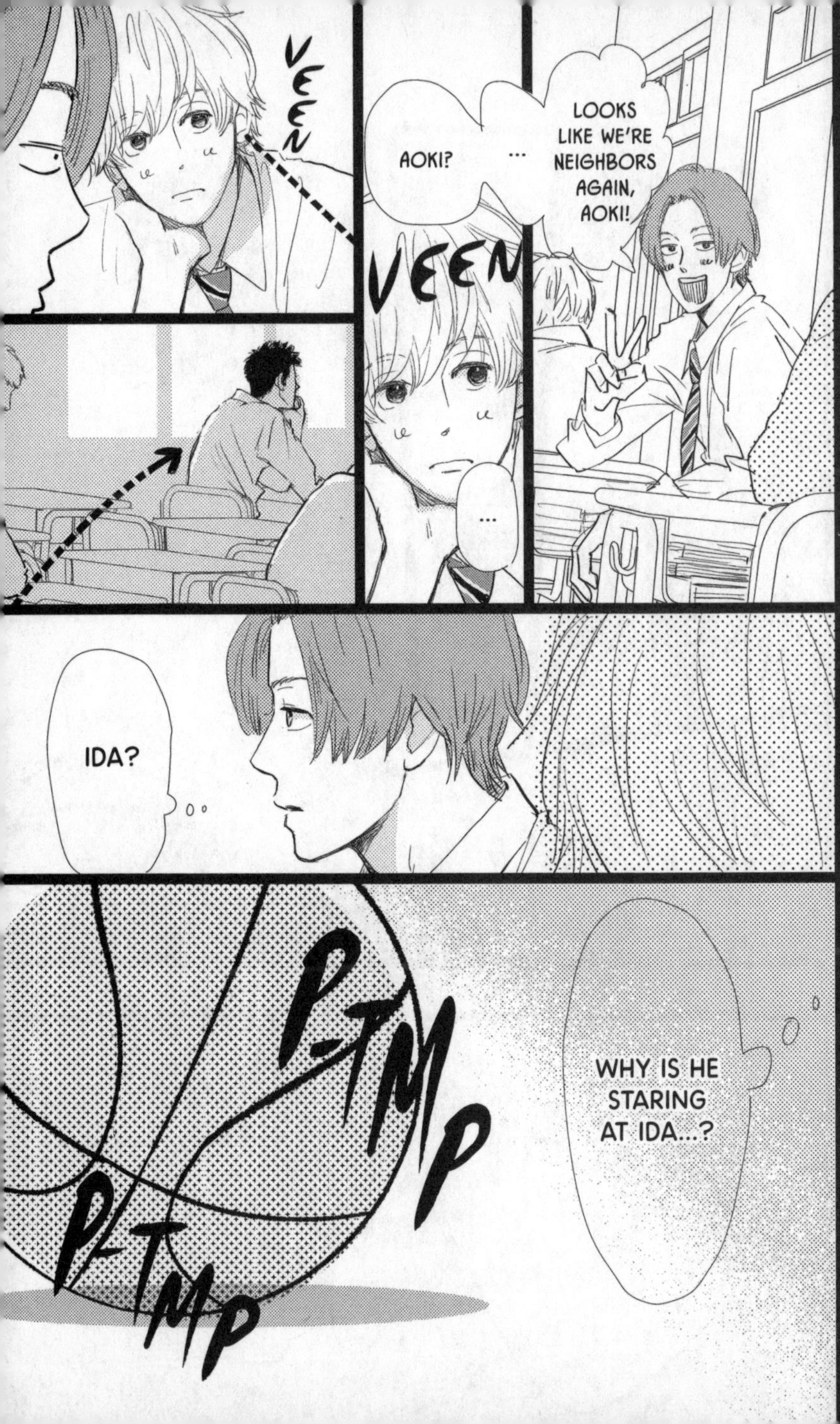
LOOKS LIKE WE'RE NEIGHBORS AGAIN, AOKI!
...
AOKI?
VEEN
...
VEEN
IDA?
WHY IS HE STARING AT IDA...?
P-TMP
P-TMP

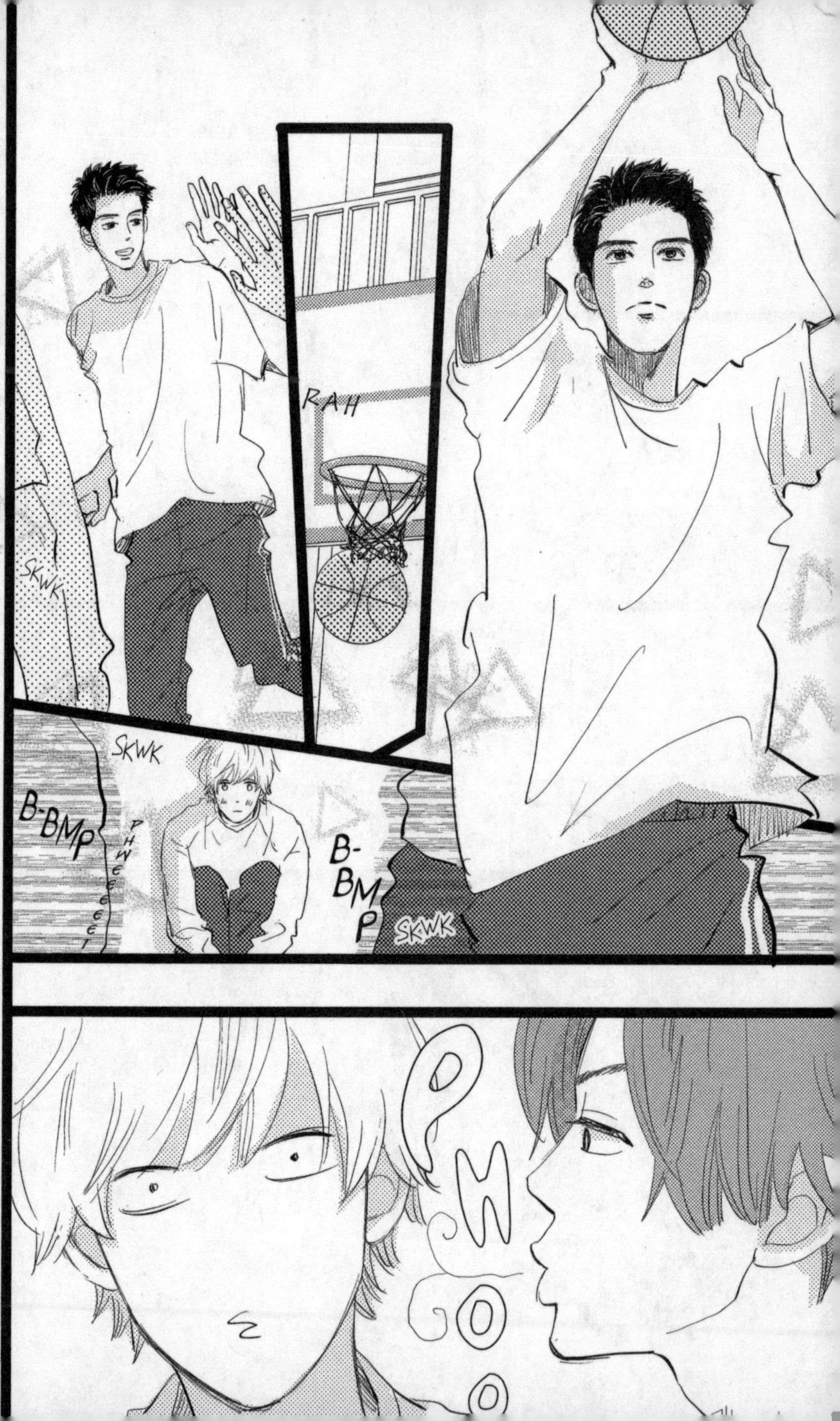
B-BMP
SKWK
RAH
SKWK
SKWK
B-BMP
PHWEEEEE!
PHOO

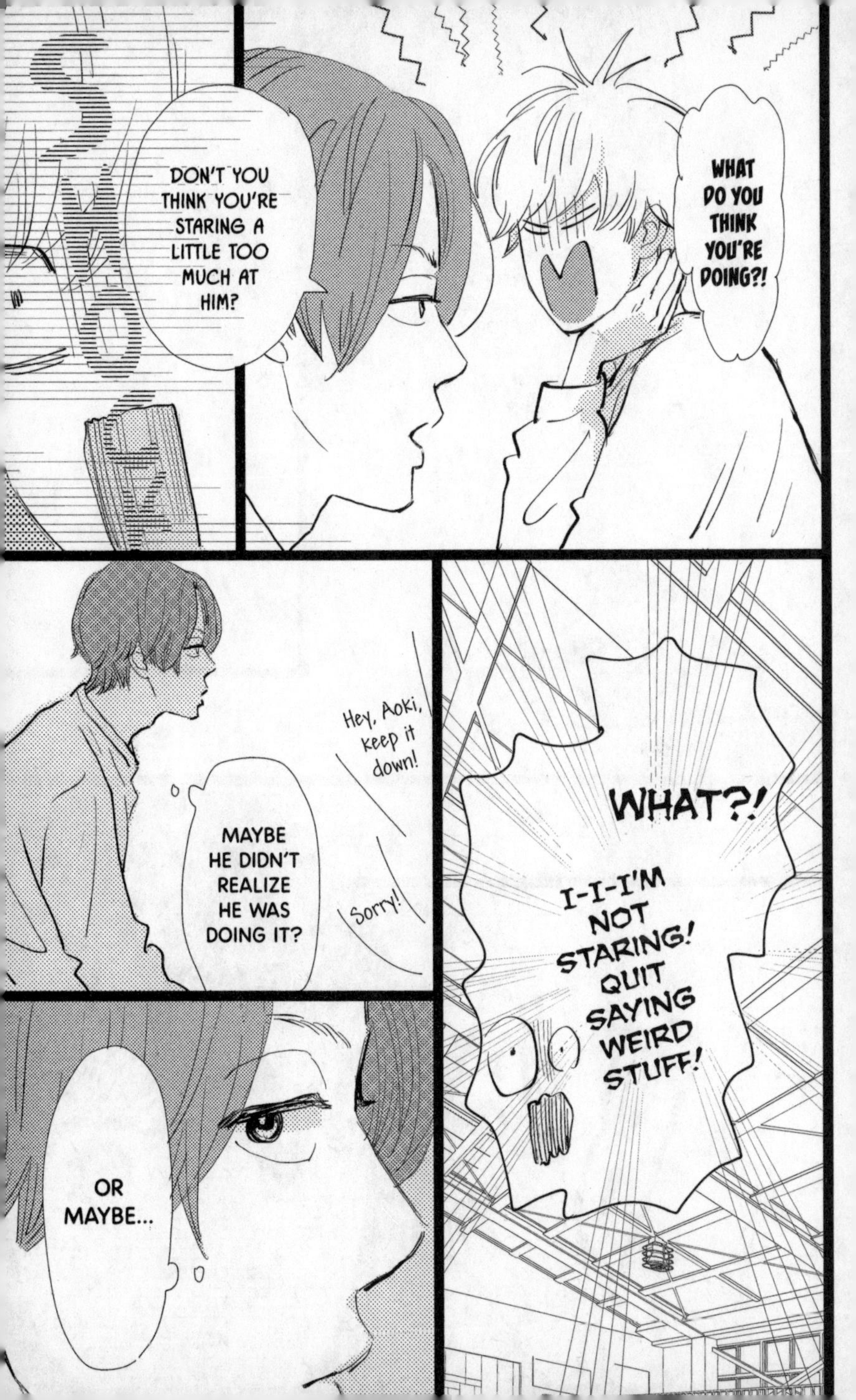
WHAT DO YOU THINK YOU'RE DOING?!
DON'T YOU THINK YOU'RE STARING A LITTLE TOO MUCH AT HIM?
WHAT?!
I-I-I'M NOT STARING! QUIT SAYING WEIRD STUFF!
Hey, Aoki, keep it down!
Sorry!
MAYBE HE DIDN'T REALIZE HE WAS DOING IT?
OR MAYBE...

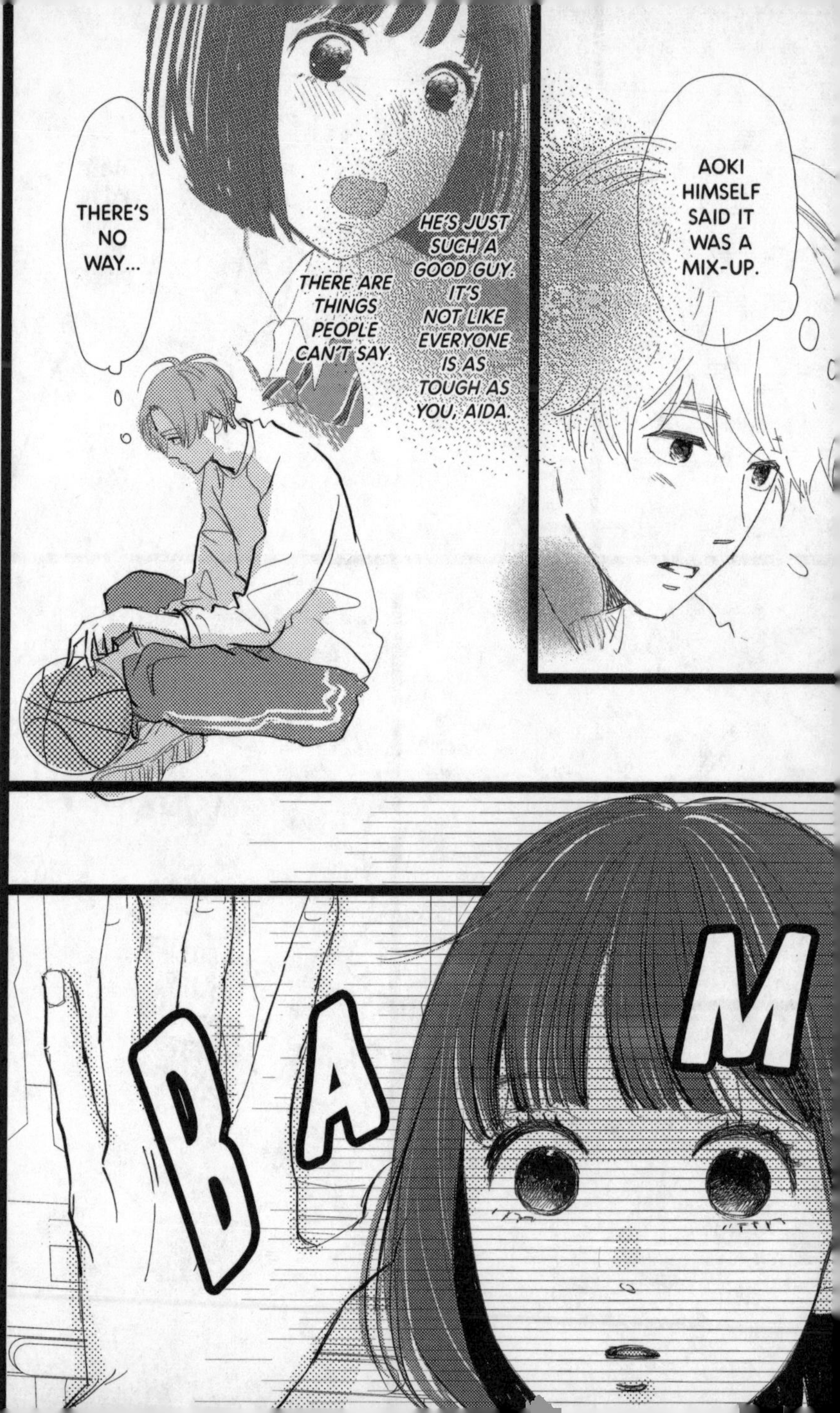
AOKI HIMSELF SAID IT WAS A MIX-UP.
HE'S JUST SUCH A GOOD GUY. IT'S NOT LIKE EVERYONE IS AS TOUGH AS YOU, AIDA.
THERE ARE THINGS PEOPLE CAN'T SAY.
THERE'S NO WAY...
BAM

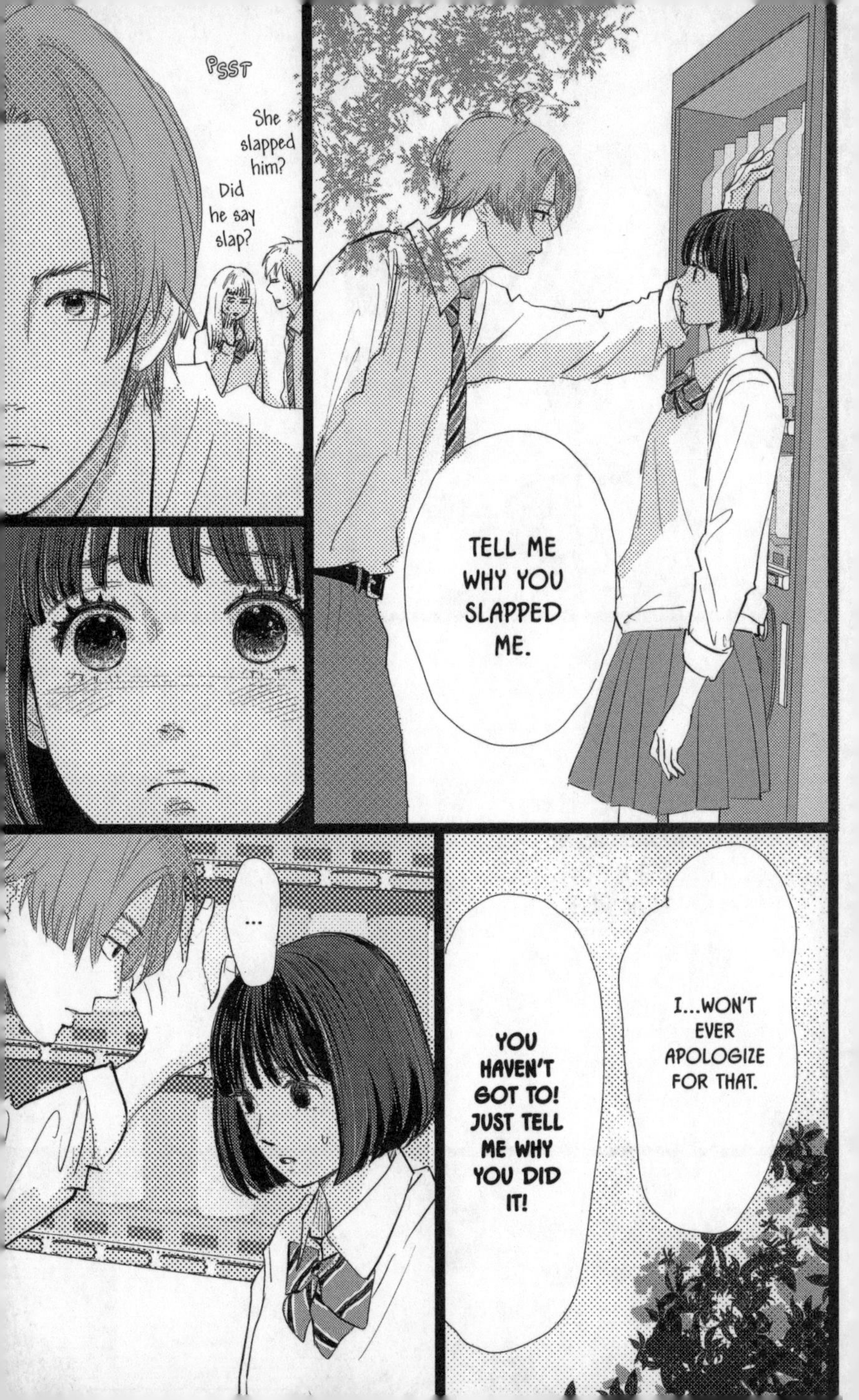
TELL ME WHY YOU SLAPPED ME.
PSST
She slapped him?
Did he say slap?
I...WON'T EVER APOLOGIZE FOR THAT.
YOU HAVEN'T GOT TO! JUST TELL ME WHY YOU DID IT!
...

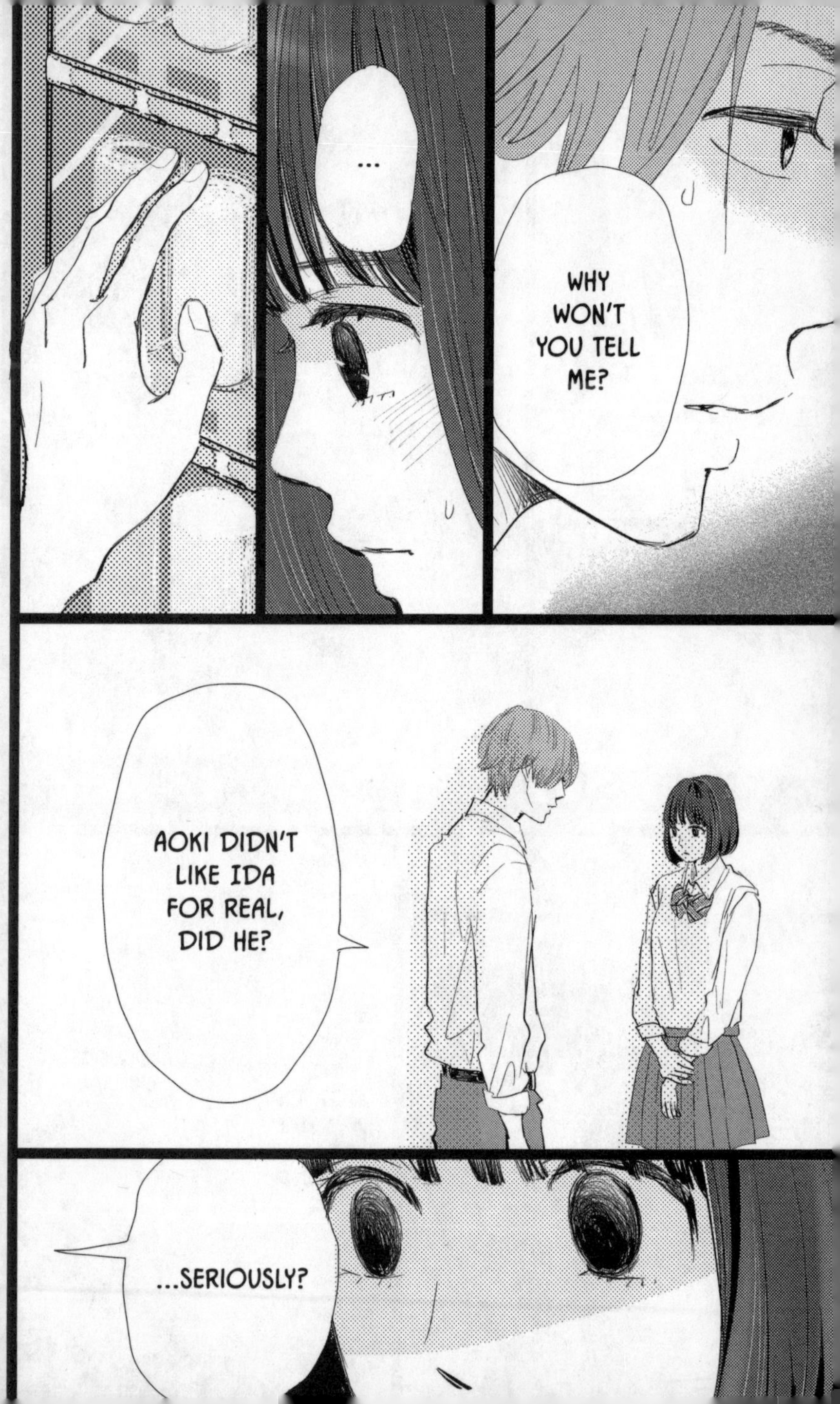
WHY WON'T YOU TELL ME?
...
AOKI DIDN'T LIKE IDA FOR REAL, DID HE?
...SERIOUSLY?

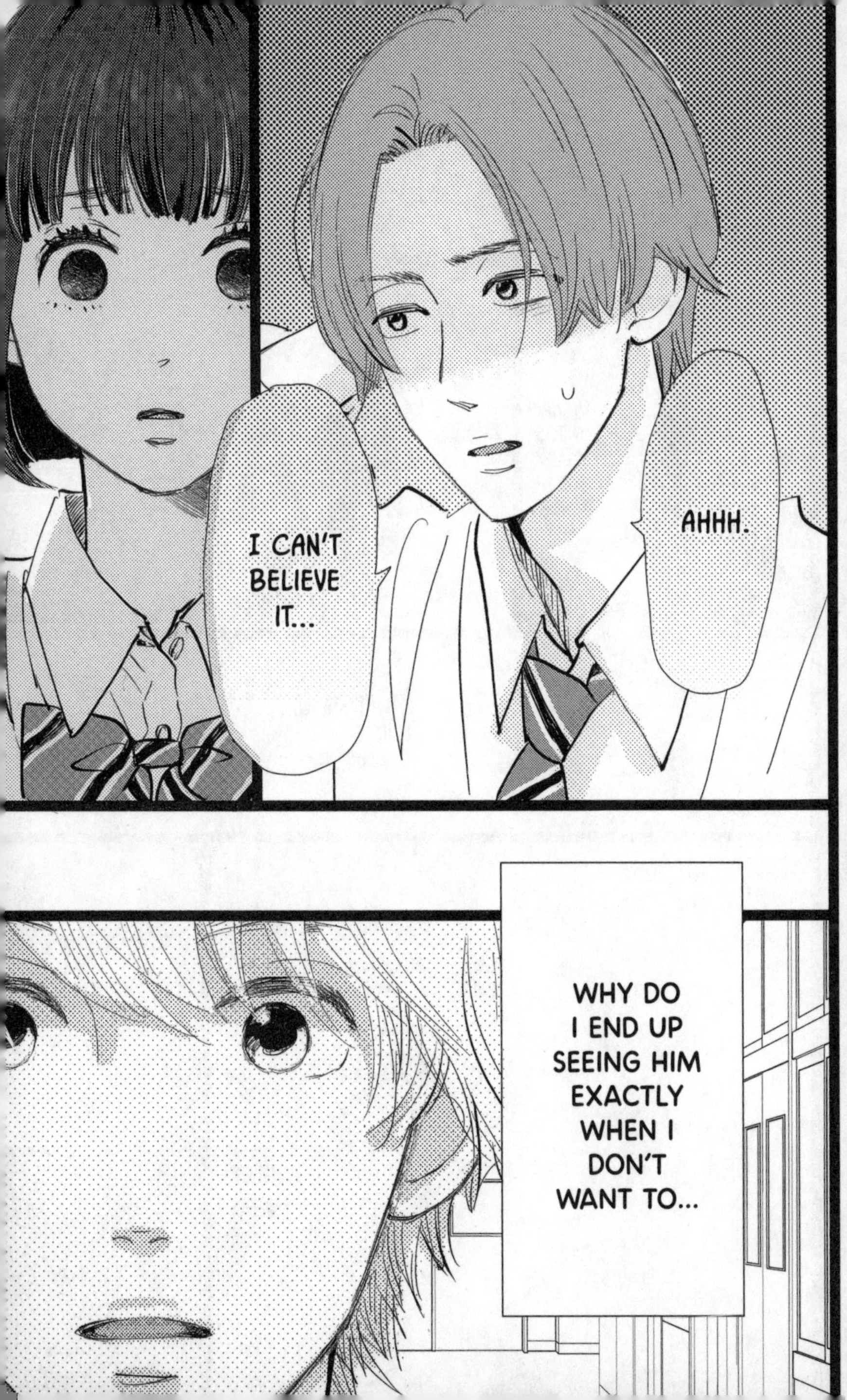
AHHH.
I CAN'T BELIEVE IT...
WHY DO I END UP SEEING HIM EXACTLY WHEN I DON'T WANT TO...

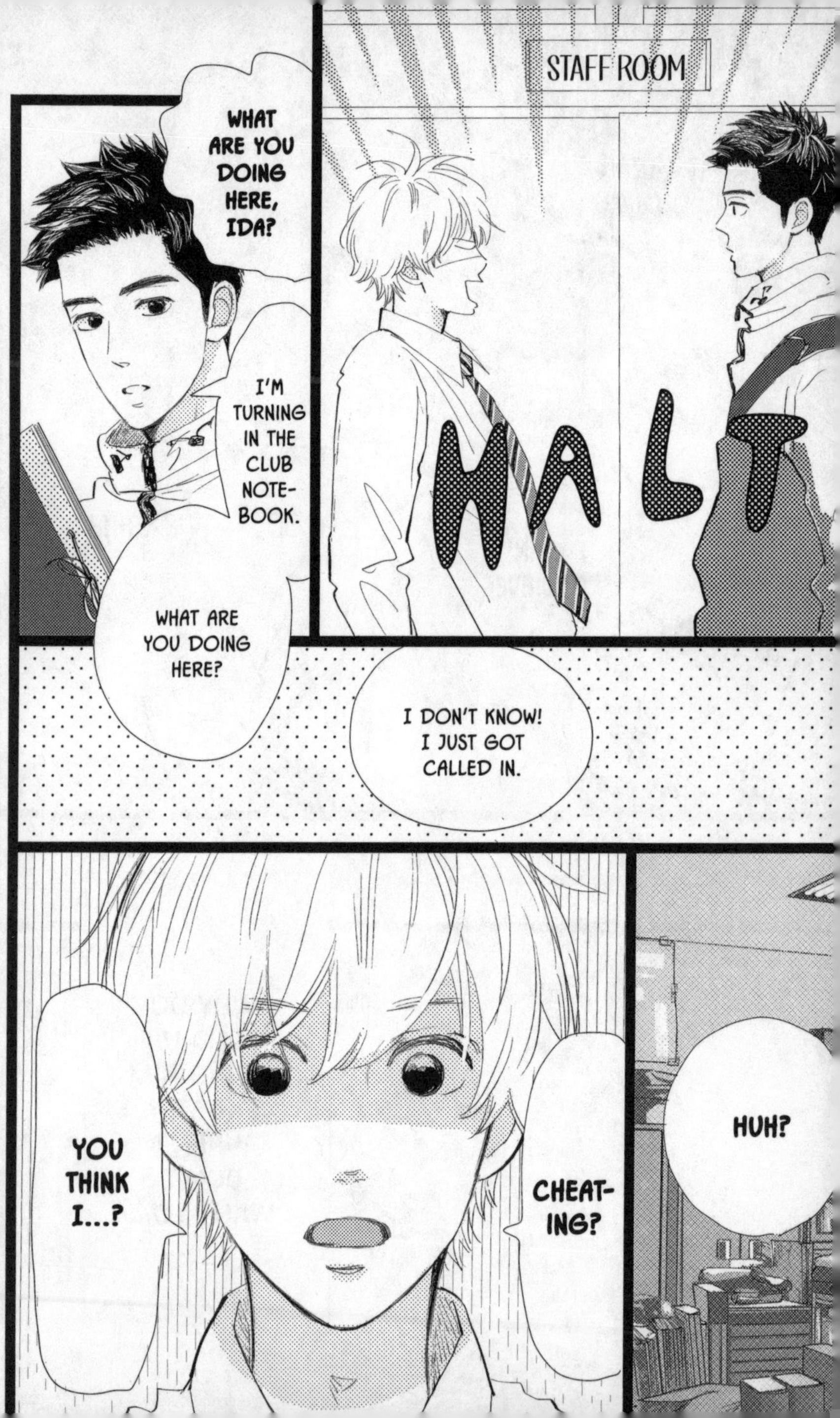
STAFF ROOM
HALT
WHAT ARE YOU DOING HERE, IDA?
I'M TURNING IN THE CLUB NOTE-BOOK.
WHAT ARE YOU DOING HERE?
I DON'T KNOW! I JUST GOT CALLED IN.
HUH?
CHEAT-ING?
YOU THINK I...?

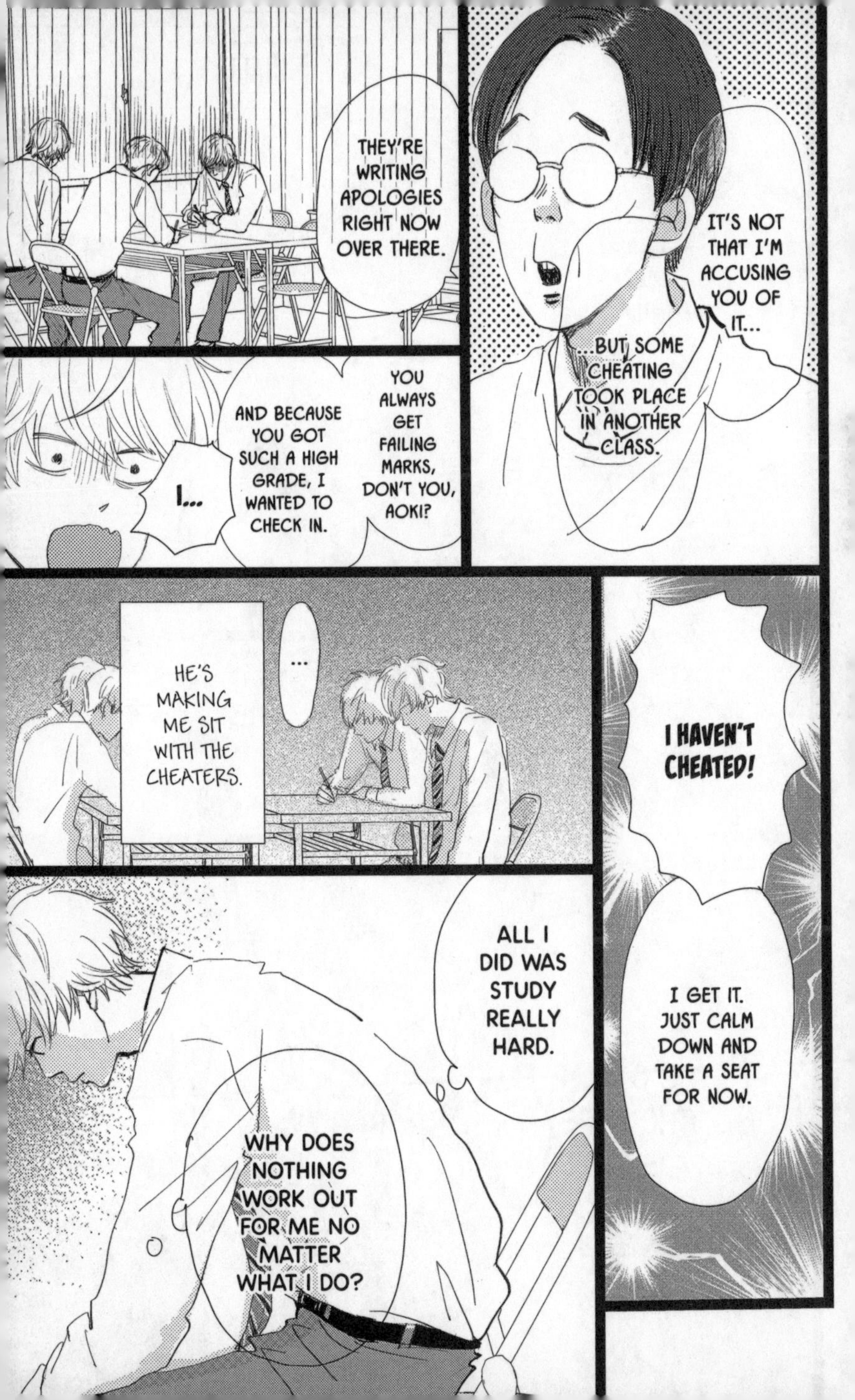
IT'S NOT THAT I'M ACCUSING YOU OF IT...
...BUT SOME CHEATING TOOK PLACE IN ANOTHER CLASS.
THEY'RE WRITING APOLOGIES RIGHT NOW OVER THERE.
YOU ALWAYS GET FAILING MARKS, DON'T YOU, AOKI?
AND BECAUSE YOU GOT SUCH A HIGH GRADE, I WANTED TO CHECK IN.
I...
I HAVEN'T CHEATED!
I GET IT. JUST CALM DOWN AND TAKE A SEAT FOR NOW.
...
HE'S MAKING ME SIT WITH THE CHEATERS.
ALL I DID WAS STUDY REALLY HARD.
WHY DOES NOTHING WORK OUT FOR ME NO MATTER WHAT I DO?

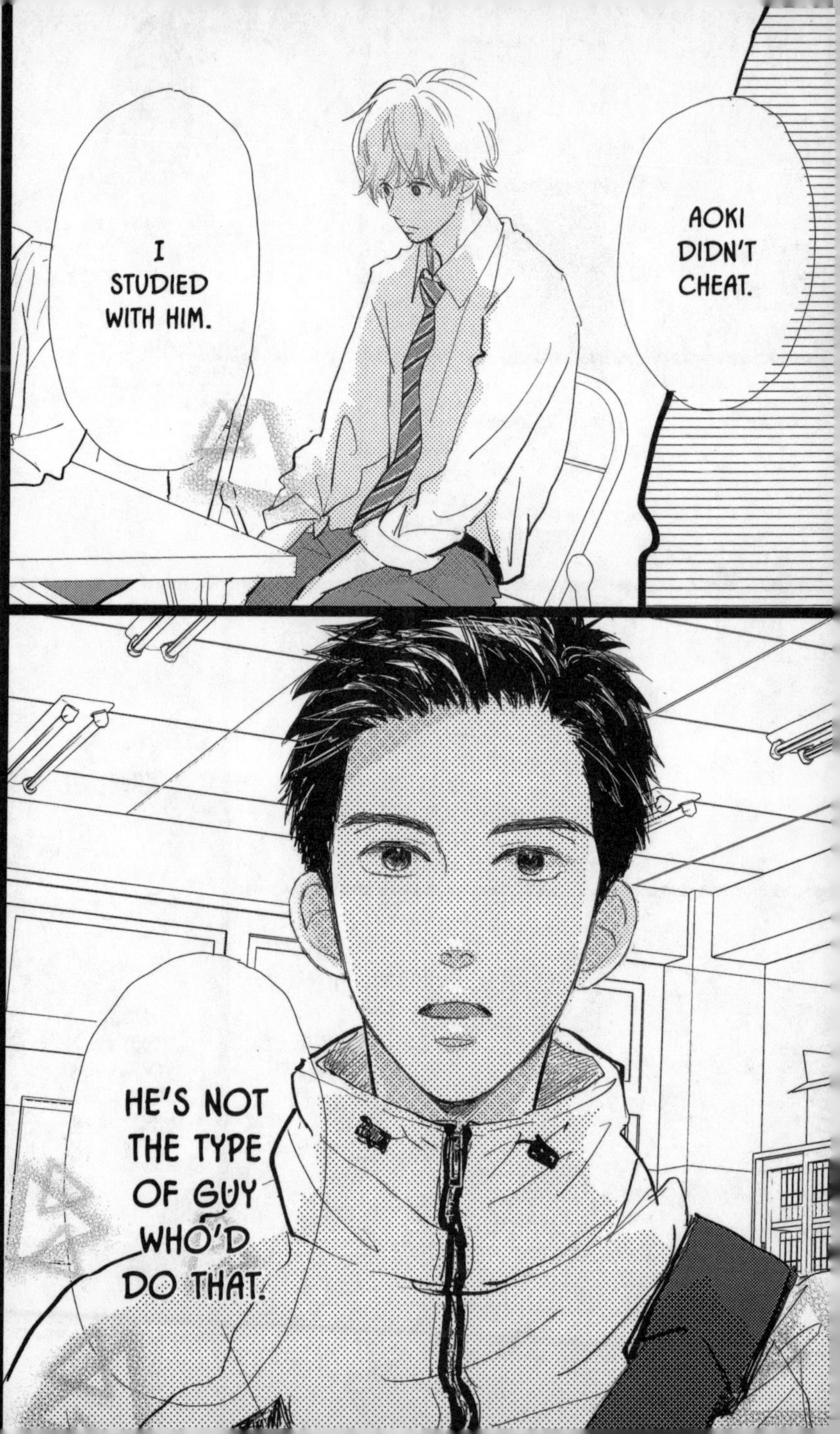
AOKI DIDN'T CHEAT.
I STUDIED WITH HIM.
HE'S NOT THE TYPE OF GUY WHO'D DO THAT.

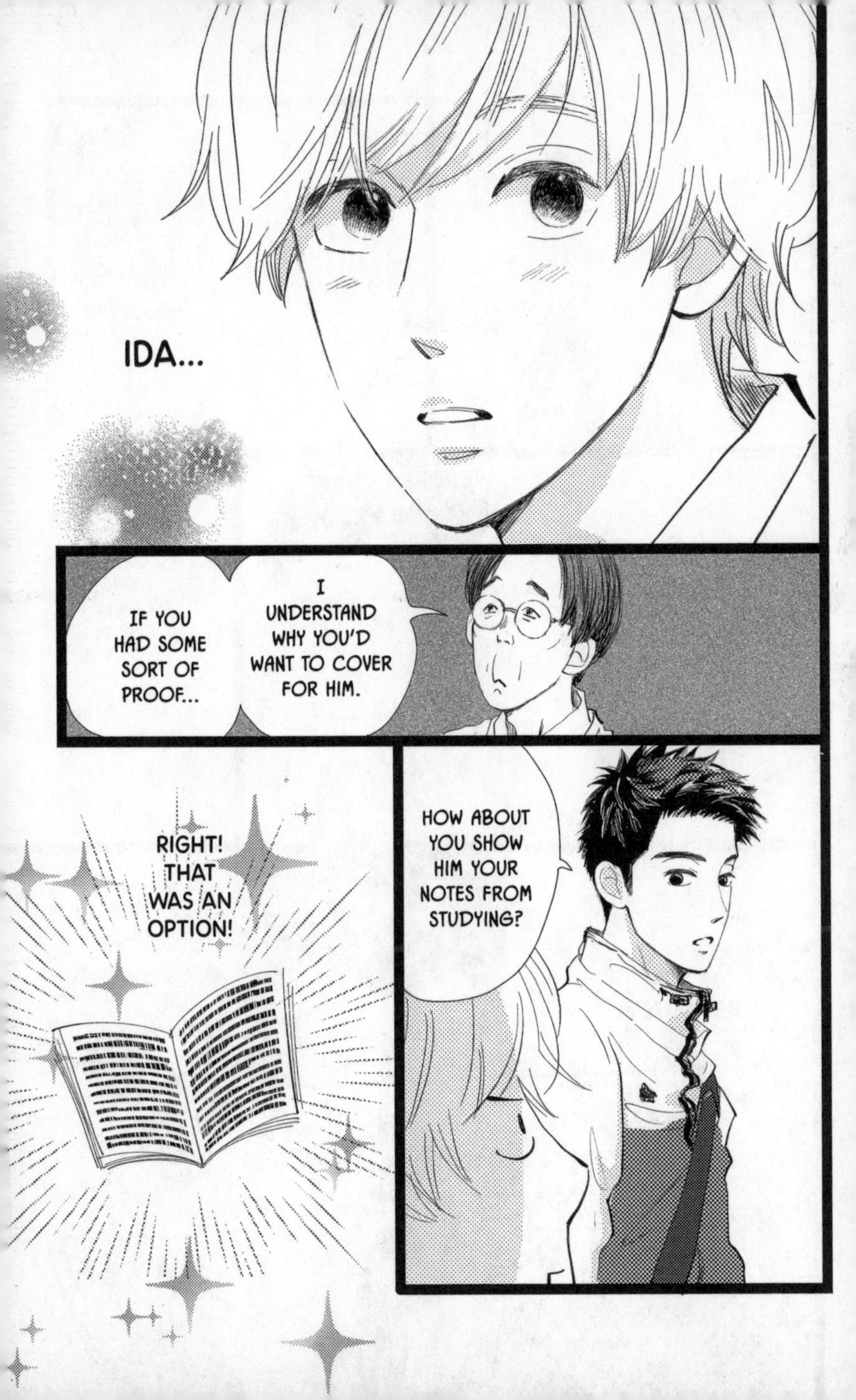
IDA...
I UNDERSTAND WHY YOU'D WANT TO COVER FOR HIM.
IF YOU HAD SOME SORT OF PROOF...
HOW ABOUT YOU SHOW HIM YOUR NOTES FROM STUDYING?
RIGHT! THAT WAS AN OPTION!

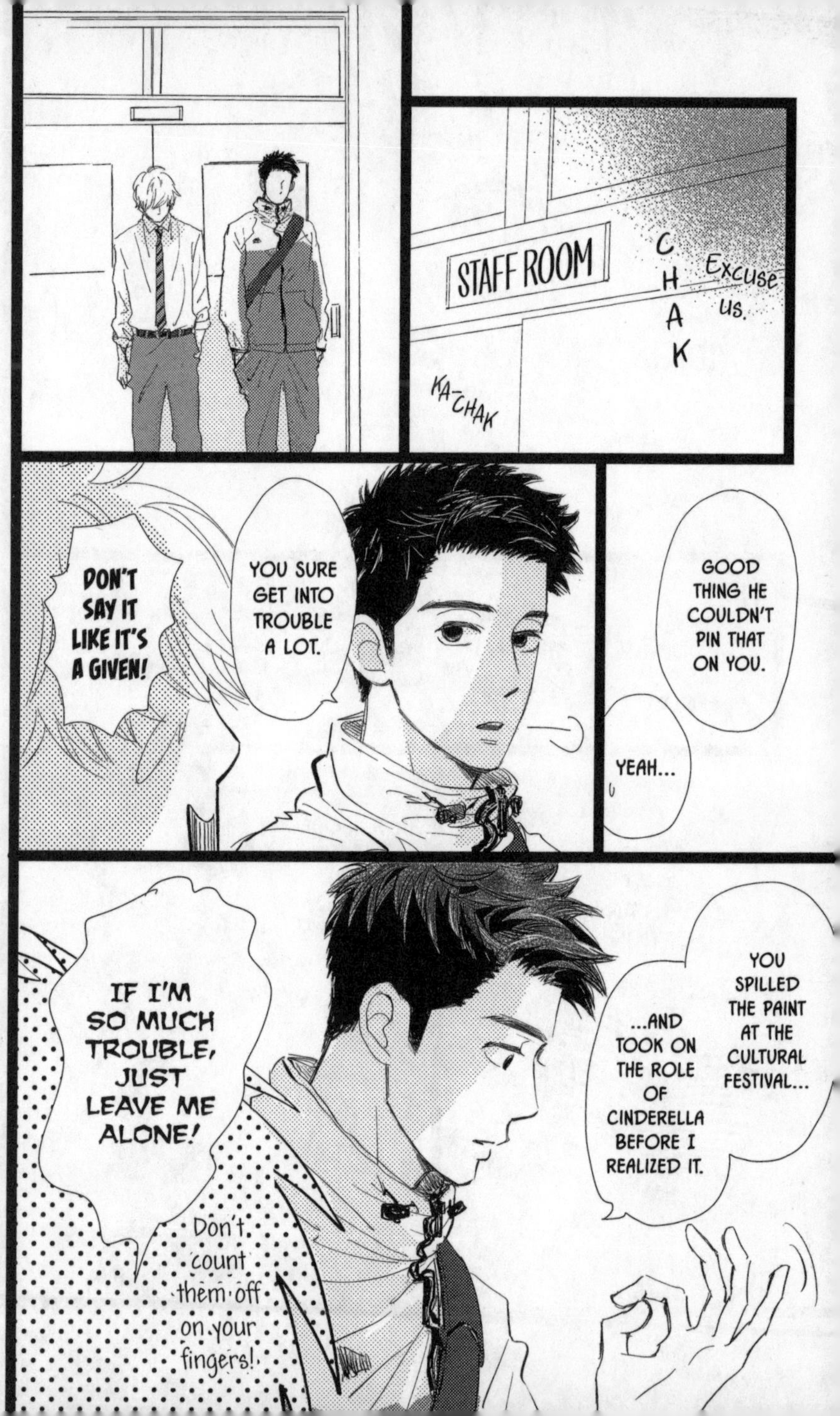
Excuse us.
CHAK
STAFF ROOM
KA-CHAK
GOOD THING HE COULDN'T PIN THAT ON YOU.
YEAH...
YOU SURE GET INTO TROUBLE A LOT.
DON'T SAY IT LIKE IT'S A GIVEN!
YOU SPILLED THE PAINT AT THE CULTURAL FESTIVAL...
...AND TOOK ON THE ROLE OF CINDERELLA BEFORE I REALIZED IT.
IF I'M SO MUCH TROUBLE, JUST LEAVE ME ALONE!
Don't count them off on your fingers!

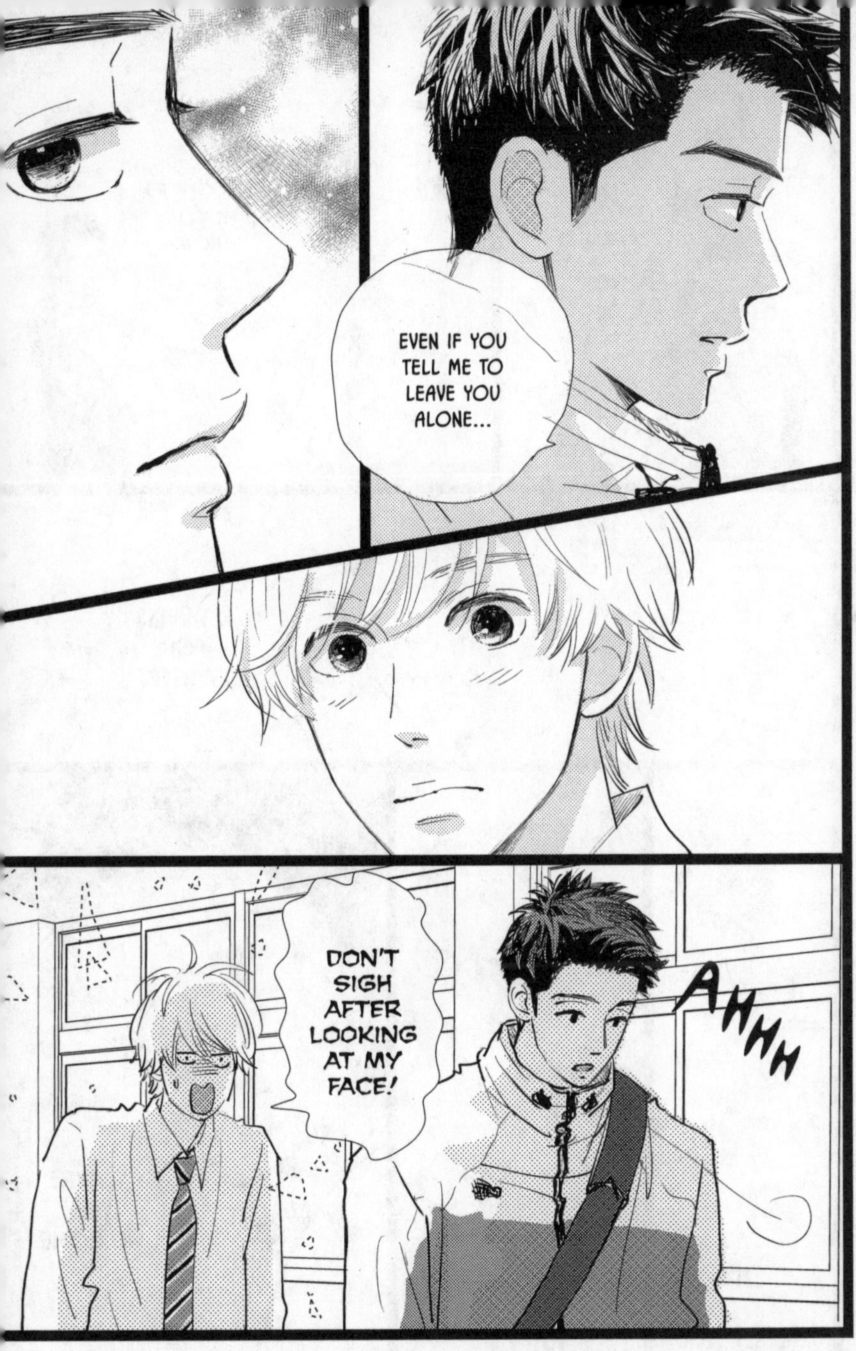
EVEN IF YOU TELL ME TO LEAVE YOU ALONE...
AHHH
DON'T SIGH AFTER LOOKING AT MY FACE!

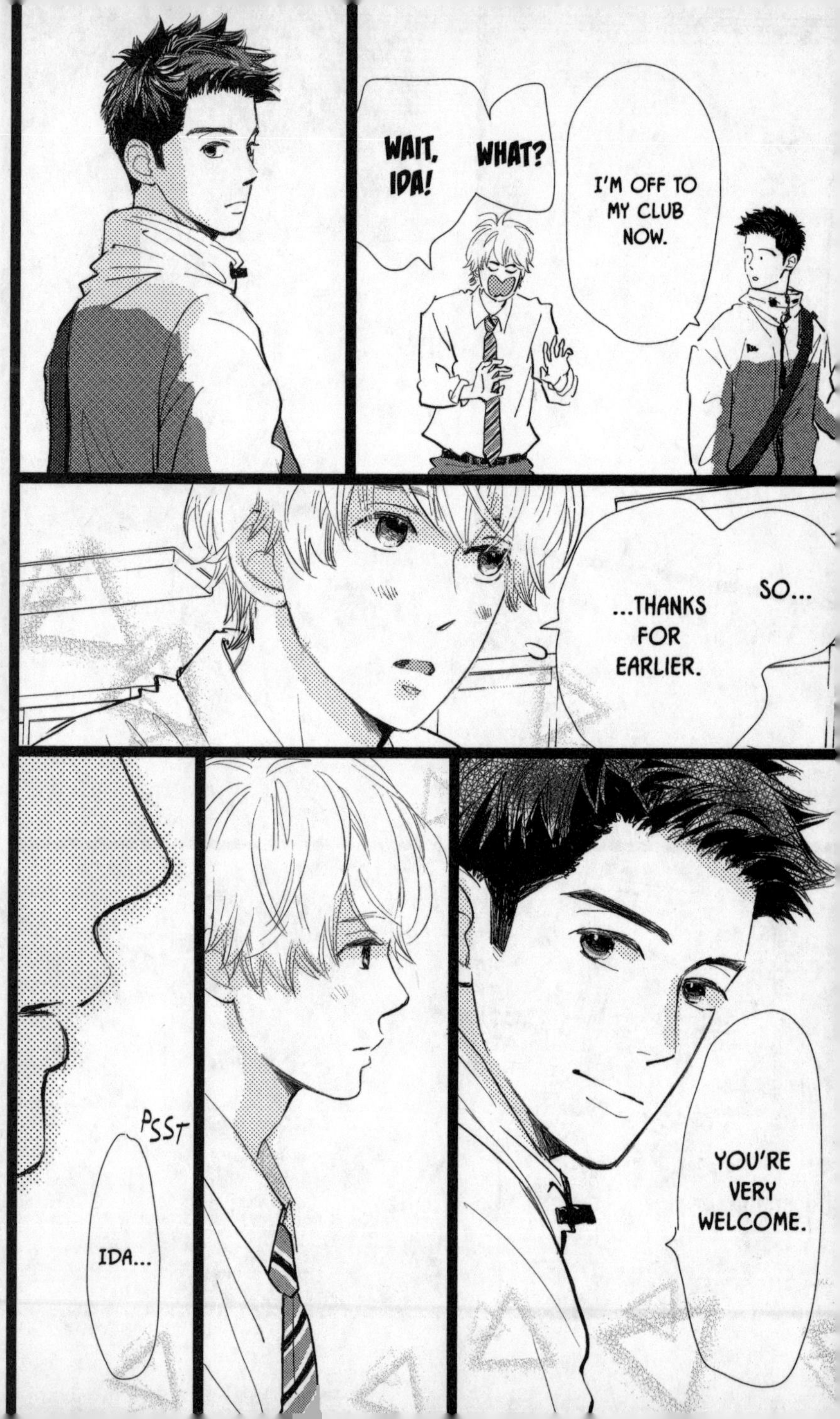
I'M OFF TO MY CLUB NOW.
WHAT?
WAIT, IDA!
SO...
...THANKS FOR EARLIER.
YOU'RE VERY WELCOME.
PSST
IDA...

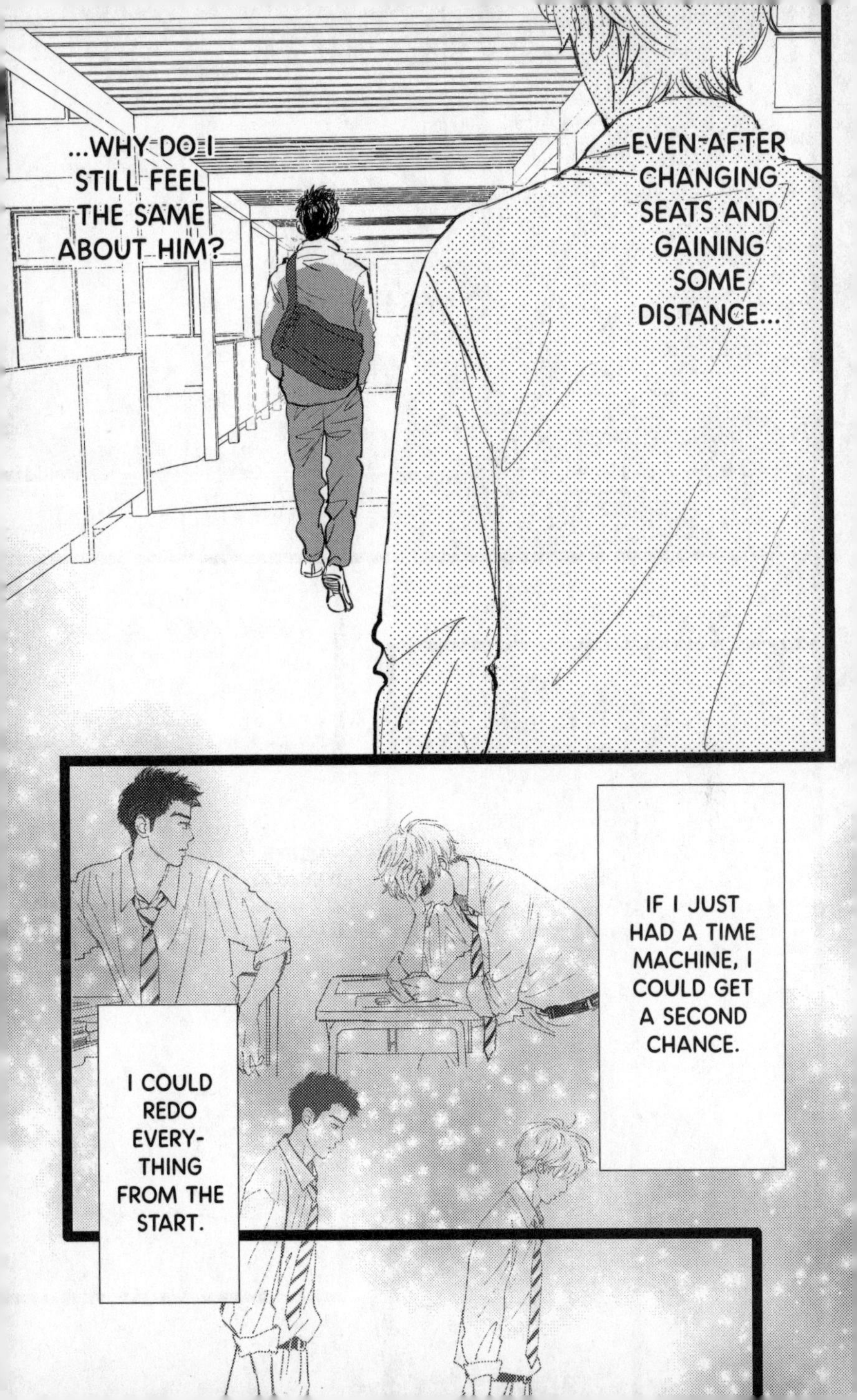
EVEN AFTER CHANGING SEATS AND GAINING SOME DISTANCE...
...WHY DO I STILL FEEL THE SAME ABOUT HIM?
IF I JUST HAD A TIME MACHINE, I COULD GET A SECOND CHANCE.
I COULD REDO EVERY-THING FROM THE START.

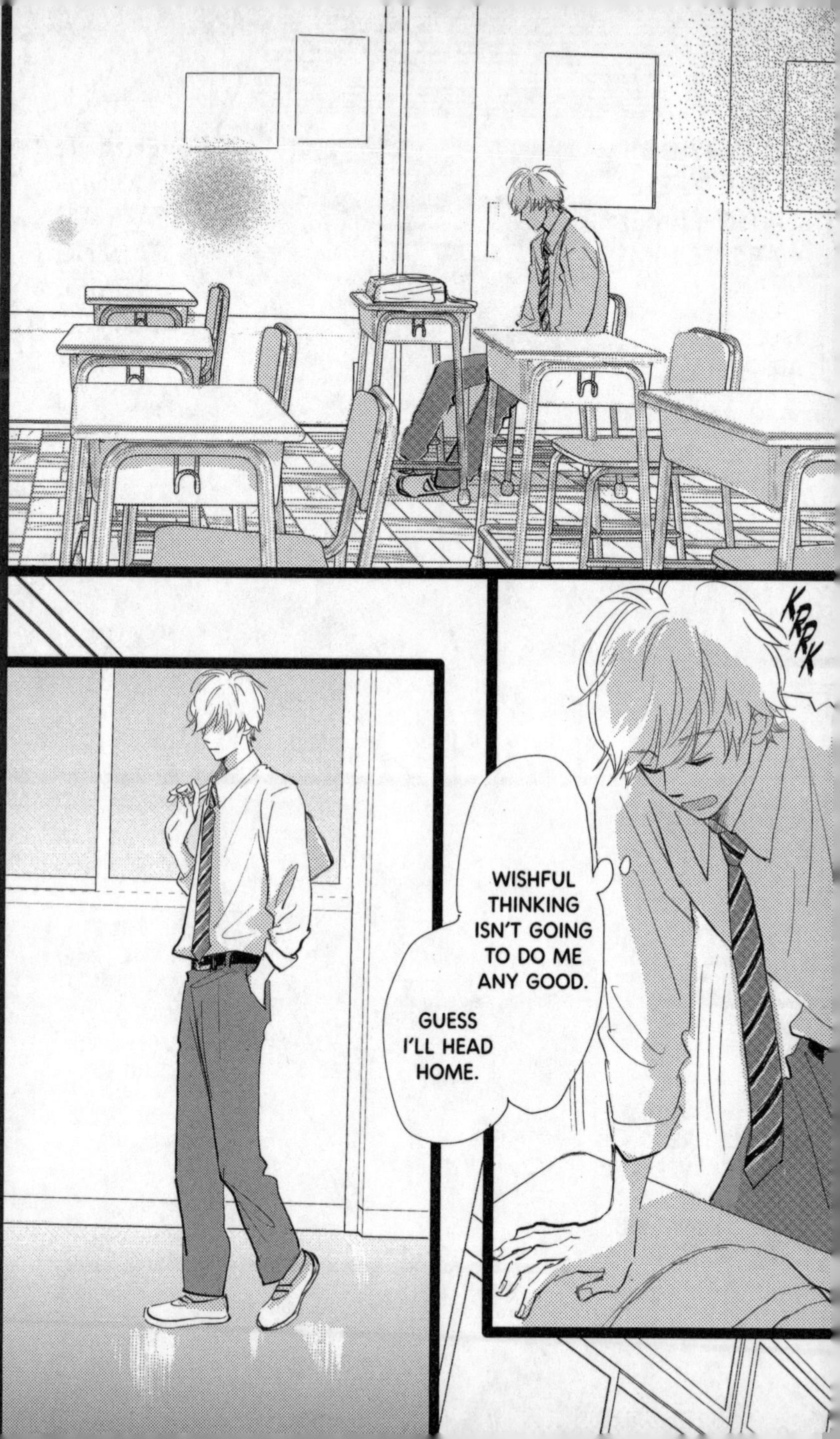
KRRK
WISHFUL THINKING ISN'T GOING TO DO ME ANY GOOD.
GUESS I'LL HEAD HOME.

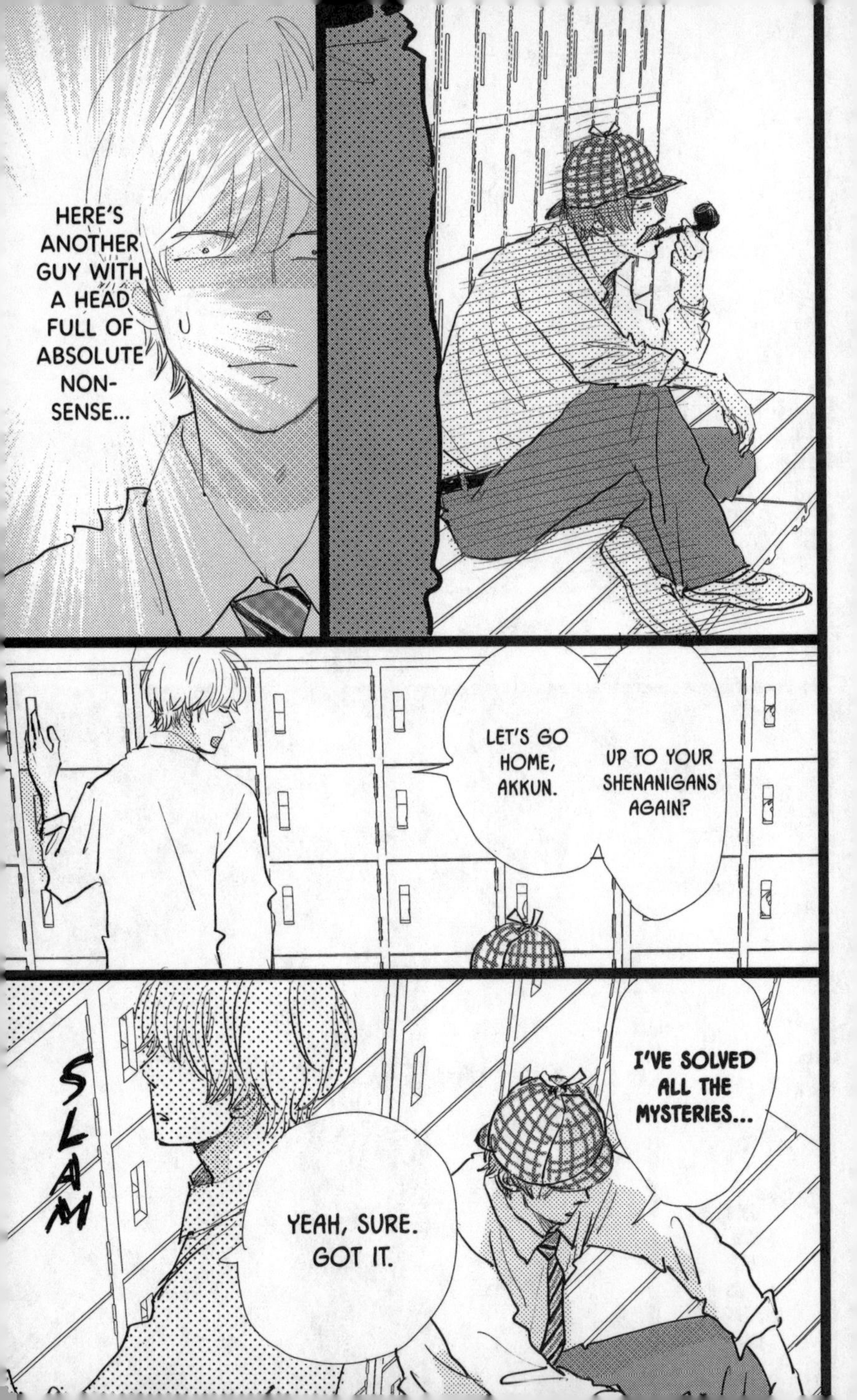
HERE'S ANOTHER GUY WITH A HEAD FULL OF ABSOLUTE NON-SENSE...
UP TO YOUR SHENANIGANS AGAIN?
LET'S GO HOME, AKKUN.
I'VE SOLVED ALL THE MYSTERIES...
YEAH, SURE. GOT IT.
SLAM

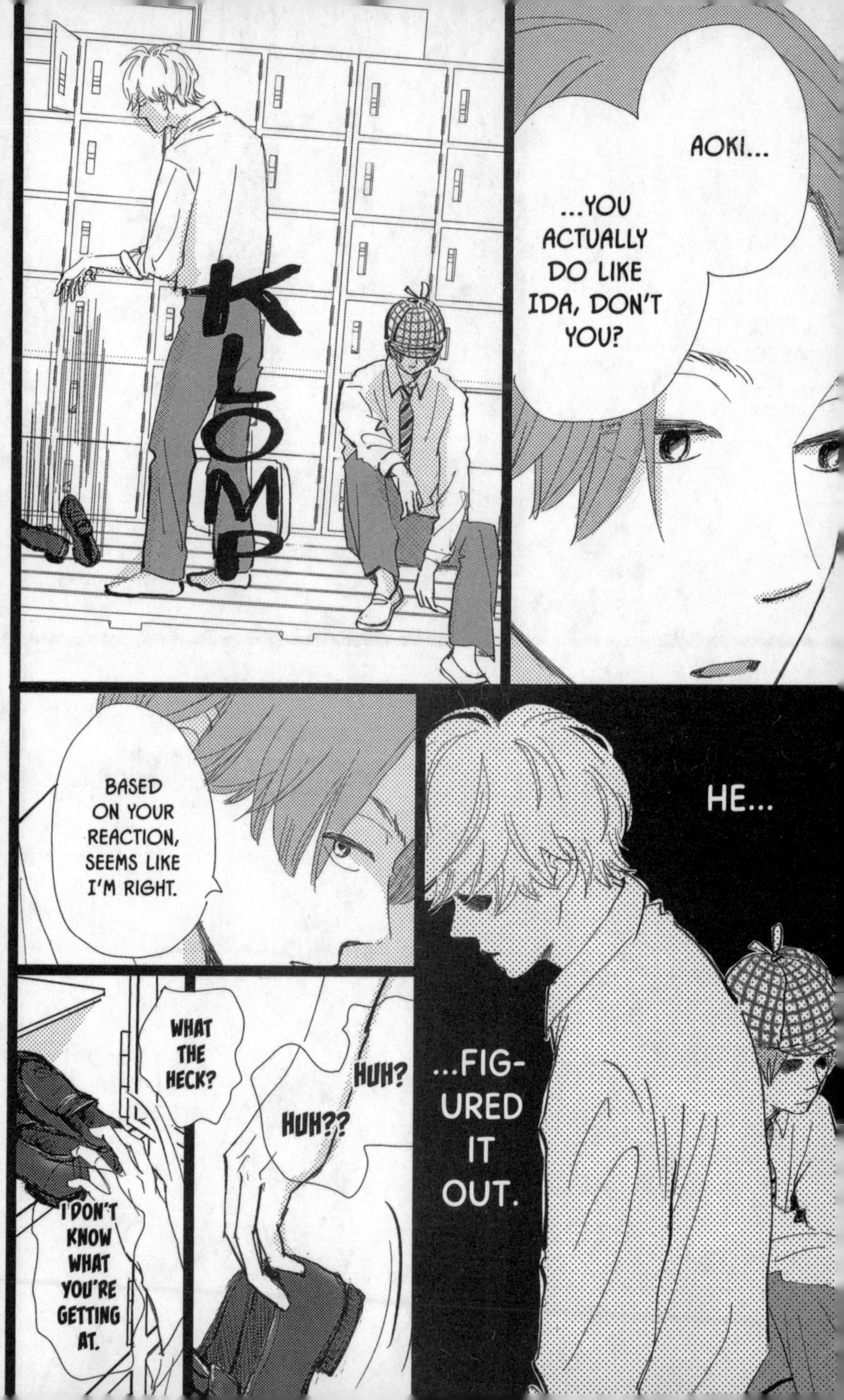
AOKI...
...YOU ACTUALLY DO LIKE IDA, DON'T YOU?
KLOMP
HE...
...FIG-URED IT OUT.
BASED ON YOUR REACTION, SEEMS LIKE I'M RIGHT.
HUH?
HUH??
WHAT THE HECK?
I DON'T KNOW WHAT YOU'RE GETTING AT.

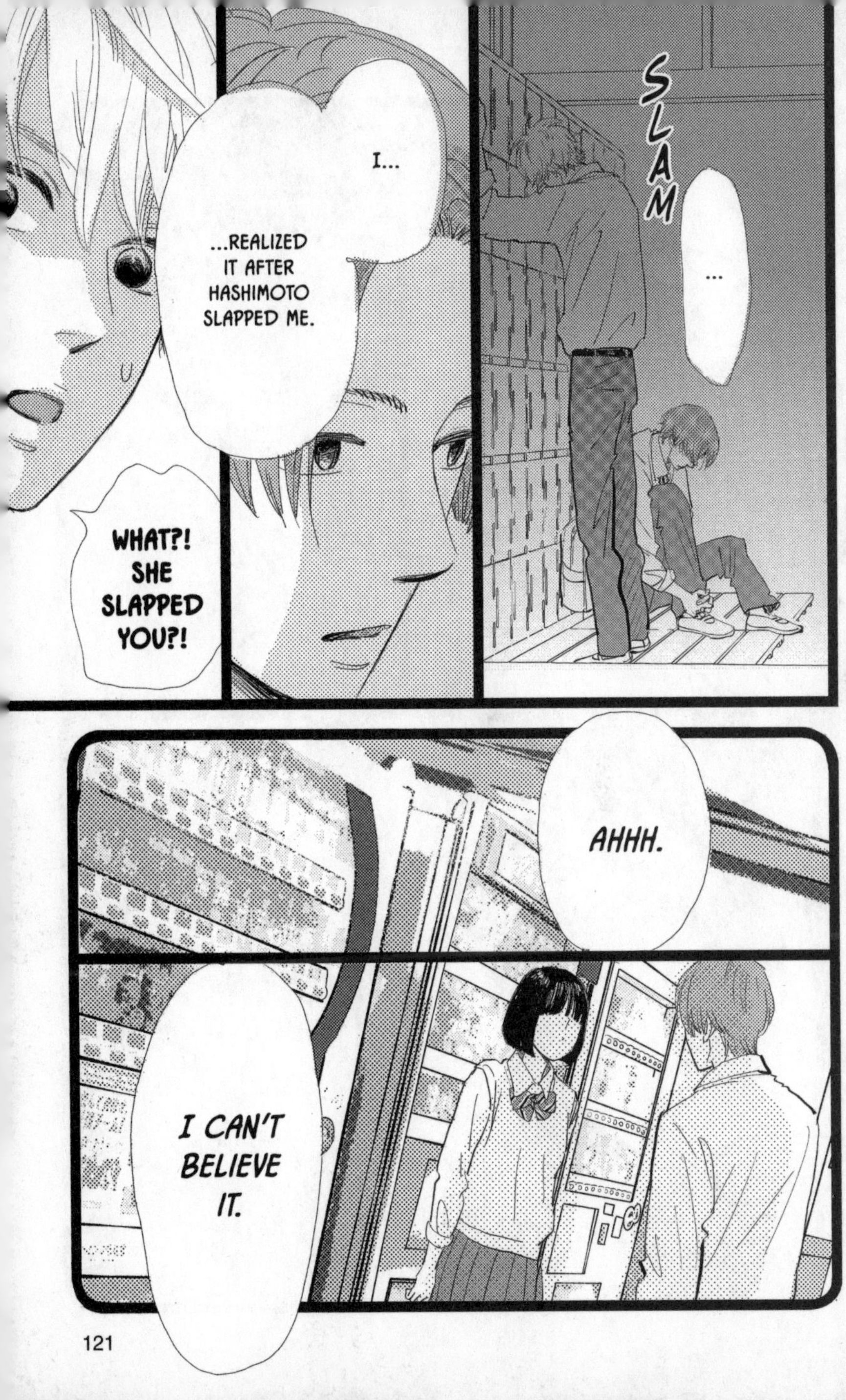
SLAM
...
I...
...REALIZED IT AFTER HASHIMOTO SLAPPED ME.
WHAT?! SHE SLAPPED YOU?!
AHHH.
I CAN'T BELIEVE IT.

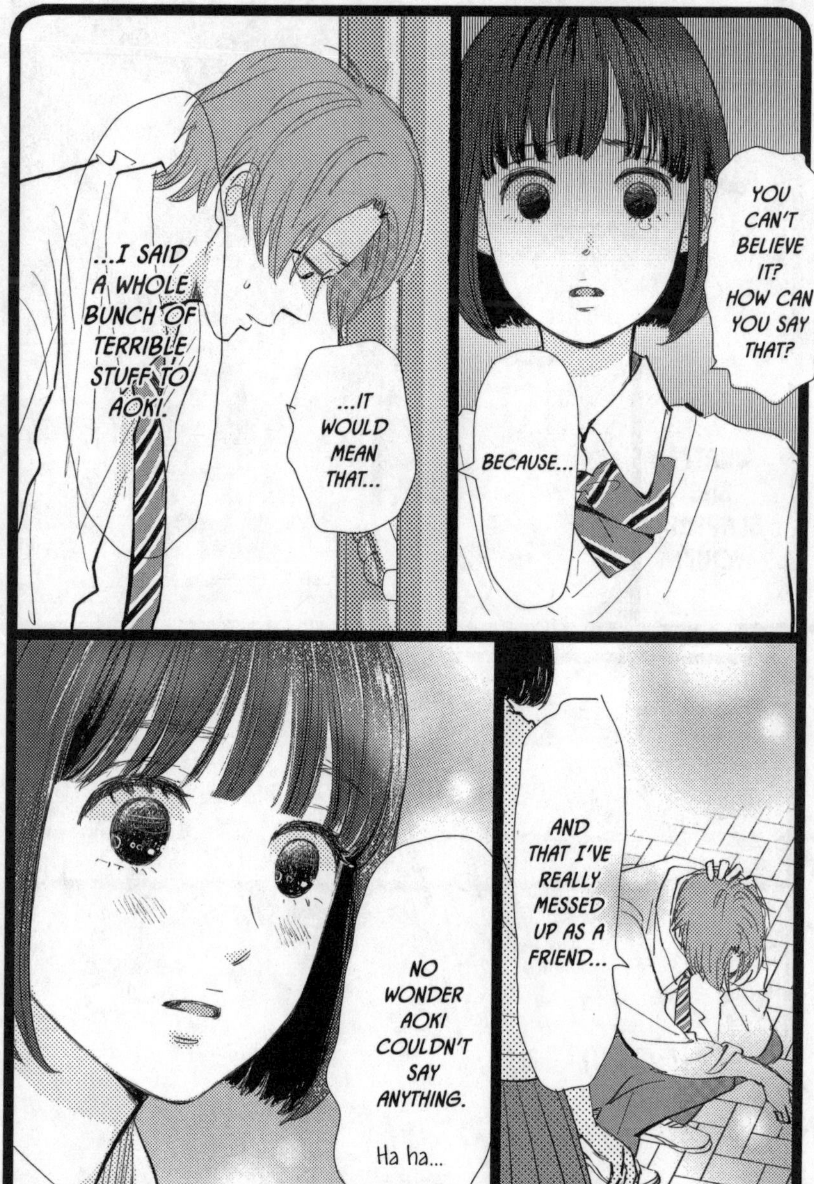
YOU CAN'T BELIEVE IT? HOW CAN YOU SAY THAT?
BECAUSE...
...IT WOULD MEAN THAT...
...I SAID A WHOLE BUNCH OF TERRIBLE STUFF TO AOKI.
AND THAT I'VE REALLY MESSED UP AS A FRIEND...
NO WONDER AOKI COULDN'T SAY ANYTHING.
Ha ha...

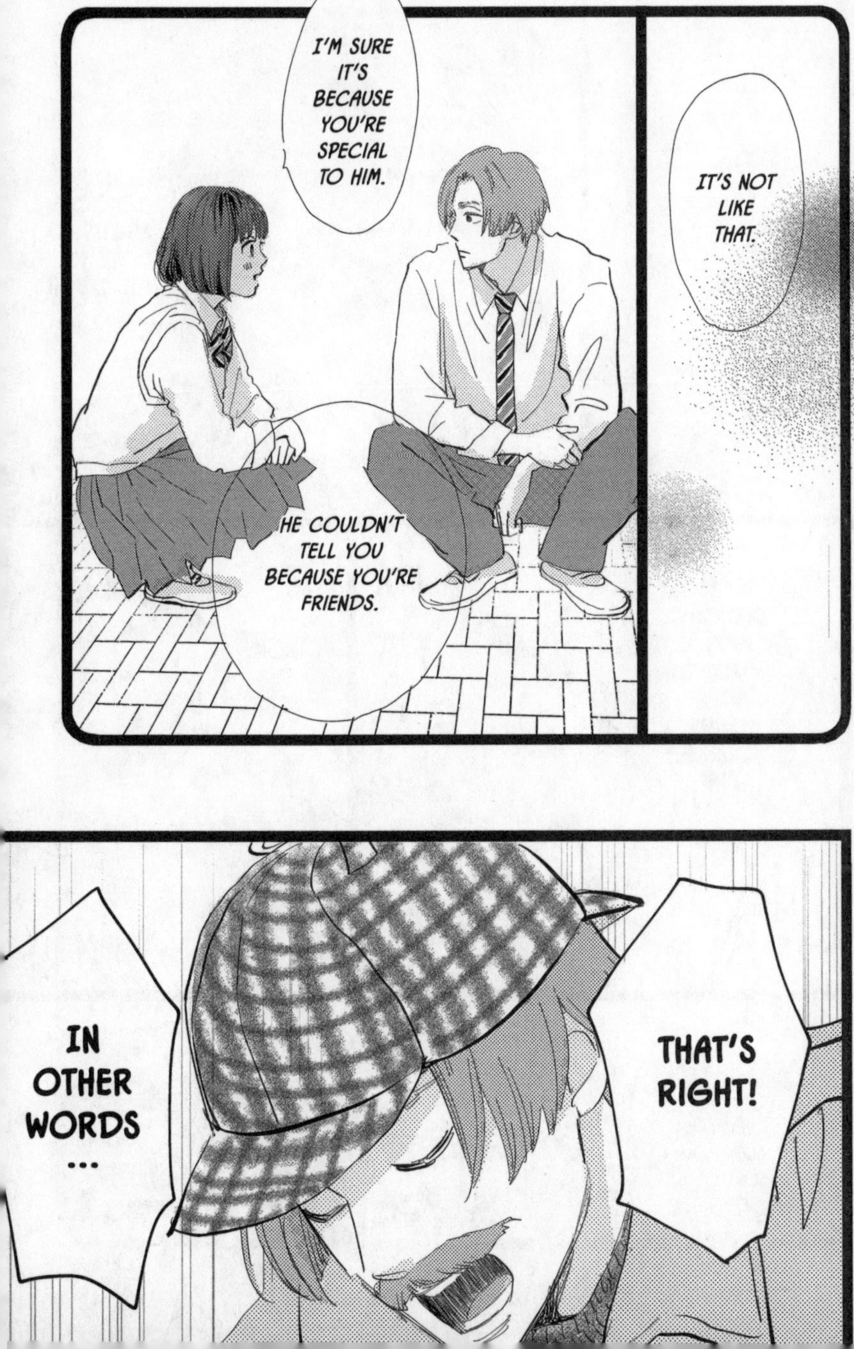
IT'S NOT LIKE THAT.
I'M SURE IT'S BECAUSE YOU'RE SPECIAL TO HIM.
HE COULDN'T TELL YOU BECAUSE YOU'RE FRIENDS.
THAT'S RIGHT!
IN OTHER WORDS ...

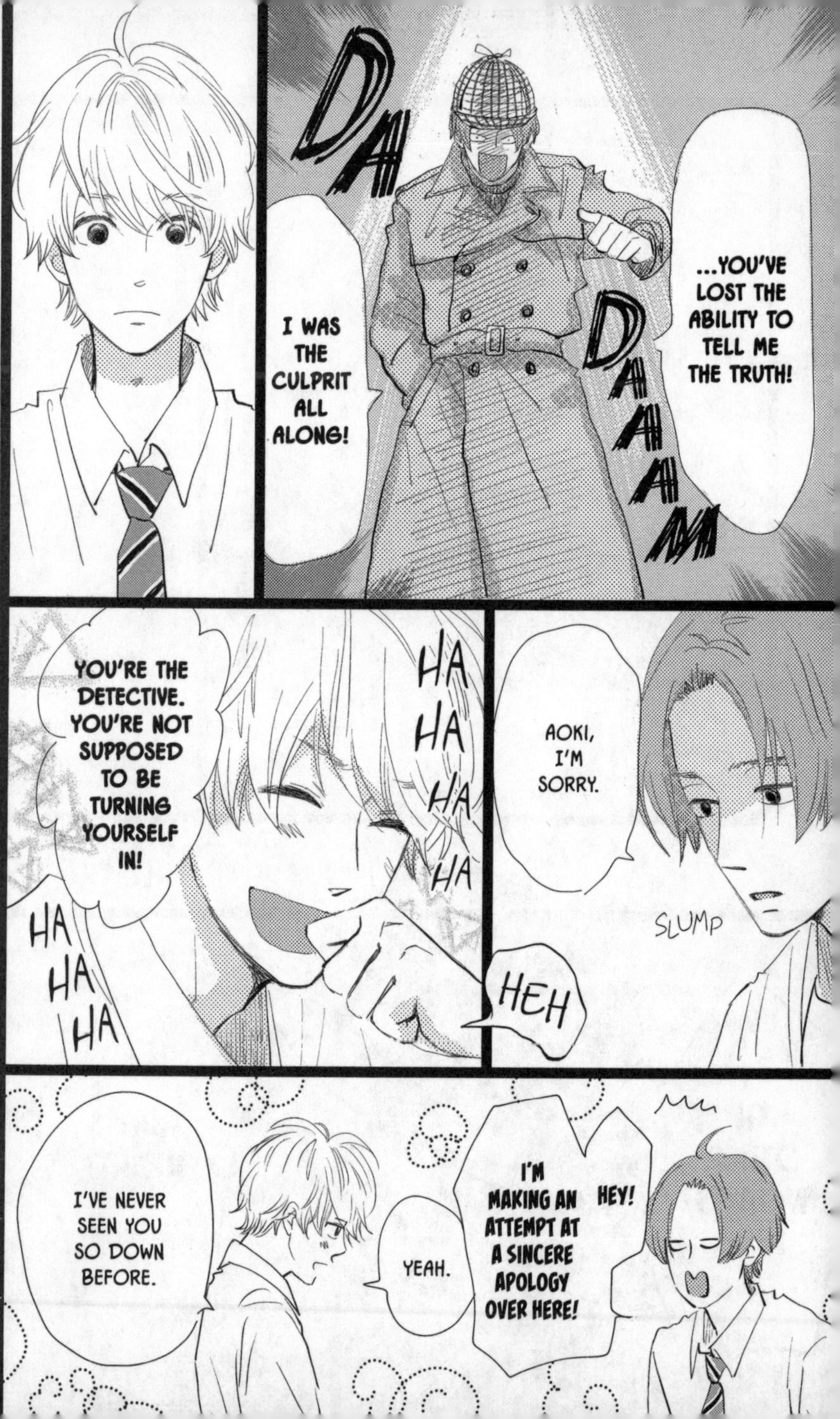
...YOU'VE LOST THE ABILITY TO TELL ME THE TRUTH!
DA
DAAAM
I WAS THE CULPRIT ALL ALONG!
AOKI, I'M SORRY.
SLUMP
HEH
HA HA HA HA
YOU'RE THE DETECTIVE. YOU'RE NOT SUPPOSED TO BE TURNING YOURSELF IN!
HA HA HA
HEY!
I'M MAKING AN ATTEMPT AT A SINCERE APOLOGY OVER HERE!
YEAH.
I'VE NEVER SEEN YOU SO DOWN BEFORE.

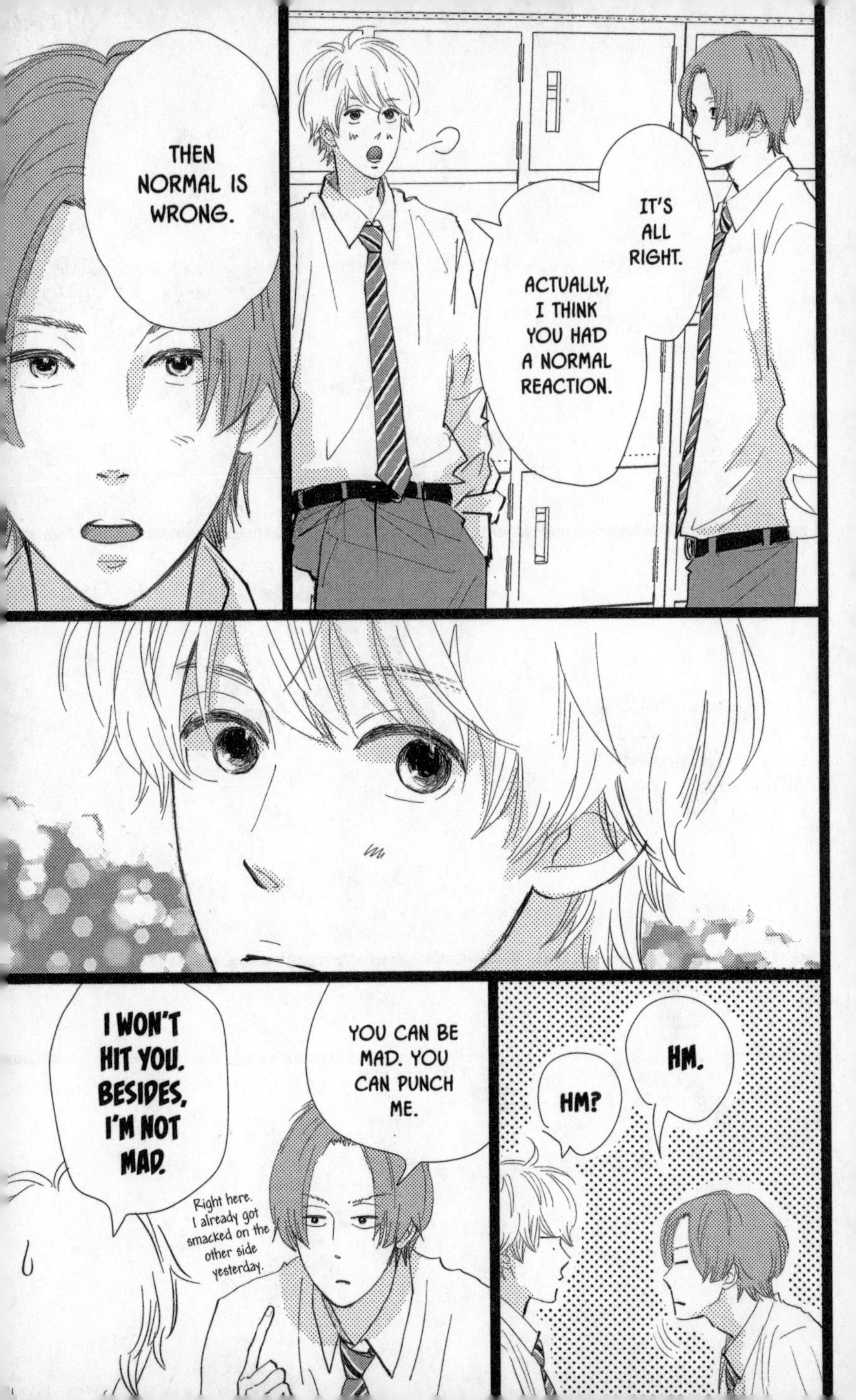
IT'S ALL RIGHT.
ACTUALLY, I THINK YOU HAD A NORMAL REACTION.
THEN NORMAL IS WRONG.
HM.
HM?
YOU CAN BE MAD. YOU CAN PUNCH ME.
I WON'T HIT YOU. BESIDES, I'M NOT MAD.
Right here. I already got smacked on the other side yesterday.

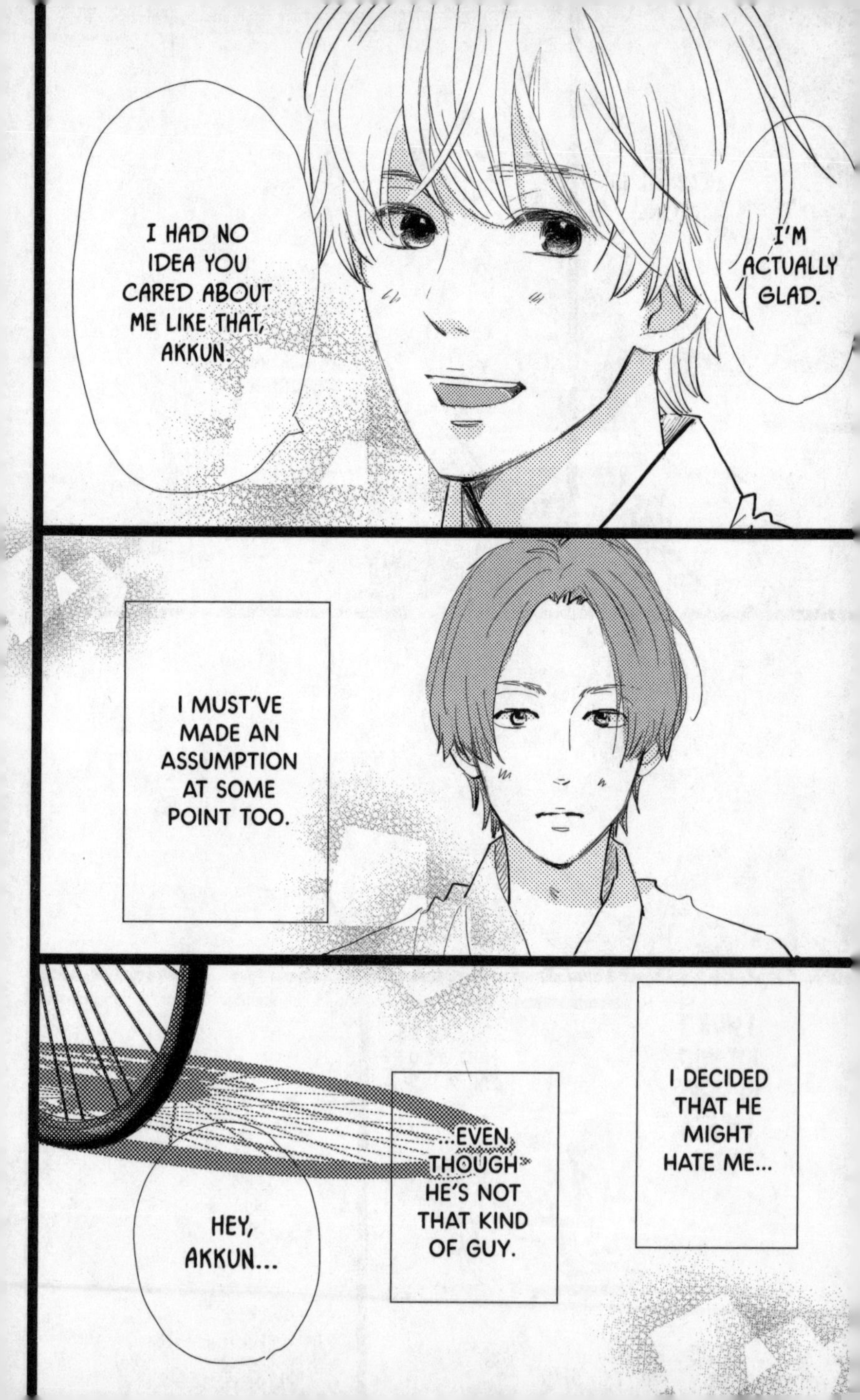
I'M ACTUALLY GLAD.
I HAD NO IDEA YOU CARED ABOUT ME LIKE THAT, AKKUN.
I MUST'VE MADE AN ASSUMPTION AT SOME POINT TOO.
I DECIDED THAT HE MIGHT HATE ME...
...EVEN THOUGH HE'S NOT THAT KIND OF GUY.
HEY, AKKUN...

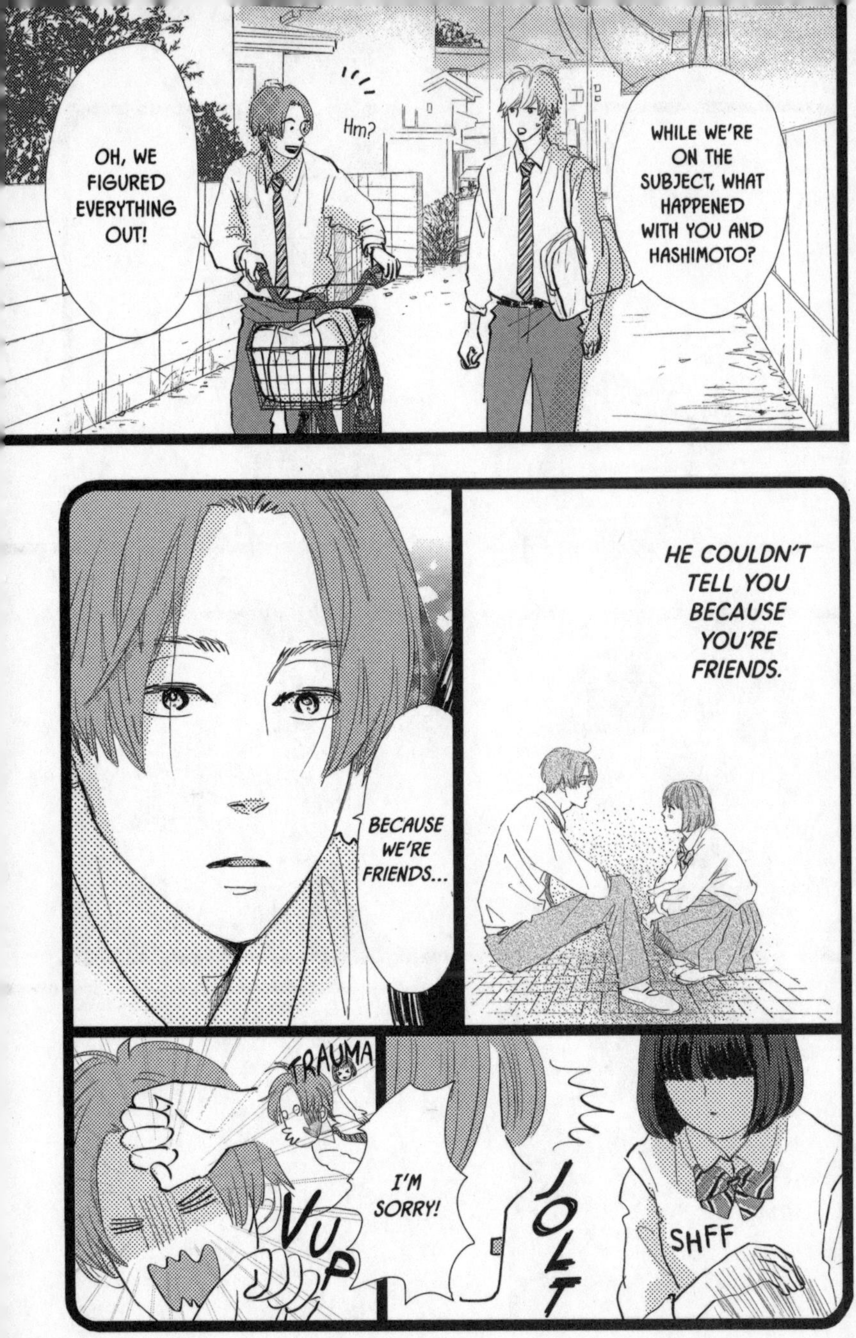
WHILE WE'RE ON THE SUBJECT, WHAT HAPPENED WITH YOU AND HASHIMOTO?
Hm?
OH, WE FIGURED EVERYTHING OUT!
HE COULDN'T TELL YOU BECAUSE YOU'RE FRIENDS.
BECAUSE WE'RE FRIENDS...
SHFF
JOLT
I'M SORRY!
TRAUMA
VUP

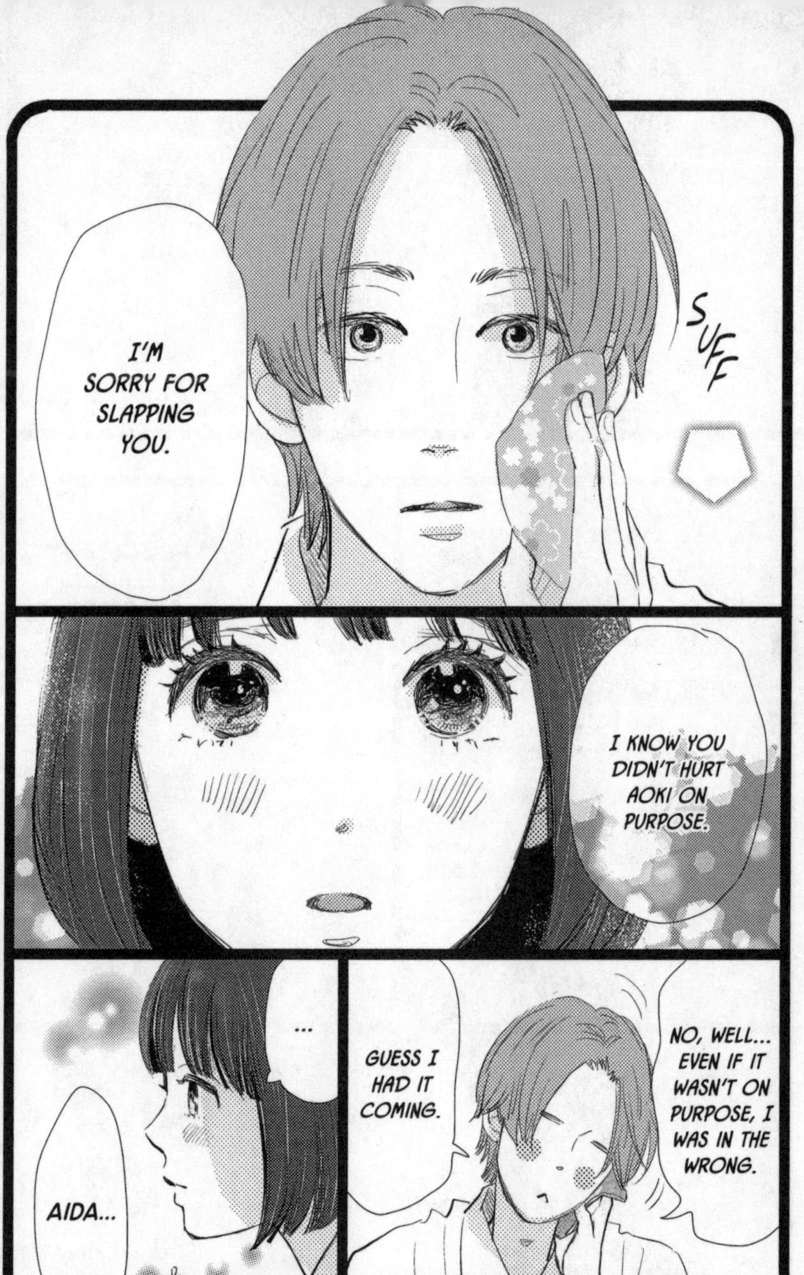
SUFF
I'M SORRY FOR SLAPPING YOU.
I KNOW YOU DIDN'T HURT AOKI ON PURPOSE.
NO, WELL... EVEN IF IT WASN'T ON PURPOSE, I WAS IN THE WRONG.
GUESS I HAD IT COMING.
...
AIDA...

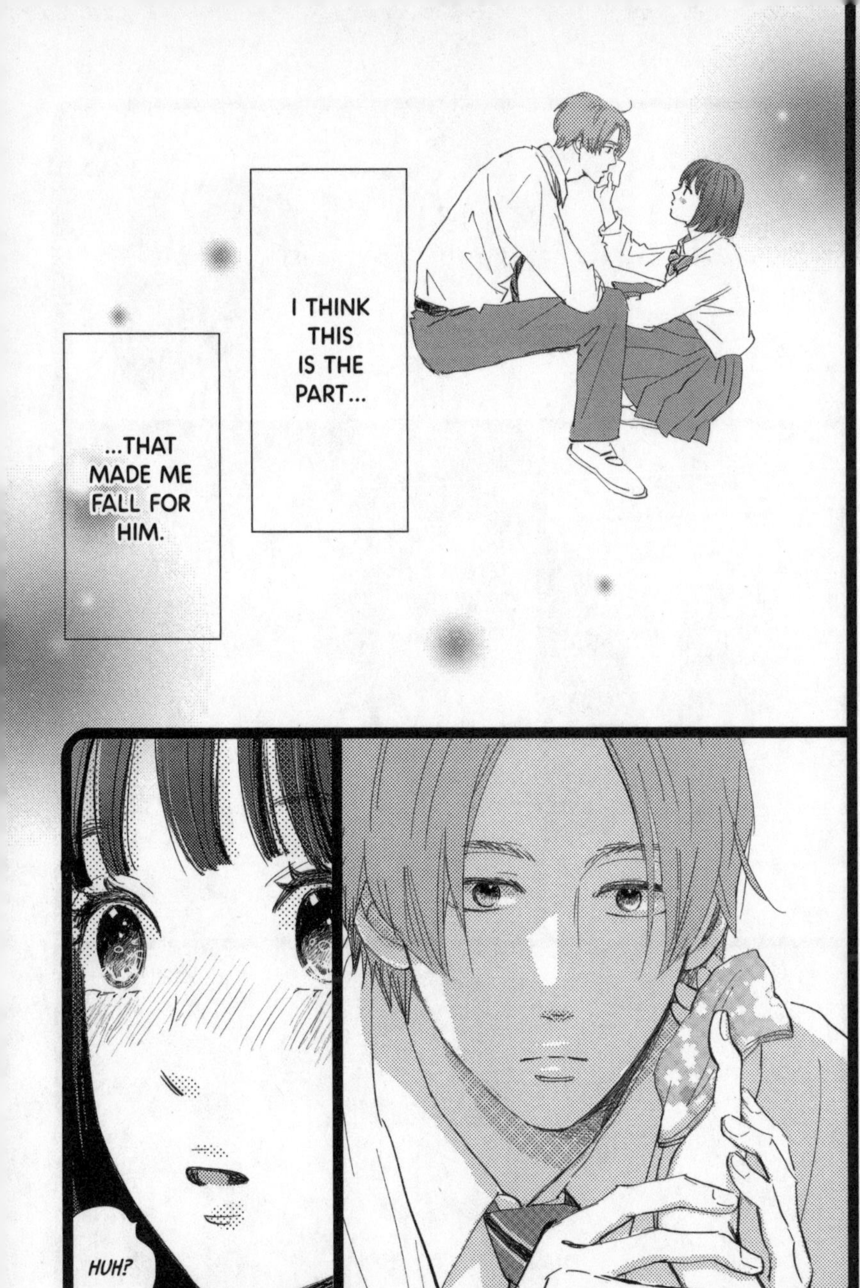
I THINK THIS IS THE PART...
...THAT MADE ME FALL FOR HIM.
HUH?

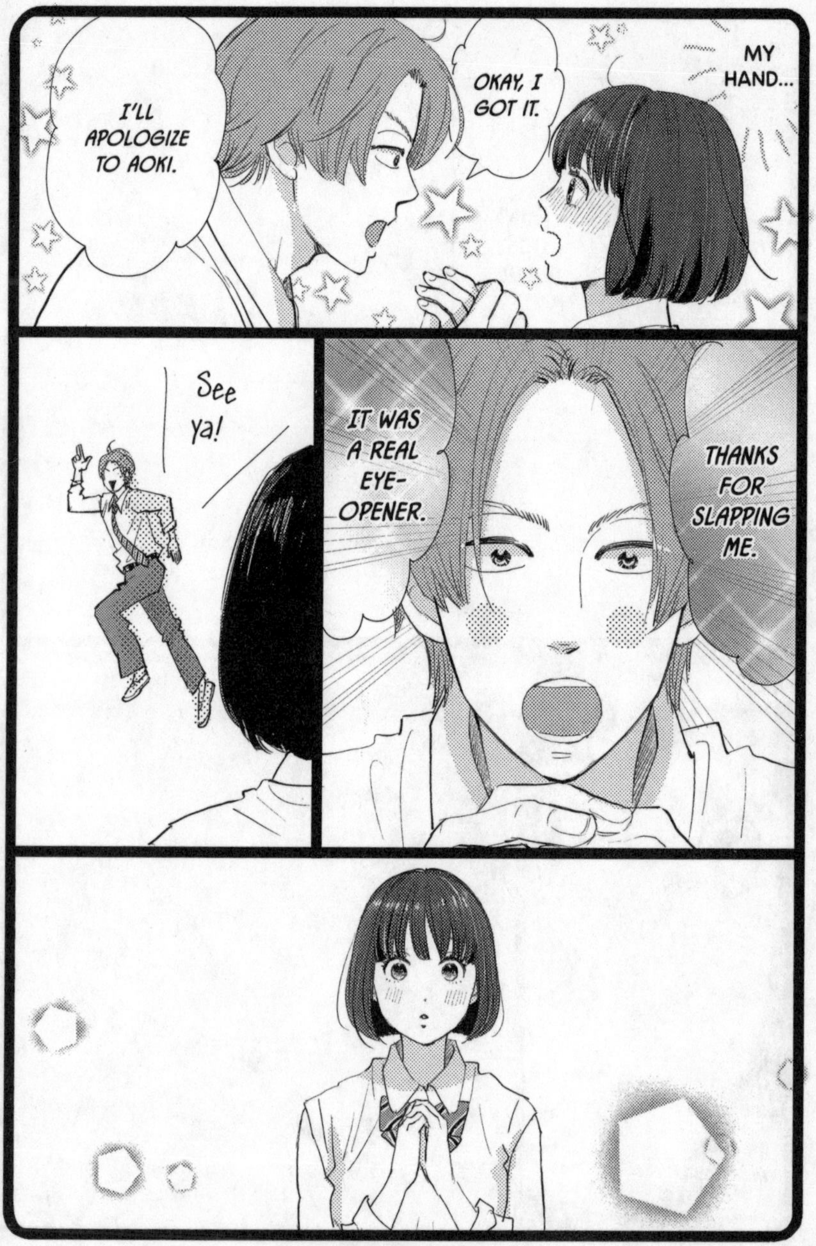
MY HAND...
OKAY, I GOT IT.
I'LL APOLOGIZE TO AOKI.
THANKS FOR SLAPPING ME.
IT WAS A REAL EYE-OPENER.
See ya!

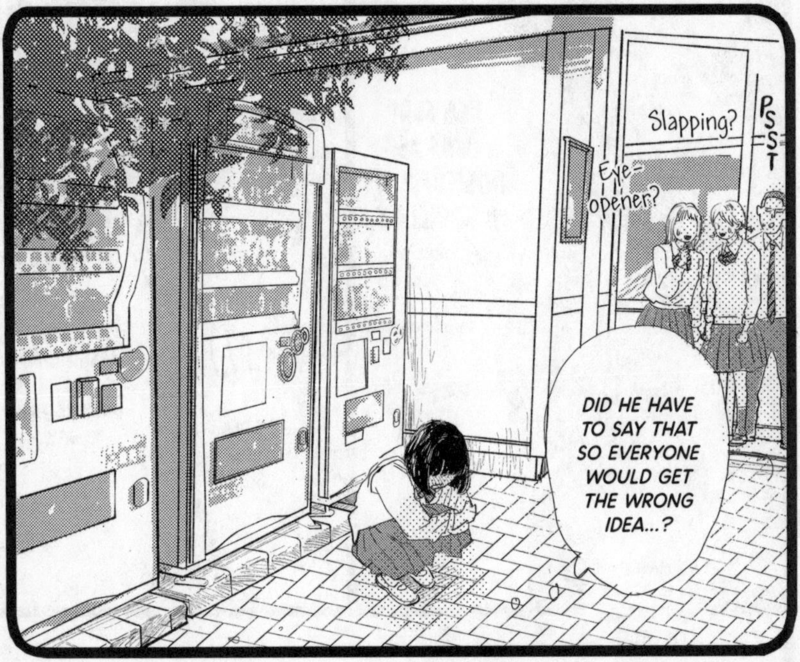
PSST
Slapping?
Eye-opener?
DID HE HAVE TO SAY THAT SO EVERYONE WOULD GET THE WRONG IDEA...?

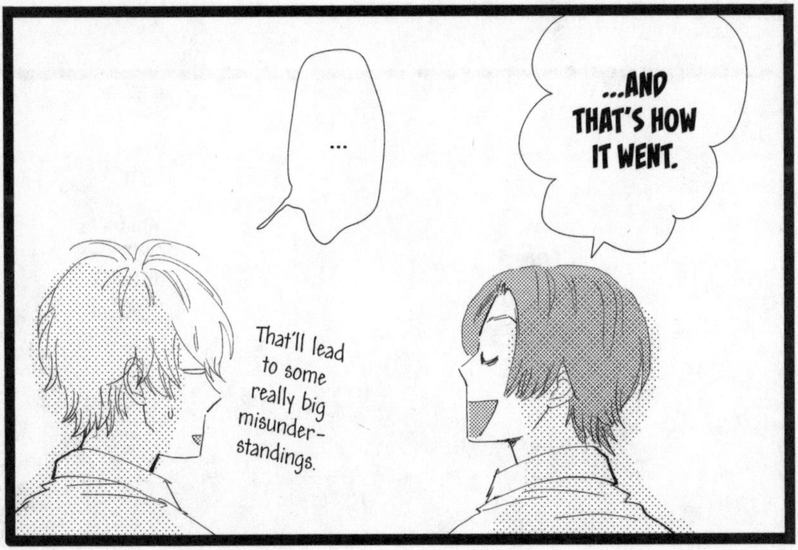
...AND THAT'S HOW IT WENT.
...
That'll lead to some really big misunder-standings.

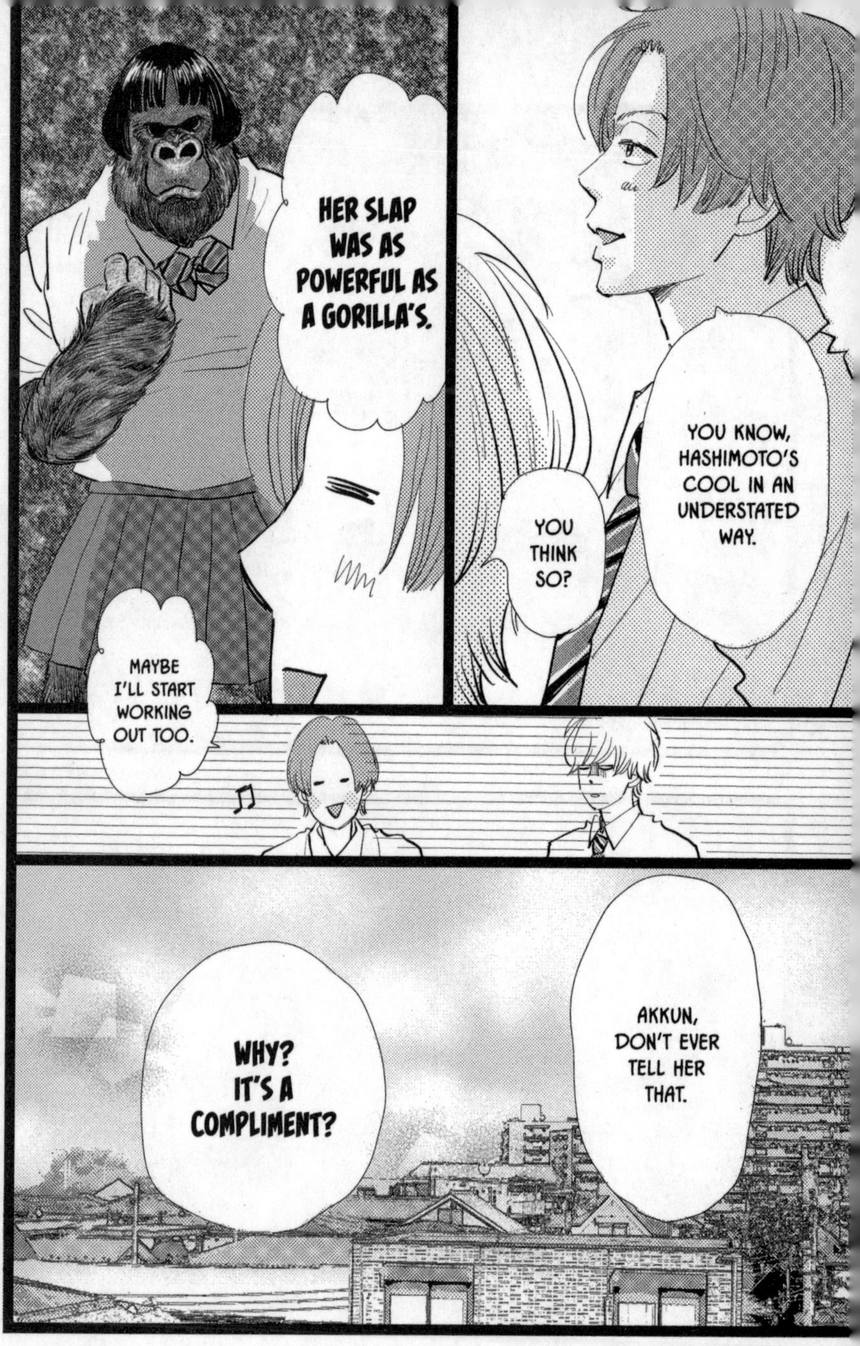
YOU KNOW, HASHIMOTO'S COOL IN AN UNDERSTATED WAY.
YOU THINK SO?
HER SLAP WAS AS POWERFUL AS A GORILLA'S.
MAYBE I'LL START WORKING OUT TOO.
AKKUN, DON'T EVER TELL HER THAT.
WHY? IT'S A COMPLIMENT?

Chapter 9

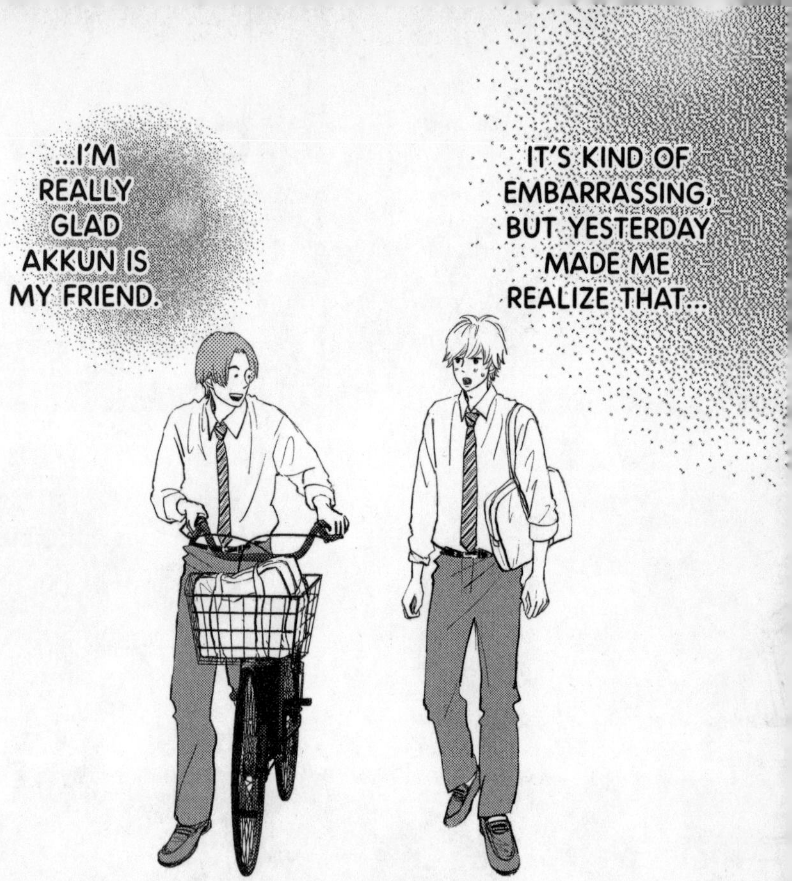
IT'S KIND OF EMBARRASSING, BUT YESTERDAY MADE ME REALIZE THAT...
...I'M REALLY GLAD AKKUN IS MY FRIEND.

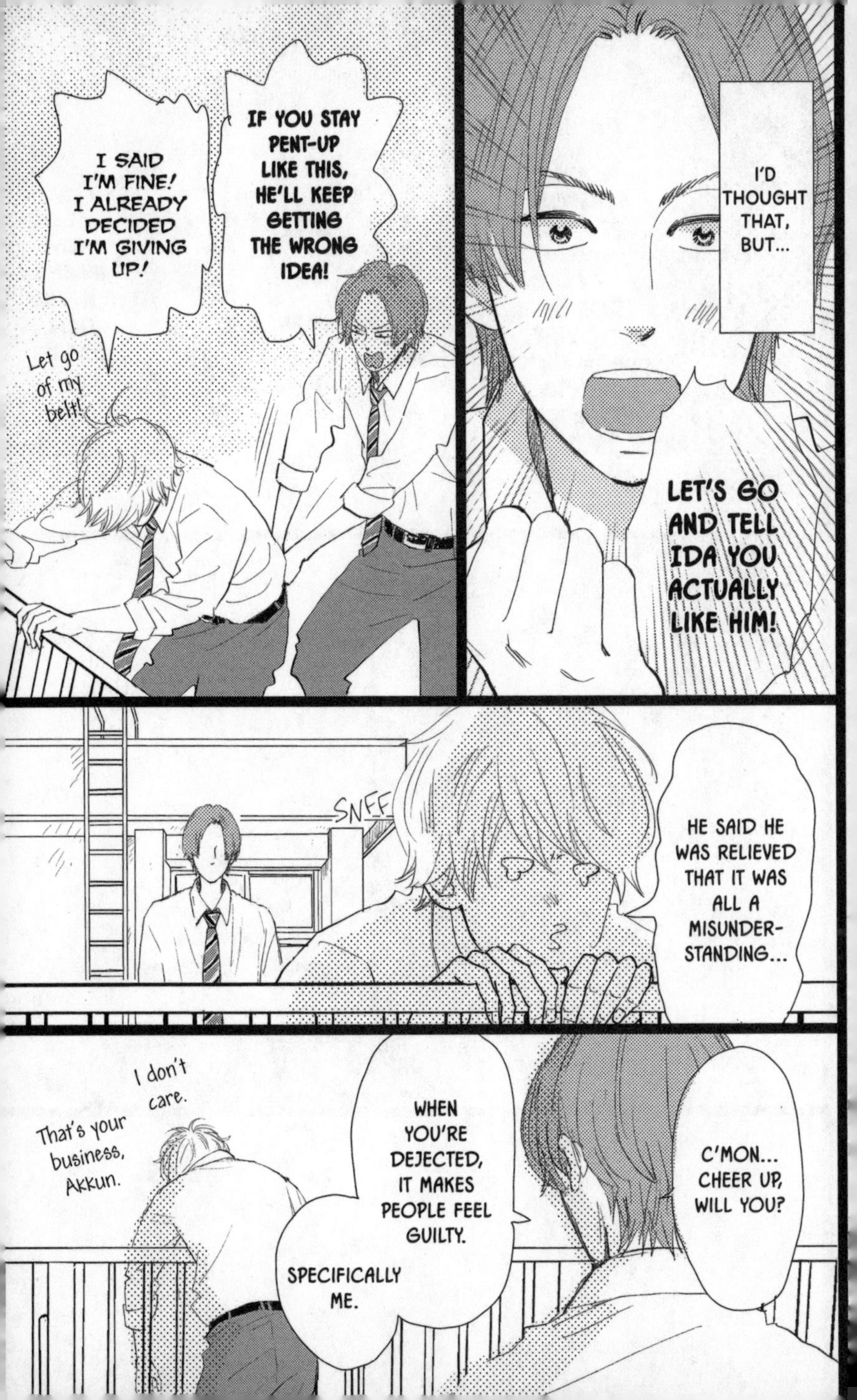
I'D THOUGHT THAT, BUT...
LET'S GO AND TELL IDA YOU ACTUALLY LIKE HIM!
IF YOU STAY PENT-UP LIKE THIS, HE'LL KEEP GETTING THE WRONG IDEA!
I SAID I'M FINE! I ALREADY DECIDED I'M GIVING UP!
Let go of my belt!
HE SAID HE WAS RELIEVED THAT IT WAS ALL A MISUNDER-STANDING...
SNFF
C'MON... CHEER UP, WILL YOU?
WHEN YOU'RE DEJECTED, IT MAKES PEOPLE FEEL GUILTY.
SPECIFICALLY ME.
I don't care.
That's your business, Akkun.

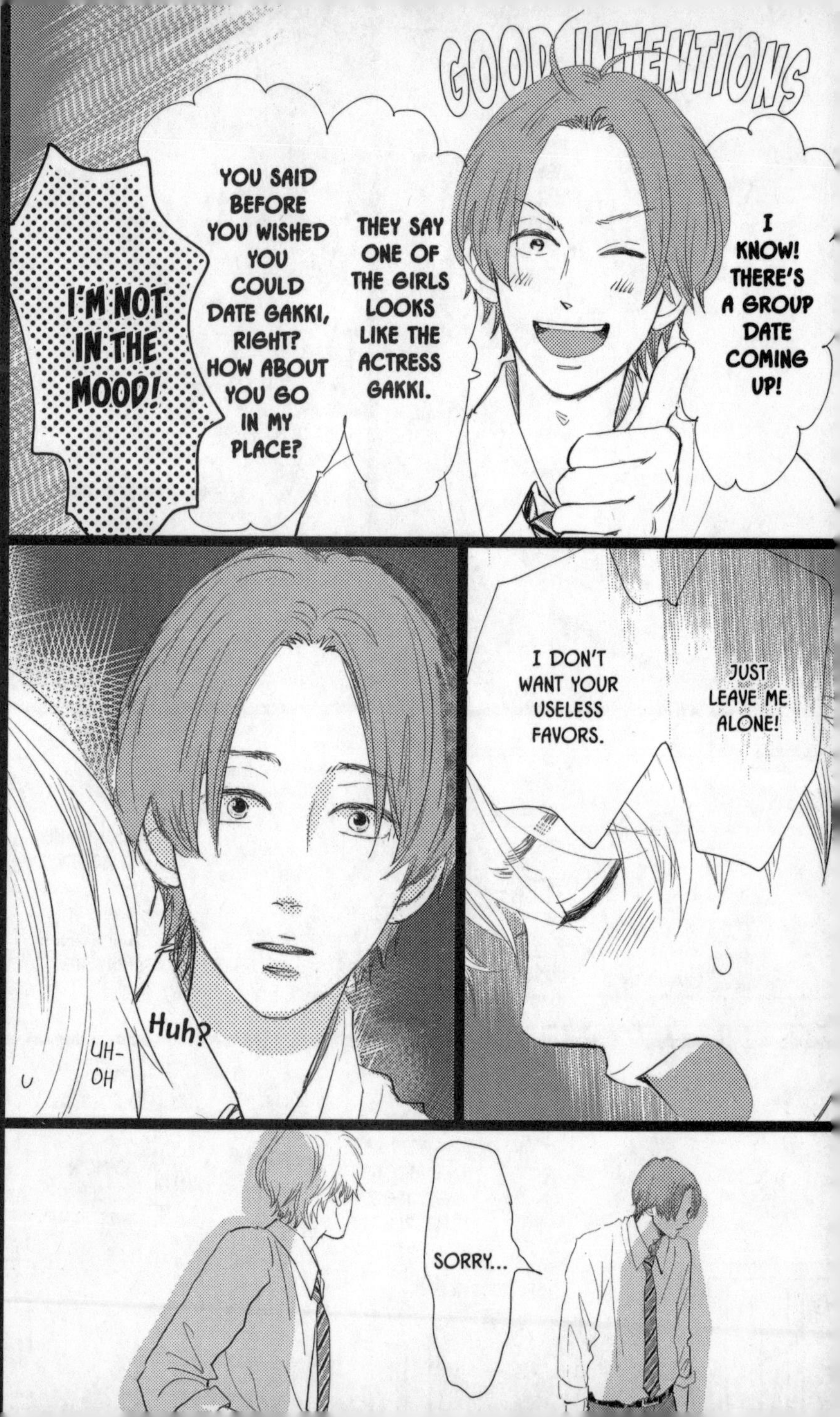
GOOD INTENTIONS
I KNOW! THERE'S A GROUP DATE COMING UP!
THEY SAY ONE OF THE GIRLS LOOKS LIKE THE ACTRESS GAKKI.
YOU SAID BEFORE YOU WISHED YOU COULD DATE GAKKI, RIGHT? HOW ABOUT YOU GO IN MY PLACE?
I'M NOT IN THE MOOD!
JUST LEAVE ME ALONE!
I DON'T WANT YOUR USELESS FAVORS.
Huh?
UH-OH
SORRY...

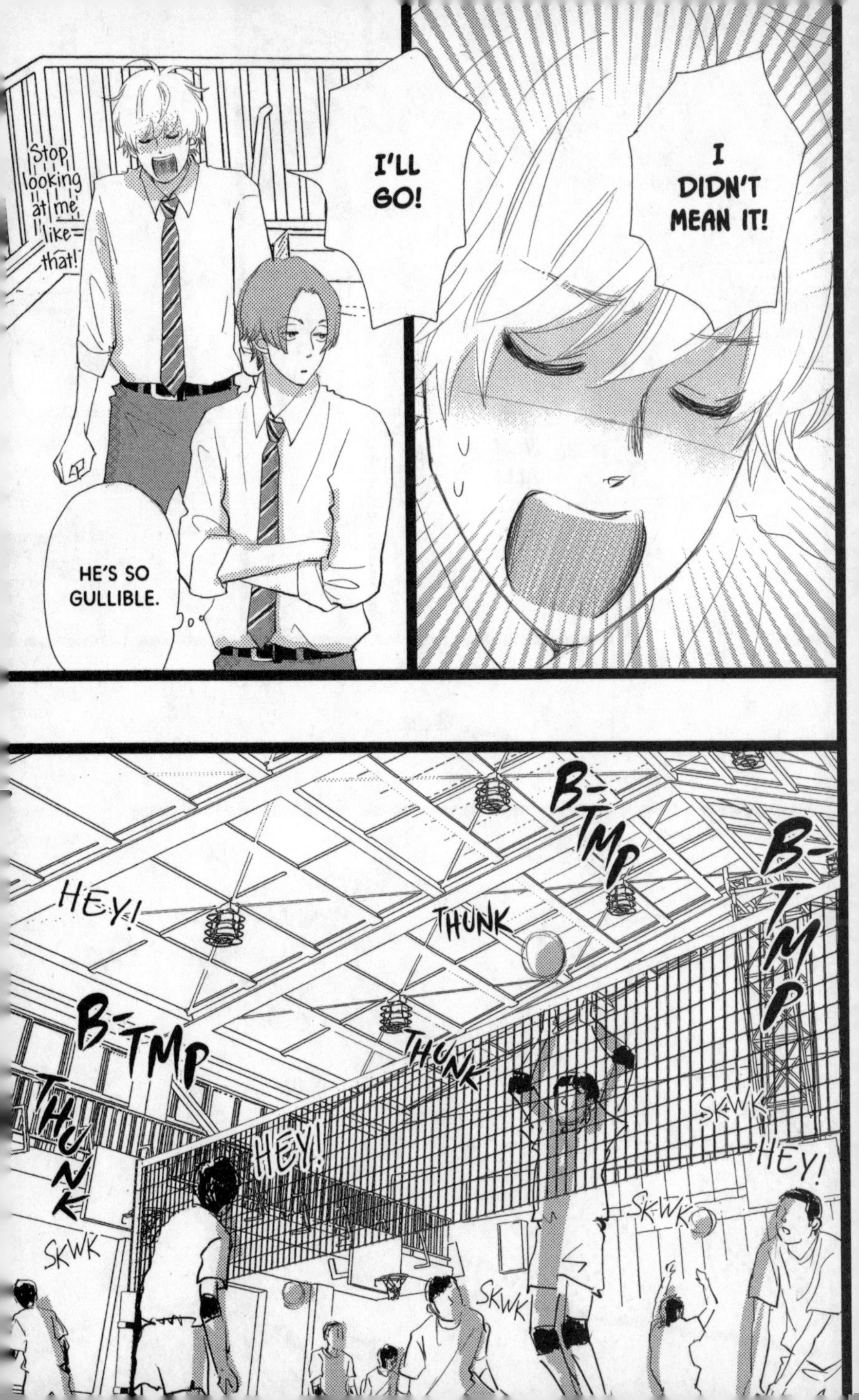
I DIDN'T MEAN IT!
I'LL GO!
Stop looking at me like that!
HE'S SO GULLIBLE.
B-TMP
B-TMP
THUNK
HEY!
THUNK
B-TMP
THUNK
HEY!
SKWK
HEY!
SKWK
SKWK
SKWK

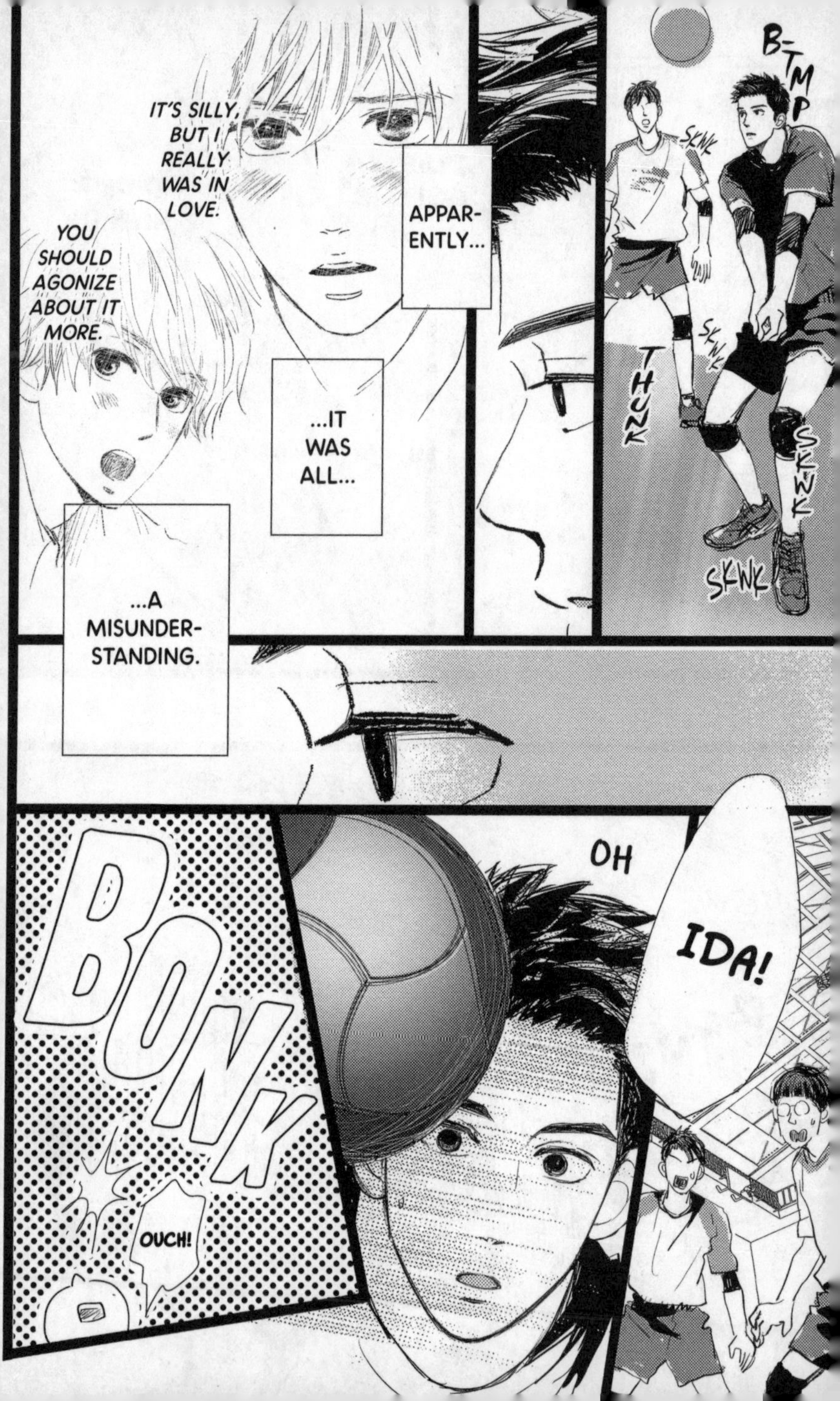

B-TMP
SKWK
SKWK
THUNK
SKWK
SKWK
APPARENTLY...
IT'S SILLY, BUT I REALLY WAS IN LOVE.
YOU SHOULD AGONIZE ABOUT IT MORE.
...IT WAS ALL...
...A MISUNDERSTANDING.
OH
IDA!
BONK
OUCH!

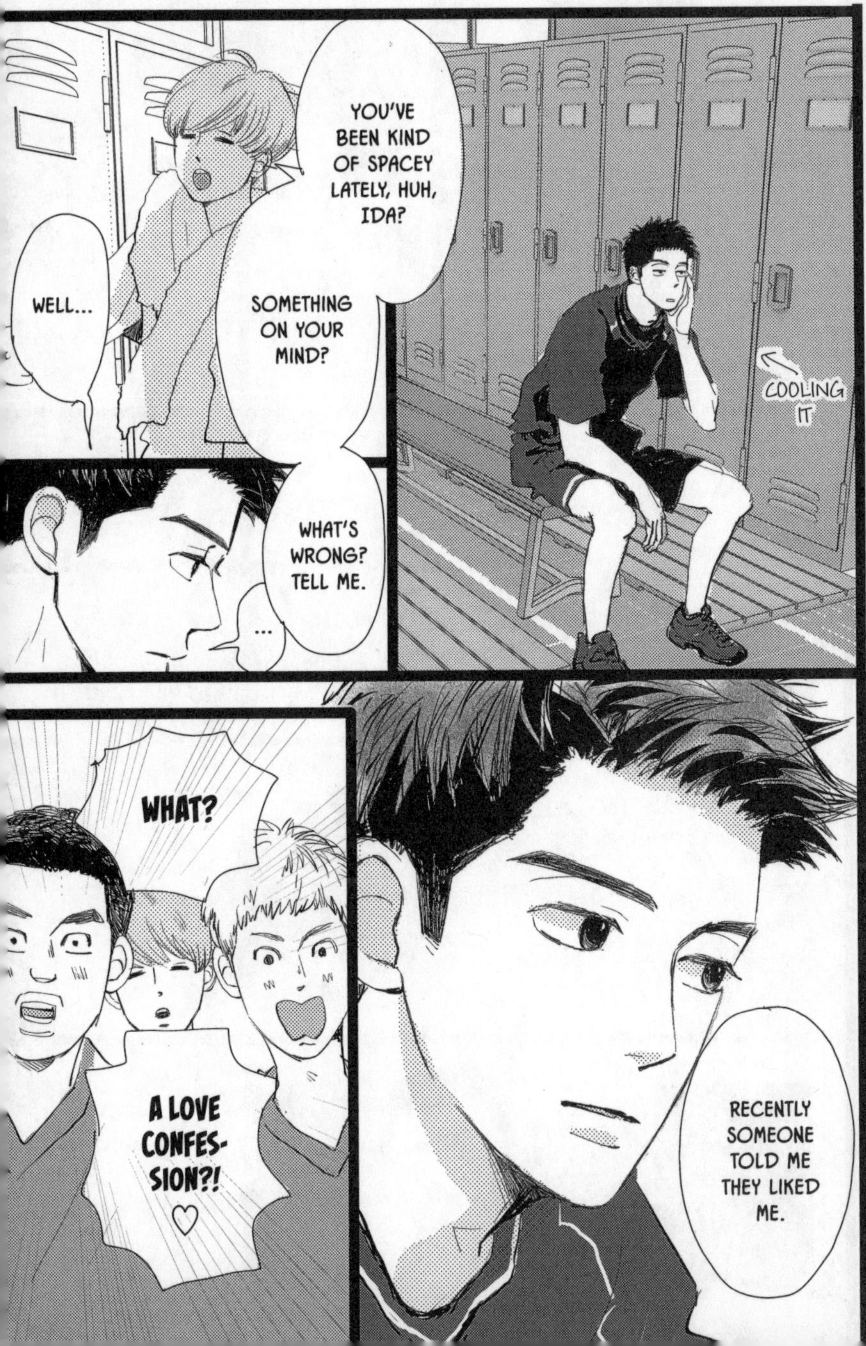
YOU'VE BEEN KIND OF SPACEY LATELY, HUH, IDA?
COOLING IT
SOMETHING ON YOUR MIND?
WELL...
WHAT'S WRONG? TELL ME.
...
RECENTLY SOMEONE TOLD ME THEY LIKED ME.
WHAT?
A LOVE CONFES-SION?! ♡

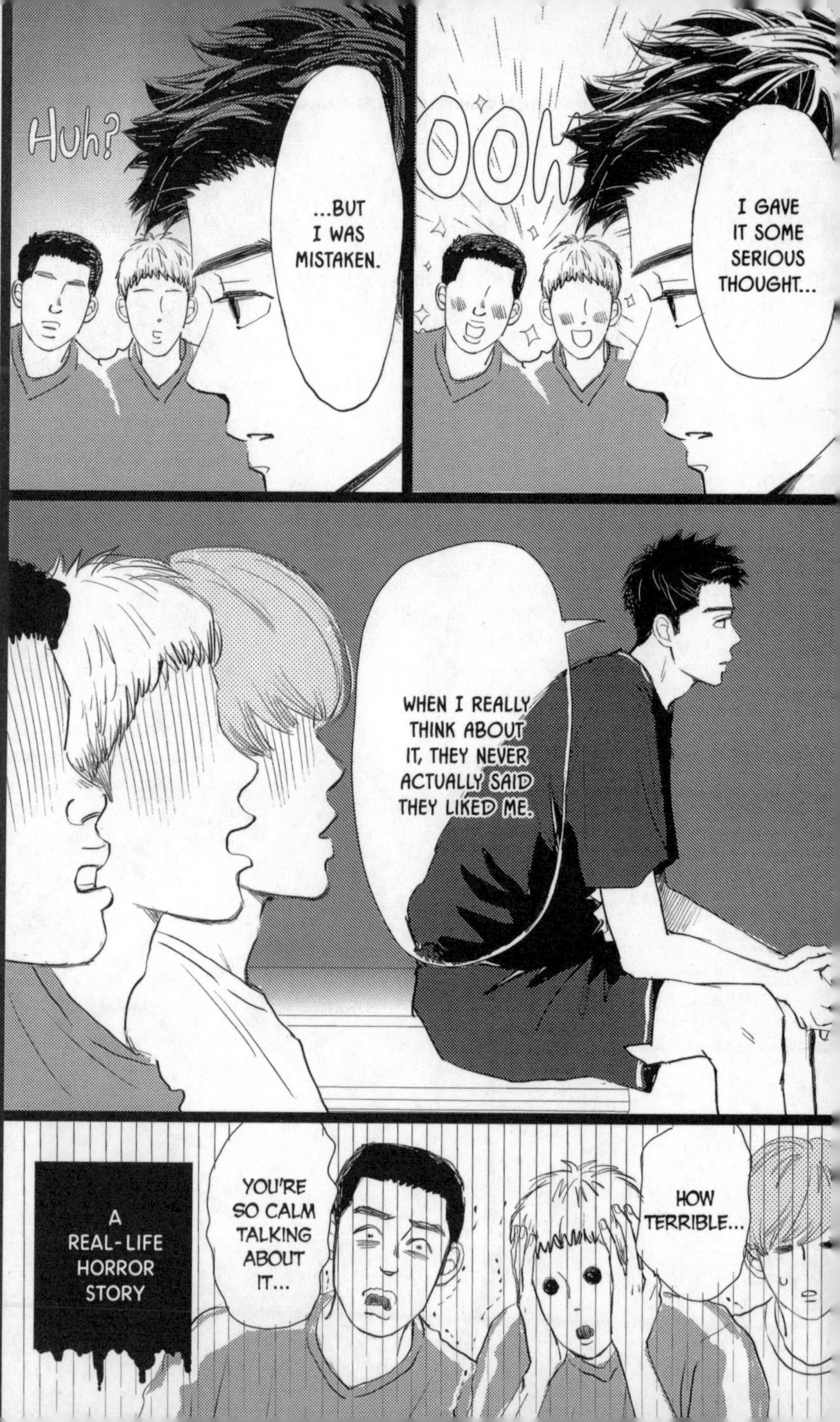
I GAVE IT SOME SERIOUS THOUGHT...
OOH
...BUT I WAS MISTAKEN.
Huh?
WHEN I REALLY THINK ABOUT IT, THEY NEVER ACTUALLY SAID THEY LIKED ME.
HOW TERRIBLE...
YOU'RE SO CALM TALKING ABOUT IT...
A REAL-LIFE HORROR STORY

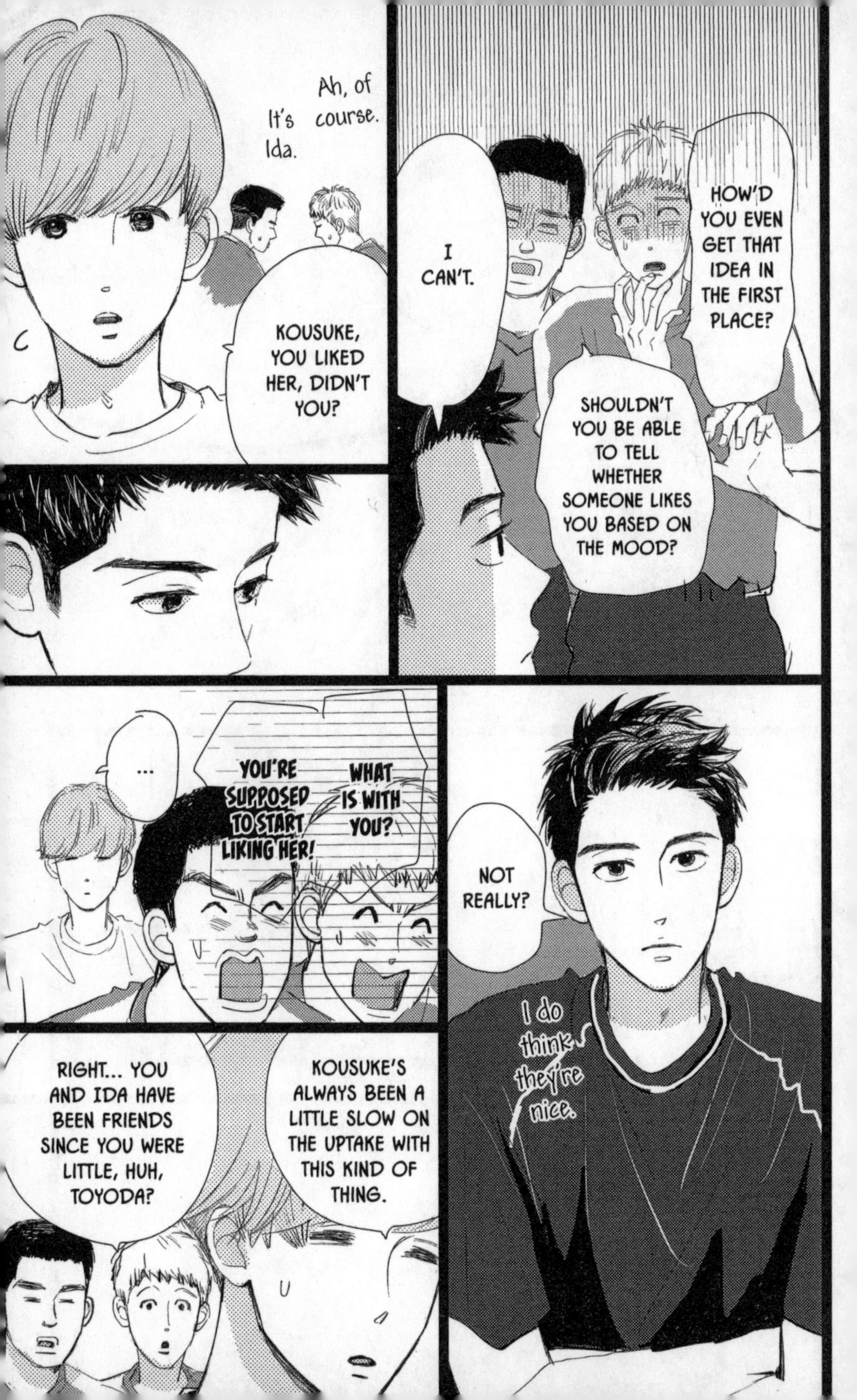
HOW'D YOU EVEN GET THAT IDEA IN THE FIRST PLACE?
I CAN'T.
SHOULDN'T YOU BE ABLE TO TELL WHETHER SOMEONE LIKES YOU BASED ON THE MOOD?
Ah, of course.
It's Ida.
KOUSUKE, YOU LIKED HER, DIDN'T YOU?
NOT REALLY?
I do think they're nice.
WHAT IS WITH YOU?
YOU'RE SUPPOSED TO START LIKING HER!
...
KOUSUKE'S ALWAYS BEEN A LITTLE SLOW ON THE UPTAKE WITH THIS KIND OF THING.
RIGHT... YOU AND IDA HAVE BEEN FRIENDS SINCE YOU WERE LITTLE, HUH, TOYODA?

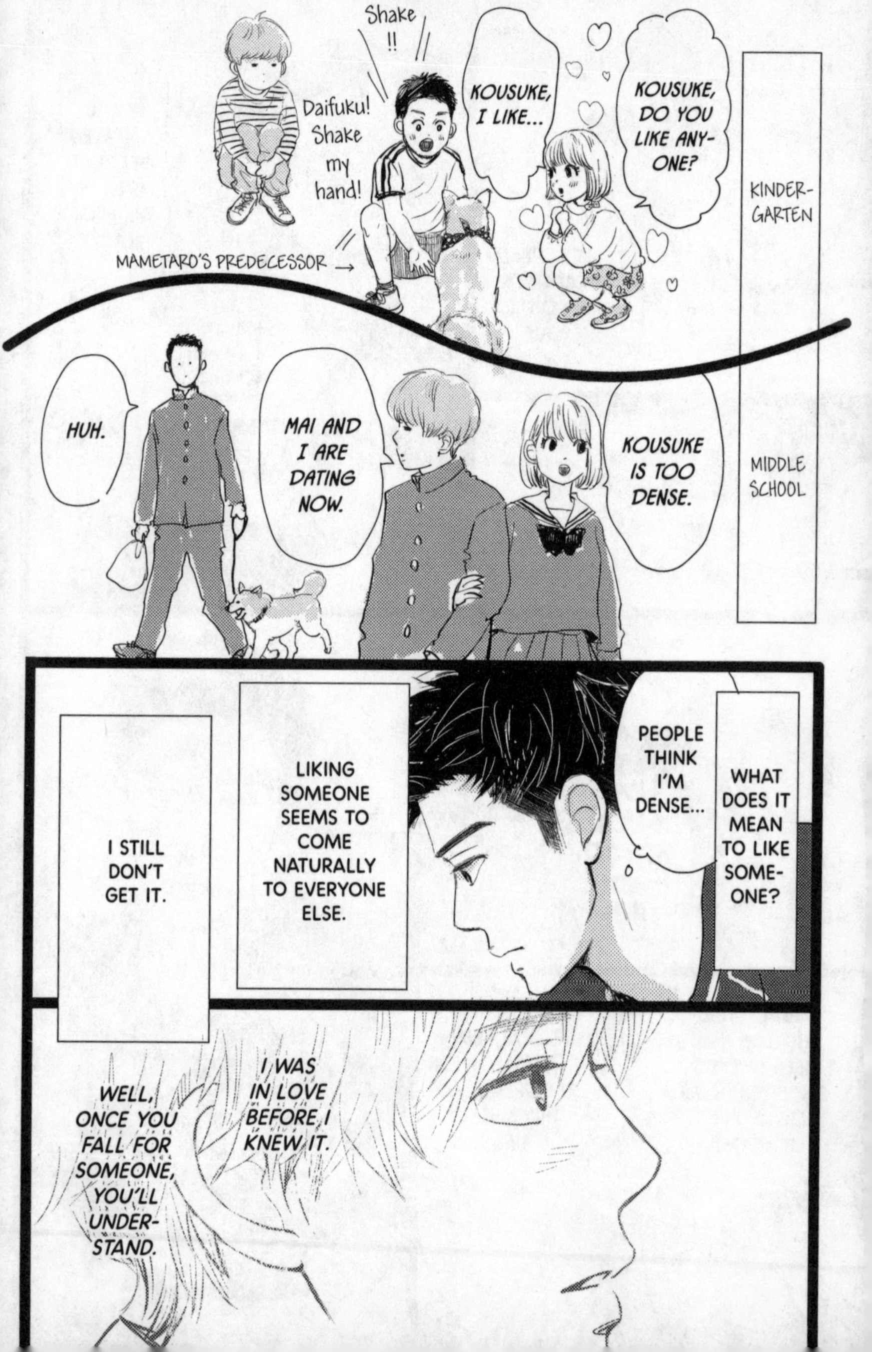
KINDERGARTEN
KOUSUKE, DO YOU LIKE ANYONE?
KOUSUKE, I LIKE...
Shake !!
Daifuku! Shake my hand!
MAMETARO'S PREDECESSOR →
MIDDLE SCHOOL
KOUSUKE IS TOO DENSE.
MAI AND I ARE DATING NOW.
HUH.
WHAT DOES IT MEAN TO LIKE SOMEONE?
PEOPLE THINK I'M DENSE...
LIKING SOMEONE SEEMS TO COME NATURALLY TO EVERYONE ELSE.
I STILL DON'T GET IT.
I WAS IN LOVE BEFORE I KNEW IT.
WELL, ONCE YOU FALL FOR SOMEONE, YOU'LL UNDERSTAND.

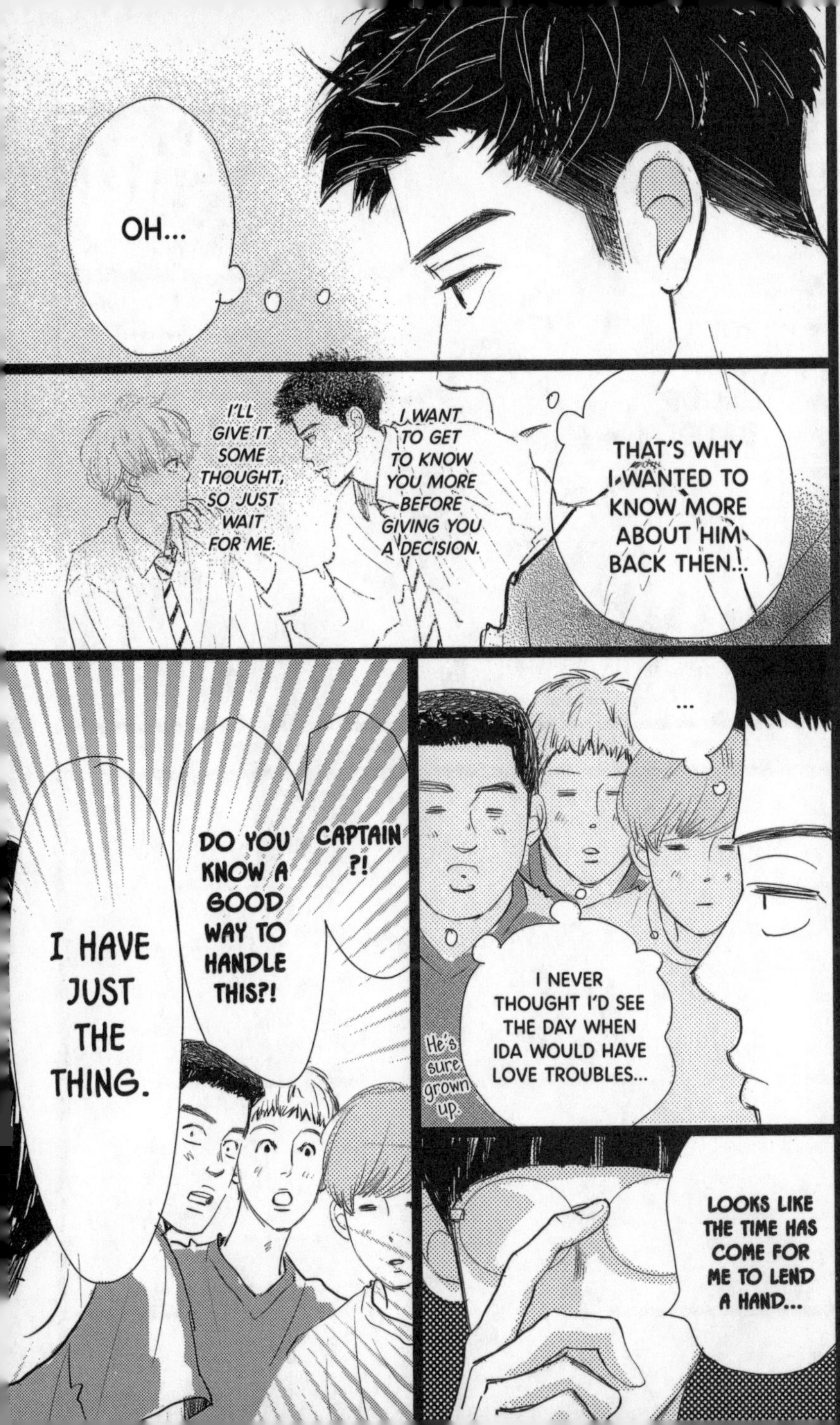
OH...
THAT'S WHY I WANTED TO KNOW MORE ABOUT HIM BACK THEN...
I WANT TO GET TO KNOW YOU MORE BEFORE GIVING YOU A DECISION.
I'LL GIVE IT SOME THOUGHT, SO JUST WAIT FOR ME.
...
I NEVER THOUGHT I'D SEE THE DAY WHEN IDA WOULD HAVE LOVE TROUBLES...
He's sure grown up.
LOOKS LIKE THE TIME HAS COME FOR ME TO LEND A HAND...
CAPTAIN?!
DO YOU KNOW A GOOD WAY TO HANDLE THIS?!
I HAVE JUST THE THING.

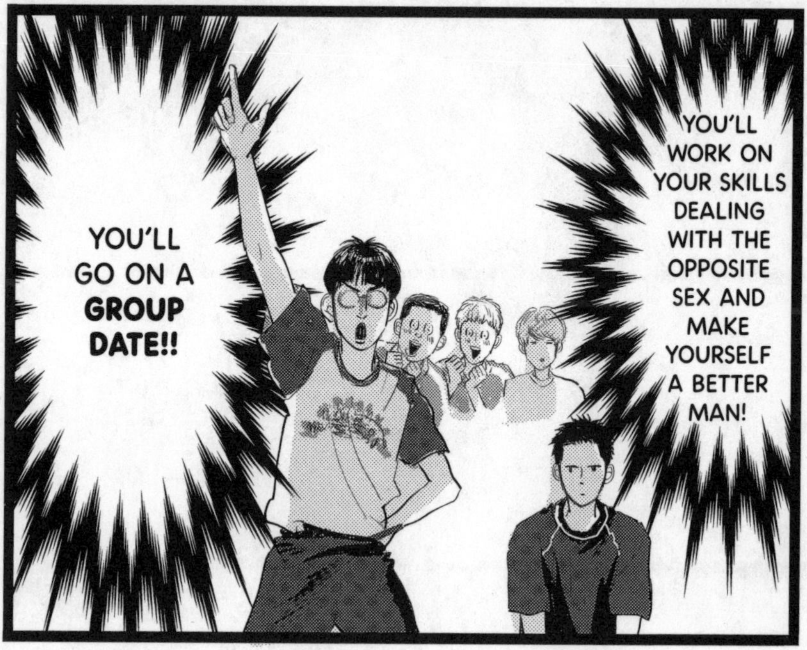
YOU'LL WORK ON YOUR SKILLS DEALING WITH THE OPPOSITE SEX AND MAKE YOURSELF A BETTER MAN!
YOU'LL GO ON A **GROUP DATE!!**

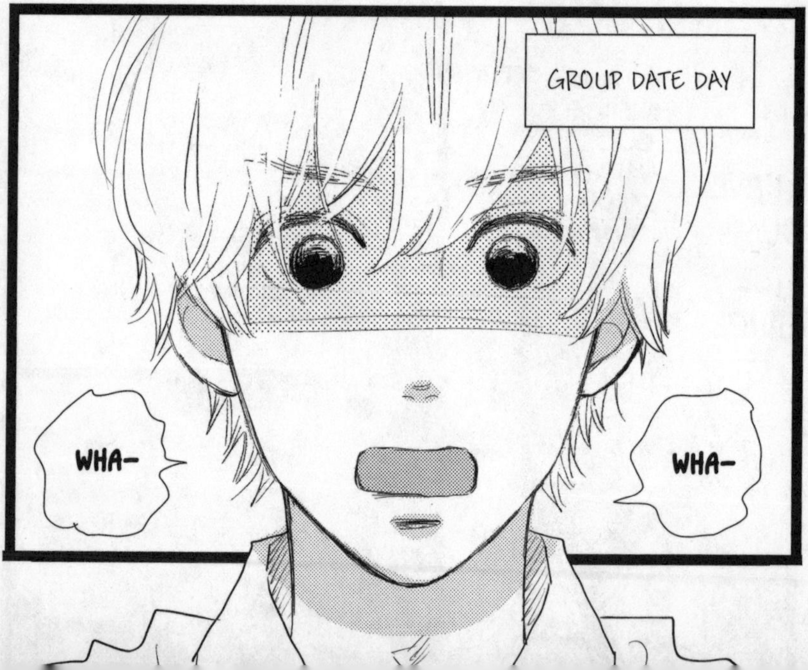
GROUP DATE DAY
WHA-
WHA-

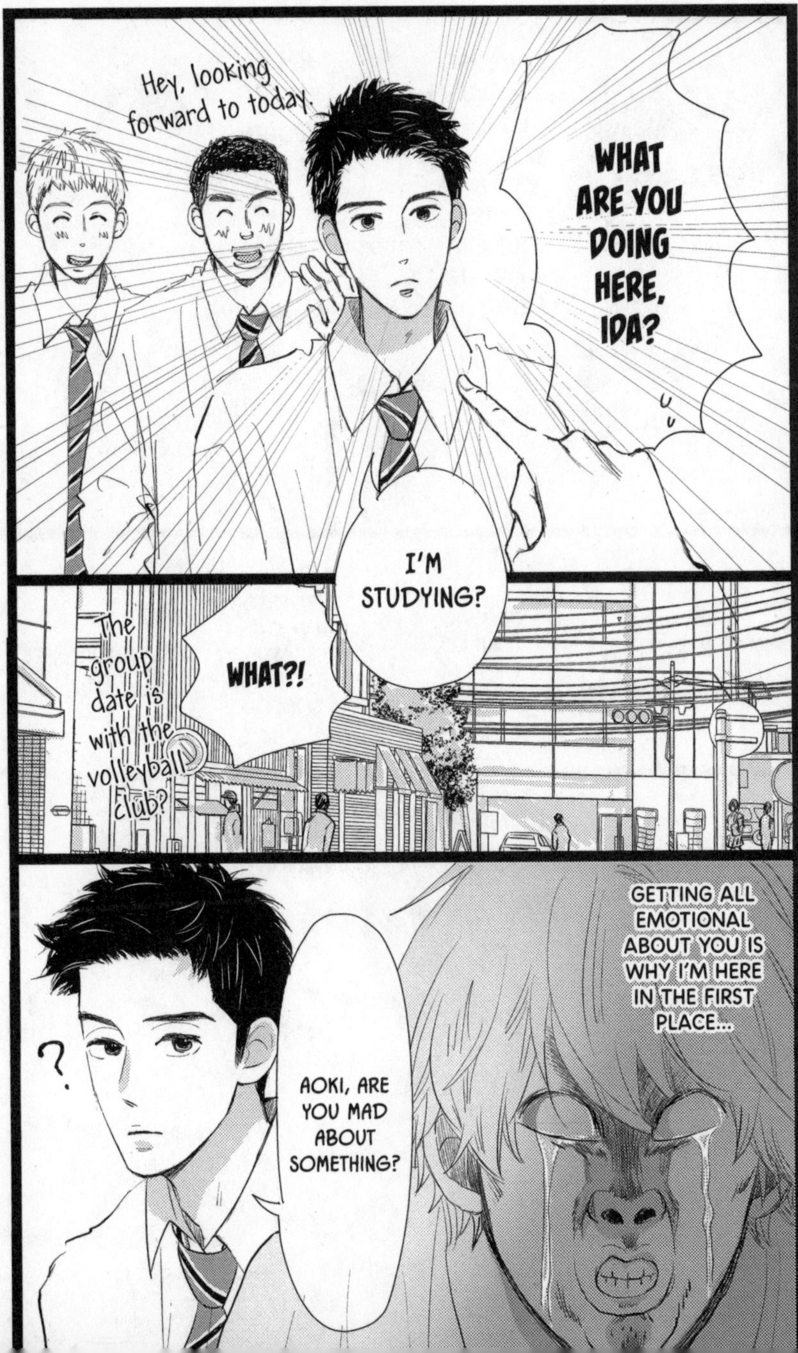
WHAT ARE YOU DOING HERE, IDA?
Hey, looking forward to today.
I'M STUDYING?
WHAT?!
The group date is with the volleyball club?
GETTING ALL EMOTIONAL ABOUT YOU IS WHY I'M HERE IN THE FIRST PLACE...
AOKI, ARE YOU MAD ABOUT SOMETHING?
?

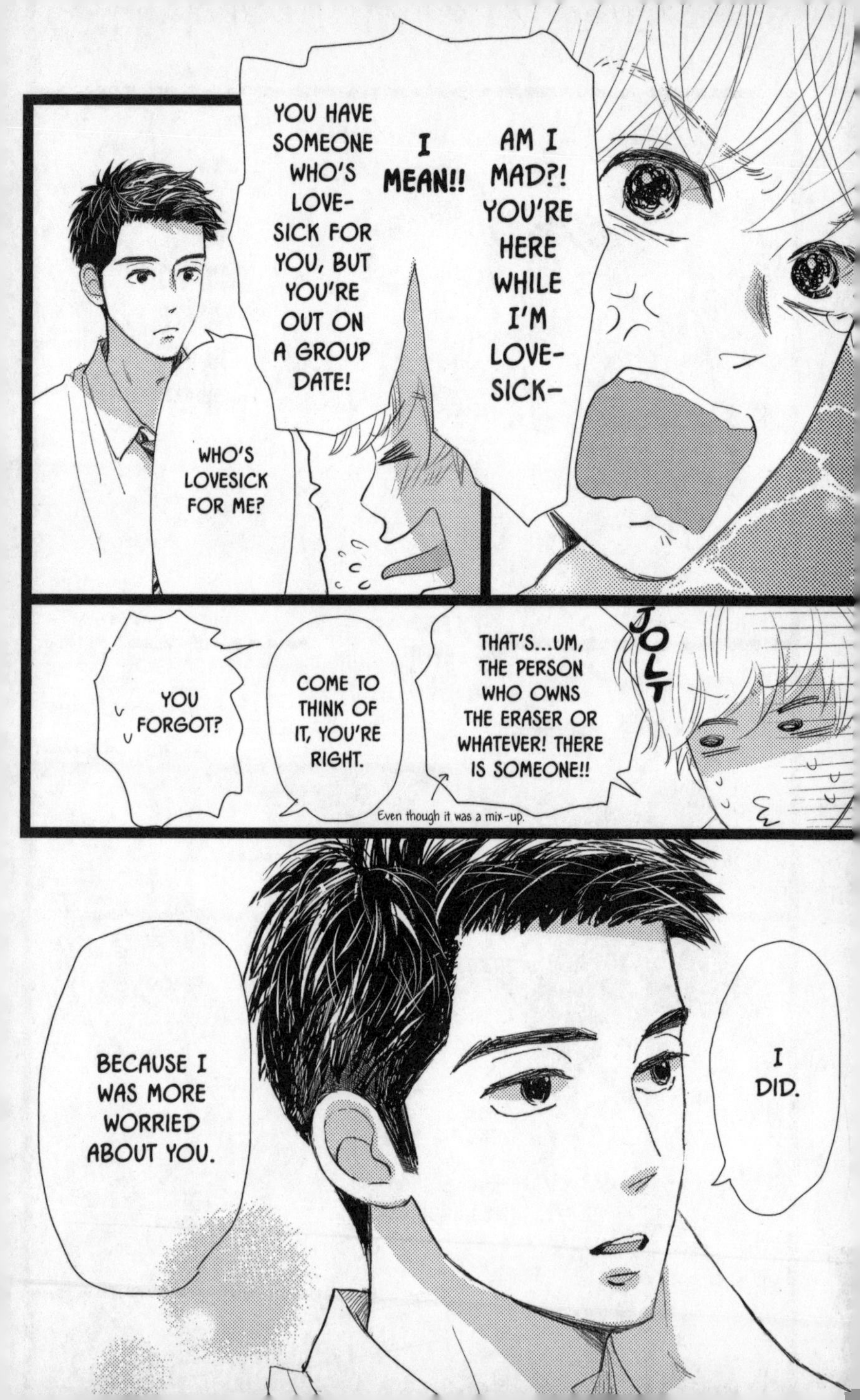
AM I MAD?! YOU'RE HERE WHILE I'M LOVE-SICK-
I MEAN!!
YOU HAVE SOMEONE WHO'S LOVE-SICK FOR YOU, BUT YOU'RE OUT ON A GROUP DATE!
WHO'S LOVESICK FOR ME?
JOLT
THAT'S...UM, THE PERSON WHO OWNS THE ERASER OR WHATEVER! THERE IS SOMEONE!!
Even though it was a mix-up.
COME TO THINK OF IT, YOU'RE RIGHT.
YOU FORGOT?
I DID.
BECAUSE I WAS MORE WORRIED ABOUT YOU.

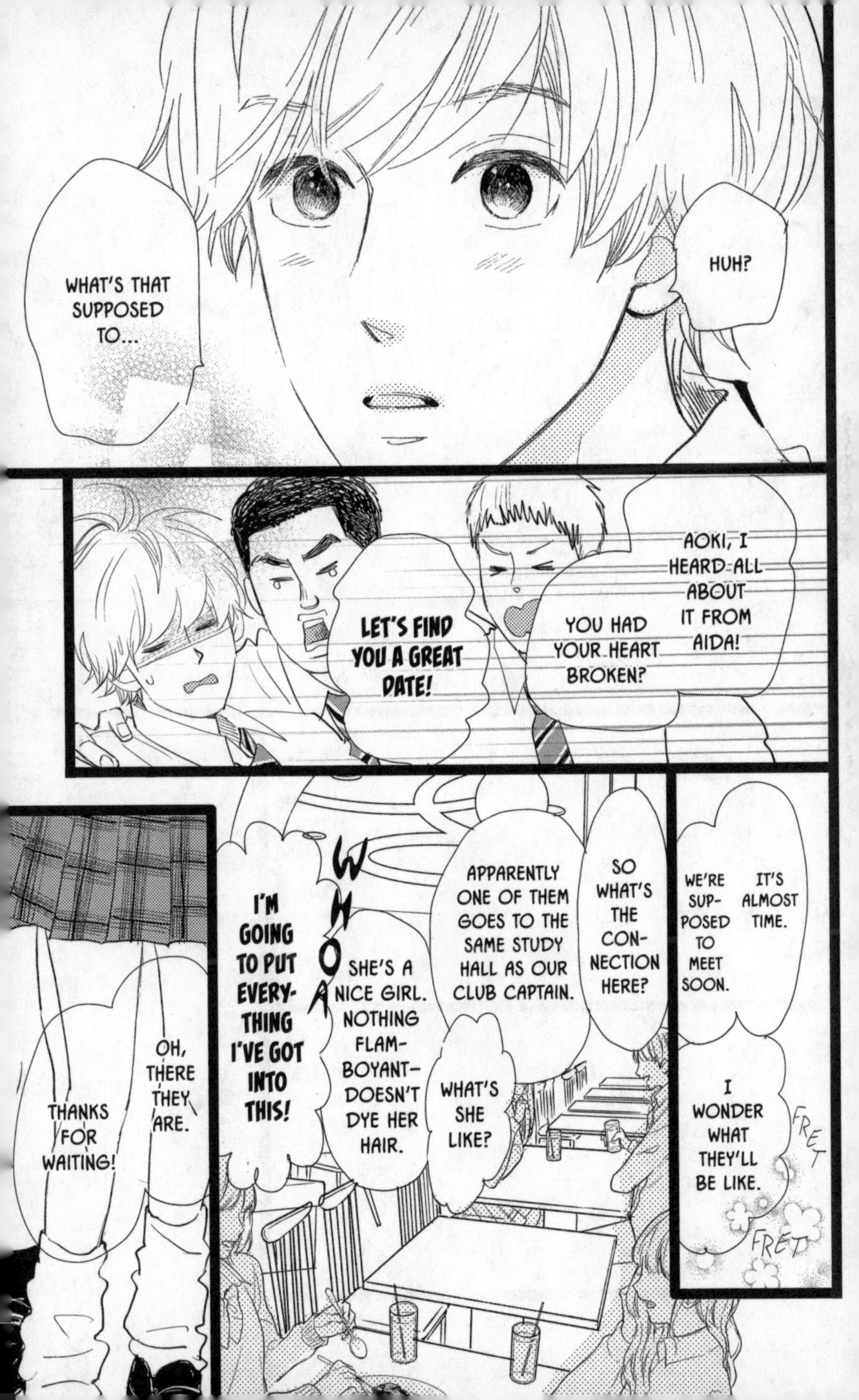
HUH?
WHAT'S THAT SUPPOSED TO...
AOKI, I HEARD ALL ABOUT IT FROM AIDA!
YOU HAD YOUR HEART BROKEN?
LET'S FIND YOU A GREAT DATE!
IT'S ALMOST TIME.
WE'RE SUPPOSED TO MEET SOON.
I WONDER WHAT THEY'LL BE LIKE.
FRET
FRET
SO WHAT'S THE CONNECTION HERE?
APPARENTLY ONE OF THEM GOES TO THE SAME STUDY HALL AS OUR CLUB CAPTAIN.
WHAT'S SHE LIKE?
SHE'S A NICE GIRL. NOTHING FLAMBOYANT— DOESN'T DYE HER HAIR.
WHOA
I'M GOING TO PUT EVERYTHING I'VE GOT INTO THIS!
OH, THERE THEY ARE.
THANKS FOR WAITING!

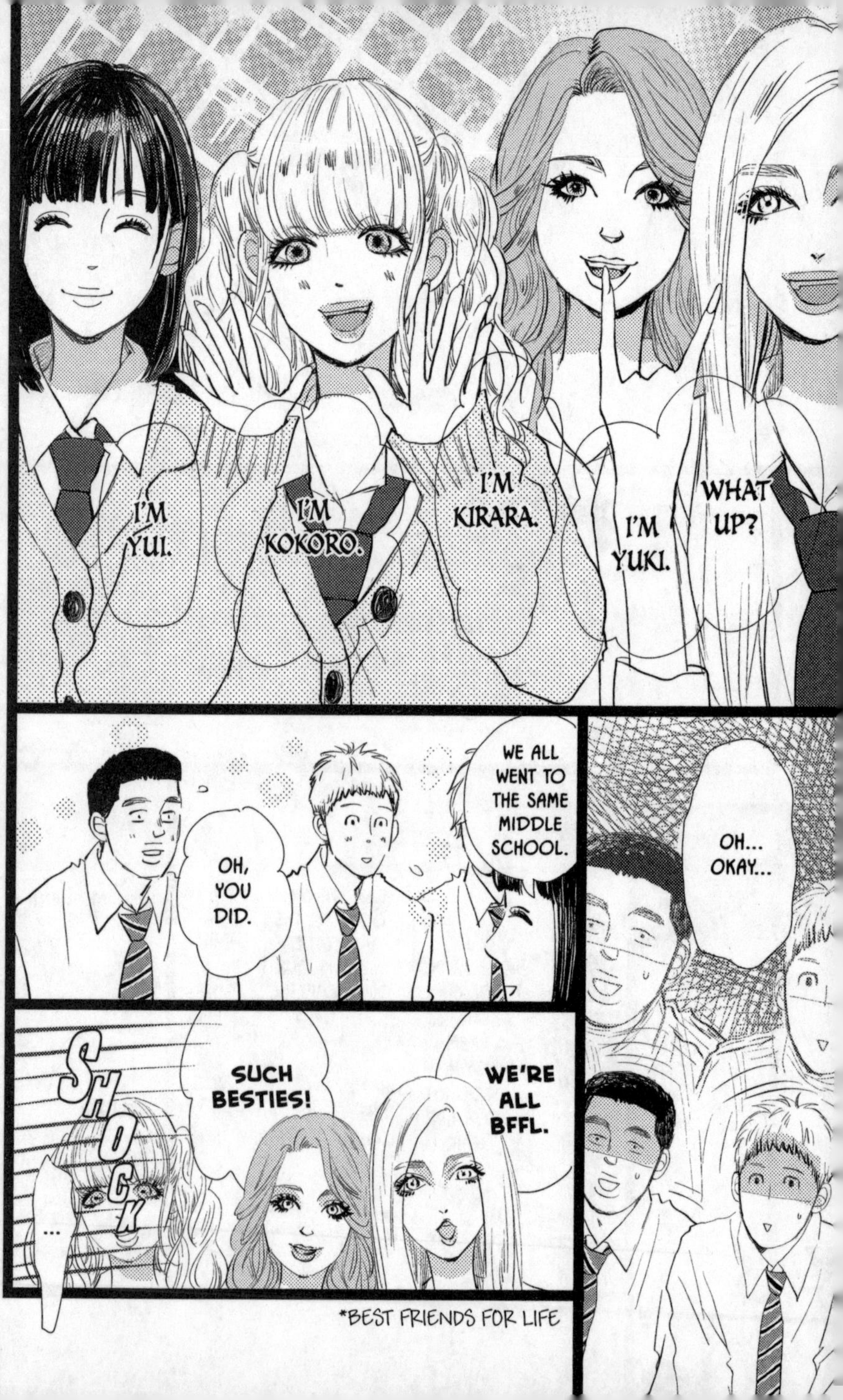
WHAT UP?
I'M YUKI.
I'M KIRARA.
I'M KOKORO.
I'M YUI.
OH... OKAY...
WE ALL WENT TO THE SAME MIDDLE SCHOOL.
OH, YOU DID.
WE'RE ALL BFFL.
SUCH BESTIES!
SHOCK
...
*BEST FRIENDS FOR LIFE

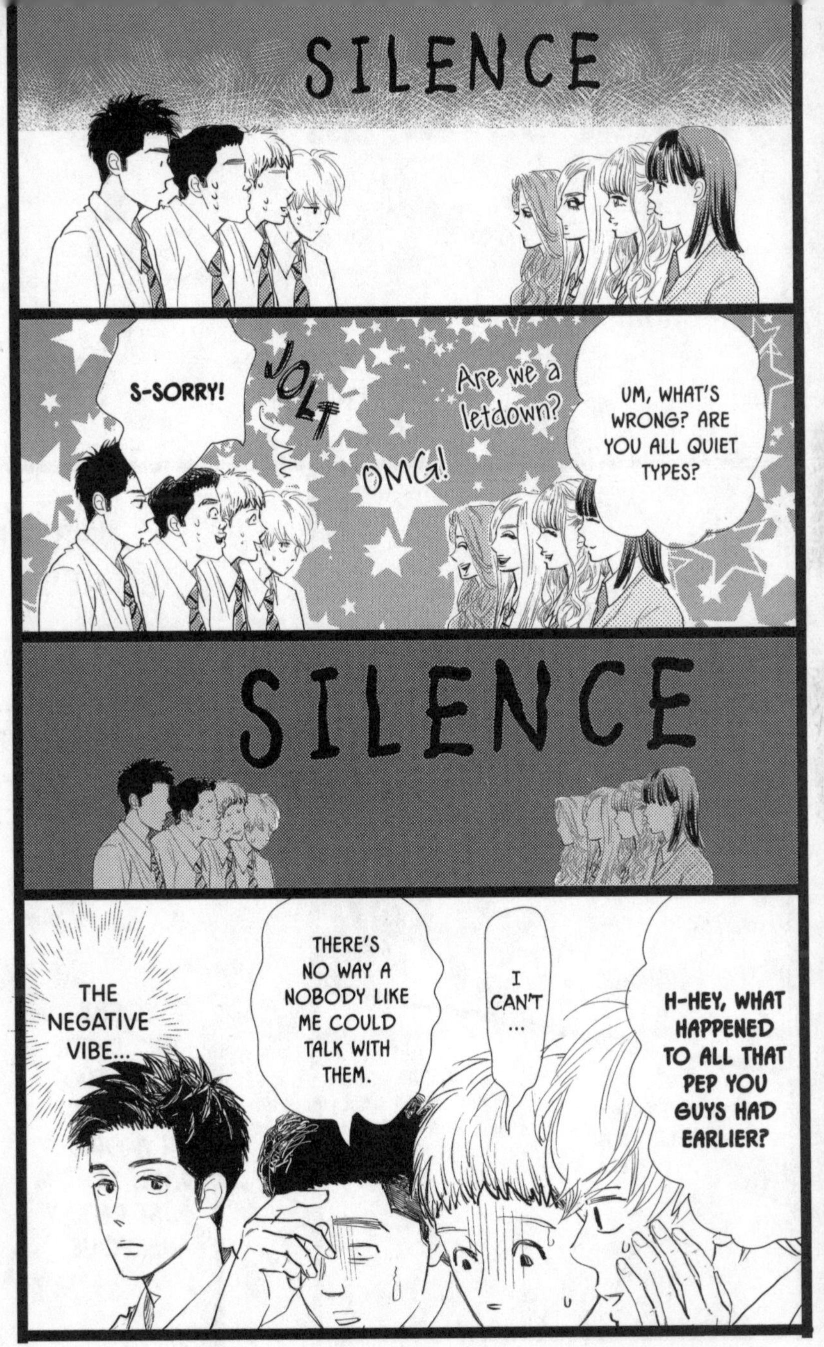
SILENCE
UM, WHAT'S WRONG? ARE YOU ALL QUIET TYPES?
Are we a letdown?
OMG!
JOLT
S-SORRY!
SILENCE
H-HEY, WHAT HAPPENED TO ALL THAT PEP YOU GUYS HAD EARLIER?
I CAN'T ...
THERE'S NO WAY A NOBODY LIKE ME COULD TALK WITH THEM.
THE NEGATIVE VIBE...

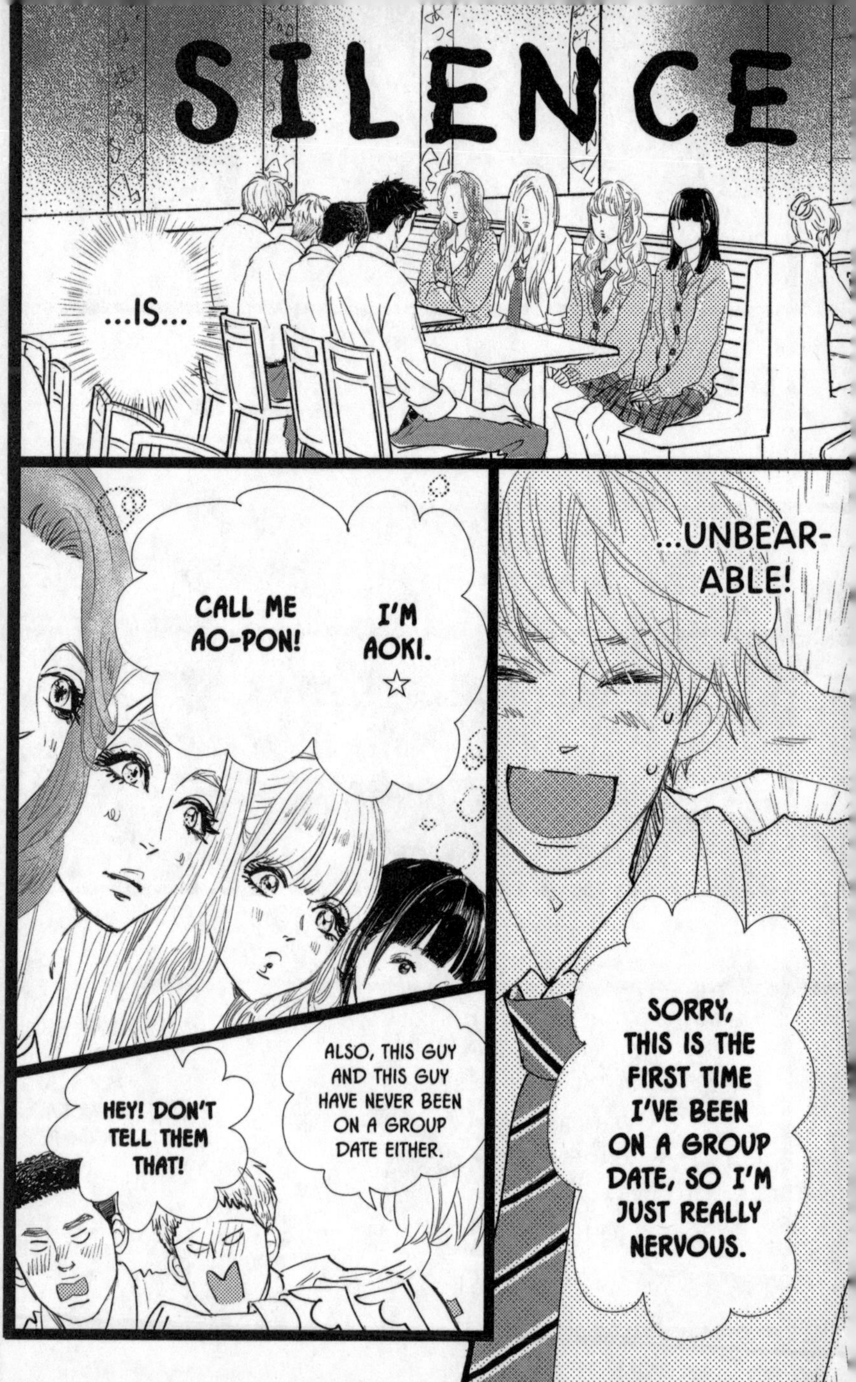
SILENCE
...IS...
...UNBEARABLE!
SORRY, THIS IS THE FIRST TIME I'VE BEEN ON A GROUP DATE, SO I'M JUST REALLY NERVOUS.
I'M AOKI. ☆
CALL ME AO-PON!
ALSO, THIS GUY AND THIS GUY HAVE NEVER BEEN ON A GROUP DATE EITHER.
HEY! DON'T TELL THEM THAT!

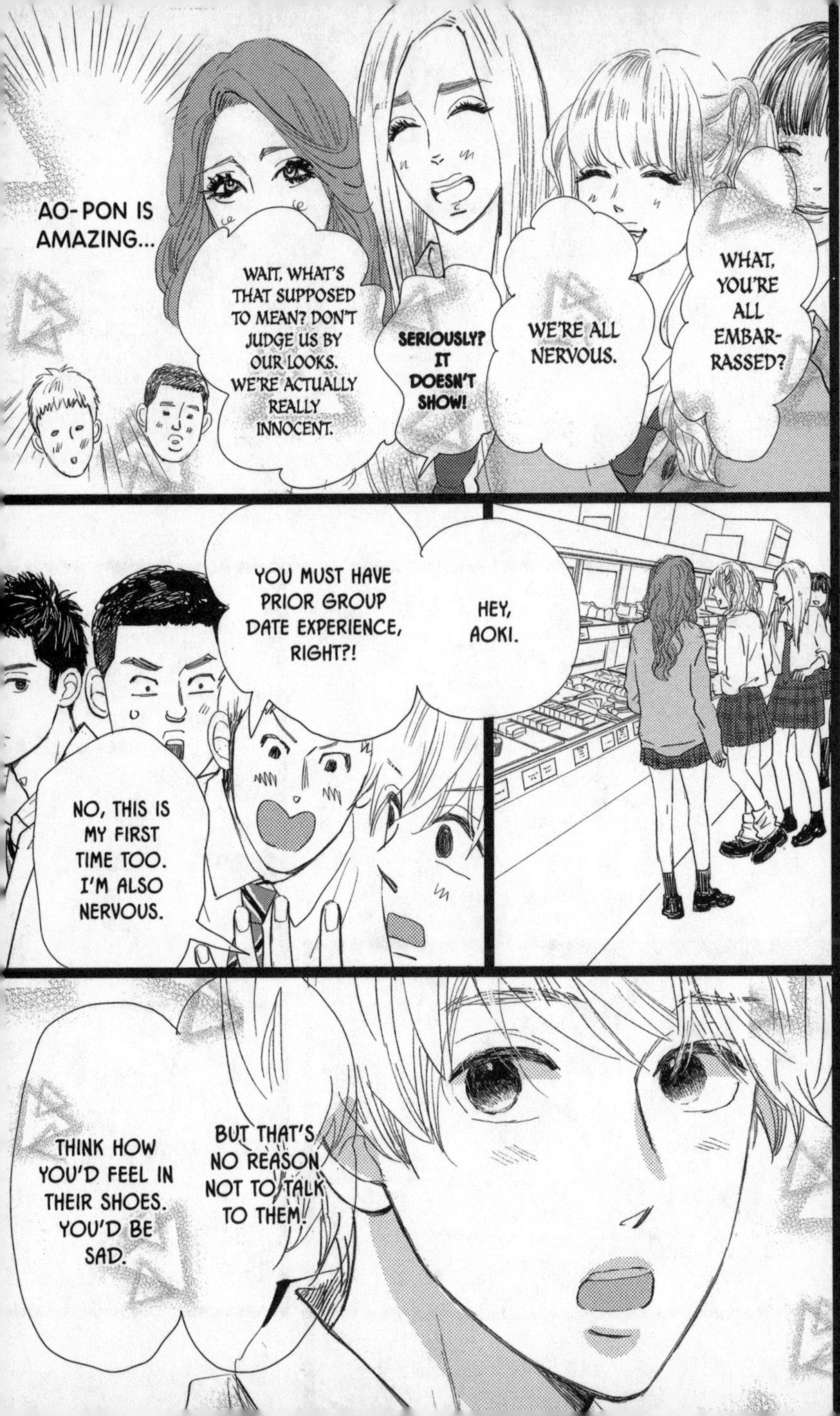

WHAT, YOU'RE ALL EMBARRASSED?
WE'RE ALL NERVOUS.
SERIOUSLY? IT DOESN'T SHOW!
WAIT, WHAT'S THAT SUPPOSED TO MEAN? DON'T JUDGE US BY OUR LOOKS. WE'RE ACTUALLY REALLY INNOCENT.
AO-PON IS AMAZING...
HEY, AOKI.
YOU MUST HAVE PRIOR GROUP DATE EXPERIENCE, RIGHT?!
NO, THIS IS MY FIRST TIME TOO. I'M ALSO NERVOUS.
BUT THAT'S NO REASON NOT TO TALK TO THEM.
THINK HOW YOU'D FEEL IN THEIR SHOES. YOU'D BE SAD.

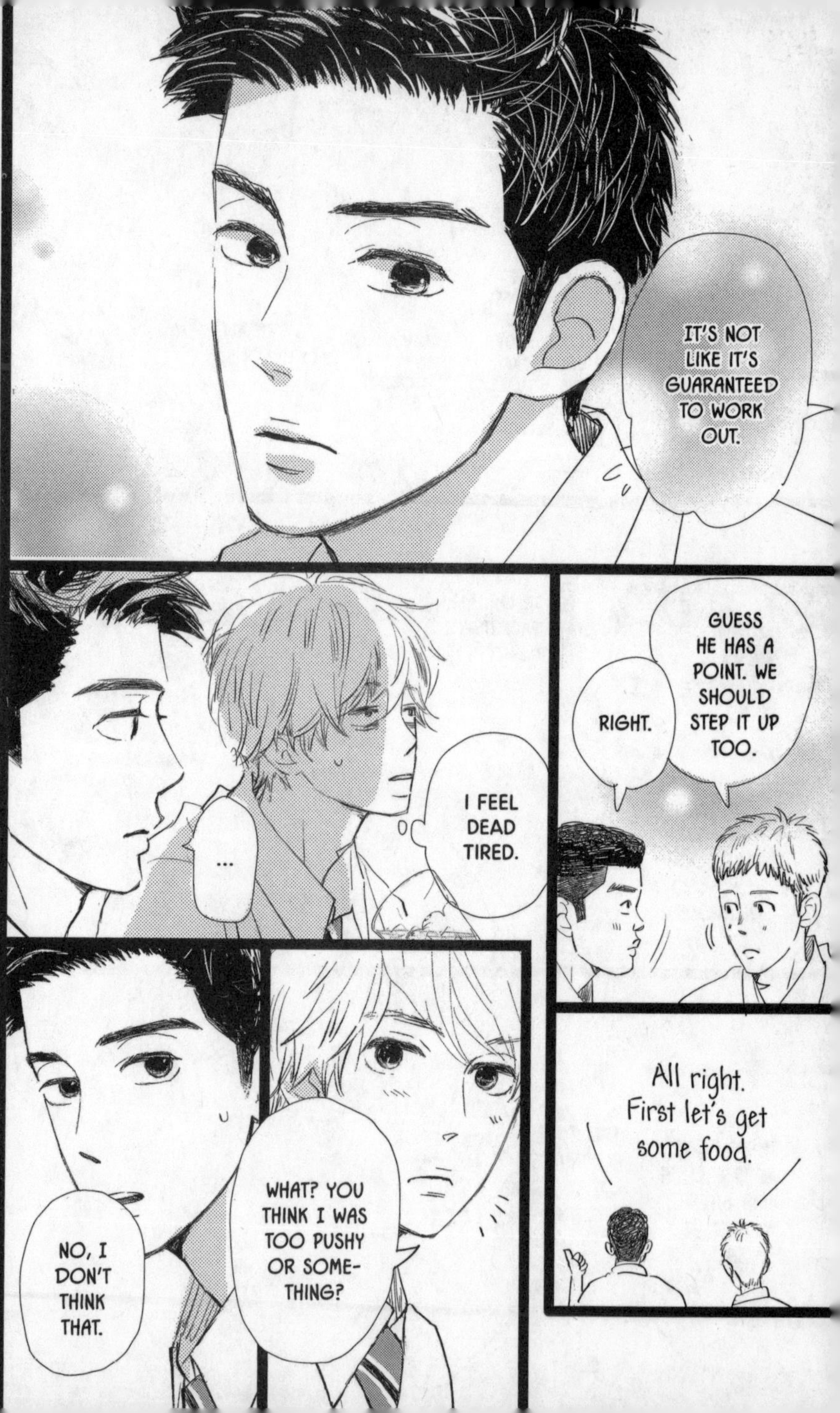
IT'S NOT LIKE IT'S GUARANTEED TO WORK OUT.
GUESS HE HAS A POINT. WE SHOULD STEP IT UP TOO.
RIGHT.
I FEEL DEAD TIRED.
...
WHAT? YOU THINK I WAS TOO PUSHY OR SOME-THING?
NO, I DON'T THINK THAT.
All right. First let's get some food.

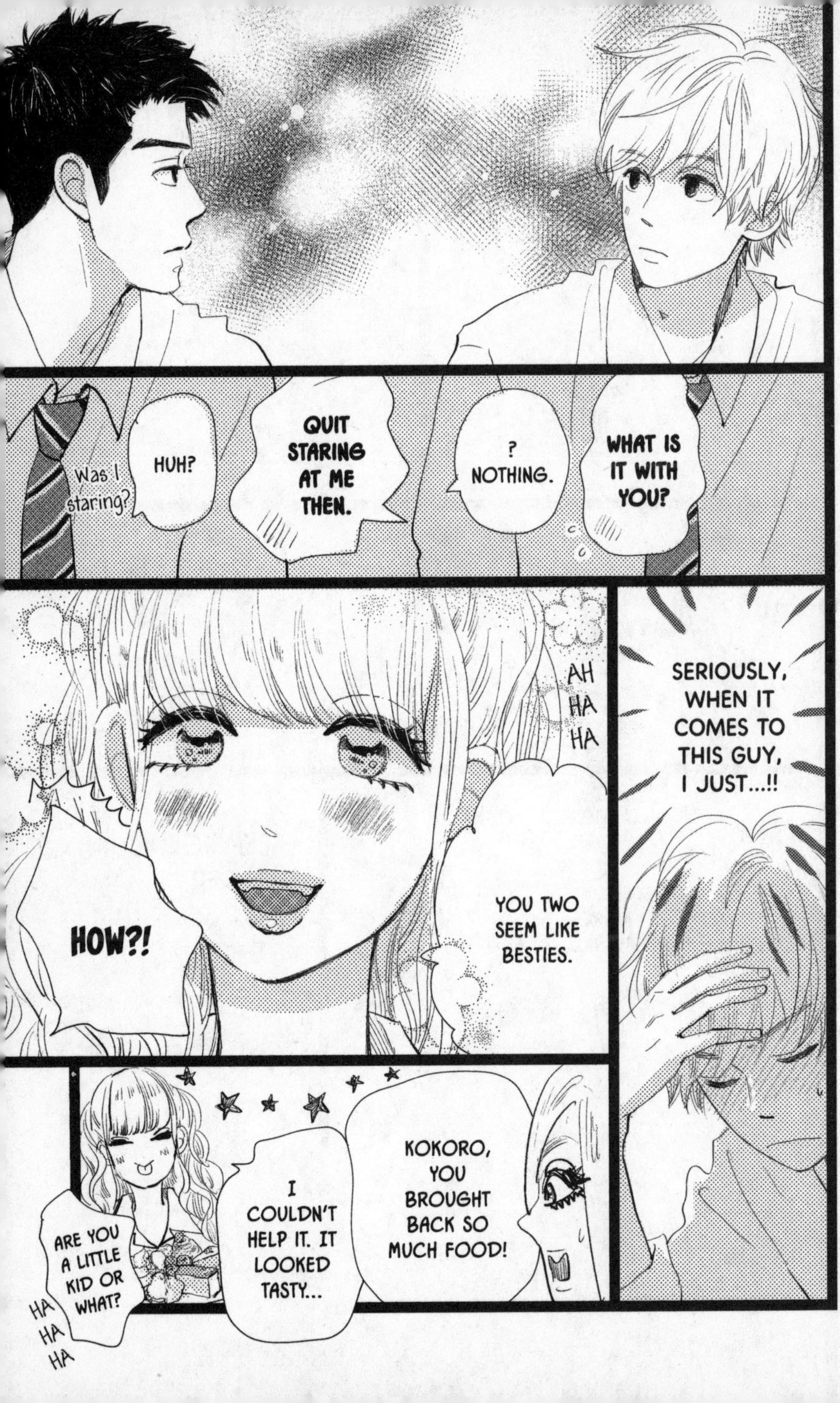
WHAT IS IT WITH YOU?
? NOTHING.
QUIT STARING AT ME THEN.
HUH?
Was I staring?
SERIOUSLY, WHEN IT COMES TO THIS GUY, I JUST...!!
AH HA HA
YOU TWO SEEM LIKE BESTIES.
HOW?!
KOKORO, YOU BROUGHT BACK SO MUCH FOOD!
I COULDN'T HELP IT. IT LOOKED TASTY...
ARE YOU A LITTLE KID OR WHAT?
HA HA HA

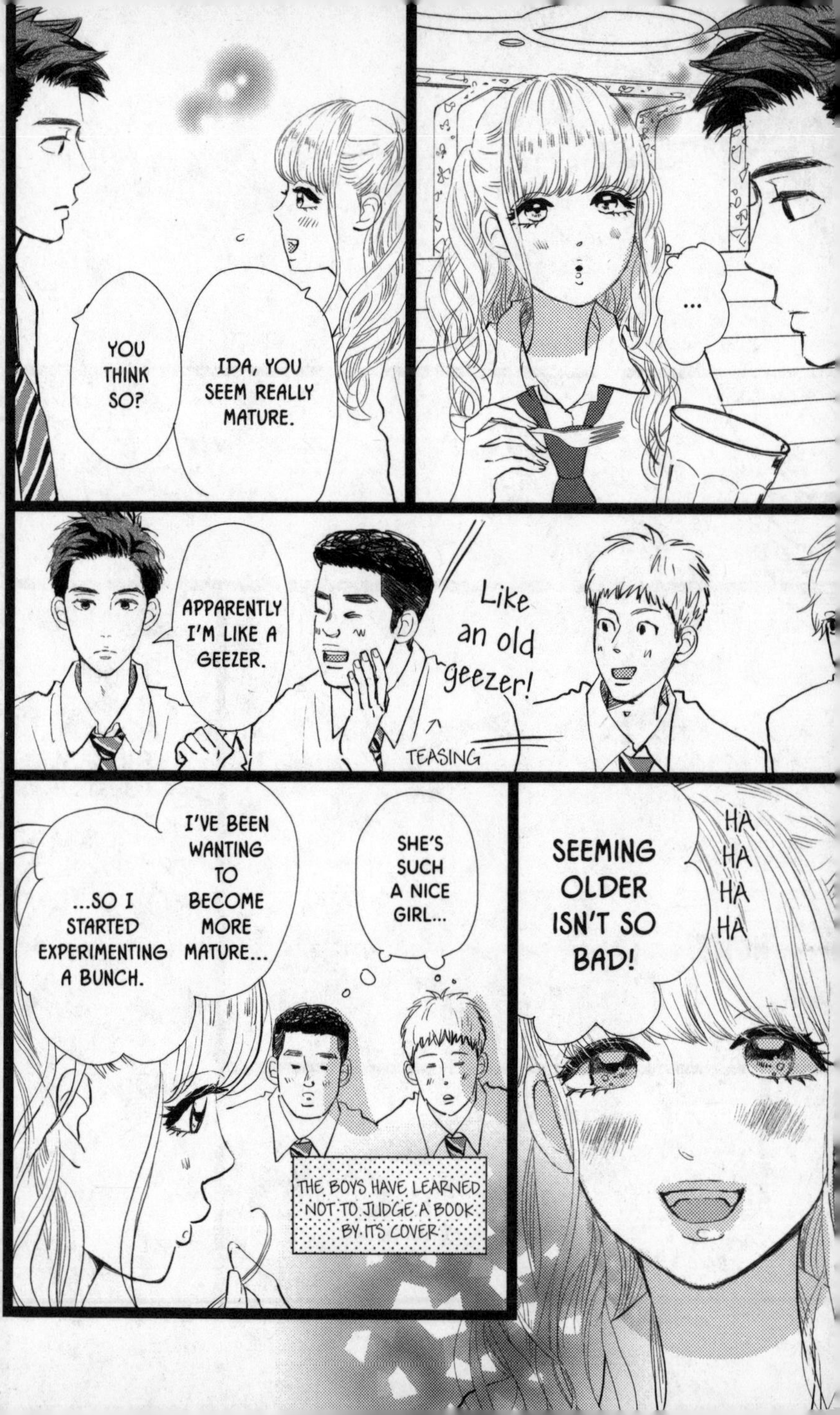
...
IDA, YOU SEEM REALLY MATURE.
YOU THINK SO?
Like an old geezer!
TEASING
APPARENTLY I'M LIKE A GEEZER.
HA HA HA HA
SEEMING OLDER ISN'T SO BAD!
SHE'S SUCH A NICE GIRL...
I'VE BEEN WANTING TO BECOME MORE MATURE...
...SO I STARTED EXPERIMENTING A BUNCH.
THE BOYS HAVE LEARNED NOT TO JUDGE A BOOK BY ITS COVER.

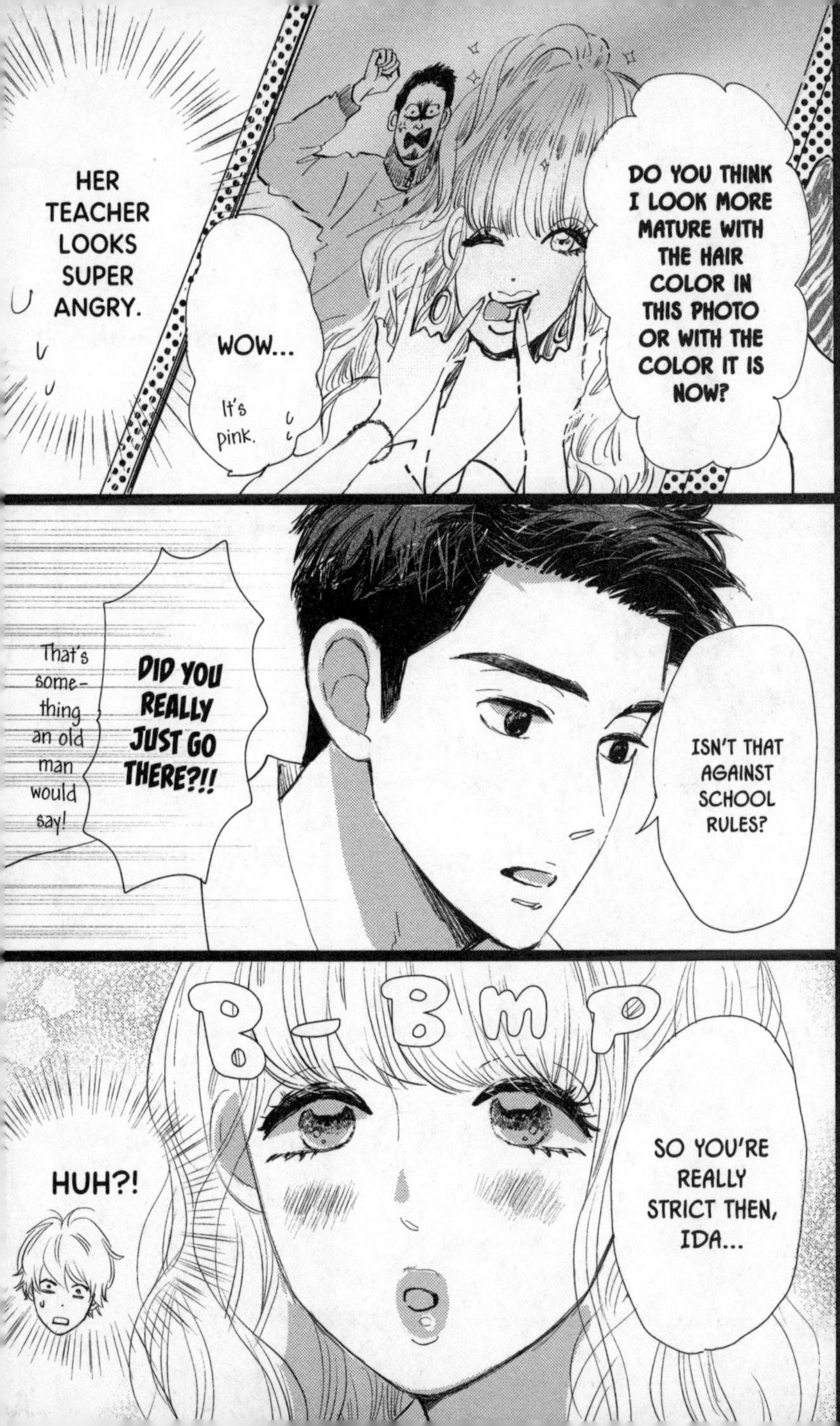
DO YOU THINK I LOOK MORE MATURE WITH THE HAIR COLOR IN THIS PHOTO OR WITH THE COLOR IT IS NOW?
WOW...
It's pink.
HER TEACHER LOOKS SUPER ANGRY.
ISN'T THAT AGAINST SCHOOL RULES?
DID YOU REALLY JUST GO THERE?!!
That's some-thing an old man would say!
B-BMP
SO YOU'RE REALLY STRICT THEN, IDA...
HUH?!

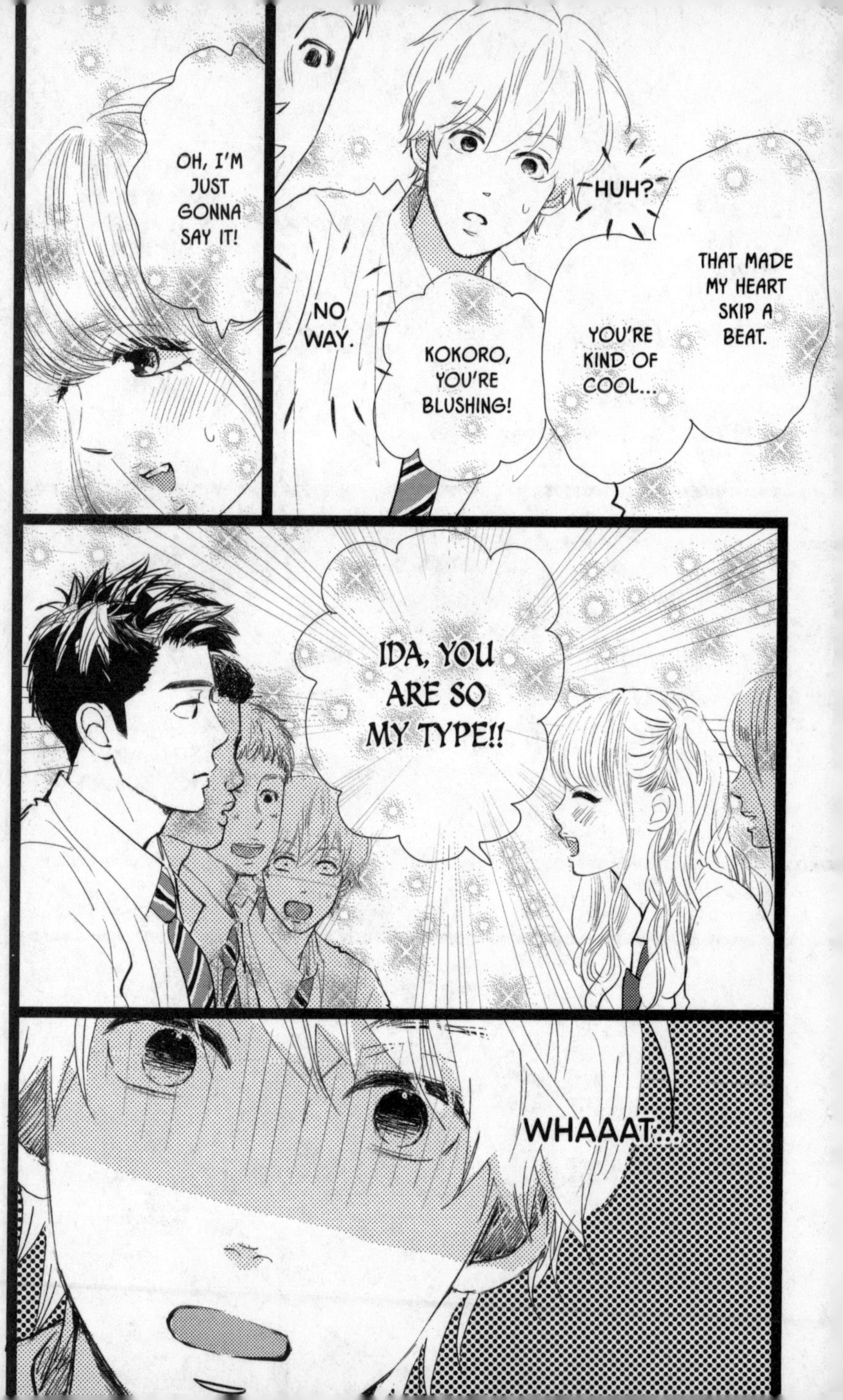
THAT MADE MY HEART SKIP A BEAT.
HUH?
YOU'RE KIND OF COOL...
KOKORO, YOU'RE BLUSHING!
NO WAY.
OH, I'M JUST GONNA SAY IT!
IDA, YOU ARE SO MY TYPE!!
WHAAAT...

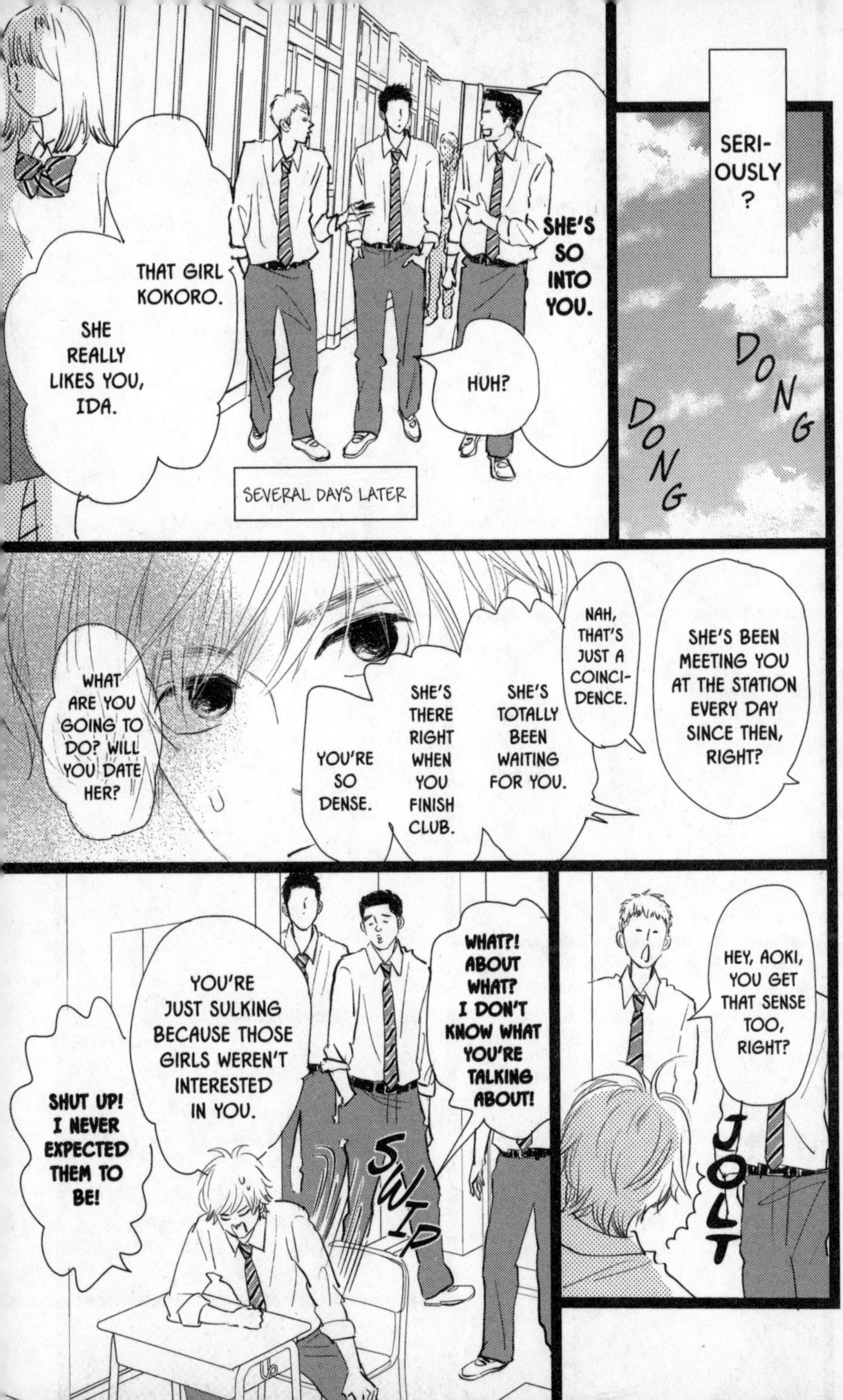
SERI-OUSLY?
DONG
DONG
SHE'S SO INTO YOU.
THAT GIRL KOKORO.
SHE REALLY LIKES YOU, IDA.
HUH?
SEVERAL DAYS LATER
SHE'S BEEN MEETING YOU AT THE STATION EVERY DAY SINCE THEN, RIGHT?
NAH, THAT'S JUST A COINCIDENCE.
SHE'S TOTALLY BEEN WAITING FOR YOU.
SHE'S THERE RIGHT WHEN YOU FINISH CLUB.
YOU'RE SO DENSE.
WHAT ARE YOU GOING TO DO? WILL YOU DATE HER?
HEY, AOKI, YOU GET THAT SENSE TOO, RIGHT?
JOLT
WHAT?! ABOUT WHAT? I DON'T KNOW WHAT YOU'RE TALKING ABOUT!
YOU'RE JUST SULKING BECAUSE THOSE GIRLS WEREN'T INTERESTED IN YOU.
SWIP
SHUT UP! I NEVER EXPECTED THEM TO BE!

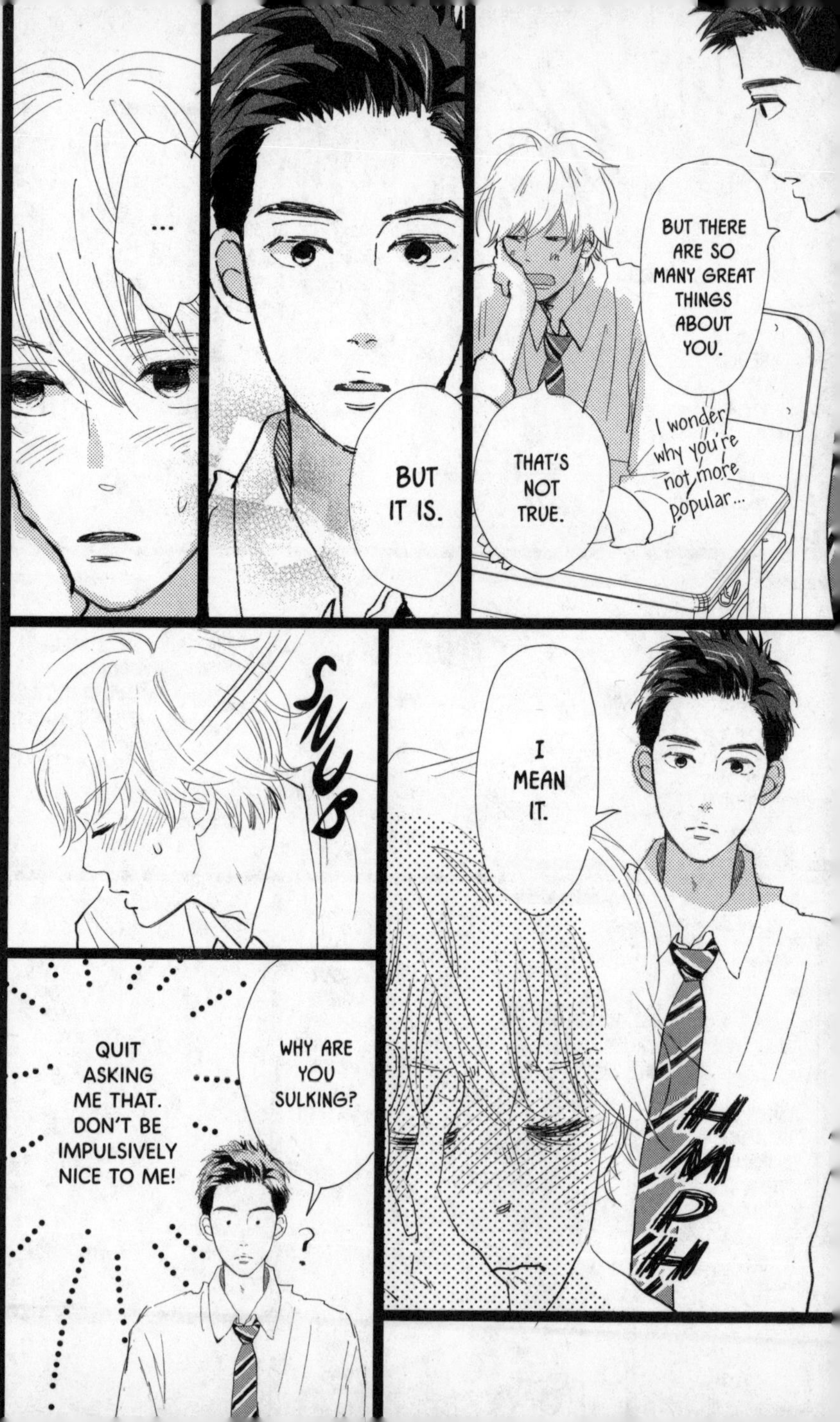
BUT THERE ARE SO MANY GREAT THINGS ABOUT YOU.
I wonder why you're not more popular...
THAT'S NOT TRUE.
BUT IT IS.
...
I MEAN IT.
HMPH
SNUB
WHY ARE YOU SULKING?
?
QUIT ASKING ME THAT. DON'T BE IMPULSIVELY NICE TO ME!

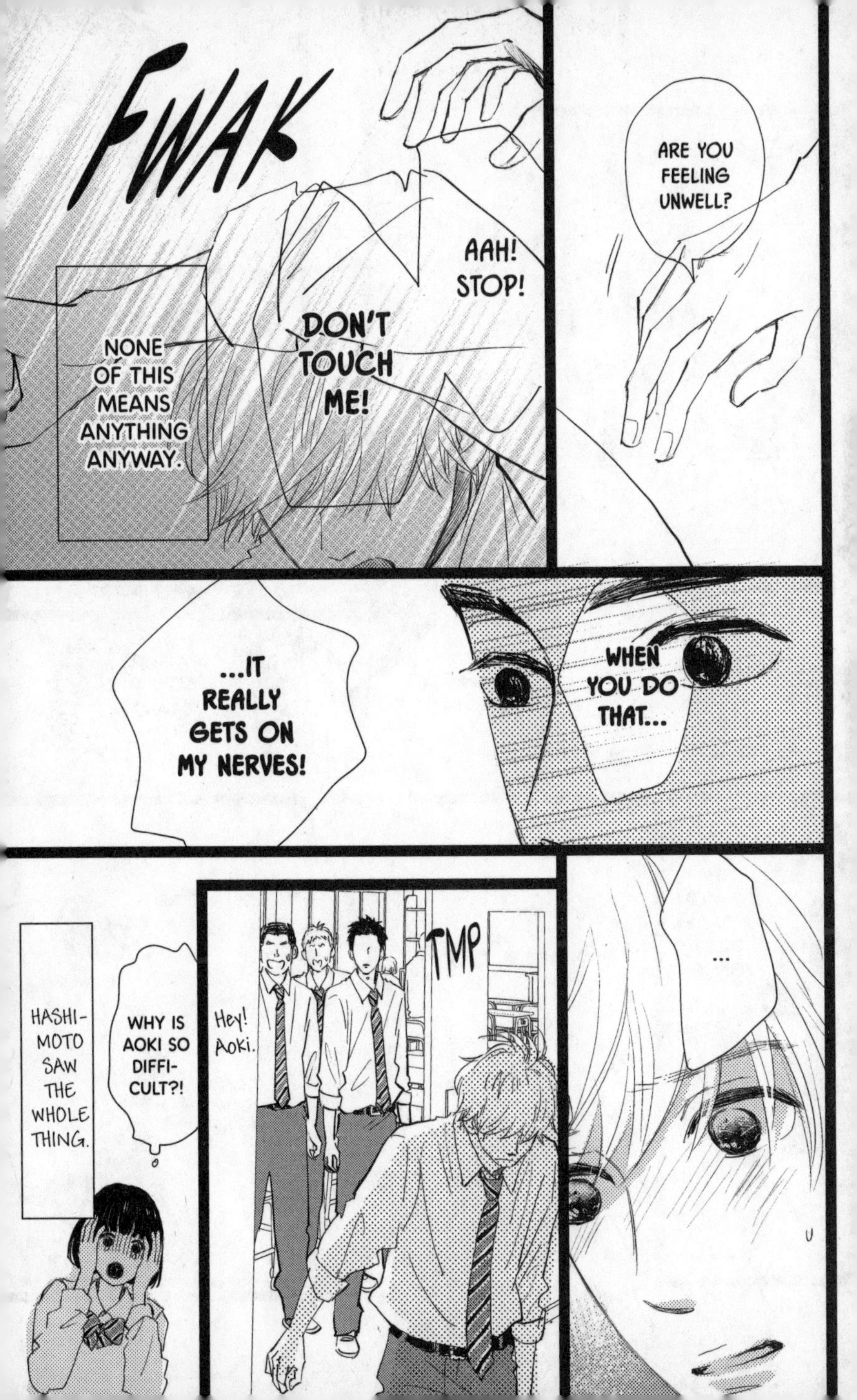
ARE YOU FEELING UNWELL?
FWAK
AAH! STOP!
DON'T TOUCH ME!
NONE OF THIS MEANS ANYTHING ANYWAY.
WHEN YOU DO THAT...
...IT REALLY GETS ON MY NERVES!
...
TMP
Hey! Aoki.
WHY IS AOKI SO DIFFICULT?!
HASHIMOTO SAW THE WHOLE THING.

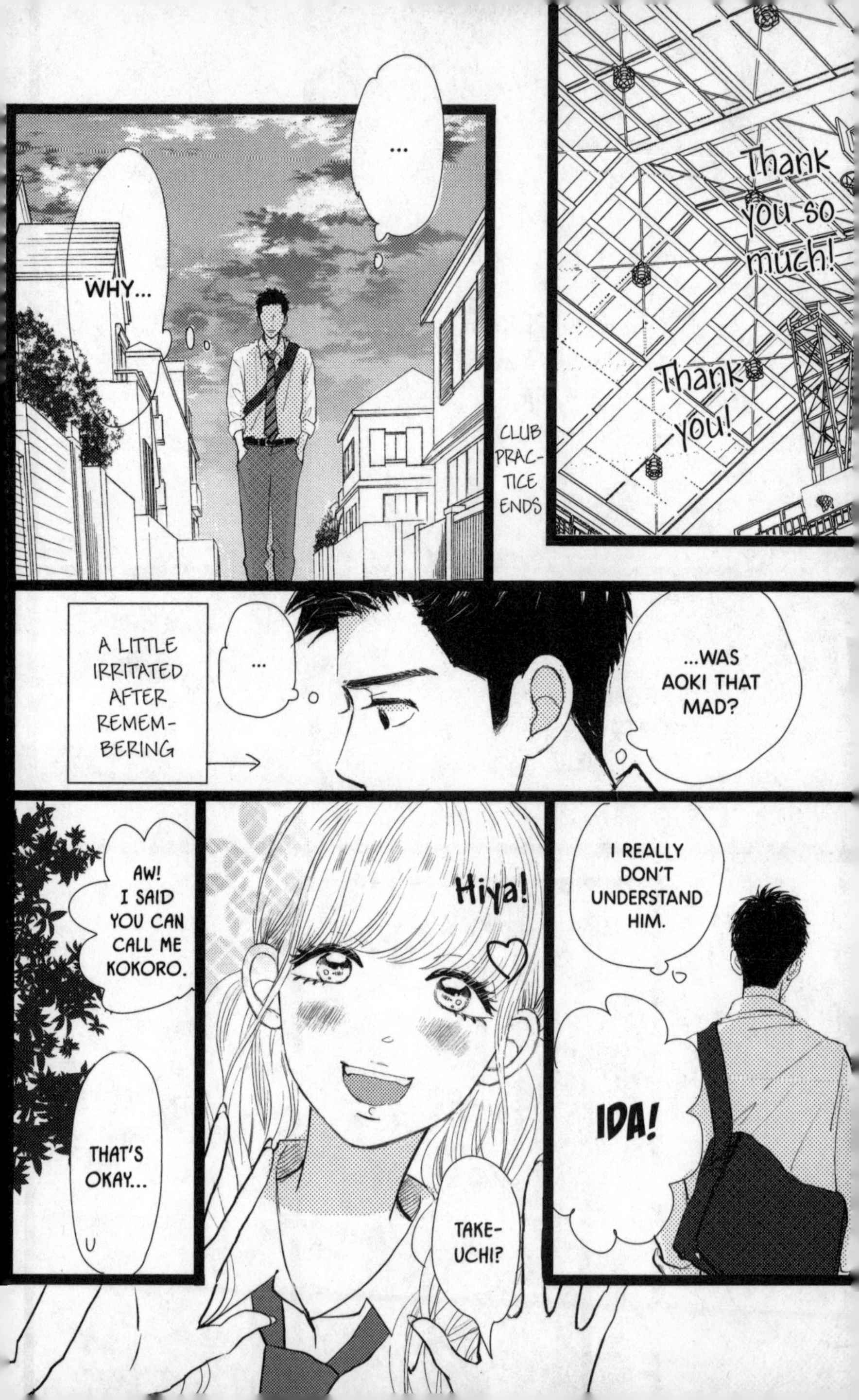
Thank you so much!
Thank you!
CLUB PRACTICE ENDS
...
WHY...
...WAS AOKI THAT MAD?
...
A LITTLE IRRITATED AFTER REMEMBERING
I REALLY DON'T UNDERSTAND HIM.
IDA!
Hiya!
TAKE-UCHI?
AW! I SAID YOU CAN CALL ME KOKORO.
THAT'S OKAY...

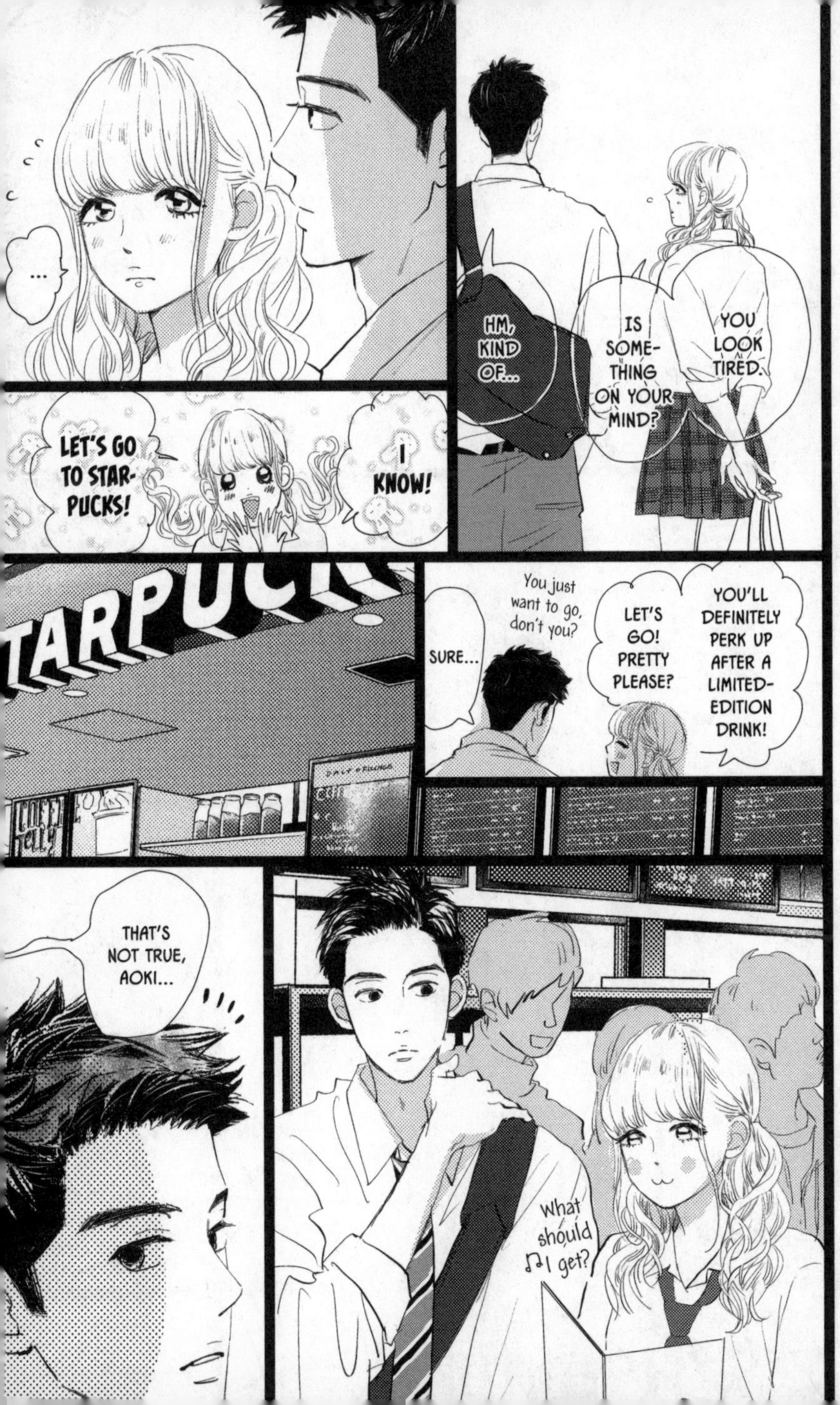
YOU LOOK TIRED.
IS SOMETHING ON YOUR MIND?
HM, KIND OF...
...
I KNOW!
LET'S GO TO STARPUCKS!
YOU'LL DEFINITELY PERK UP AFTER A LIMITED-EDITION DRINK!
LET'S GO! PRETTY PLEASE?
You just want to go, don't you?
SURE...
What should ♫ I get?
THAT'S NOT TRUE, AOKI...

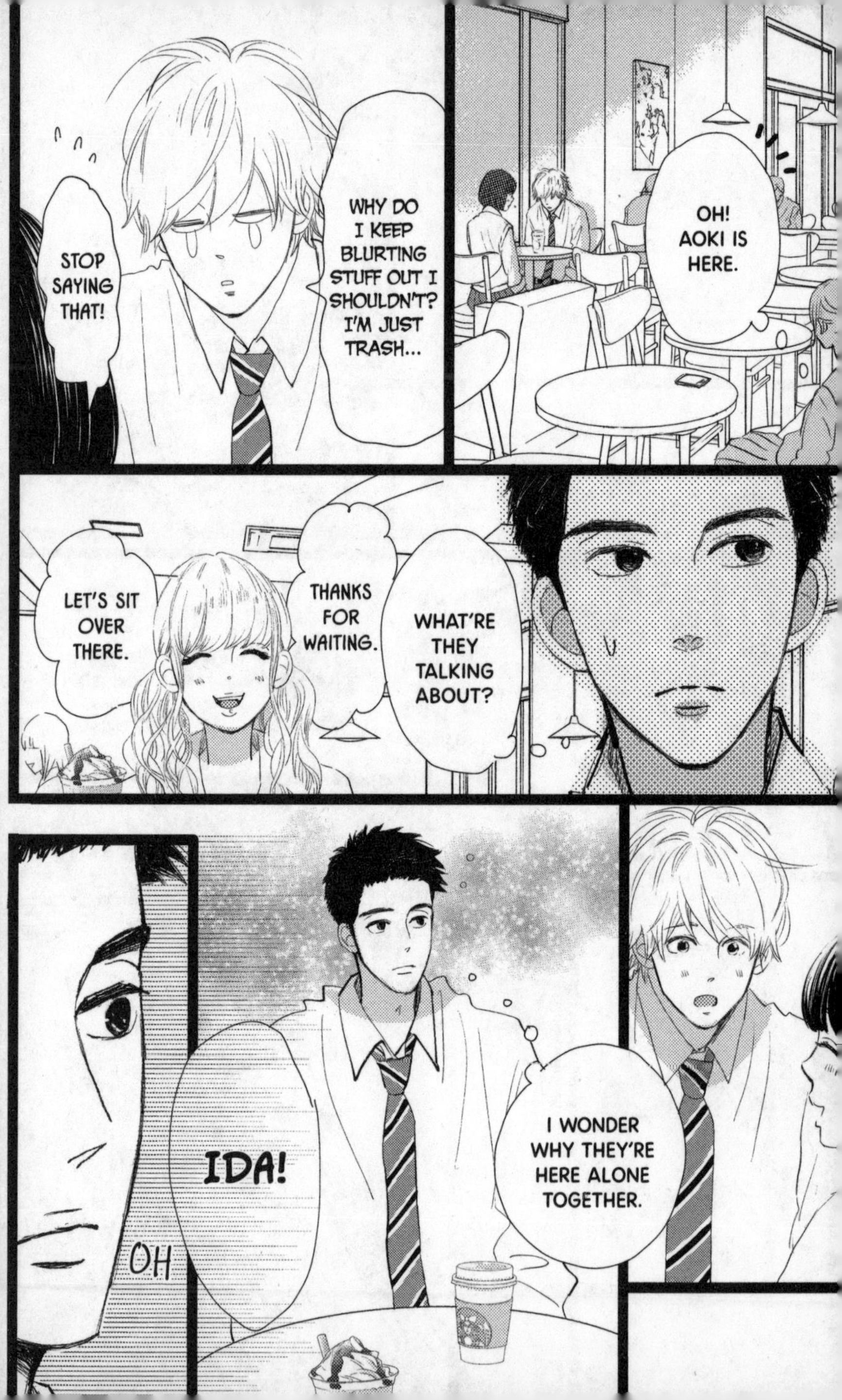
OH! AOKI IS HERE.
WHY DO I KEEP BLURTING STUFF OUT I SHOULDN'T? I'M JUST TRASH...
STOP SAYING THAT!
WHAT'RE THEY TALKING ABOUT?
THANKS FOR WAITING.
LET'S SIT OVER THERE.
I WONDER WHY THEY'RE HERE ALONE TOGETHER.
IDA!
OH

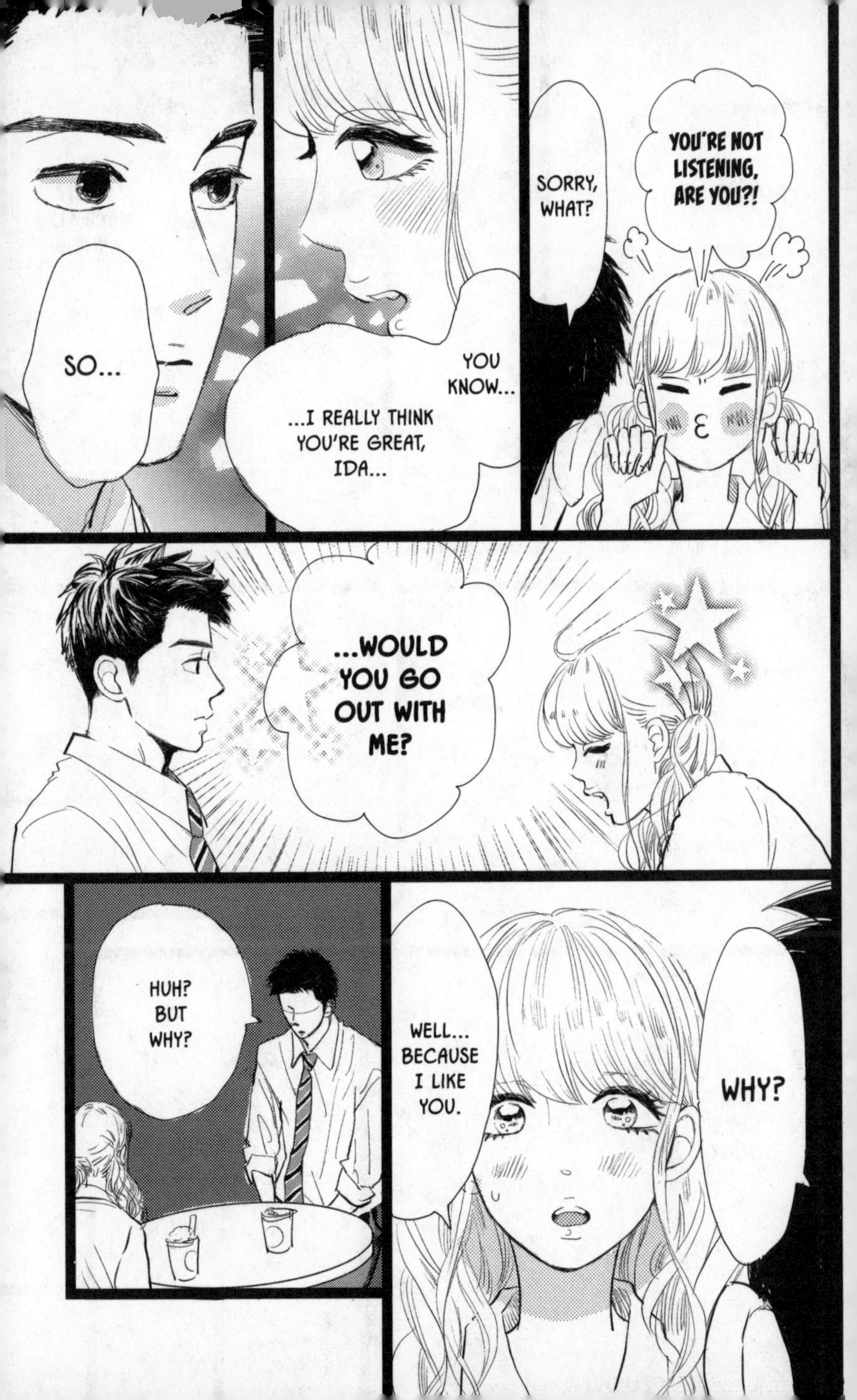
YOU'RE NOT LISTENING, ARE YOU?!
SORRY, WHAT?
YOU KNOW...
...I REALLY THINK YOU'RE GREAT, IDA...
SO...
...WOULD YOU GO OUT WITH ME?
WHY?
WELL... BECAUSE I LIKE YOU.
HUH? BUT WHY?

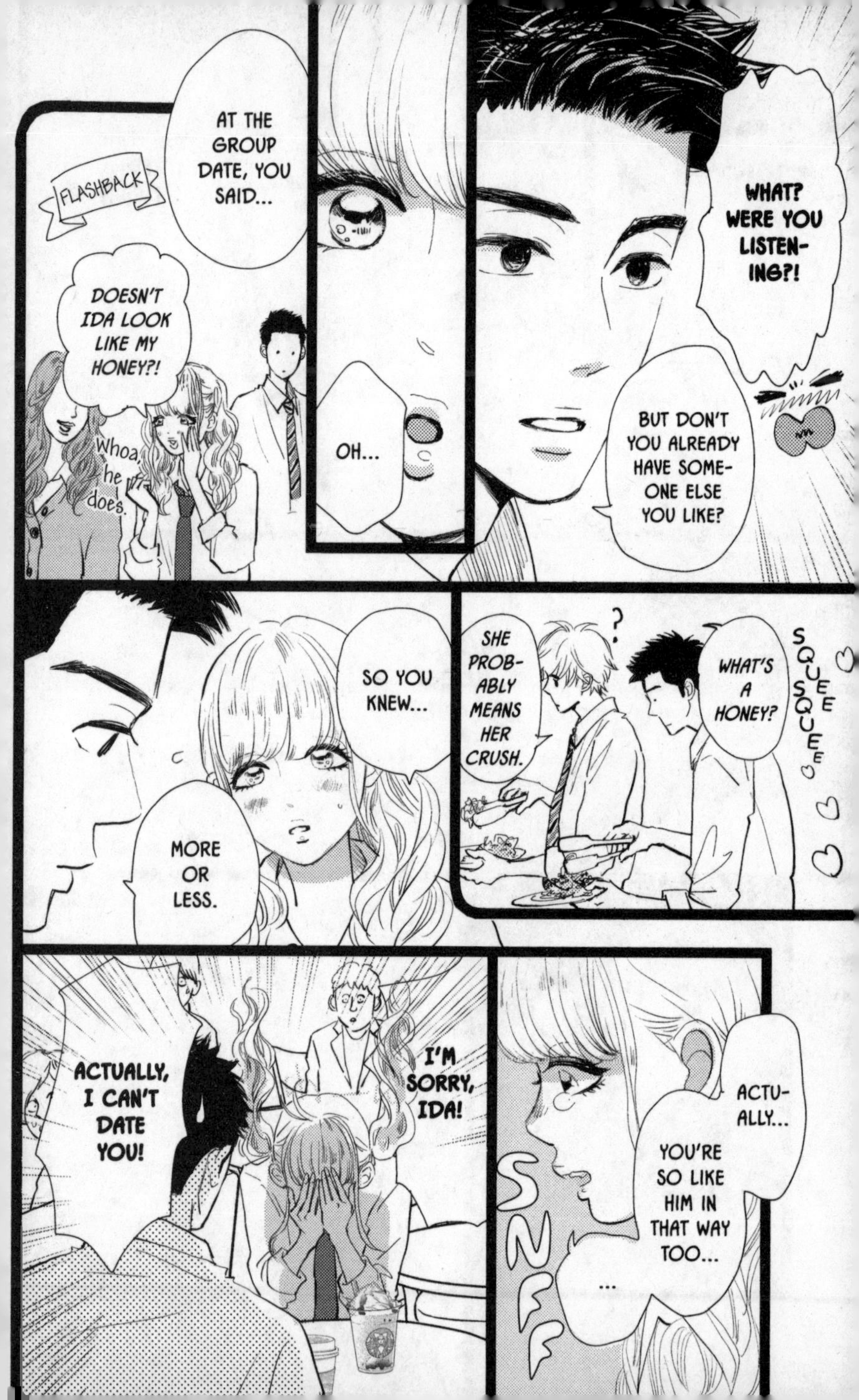
WHAT? WERE YOU LISTEN-ING?!
BUT DON'T YOU ALREADY HAVE SOME-ONE ELSE YOU LIKE?
OH...
AT THE GROUP DATE, YOU SAID...
FLASHBACK
DOESN'T IDA LOOK LIKE MY HONEY?!
Whoa, he does.
SQUEE SQUEE
WHAT'S A HONEY?
?
SHE PROBABLY MEANS HER CRUSH.
SO YOU KNEW...
MORE OR LESS.
ACTU-ALLY...
YOU'RE SO LIKE HIM IN THAT WAY TOO...
SNFF
...
I'M SORRY, IDA!
ACTUALLY, I CAN'T DATE YOU!

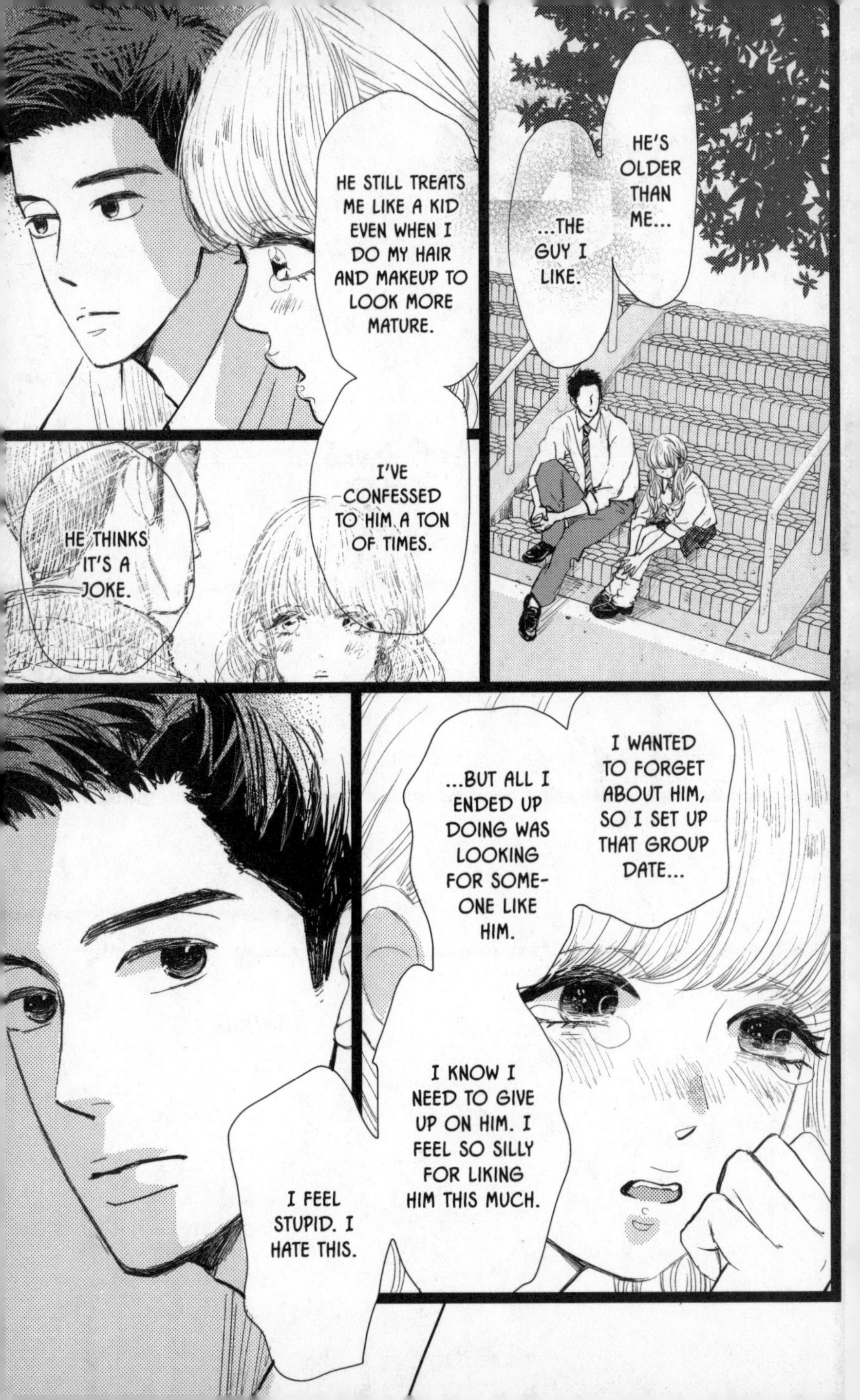
HE'S OLDER THAN ME...
...THE GUY I LIKE.
HE STILL TREATS ME LIKE A KID EVEN WHEN I DO MY HAIR AND MAKEUP TO LOOK MORE MATURE.
I'VE CONFESSED TO HIM A TON OF TIMES.
HE THINKS IT'S A JOKE.
I WANTED TO FORGET ABOUT HIM, SO I SET UP THAT GROUP DATE...
...BUT ALL I ENDED UP DOING WAS LOOKING FOR SOME-ONE LIKE HIM.
I KNOW I NEED TO GIVE UP ON HIM. I FEEL SO SILLY FOR LIKING HIM THIS MUCH.
I FEEL STUPID. I HATE THIS.

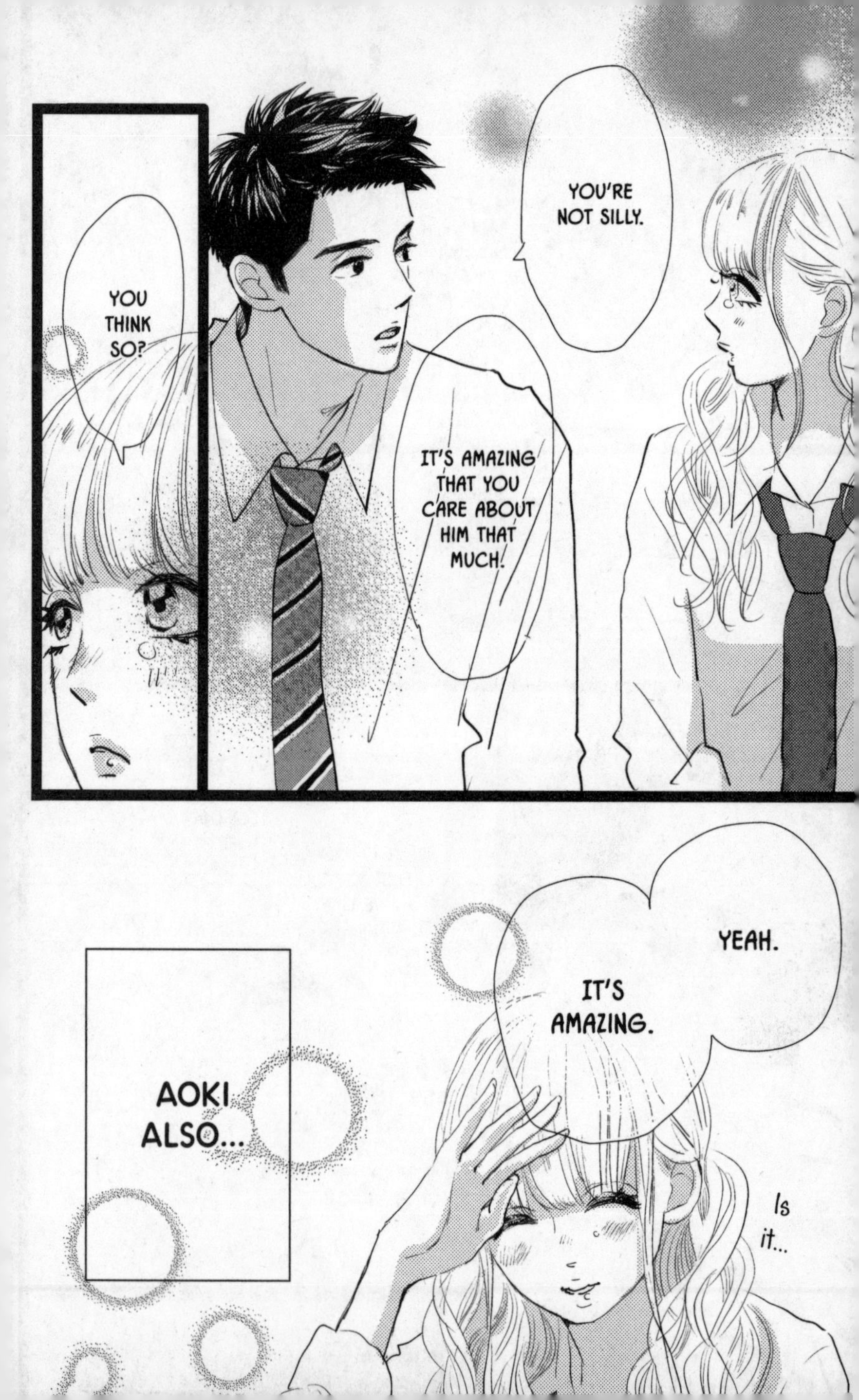
YOU'RE NOT SILLY.
IT'S AMAZING THAT YOU CARE ABOUT HIM THAT MUCH!
YOU THINK SO?
YEAH.
IT'S AMAZING.
Is it...
AOKI ALSO...

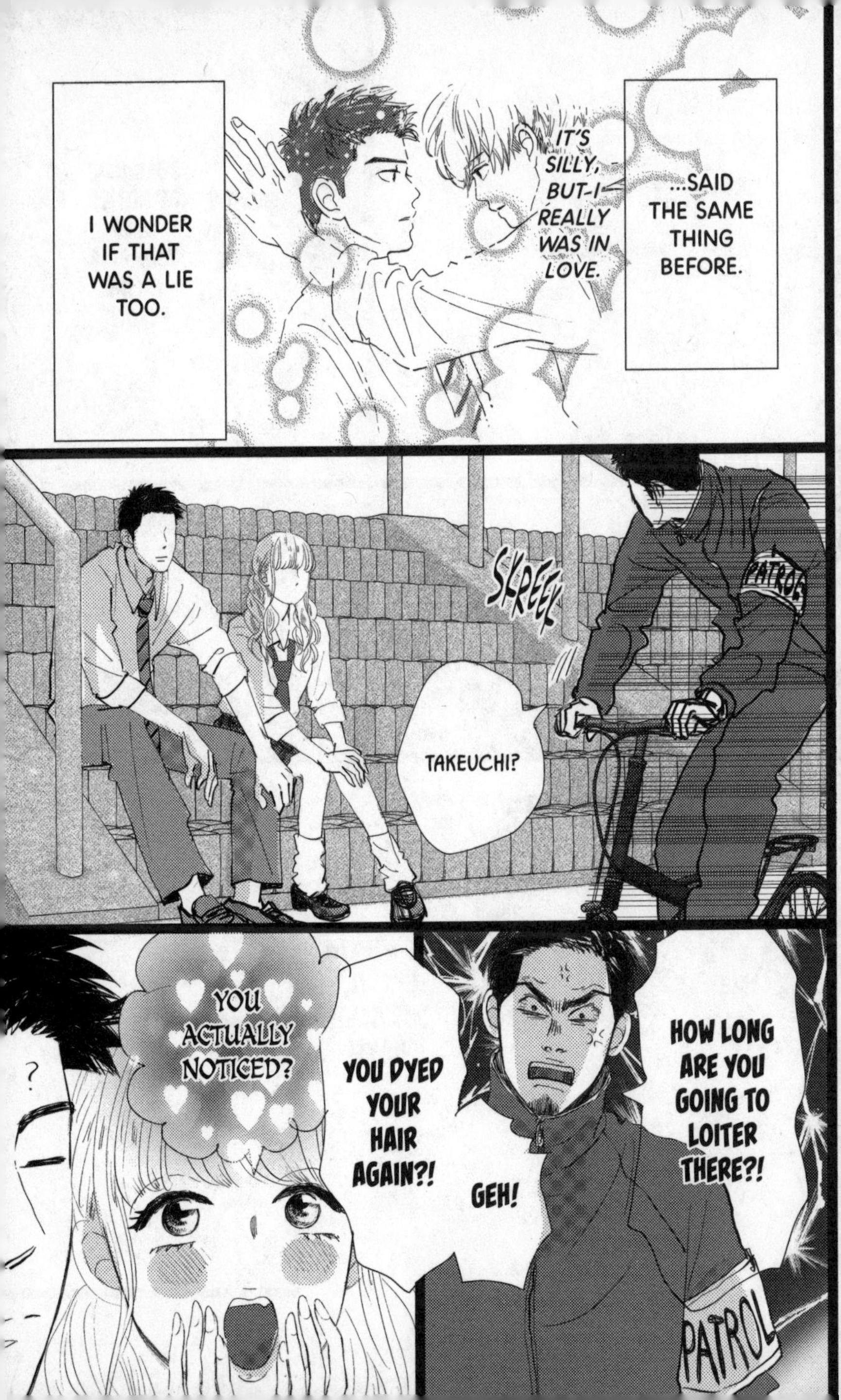
IT'S SILLY, BUT-I REALLY WAS IN LOVE.
...SAID THE SAME THING BEFORE.
I WONDER IF THAT WAS A LIE TOO.
PATROL
SKREEK
TAKEUCHI?
HOW LONG ARE YOU GOING TO LOITER THERE?!
PATROL
GEH!
YOU DYED YOUR HAIR AGAIN?!
YOU ACTUALLY NOTICED?
?

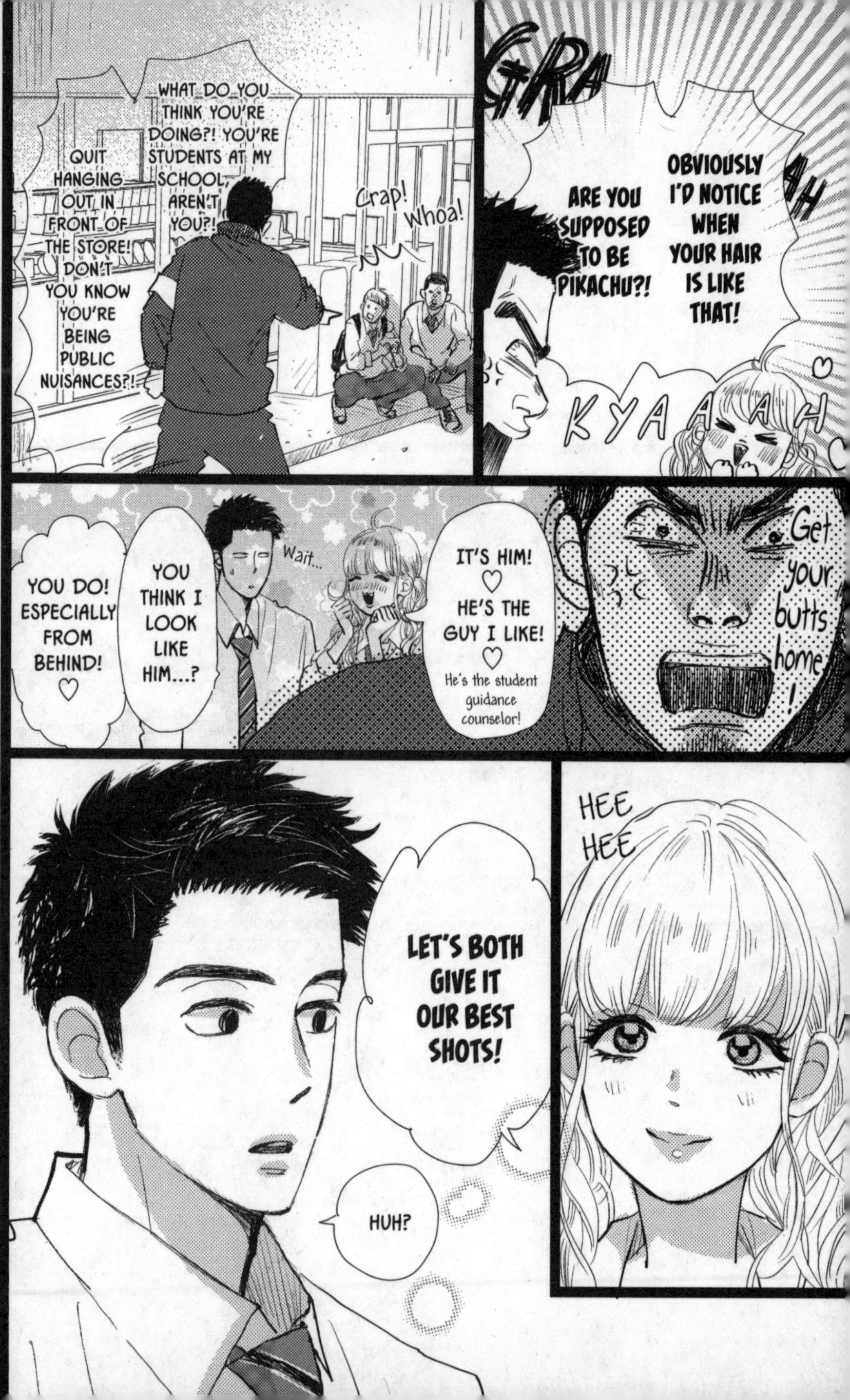
GRAAH
OBVIOUSLY I'D NOTICE WHEN YOUR HAIR IS LIKE THAT!
ARE YOU SUPPOSED TO BE PIKACHU?!
KYAAAH
WHAT DO YOU THINK YOU'RE DOING?! YOU'RE STUDENTS AT MY SCHOOL, AREN'T YOU?!
QUIT HANGING OUT IN FRONT OF THE STORE! DON'T YOU KNOW YOU'RE BEING PUBLIC NUISANCES?!
Crap!
Whoa!
Get your butts home!
IT'S HIM! ♡ HE'S THE GUY I LIKE! ♡
He's the student guidance counselor!
Wait...
YOU THINK I LOOK LIKE HIM...?
YOU DO! ESPECIALLY FROM BEHIND! ♡
HEE HEE
LET'S BOTH GIVE IT OUR BEST SHOTS!
HUH?

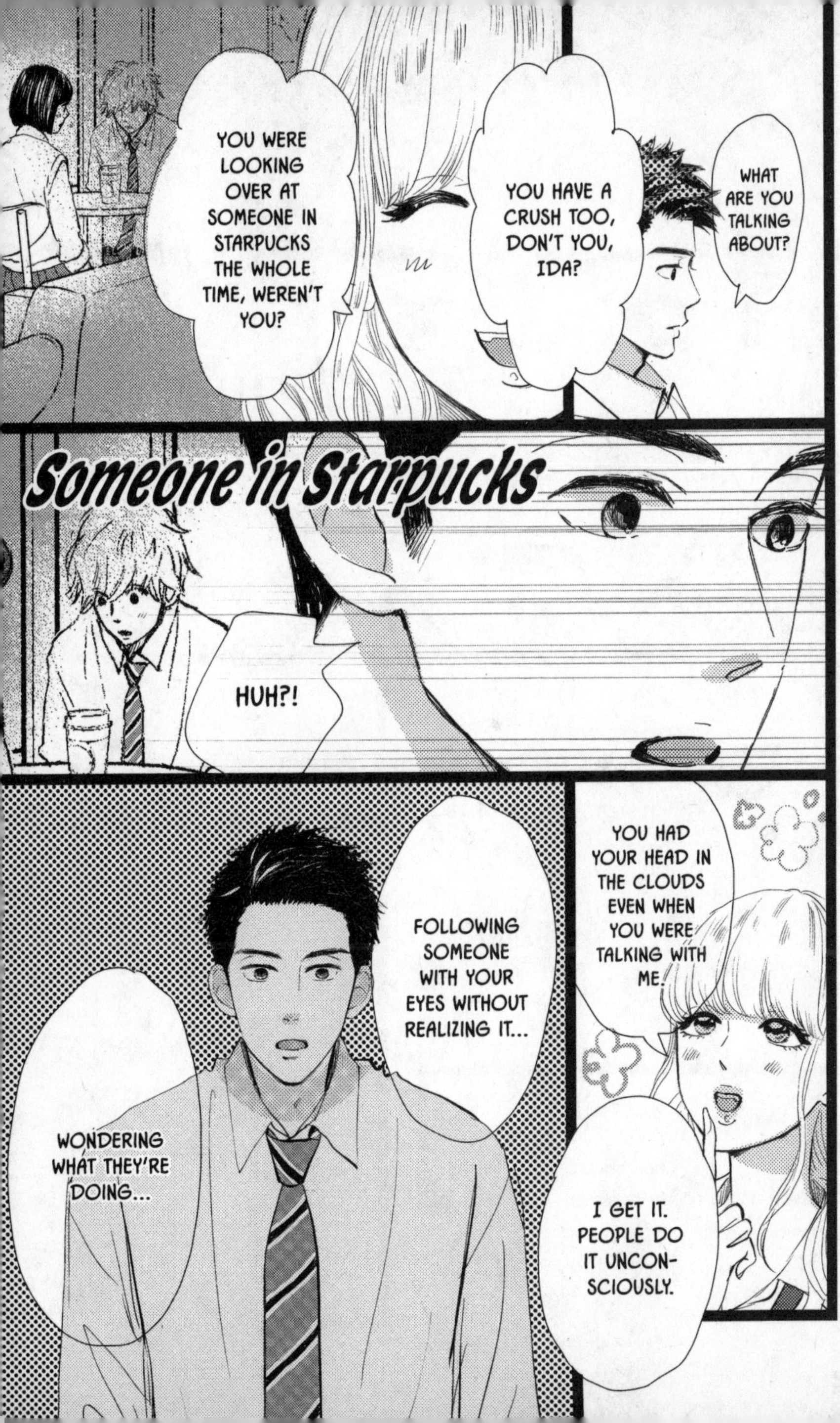
WHAT ARE YOU TALKING ABOUT?
YOU HAVE A CRUSH TOO, DON'T YOU, IDA?
YOU WERE LOOKING OVER AT SOMEONE IN STARPUCKS THE WHOLE TIME, WEREN'T YOU?
Someone in Starpucks
HUH?!
YOU HAD YOUR HEAD IN THE CLOUDS EVEN WHEN YOU WERE TALKING WITH ME.
I GET IT. PEOPLE DO IT UNCON-SCIOUSLY.
FOLLOWING SOMEONE WITH YOUR EYES WITHOUT REALIZING IT...
WONDERING WHAT THEY'RE DOING...

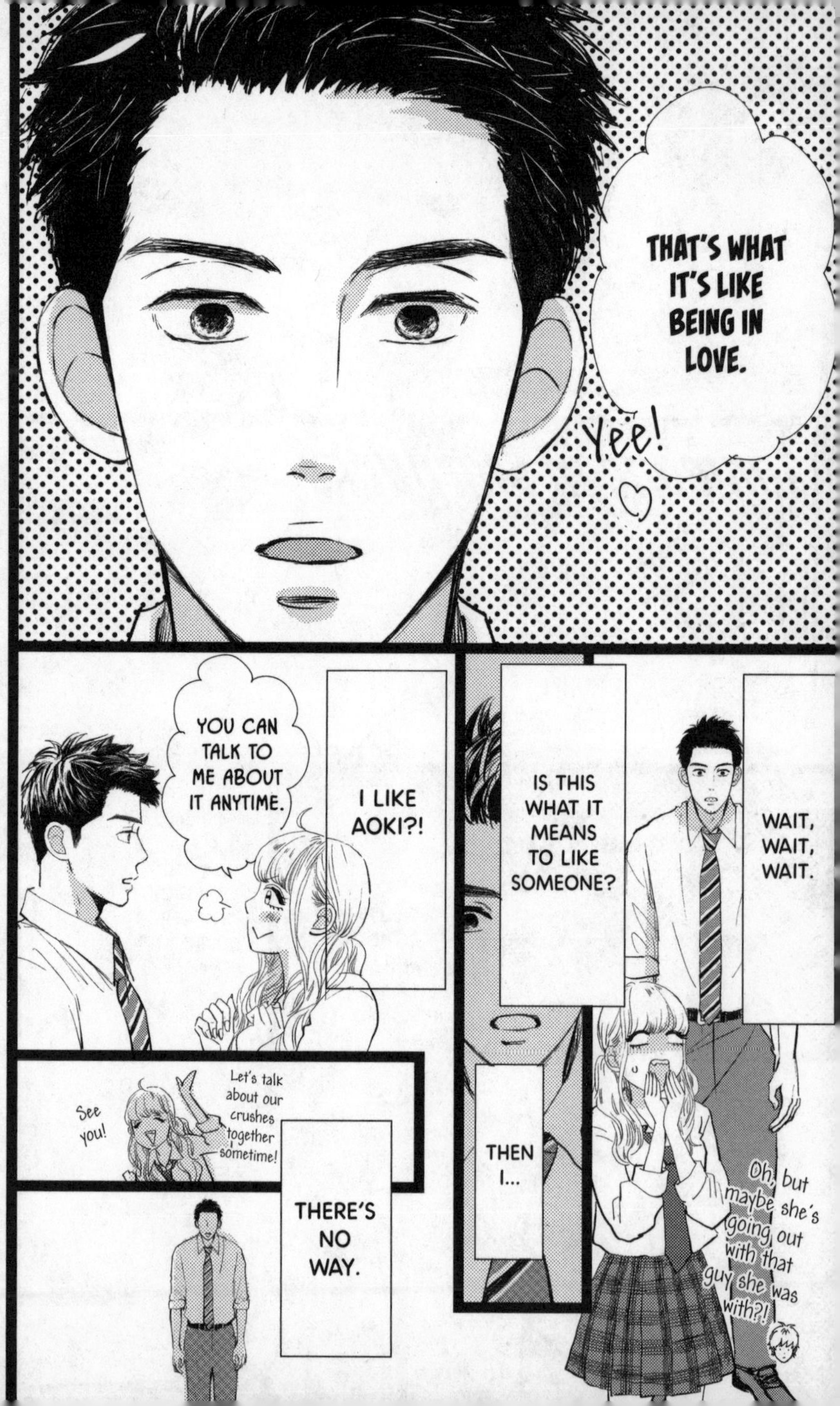
THAT'S WHAT IT'S LIKE BEING IN LOVE.
Yee!
WAIT, WAIT, WAIT.
Oh, but maybe she's going out with that guy she was with?!
IS THIS WHAT IT MEANS TO LIKE SOMEONE?
THEN I...
I LIKE AOKI?!
YOU CAN TALK TO ME ABOUT IT ANYTIME.
Let's talk about our crushes together sometime!
See you!
THERE'S NO WAY.

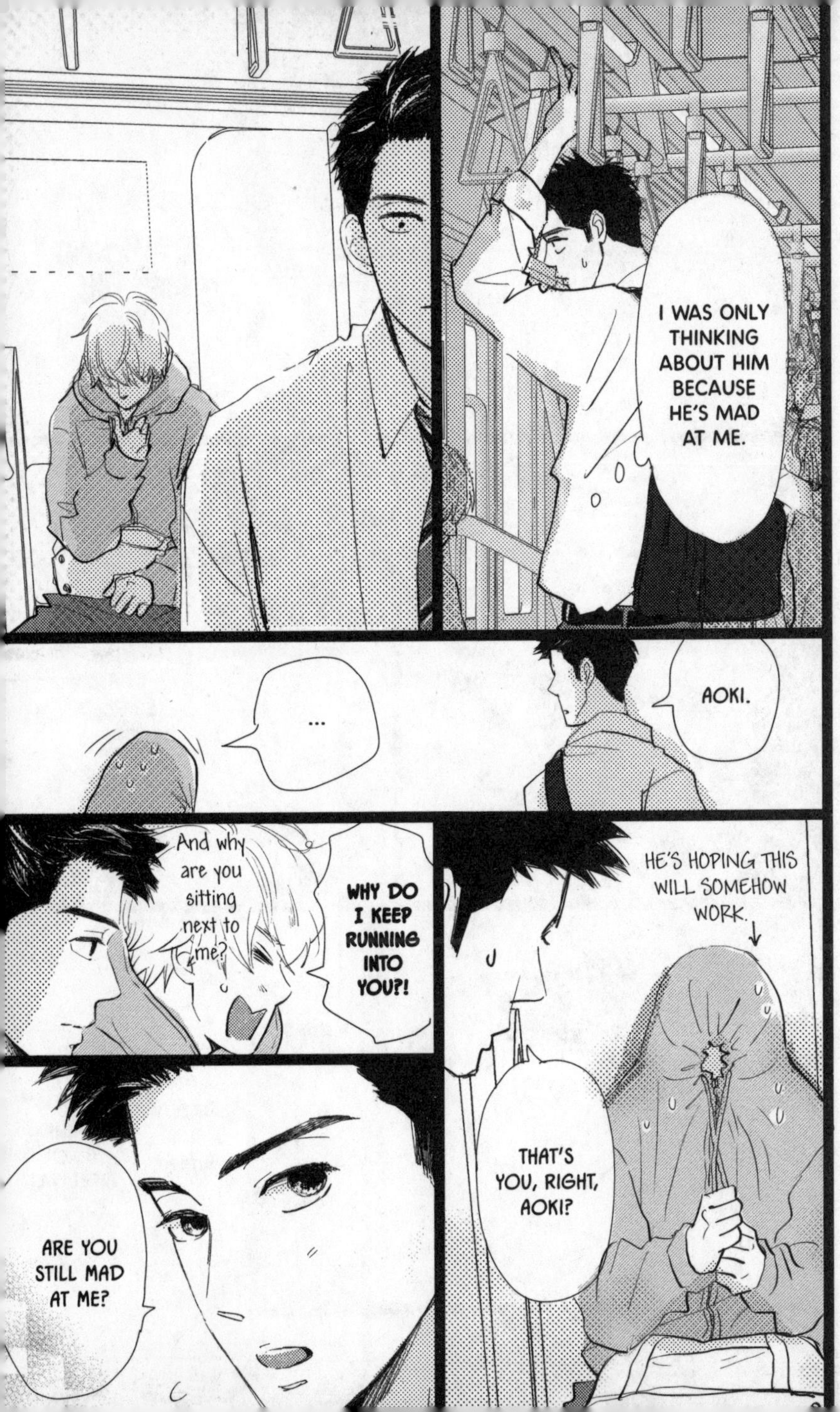
I WAS ONLY THINKING ABOUT HIM BECAUSE HE'S MAD AT ME.
AOKI.
...
HE'S HOPING THIS WILL SOMEHOW WORK.
THAT'S YOU, RIGHT, AOKI?
WHY DO I KEEP RUNNING INTO YOU?!
And why are you sitting next to me?
ARE YOU STILL MAD AT ME?

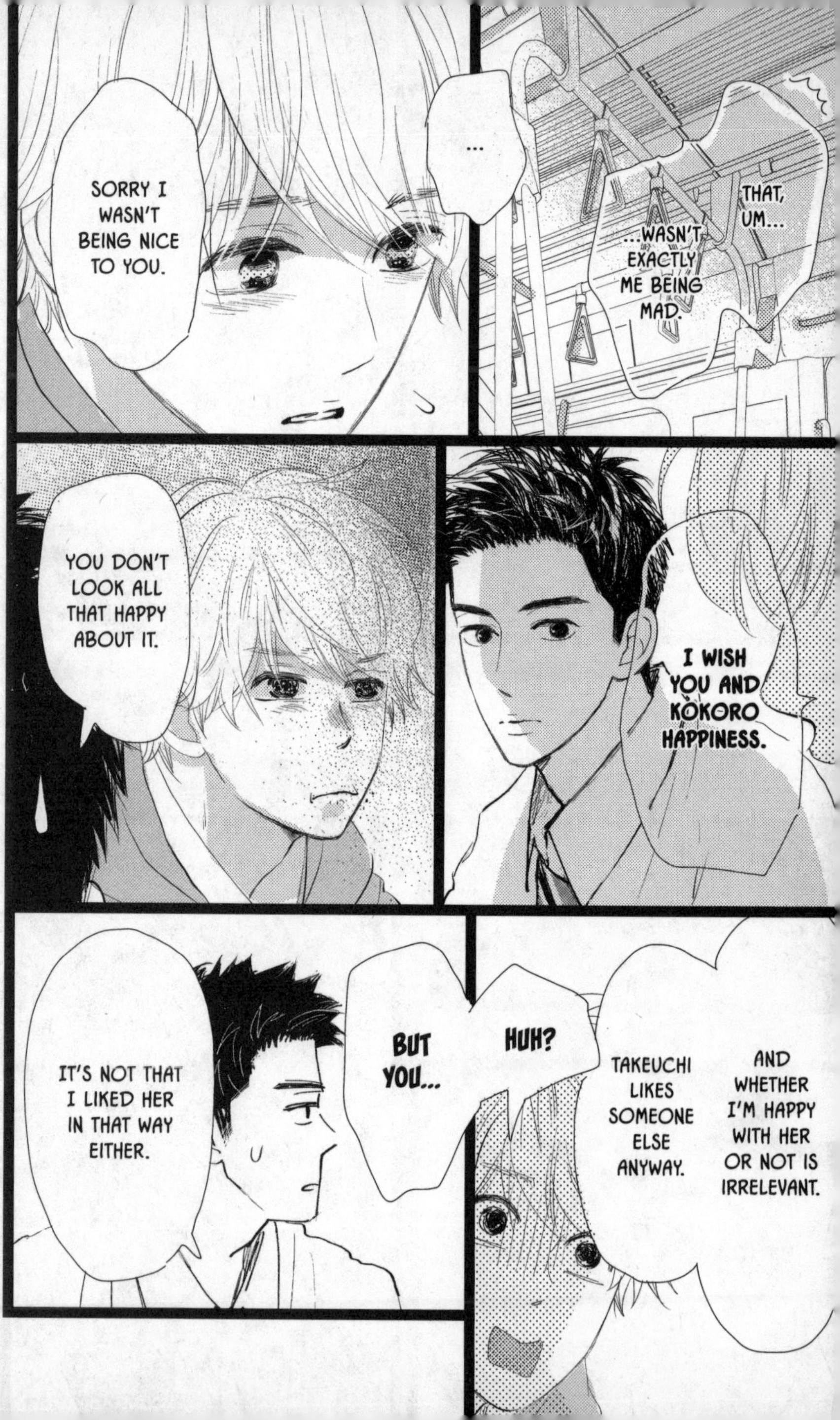
...
THAT, UM...
...WASN'T EXACTLY ME BEING MAD.
SORRY I WASN'T BEING NICE TO YOU.
I WISH YOU AND KOKORO HAPPINESS.
YOU DON'T LOOK ALL THAT HAPPY ABOUT IT.
TAKEUCHI LIKES SOMEONE ELSE ANYWAY.
AND WHETHER I'M HAPPY WITH HER OR NOT IS IRRELEVANT.
HUH?
BUT YOU...
IT'S NOT THAT I LIKED HER IN THAT WAY EITHER.

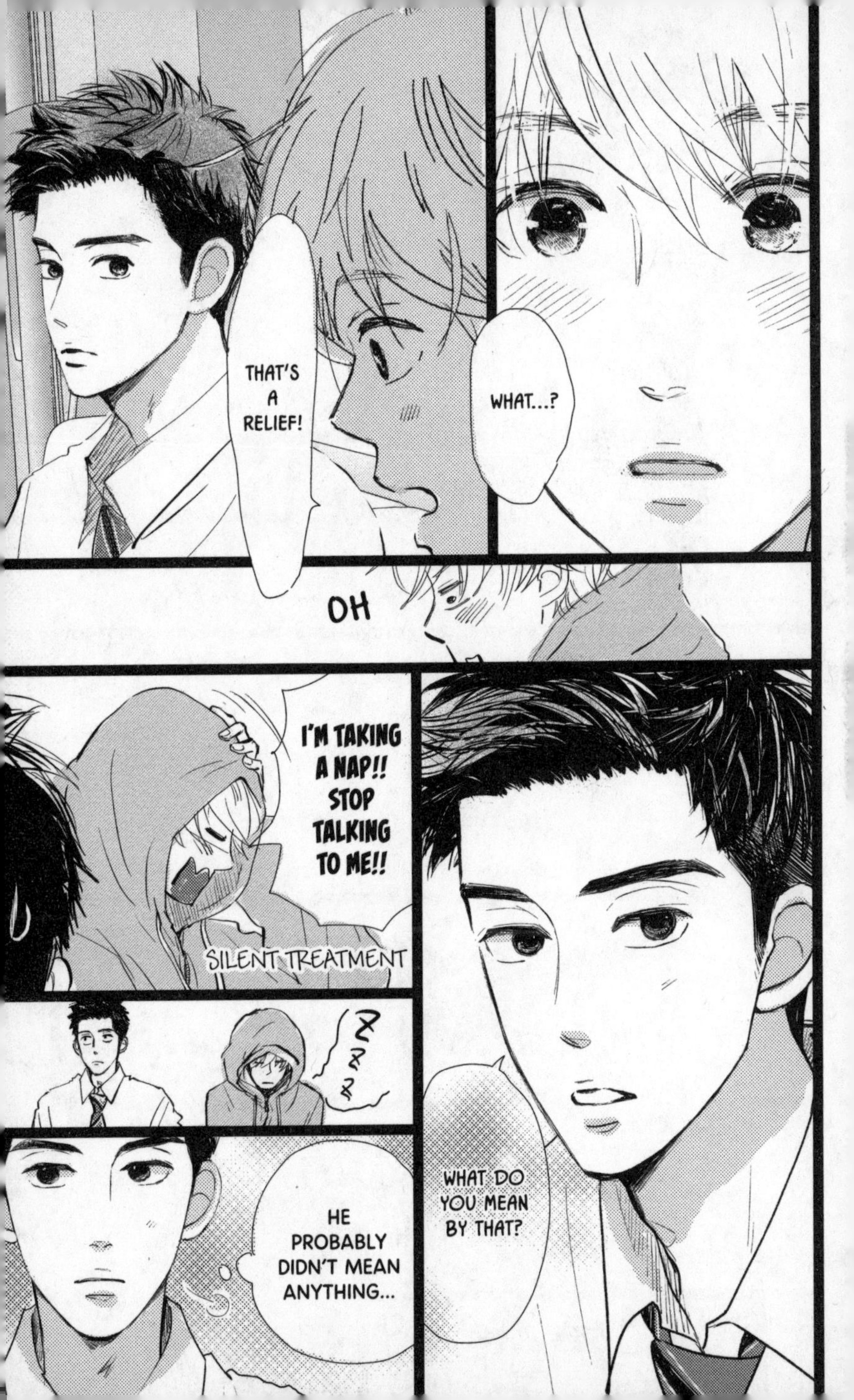
WHAT...?
THAT'S A RELIEF!
OH
WHAT DO YOU MEAN BY THAT?
I'M TAKING A NAP!! STOP TALKING TO ME!!
SILENT TREATMENT
HE PROBABLY DIDN'T MEAN ANYTHING...

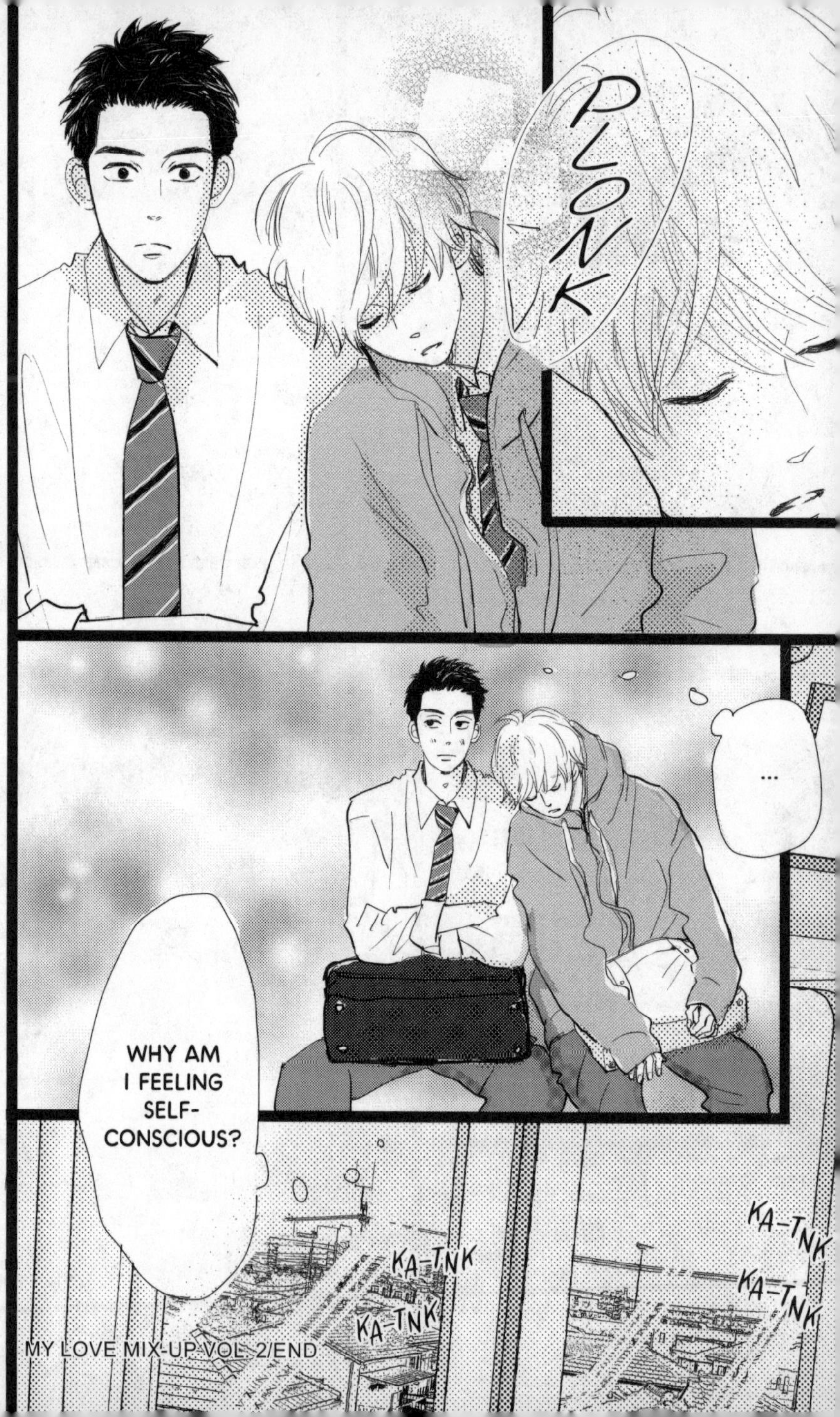
PLONK
...
WHY AM I FEELING SELF-CONSCIOUS?
KA-TNK
KA-TNK
KA-TNK
KA-TNK
MY LOVE MIX-UP VOL. 2/END

My Love Mix-Up!
Volume 2 is released!
Thank you so very much!!!

To all you readers who picked up this book, and to everyone who was involved in getting it into your hands, thank you very much!! I always look forward to receiving Hinekure's manuscripts to see all the difficult parts turn out amazingly. It's truly great... I really respect Hinekure in that way. I'm looking forward to the third volume already. I want to thank my assistant Amane Koyama.
(She can draw anything. ↑Her LINE icon is so cute and heartwarming.)
Thank you for everything, Sawada (my editor).   Aruko

My Love Mix-Up! Volume 2! Thank you so much!!

I'm Hinekure, and I'm in charge of the story. Thank you so very much for picking up the next volume of this series. I came across the old manuscript (or rather notes and good ideas) for *My Love Mix-Up!* the other day. I was surprised at how terrible I was back then. I'm still in the process of learning even now... I've been thinking about how much the story has developed after talking to Aruko and to my editor daily, and from the reader comments... I'm filled with gratitude right now. I'm going to work hard on volume 3!!!

The emotion!
Hashi-moto

Akkun
It's old!

Sorry the story-boards are late.
Ida

Aoki

Something that made me happy recently was getting Valentine's Day chocolates from my editor. Something that made me sad was that I couldn't jump rope (from the front) more than four times in a row.

Aruko

I'm super, super, super grateful for volume 2. All the love is for Aruko, my editor, and also the readers...! I'd be so happy if you'd continue keeping an eye on this and enjoying it.

Wataru Hinekure

Aruko is from Ishikawa Prefecture in Japan and was born on July 26 (a Leo!). She made her manga debut with *Ame Nochi Hare* (Clear After the Rain). Her other works include *Yasuko to Kenji*, and her hobbies include laughing and getting lost.

Wataru Hinekure is a night owl. *My Love Mix-Up!* is Hinekure's first work.

My Love Mix-Up!

Vol. 2
Shojo Beat Edition

STORY BY
Wataru Hinekure

ART BY
Aruko

Translation & Adaptation/Jan Cash
Touch-Up Art & Lettering/Inori Fukuda Trant
Design/Yukiko Whitley
Editor/Nancy Thistlethwaite

Printed in the U.S.A.

Published by VIZ Media, LLC
P.O. Box 77010
San Francisco, CA 94107

10 9 8 7 6 5 4 3 2 1
First printing, January 2022

PARENTAL ADVISORY
MY LOVE MIX-UP! is rated T for Teen and is
recommended for ages 13 and up. No cinnamon
rolls were harmed in the making of this manga.

viz.com   shojobeat.com

Sweet Blue Flowers

Story and Art by **Takako Shimura**

Akira Okudaira is starting high school and is ready for exciting new experiences. And on the first day of school, she runs into her best friend from kindergarten at the train station! Now Akira and Fumi have the chance to rekindle their friendship, but life has gotten a lot more complicated since they were kids…

Collect the series!

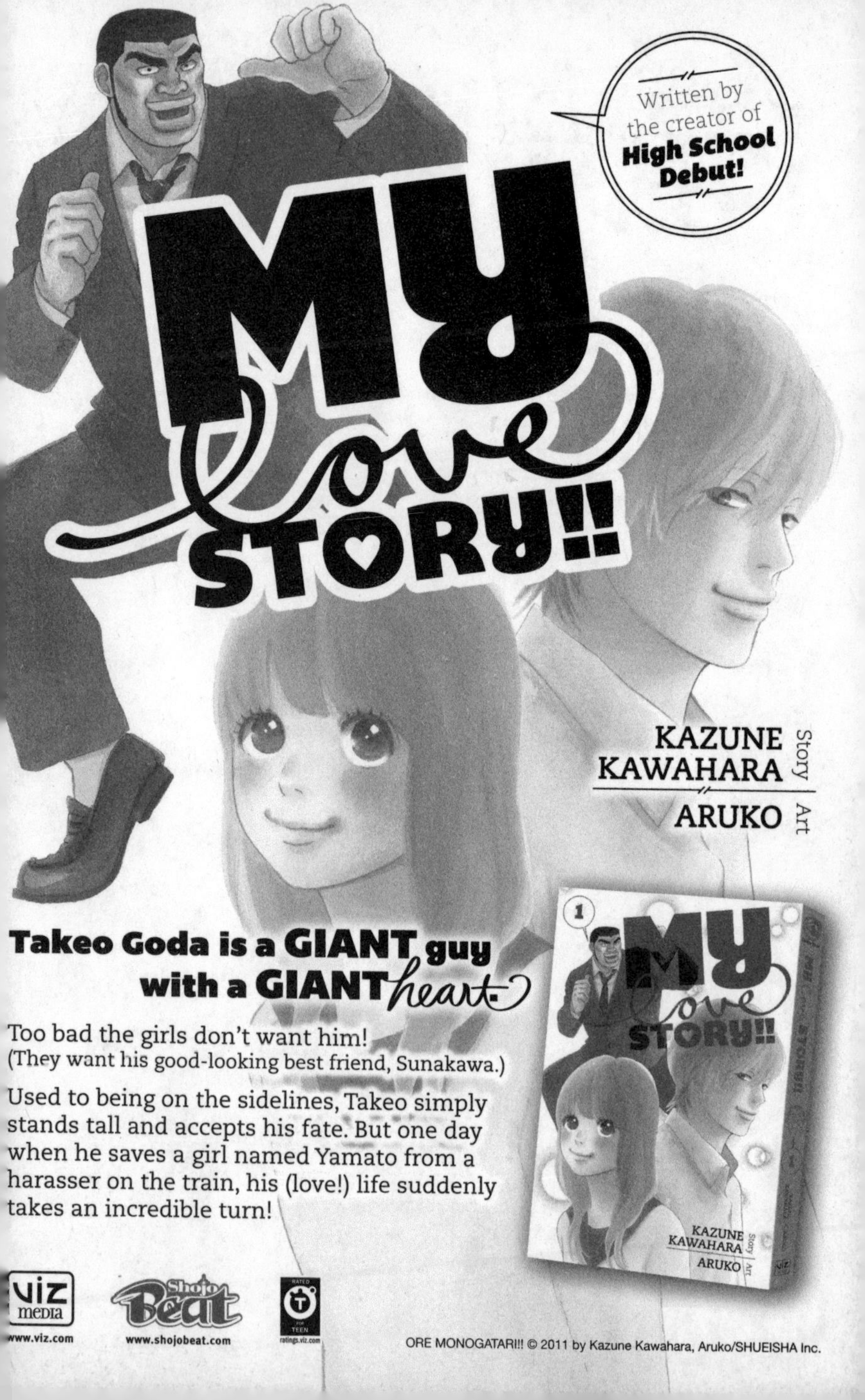
Written by the creator of High School Debut!
MY love STORY!!
KAZUNE KAWAHARA Story
ARUKO Art
Takeo Goda is a GIANT guy with a GIANT heart
Too bad the girls don't want him! (They want his good-looking best friend, Sunakawa.)
Used to being on the sidelines, Takeo simply stands tall and accepts his fate. But one day when he saves a girl named Yamato from a harasser on the train, his (love!) life suddenly takes an incredible turn!
1
MY love STORY!!
KAZUNE KAWAHARA Story
ARUKO Art
viz media
www.viz.com
Shojo Beat
www.shojobeat.com
RATED T FOR TEEN
ratings.viz.com
ORE MONOGATARI!! © 2011 by Kazune Kawahara, Aruko/SHUEISHA Inc.

SHORTCAKE CAKE

STORY AND ART BY
suu Morishita

An unflappable girl and a cast of lovable roommates at a boardinghouse create bonds of friendship and romance!

When Ten moves out of her parents' home in the mountains to live in a boardinghouse, she finds herself becoming fast friends with her male roommates. But can love and romance be far behind?

RATED T TEEN

VIZ

Shojo Beat Romances by IO SAKISAKA

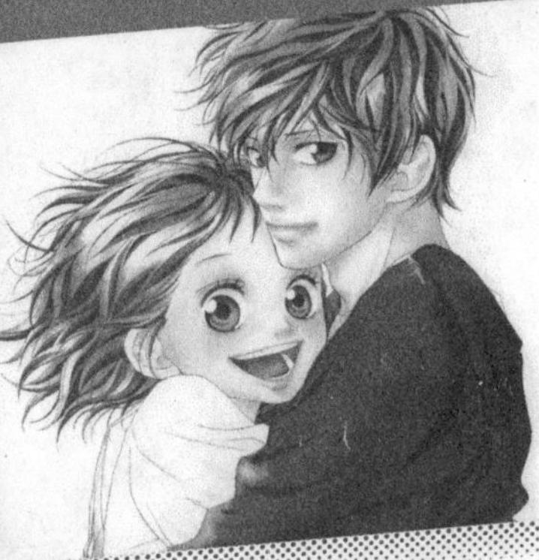

STROBE EDGE

When Ninako meets Ren, the handsome, enigmatic guy that all the girls worship, her life takes an unexpected turn. With just a few words and a smile, he changes her world...

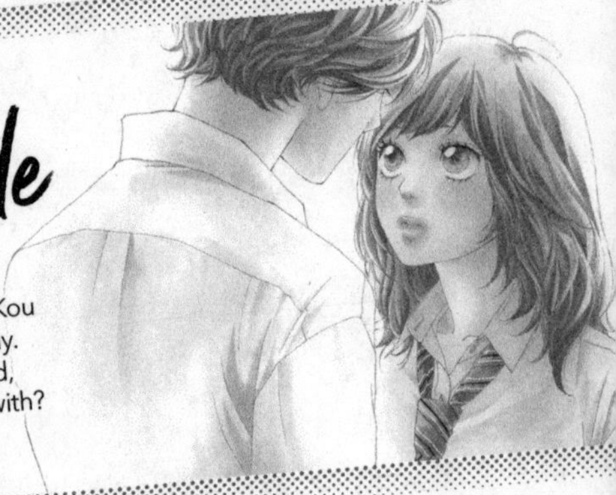

Ao Haru Ride

As soon as Futaba realized she really liked Kou in junior high, he had already moved away. Now, in high school, Kou has reappeared, but is he still the same boy she fell in love with?

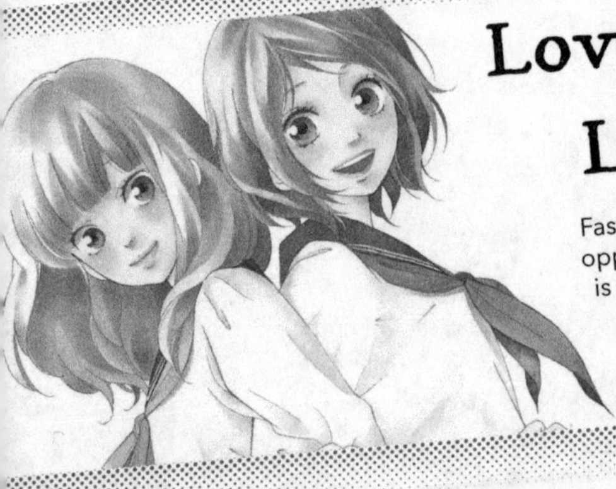

Love Me, Love Me Not

Fast friends Yuna and Akari are complete opposites—Yuna is an idealist, while Akari is a realist. When lady-killer Rio and the oblivious Kazuomi join their ranks, love and friendship become quite complicated!

RATED T TEEN

VIZ

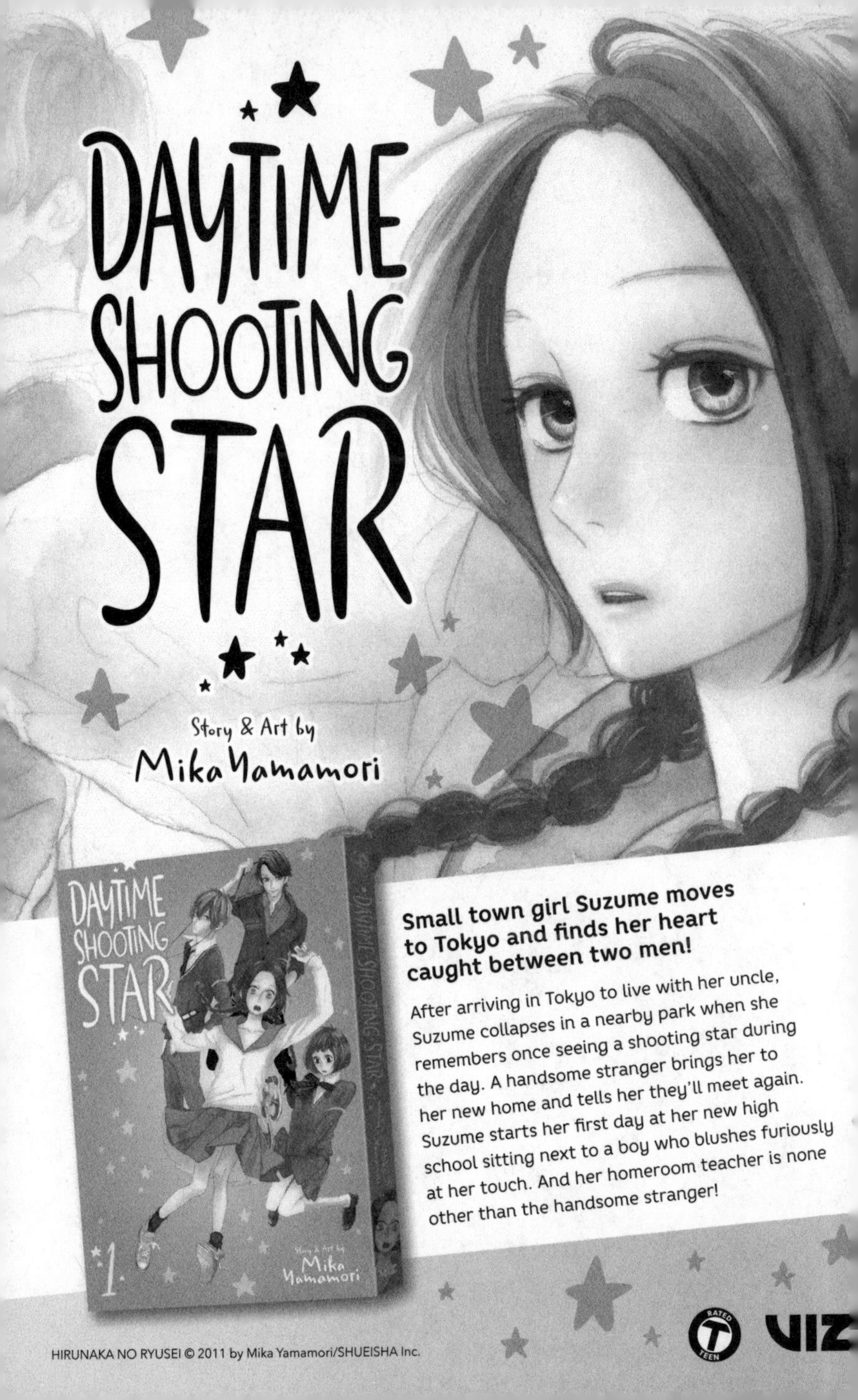
DAYTIME SHOOTING STAR
Story & Art by
Mika Yamamori
DAYTIME SHOOTING STAR
1
Story & Art by Mika Yamamori
Small town girl Suzume moves to Tokyo and finds her heart caught between two men!
After arriving in Tokyo to live with her uncle, Suzume collapses in a nearby park when she remembers once seeing a shooting star during the day. A handsome stranger brings her to her new home and tells her they'll meet again. Suzume starts her first day at her new high school sitting next to a boy who blushes furiously at her touch. And her homeroom teacher is none other than the handsome stranger!
RATED T TEEN
VIZ
HIRUNAKA NO RYUSEI © 2011 by Mika Yamamori/SHUEISHA Inc.

Stop!

You may be reading the wrong way.

In keeping with the original Japanese comic format, this book reads from right to left—so action, sound effects, and word balloons are completely reversed to preserve the orientation of the original artwork. Check out the diagram shown here to get the hang of things, and then turn to the other side of the book to get started!

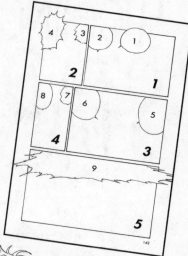